Richard Hobson
of Liverpool

Hon. Canon of Liverpool, and for thirty-three years
Vicar of St Nathaniel's, Windsor, Liverpool

Richard Hobson of Liverpool

The Autobiography of a Faithful Pastor

THE BANNER OF TRUTH TRUST

THE BANNER OF TRUTH TRUST
3 Murrayfield Road, Edinburgh EH12 6EL, UK
P.O. Box 621, Carlisle, PA 17013, USA

*

First published as *What Hath God Wrought*, 1903

First Banner of Truth edition, 2003

ISBN 0 85151 845 1

*

Printed and bound in Great Britain
at the University Press,
Cambridge

To the ever blessed memory of
a darling and beloved
Mother
this book is dedicated in token of
abiding filial affection and love
by her son
Richard

Illustrations

Everton in 1925   *Front endpaper*
Church Street, Liverpool, 1886   *Back endpaper*
Richard Hobson   *Frontispiece, facing title page*

Between pages 168 and 169

Richard Hobson at the age of 19

Patrick William McConvill (see pp. 24–6 and Appendix A)

Dr R. P. Blakeney (see pp. 37, 41–8)

The Cellar at 6 Oliver Street, Windsor (see pp. ix, 50)

St Nathaniel's Ragged School

The interior of St Nathaniel's Church

The 'Little Hell' (see pp. 49, 113–5)

Mrs Catharine Hobson, the author's mother

J. C. Ryle, first Bishop of Liverpool

The Windsor Mission Hall (see pp. 151–3)

The Jubilee Memorial Hall (see pp. 183–5)

St Nathaniel's Vicarage (see p. 206)

F. C. Chavasse, second Bishop of Liverpool (see pp. xxi, 295)

Alfred Butterworth, J.P. (see p. 324)

Officers of St Nathaniel's Church in 1901

Richard Hobson in 1893 (see p. 229)

Contents

Illustrations   vi

Biographical Sketch   ix

Author's Prefaces   xvii

Introduction   xxiii

PART 1: CHILDHOOD, YOUTH AND MINISTRY   1

PART 2: AGENT OF THE IRISH CHURCH MISSIONS   16

PART 3: STUDENT OF ST AIDAN'S COLLEGE, BIRKENHEAD   34

PART 4: CURATE OF CHRIST CHURCH, BIRKENHEAD   41

PART 5: VICAR OF ST NATHANIEL'S, WINDSOR, LIVERPOOL: Diary Extracts for 1868–69   49

      Diary Extracts for 1870   55

      Diary Extracts for 1871   69

      Diary Extracts for 1872   75

      Diary Extracts for 1873   83

      Diary Extracts for 1874   90

      Diary Extracts for 1875   97

      Diary Extracts for 1876   105

      Diary Extracts for 1877   111

      Diary Extracts for 1878   118

      Diary Extracts for 1879   127

Diary Extracts for 1880   134

Diary Extracts for 1881   143

Diary Extracts for 1882   149

Diary Extracts for 1883   156

Diary Extracts for 1884   163

Diary Extracts for 1885   168

Diary Extracts for 1886   176

Diary Extracts for 1887   182

Diary Extracts for 1888   189

Diary Extracts for 1889   195

Diary Extracts for 1890   202

Diary Extracts for 1891   208

Diary Extracts for 1892   216

Diary Extracts for 1893   228

Diary Extracts for 1894   238

Diary Extracts for 1895   246

Diary Extracts for 1896   255

Diary Extracts for 1897   263

Diary Extracts for 1898   272

Diary Extracts for 1899   278

Diary Extracts for 1900   287

Diary Extracts for 1901   297

'My Eventide' (added to the Fourth Edition, 1913)   311

Appendices A – T   329

Biographical Sketch

In the month of November 1868, Richard Hobson, at the age of 37 years, began his ministry in a newly-formed parish, soon to be known as St Nathaniel's, in the district of Windsor, Liverpool. A church building was in process of erection, but not ready for use. And so the new minister conducted his first service in the cellar of 6 Oliver Street. Six people were present, Richard Hobson plus a congregation of five, consisting of three women, one elderly man, and, as Hobson put it, 'a little fellow who sat on a creaky stool'. Hobson sang 'Rock of Ages' and 'There is a fountain filled with blood', read the parable of the lost sheep, prayed twice, and presumably made the gospel plain (though he does not say so in his autobiography, here reprinted). But he was able to record: 'What it was that went home to him I know not, but, oh, wondrous grace, that one man was quickened by the Holy Spirit – the first drop of the coming shower, and, in later years that little lad was led to the Lord, became a communicant and lived the rest of his life in the fear and love of God.'

At the end of Hobson's ministry of thirty-three years, the congregation had grown from five to some 3,000 worshippers each Lord's day; and the tiny cellar had been replaced by a large church building, and three church halls (Windsor Street Mission Hall, Harding Street Mission Room and the Jubilee Memorial Hall) – all of which were used for Sunday worship. At the heart of this change was an outstanding pastoral ministry which resulted in great blessing to very many. For all this, Hobson himself would have been the first to give all the glory to God.

THE MAN AND HIS MINISTRY

What kind of man was Hobson? First, he never married, though he believed that a married ministry had many advantages over a celibate one. But it seemed, he said, 'as if God had kept me single for Himself'. (Perhaps a good wife would have helped him to cultivate a more moderate use of his energies!)

Second, he was a man who inspired the true affection and support of J. C. Ryle, appointed the first Bishop of the newly-formed diocese of Liverpool in 1880. Hobson was delighted with the appointment, and had the joy of welcoming the Bishop to St Nathaniel's whenever he was not engaged somewhere else. Ryle loved the pure gospel, a simple, hearty service and the manifest power of the Holy Spirit in the midst, evidenced by the quickening of dead souls, all of which he found at St Nathaniel's. He preached at the church every year on Whit Sunday at the annual confirmation service and on many other occasions. The church was usually packed to overflowing for these visits, since the congregation appreciated Ryle's clear proclamation of the Word.

Towards the end of his life, in 1899, the Bishop and his family came to the Christmas morning service at St Nathaniel's. His health was declining and he was bowed down. At the Communion the Bishop came to the rail with his children, who knelt on either side of him. Hobson recalled, 'For a moment I felt almost overcome; which he must have perceived, for, looking at me, he said softly, "Go on".' They stayed until the rest of the congregation had gone. Hobson went to the Bishop who reached out his hand and drew him to him, saying: 'This is the last time; God bless you; we shall meet in heaven.' Ryle could not suppress the big tears that trickled down his furrowed cheeks. Before he died, he gave Hobson the Bible he had been using on his study table for over fifty years. He wrote in it, 'Given to R. Hobson by J. C. Ryle, First Bishop of Liverpool, with very much Christian love, 22nd January 1900.' Hobson thanked him most warmly and assured him that he would value his gift more than anything. That gift and those words tell us much about the mutual affection and esteem of the two men.

Thirdly, he was a man who inspired great love and affection from his congregation. They saw in him a true and sincere pastor who cared for Christ's sheep, and especially the lambs of the flock, ensuring that they had a plentiful supply of the milk of the Word. In 1883, he was offered another parish away from the city area by Bishop Ryle, on account of increasing insomnia, a sign of stress due to overwork. He was drawn to it for a number of reasons, and accepted the offer, but a deputation of men from the church begged him to reconsider his decision.

He was overcome by their evident love and affection for him, and agreed to write a letter to the Bishop withdrawing his resignation. The men took it, as a body, to the Bishop's residence. The Bishop saw and heard them, and later told Hobson: 'I think if I had not agreed with your withdrawal, they would have knocked my head off.' Hobson never regretted his decision, and showed his deep affection for the people of St. Nathaniel's by staying happily with them until his retirement in 1901.

Fourthly, Hobson was a man with a great burden and passion for the lost. As he looked back over his years at St Nathaniel's, he was thankful to the Lord for the many who had been saved under his ministry, but he felt deeply for the great majority in his parish who remained without Christ. He described the essence of true pastoral care as 'travailing for souls', which, he said, 'is a part of a true minister's and evangelist's work . . . not seen of men, being that which, in the privacy of God's presence, engages the mind and the heart. To travail for souls,' he continued, 'is to hope, long, yearn, watch, wait, pray, agonise for, and to expect, the new birth of souls through the Word – for of his own will begat He us with the word of truth. In this God is sovereign; He works as, and by whom, and when, and where, He pleases.'

Hobson seemed to have a special place in his heart for the backslider. A local doctor who came to believe on the Lord Jesus later read a book which attacked Christianity and made shipwreck of his faith, leaving the church in consequence. However Hobson 'resolved to pray for for him', and continued to do so for ten years, keeping in friendly contact with him throughout. Then, as the doctor's health began to decline, Hobson was able to visit him and speak to him about the things of God and the need of his heart. The Lord had been dealing graciously with him, and it was not long before Hobson saw him return to the Lord. This made Hobson thank God for the promise, 'I will heal their backsliding, I will love them freely', and he added, 'It is well for all of us that we are in the hands of so merciful and gracious a God, as is our God and Father, in Christ Jesus.'

A fifth aspect of Hobson's life was his communion with God. He was a man of prayer, recognizing that personal communion with God could only be experienced and enjoyed through constant private prayer. Looking back on his experience, he confessed, 'I had, with others, communion with God in the church, but I never had a set time for private prayer, except by my bedside morning and evening, which from a child had always been my custom. I have also constantly cultivated habitual private communion with God, through his dear Son, in prayer. Prayer was, therefore, to me as natural as breathing: I could not go on without it. The Saviour's command to His disciples was, "As you go, preach"; to me it was "As you go, pray"; and as I went I prayed. This may not be for all the most excellent way. It was, however, that for me.'

Regarding Hobson's preaching, we may notice, sixthly, that his ministry was God-centred, Christ-centred and cross-centred. He was never ashamed of the fact that he made much of the blood of Christ at St Nathaniel's. He believed that without this emphasis, Christianity would be but a body without a soul. 'The magnetic power of the gospel', he asserted', is the priceless, precious blood of our dear Lord.'

We should also notice the emphasis he placed on prayer that the Holy Spirit should come upon the preachers of the Word. He was sensitive to criticism of the evangelicalism of the day. He granted that there was a dead evangelicalism, but insisted that it was unfair to judge a movement by poor representatives of it. For him, the gospel of true evangelicalism was not only a thoroughly biblical system of doctrine but also a mighty transforming power, warm and glowing. He took delight in quoting two sayings of Bishop Ryle: 'The people want sixteen ounces to the pound'; and, 'If you want to warm a church, put a stove in the pulpit.' But the ministers of the gospel were themselves in need: 'Oh, that God would be pleased to baptize the ministers of our church "with the Holy Ghost and with fire". This is the one, great, chief, urgent need if the church is to remain a power for good in the land.'

HOBSON'S CLOSING YEARS

Hobson retired in 1901. His health was not good. After a strenuous period of ministry at the beginning of 1901 his health gave way altogether and he came to the conviction that he should resign. Though he felt that this was the right decision, he described it as the greatest sorrow he had ever experienced, except the death of his mother, which occurred in 1898. At his farewell service on Wednesday, 9 May 1901 he preached on the text, 'I have no greater joy than to hear that my children walk in truth' (*3 John* 4). The church was full. It was a moving occasion for both minister and people, marking as it did the end of 33 years spent serving the Lord together, and experiencing His saving power in their midst.

In his retirement years Hobson felt moved to write about his inner experience of God. Though he had rejoiced in habitual fellowship with the Father and with His Son Jesus Christ, this precious and soul-absorbing fellowship was heightened to a remarkable degree in his closing years. He had known this before during a visit to Palestine when, in his own words, 'I was well nigh out of the body . . . I felt as if I could scarcely remain on the earth, even to do His will, because of the intense longing to be in God's immediate presence. I bless God', he continued, 'that this fellowship has been mine all through my eventide [as he called his closing years]: hence the restfulness, contentment, peace, happiness, and joy in God which has all along filled the soul of His worn-out servant.' He then gave thanks for the precious blood of Christ which cleanses from all sin, and added, 'From this height of privilege, how poor one's past life looks! How deficient even one's ministerial life appears! What a powerful incentive to contrition, humiliation, and repentance.'

Ten years after leaving St Nathaniel's, aged eighty, Hobson said, 'I do not feel old, for my faith, hope, and love to God and His Christ, are as strong, if not stronger than ever, while my heart is as buoyant, young, fresh, green and tender as ever. At the same time, I know that God is taking down my tabernacle, though very gently. In a word, I do know that while the house of David waxes stronger and stronger, the house of Saul waxes weaker and weaker.'

He went on, 'I shall only add that, as the time yet remaining of my earthly life must be short, I do crave the prayers of my dear friends that I may be kept in close fellowship with the Father and with His Son Jesus Christ, and that I may be used yet, despite failing strength, in bringing souls to God, which is still the ruling passion of my life.'

Richard Hobson was called to his heavenly home on 29 December 1914. Sadly, St Nathaniel's Church no longer exists, and the parish itself has apparently ceased to be. But Hobson himself lives on in glory, resting from his earthly labours, eternally happy and blessed, his works following him. In the twentieth-first century he is still, to ministers of the Word, a wonderful example of pastoral ministry; and to us all, a marvellous example of Christian compassion and concern for the salvation of the lost.

LESLIE A. RAWLINSON[1]
August 2003

[1] Mr Rawlinson attended St Nathaniel's, Liverpool, during the 1950s. He gave a fuller account of Richard Hobson at the Banner of Truth Leicester Ministers' Conference in 1999, the substance of which was published in the *Banner of Truth* magazine for July 2000, pp. 17–23.

Author's Preface to First Edition

The following reasons, amongst others, have led me to prepare for publication an outline of the story of my life.

1. That God may be glorified.

2. That my experiences may encourage 'stranded' Christian youths to trust God, and do the right.

3. That any Christian worker in a position similar to mine may through reading this narrative take fresh courage, and press on, realizing that, as 'the battle is the Lord's', He will give the victory.

4. To show that Evangelical Protestantism io still a living power, owned of God.

5. To illustrate and prove by results that teaching by contrast is one of the best methods, if indeed not the very best method, of imparting truth, whether in the pulpit, in the mission-field, or in parochial work.

6. To set forth the vital importance of individual personal dealing with souls through the Word.

7. To emphasize the great value in pastoral visitation, of teaching ' from house to house'.

With those objects in view, I have sought to give, by way of diary extracts, a plain, unvarnished account of the way by which God has led me for full seventy years, and the use He has made of me.

I feel sure that no candid-minded reader will find reasonable grounds for accusing me of desiring thereby to make a fair show in the flesh. The late Dr Temple, though Archbishop of Canterbury, had the moral courage to tell the world that he had known what it was to wear a patched jacket and mended shoes, to plough the land and thresh corn. I venture to claim that in that direction his record must give place to mine.

It is with adoring love and gratitude to my heavenly Father in Christ Jesus that I see fulfilled in me the Psalmist's words, 'He raiseth up the poor out of the dust, that He may set him with princes, even with the princes of His people.'

I earnestly desire the prayers of God's dear people that this narrative may be made a real blessing to all who read it.

R. HOBSON
Southport, 1903

Author's Preface to Second Edition

That, notwithstanding its high price, the first Edition should now be out of print, and that a second should be called for, is a cause for thankfulness.

Also, that the autobiography of a modest life, with a limited horizon, and amidst unpropitious environments, should be noticed at all, is something of a surprise; but that it should have been so widely reviewed by the Press generally is almost a wonder. Moreover, leading laymen, distinguished dignitaries of the Established Church, and eminent members of the Free Churches, have expressed the approval in kindly terms; whilst His Majesty the King has graciously accepted a copy.

Greater cause for thankfulness, however, attaches to the knowledge of souls having been brought to God by the book's perusal. To Him be all the praise.

I am venturing on the issue of a Second Edition essentially similar to the First, but at a much cheaper cost, in order that it may reach a larger circle of workers in similar spheres, for their information and encouragement.

I therefore send it forth in faith, and with prayer, that it may be further used to the glory of our Covenant God and Father in Christ Jesus.

R. HOBSON
Southport, September 1907

Author's Preface to Third Edition

The Third Edition of this Book is an answer to an honoured Publisher, who said, 'It will not sell.'

I have a pile of voluntary testimony as to how the Holy Spirit is using it.

In sending it out I venture to let the gentle reader know that in the unexpected lengthening, by God, of the eventide of my life I am not quite incapacitated by senile old age from doing anything for the Lord. That I have still the great privilege of voluntarily betimes assisting in public prayer and preaching occasionally; visiting the sick and helping in Bible and Confirmation Classes; but I wish more especially to emphasize the fact that in this, doubtless, the last decade of my life, God the Holy Spirit is being pleased to give me through simple faith more than ever of close Spirit-blessed fellowship with the Father and the Son, so that not only my cup but my saucer runs over; and thus my aged life is being filled with the Triune God, while I am waiting for the Home call.

Peace be with you. Amen.

The Author
Southport,
October 1909

[xx]

Author's Preface to Fourth Edition

It affords me real pleasure to issue the fourth Edition of my Autobiography, in faith and prayer as its predecessors; that it, too, may tell its own story in its own way to the glory of our Triune God.

I wish also to say, that while doing so, I have made some revisions and emendations; but specially, I have made a substantial addition of a whole chapter; in order to bring it up-to-date by giving a bird's eye view of the gracious and loving care of my Heavenly Father; and of the use He is making of me, in my lengthened eventide, and of signs following.

In all probability this will be my last issue thereof; as I have an undefinable feeling, that betimes my feet touch the margin of the river; and from thence well nigh, by faith,

> 'Waiting the greeting
> When I land;
> Waiting the grasp
> Of His dear hand.'

The Author
Southport,
February, 1913.

Introduction

I gladly consented to write a brief introduction to Canon Hobson's graphic description of his life and work, because the book appears to me to have a special message for the critical days in which we are at present living.

It is an evidence that the simple Gospel of our Lord Jesus Christ, when it is fully preached by a man whose live is in accordance with its teaching, has lost none of its vitality. It is still 'the power of God unto salvation to everyone that believeth'. It still meets the deepest spiritual needs of human nature, and is still 'living and active, and sharper than any two-edged sword'. Canon Hobson's simple and pathetic story shows what Christ can do amongst the poor of a great city, where the struggle for existence, and the race for wealth, and the love of pleasure, are supposed to make the soil peculiarly hard and barren.

And if the book is a witness of the power of the Gospel, it is also an evidence that the Church of England, when properly worked with faith and sympathy and devotion, is still the Church of the poor as well as of the well-to-do classes. I myself have seen the Church of St Nathaniel thronged with children from the street, bare-legged and barefooted. I have heard the modest and grateful testimony of men who look today to the Church of England as their nursing mother, and in days of degradation, poverty, and sin, first learned to know Christ through her ministrations. Canon Hobson's story is a proof that the poorest in the land may be led to love our national Church, and to support it and to work for it with a self-denial and enthusiasm which put to shame many of our educated people.

Above all, the book teaches what we all know so well and yet fail to realize, tbat it is not by might, nor by power, but by God's Spirit, that the hearts of men are turned to Him, and the kingdom of God extended upon earth. Given a firm faith m the unseen God, a living trust in a living Christ, daily dependence on the Holy Spirit, unwavering confidence in the Bible as the Word of God, a pure and single heart, and a devoted life, there is no limit to the possibilities of usefulness which lie before the true servant of God.

That this record of what God has wrought may inspire and strengthen many, and may bring increasing glory to his Master, is, I know, the great and only motive which has led its Author to lay it before the public.

F. J. LIVERPOOL[1]

The Palace, Liverpool
January 30, 1903

[1] The Right Rev. F. J. Chavasse, D.D., successor to J. C. Ryle as Bishop of Liverpool. It was Bishop Chavasse who described Ryle as a 'man of granite with the heart of a child'.

[xxiv]

PART I.

CHILDHOOD, YOUTH, AND MINORITY.

Descent—Birth—Early impressions—Attack of measles—The parish
school—Attack of small-pox—Primitive Methodists—Aunt Frances'
Meetings—Miles and Edward J——'s jokes—The Methodist preacher's
prophecy—Irish Famine of 1846-7 — The all-important question —
Confirmation and Communion—The Misses Featherston H.—Work
under Colonel Bruen—Father's death—Garden work—Mother's efforts
—Irish Church Missions appointment—Family success.

In the middle of the eighteenth century three brothers
named Hobson, belonging to an old yeoman
family in Yorkshire, left their native county for
Ireland. One of them settled in Kilcarney, co. Wicklow,
having acquired by marriage a large part of that
township. His grandson Thomas fought in defence
of his country during the Irish Rebellion of 1798,
and left behind him records of hardships endured,
and of victories won, by the Loyalists in that Rebellion.
John, his eldest son, married Catharine Bollard, of
Coan, Glen of Imaal, co. Wicklow ; and their fourth
son, Richard Hobson, Honorary Canon of Liverpool,
and late Vicar of St. Nathaniel's, Windsor, West
Derby, Liverpool, is the subject of this autobiography.
All the family have always been strong Protestants,
and loyally attached to the Throne and Constitution.

My father, an honest man and fairly educated,
died at the comparatively early age of forty-six, leaving

his family ill provided for, and not over well equipped
for the struggle to regain a lost position. My dear
mother had early learned to trust in God and in His
blessed Son; and lived an exemplary life. She had
a cheerful, contented disposition; her wants were few;
her industry was unbounded, and her faith and hope
were unshaken even under the darkest providence;
her very look was love and home to her children,
in whose young hearts she sowed the seed of eternal
life in her own simple motherly way; as, it is not
too much to say, showed itself in the characters of
her children by the grace of God.

I was born on October 7, 1831, in the picturesque
village of Donard, co. Wicklow; and I thank God
that I was born into this world, and that during my
temporary passage through it I have obtained, as God's
free gift, eternal life, by the quickening power of the
Holy Spirit, 'the Author and Giver of life.' I have
often thought whether, in answer to the prayer of
faith, that great gift may not have been bestowed
upon me in baptism, since from my earliest recollection
I have had a delight in 'the things of God.' Why
should it not have been? Prayer was specially offered
in the baptismal service for my spiritual regeneration;
and, not only so, but in the same service God was
thanked, in the language of faith, hope, and love,
for so great a gift. That is quite a different thing from
the *opus operatum* doctrine of Rome and Rome's
imitators.

During my ministerial life I have had a growing
appreciation of the baptismal service, and have often
been grieved at the apparent hurry in which it is rushed
through, as if the act *per se* on the one side, and ' get
it over ' on the other, were sufficient; causing one
to think that the need of pleading, in prayer and faith,
for the regeneration of the child could hardly be very
deeply felt.

When only five months old I suffered from a severe
quinsy, but the skill of a neighbouring medical man
was blessed to my recovery: God had work for me

to do. When about four years of age, hearing one day a loud clapping in one of the rooms, I ran to the door, but was at once ordered away. An Orange Lodge was being held, and I soon got the impression that an Orangeman was a Protestant; but though strongly and openly attached to the Protestantism of Orangeism, I never became a member of that honourable organization.

A cousin once took me by the hand to have a stroll in the fields, and deeply impressed my young mind by kneeling down in a dry ditch to pray. I felt filled with awe. One evening I wandered into the parish school, and saw three girls who had met, I learned afterwards, for a prayer-meeting. Finding no one came to conduct it, they rose and sang the evening hymn, ' Glory to Thee, my God, this night,' which I thought just lovely! How precious are such impressions made upon the mind of a child, and how likely to be, as in this instance they certainly were, permanent and abiding, forming possibly the characteristics of the life in after-years!

The first prize I received, in Donard Sunday-school, when about six years old, was a New Testament, which I carried home with great joy.

At this time my father took a farm in Woodenboley, two miles outside Donard, where he and darling mother laboured night and day for seven years. But they could not make it pay, the rental being too high. Ah, if the landlords of Ireland, as a class, had been humanely considerate of their tenants, they would not be in the position they occupy to-day! This farm was in the parish of Holywood Eustace, and I attended a small Sunday-school in the church, though two miles off. I recollect being impressed in the service by the collect, ' Stir up, we beseech Thee, O Lord, the wills of Thy faithful people.' The minister was a good man, who used sometimes to visit us. I felt half timid of him, and at times, on taking the bridle as I handed his horse over to him, he would say, ' Thank you,' but without either a smile, or a pat on the head, for the little fellow who waited on him. I well remember that when there I had the measles, from which I slowly recovered, and, awakening from a state of semicoma, the crisis having passed, I saw my father and mother kneeling at my bedside. My father was weeping aloud. In rising from prayer he walked about the room. I heard him say : ' I would part with any of my children rather than with poor Richard.' I then heard mother whisper to him : ' John, his eyes are open.' ' How are you, my child ? ' she inquired. ' I am very well,' I replied ; when my father sobbed, and left, saying : ' Thank God, he is spared ! '

As a child I grew very fast, but was not strong, suffering greatly from headache.

It was now seen that I had a disposition to learn ; so on the visit of my grandmother, Hobson, who, with my grandfather and family, resided at Mill Park, Hacketstown, co. Carlow, about ten miles away, it was arranged for me to live there, and go to the parish school, which was carried out, I being about seven years old. This new opening brought me under the notice of two of the rector's daughters, the Misses Featherston H., who lived only to serve God, not merely in the day and Sunday-school, but as constant visitors in the parish. The rector was a gentlemanly man, of good birth ; and an earnest preacher ; but I always felt afraid of him. While respected, he was not much beloved. Oh, what a mistake it is for the minister of Christ not to have a word, a smile, for the young as well as for the old, at all times ! His two eldest angelic daughters won the hearts of all, especially of the children, as they did mine, and were the means, in God's hand, of winning me still more to Him, and of enabling me, though only yet a lad, to confess His Name. It was at Mill Park my kind and tender grandmother nursed me through the small-pox, which was then prevalent there. In my case it was of a very light type. I remember how my face was constantly covered with cream to remove the scab on the decline of the loathsome disease. The slight marks left wore away in time.

Here, again, was the hand of God. Blessings on His Name !

About this time my father's youngest sister, Frances, eighteen years of age, was brought to the Lord through the instrumentality of a Primitive Methodist preacher, who, in his monthly rounds, was accustomed to be ' stopped ' at my grandfather's, and at the houses of two of my father's married sisters who lived in the neighbourhood. The Primitive Methodists in Ireland were then strong Churchpeople, though followers of John Wesley, who wished the movement bearing his name to be a lay missionary body in the Church. I know that in that part they were a real blessing to numbers, as well as a strength to the church itself. They were to be seen in procession on a Sunday morning, going to church, singing hymns as they went.

The preacher's day was looked forward to with real pleasure, relatives and friends being invited to meet the good man at ' high tea,' and then to attend the preaching, consisting of an earnest Gospel address, with, of course, hymns and prayers, led by himself or some of those present. What more calculated to keep alive true religion, and to foster goodwill and fellowship ! These meetings, which I now regularly attended, were not joined in by the rector and his family, who, however, wisely, never spoke against them. My aunt Frances used to have a class-meeting once a week, in which each one had an opportunity of telling of the Lord's dealings with his or her soul. There was one Miles J., a gentlemanly fellow, a chum of my youngest uncle, who ' cared for none of those things.' He said to him : ' I hear that Frances holds a meeting in your father's house, and that she shakes hands with each one on leaving. Let's get into the kitchen on the next evening, and as the people are going out I can get amongst them, and will kiss Frances.' ' Well, if you like,' said uncle. The evening came, they were both in the kitchen. Aunt, knowing they were there, was a little perturbed, yet she went on with the meeting. She purposely had the parlour-

door left open. Every word uttered was heard by
them, and after her address the people went away
as usual. Meantime the Lord had spoken to the heart
of Miles, and soon after, he was the conductor of that
very meeting !

My aunt used also to hold prayer-meetings in the
parish. Finding she could not rely upon herself to
start the hymn-tunes in the right key, and discovering
that at school I had been taught well-known long, short
and common metre, tunes in the proper pitch, she
requisitioned me for the work, and used to take me
with her to lead the singing. This was my first effort
for God, for which I most humbly and sincerely thank
Him. It was a joy to me to accompany my aunt, which
I did more or less for a few years. I could fill a small
volume with the blessed results which came under
my own notice at these meetings. Is it any wonder
that in after-years I loved such meetings ? Let me
give one case only. My aunt conducted one of her
little meetings in a mud hut—having only a hole
in the roof for a chimney—in Ranagry Bog, where a
pious widow and her two children lived. Edward,
brother of the before named Miles, thought he would
play a trick on her, and resolved to drop a big sod of
turf down the chimney into the fire ; but as he was
approaching he heard aunt's voice in prayer, which
caused him to let the sod fall. He got away, but with
the Lord's arrow in his breast. I subsequently saw
the dear young fellow conduct that meeting, and with
streaming eyes narrate fully these particulars. Thank
God, I myself also know definitely of several brought
to the Lord in that mud cabin. How true,

> ' Jesus, where'er Thy people meet
> There they behold Thy mercy seat ;
> Where'er they seek Thee, Thou art found,
> And every place is hallowed ground ! '

Once I was late for tea at an uncle's house, on the
preacher's day. On arriving, I saw aunt, uncle, and
the preacher—who was blind from his infancy, but a
powerful expounder of the simple Gospel—having a

walk, and on coming up to them, the preacher said :
' Bring Richard here that I may cane him ' ; but making
a stroke with his stick on the road he corrected himself,
and said : ' Oh no, I shall not do that ; it may be
Richard will be preaching the Gospel when we are in
the clay.' Those words sank down into my heart ;
I little thought that they were really prophetic. How
truly the things impossible with men are possible
with God !

About this period my dear parents left Woodenboley,
and went to live at Hacketstown, whereupon I left
my grandfather's, and went to them. They had but
little remaining of the farm, except four cows and a
horse, with which to maintain their family of seven
children, and they rented a field outside the town for
the cattle. The live-stock, however, soon disappeared,
as my father could get no employment, and there
was not much sale for milk in a small town. All this
time my brothers, sisters, and I were attending the
parish and Sunday schools, and the church. I would
not for the world have missed attending, as they were
my chief delight. I sang in the church choir, and was
considered to have a sweet, true voice, of fair volume.
The only instrument was a bass fiddle ; still, I believe
we made a cheerful noise unto the Lord. Through
the kindness of a relative I had two summers' education,
under an able teacher, near Abbeyleix, Queen's County.

Now came the great famine of 1846-47, caused by the
failure of the potato crop, that being the staple food
of the people. Numbers died of hunger and sickness,
and many more would have died had not England,
with her accustomed liberality, poured in food and
clothing in abundance, of which we had a share. The
rector and his daughters took an active part in securing
and distributing this welcome relief ; indeed, the kind
man so forgot his years that he caught cold, and died
while ' the famine was yet in the land.' During the
prevalence of the visitation and consequent diseases,
I remember one Sunday morning we had no breakfast,
nor anything with which to get one ; yet I went to

church at noon, and sang in the choir as usual, but wept during the whole of the Litany, asking the Lord to send relief. On my return home there was still no food, so I then said to my dear mother : ' Give me a pillow-slip, and I will go where I feel sure some meal will be given to me.' I soon found myself at the door of the house where Miles and his brother lived. Edward opened the door, and, with tears in my eyes, I said : ' We have had nothing to eat to-day ; will your mother give me some meal ? or we may starve.' I handed him the pillow-slip, which he soon brought back filled with meal. Thanking him heartily, I ran home as hard as I could, praying, praising, and weeping. Dashing into the house, I cried out, ' I have got meal ! ' And dear mother exclaimed : ' Oh, Richard, you are a good boy ! Relief has come from one of your uncles. The food is ready ; sit down, my child ; break your fast.' And we all ate.

As an honest man my father was now obliged to leave even the fairly comfortable house in which we lived, and to go into a small house, wretchedly thatched, not weather-proof, with an earthen floor, in the lowest part of the town. A van was not required to remove the furniture left. When it rained heavily I used to help mother to ladle out the water in buckets. There were only three dry spots, where we lay on beds—two of which were on boards slightly raised from the floor— with scarcely any bed-clothing. There was not much to eat, we some days having only one meal, and that of stewed turnips and a little flour, with Indian meal bread, but no meat. Any second meal was of Indian corn porridge, with or without milk.

The distress, after lasting a full year, had now reached its lowest depth. I remember at this time the rector called one day, and, looking round, said, ' I am sorry,' at the same time putting a five-shilling piece into my mother's hand. Oh, what a Godsend ! As she showed it to me she wept. I said : ' Mother, don't cry ; this will not last always.' ' No, my child—no, my child,' she replied. It is remarkable that during this trying time neither death nor disease touched any of the family.

Notwithstanding all this awful visitation, I was drinking in with childlike faith, delight and consolation, of the pure Gospel of God's free grace, from the lips of the rector's daughters, who instilled into my mind the blessed and saving truths of the grace of God, as well as the historic narratives of the Bible. The younger sister superintended the Sunday-school, besides teaching her Bible-class on the Sunday morning and evening. I was the only boy in her class, and her sisters used to call me her ' little pet.' I was with her in church one week-day, when, standing at the Communion Table, she gently put this question to me : ' Richard, are you born again ? ' I thought a moment, and replied, ' I trust so,' at which she smiled. Yes, thank God ! though only twelve years old, I had about that time realised consciously my sonship in Christ by the quickening power of the Holy Spirit, just as I do now. ' Oh, to grace how great a debtor ! ' It was soon after this that I was confirmed by the Bishop of Ossory Leighlin and Ferns. What a privilege and happiness it was to me to partake of the Lord's Supper, as it has continued to be all through my life ! Who can tell the depth and extent of the work done for God by those dear servants of the Lord in that parish, bringing into the blessed work education, culture, refinement, perseverance, devotion, faith, hope, and love ? They loved the children in the Lord. So great was my ambition to be like my teachers, especially the younger one, that one day, seeing her pass and leave her footprints on the soft road, I thought it a great thing to put my feet into them. Although nearly sixty years have passed since then, her teaching is as fresh in my mind as when I was in her class. Would that all clergymen's daughters were like those !

But this most blessed work came to an end. Owing to the death of the rector, the family had to vacate the Rectory. As the carriage drove them away, I threw myself upon the ground, and felt as if I should have

died. Thankfully do I record that they never lost
sight of me in my after-struggles—in the mission-field,
when ordained, and especially in my life-work at St.
Nathaniel's, Liverpool—giving me a daily place in
their prayers until, in a ripe old age, they obeyed the
call to come up higher. Before the new rector was
appointed, a curate was placed in charge. He was a
dear man of God, taking an interest in every good work.
I recollect his saying to me one day, ' I see, my boy,
your jacket is very much worn ; come to my lodgings
this evening, and have tea with me ; I think I have
a coat which may fit you ' ; laughingly remarking
' you are a big fellow, you know.' I felt honoured
by the invitation, and what really pleased me better,
was that the coat fitted me well, and lasted me for
some years. Thank God ! I never wanted a coat
afterwards. When I was leaving him he handed me
a book, saying : ' I want you to read those sermons,
as I believe you will, one day, be a Minister in the
Church ' ; to which I replied : ' Oh no, how could
that be ' ? But, later on, the remark constantly came
to my mind.

Relief really seemed to have come at last, in that
my father had an offer of a sort of stewardship, with
a promise of work for my eldest brother ; but there
was no opening for me. I helped in getting the family
removed, but my poor father found himself unequal
to the post. He was really a broken-down man, but
my brother did his best. I was now stranded. What
could I do, being only fifteen years old ? I was not
robust, and felt I could not do rough work even if I
got it. I still cried : ' Lord, guide me ! I know not
what to do.' My grandfather had died, two of my
uncles had emigrated to America—one of them taking
with him a younger sister of mine—and one had died.
My aged grandmother, with Aunt Frances, emigrated
soon after, leaving not one of our immediate family
in Ireland. The happy thought occurred to me that,
as my grandfather and uncles had supported the
candidature of Colonel Bruen, Oak Park, near Carlow,

as a Conservative M.P., when he was opposed by the
notorious Daniel O'Connell, whom he defeated, and
as I had heard that the Colonel had many employeès
for his extensive and beautiful grounds, I might get
in there if I had courage enough to apply. This I
resolved to do, and off I set, walking thither fourteen
miles. How I prayed, as I inquired the way, that I
might succeed! I could scarcely gain admittance
at the great gate, but the keeper at last gave way,
and I was overawed by the appearance of the grand
house and demesne. With a trembling hand I pulled
the bell, and an attendant opening the door, I asked
to see the Colonel. ' What do you want with the
Colonel ? ' he rather gruffly inquired, spying me from
head to foot. I answered : ' I want, please, to see
the Colonel.' ' I will give your message,' he replied ;
' but I do not think he will see you.' Then in the
little interval of waiting I prayed to my Father in
in heaven. Soon the Colonel came out, and at once
said : ' What do you want with me ? ' I made myself
known as well as I could, as the son and grandson
of So-and-so, when he remarked : ' I know the family
very well.' ' I want employment in your garden,'
I continued ; ' and I have brought a character from
my late Sunday-school teacher ' ; which I handed
to him. Having read it, he promptly said : ' I will
see the gardener. You go to him at once, and tell him
I said he is to employ you in the garden at six shillings
a week.' That was a man's wages. I thanked the
Colonel, and set off to the gardener, who, with his
wife, received me kindly, gave me something to eat,
as I was very hungry, and arranged for me to begin
work the following week. I walked back to Hacketstown that day, though my feet were blistered ; and
I kept the appointment.

I got lodgings at eighteenpence a week, and managed
out of my wages to send a little home each month.
What a pleasure that was to me ! The gardener and
the men were both kind and considerate of my youth.
I found gardening a very agreeable employment. It

was just what I wanted, in that it gradually strengthened and developed my whole physique. Whilst there I got rid for ever of distressing headaches, and had many a lesson in God's goodness and bountifulness as seen in flowers, fruits, and vegetables. Truly God's voice is everywhere, if there are ears to hear it!

I soon found my way to Paynstown church service, conducted in the house of the Colonel's chaplain, and Sunday-school near to, also conducted by him, one of the best of men. This service was only intended for the Colonel's family, household servants, and Protestant employeès. I received from the Colonel, for regular attendance at the Sunday-school, a prize, entitled ' The Christian Youth's Book.' I never read a more suitable and excellent book than that, which I still possess. All this time I was getting most distressing news from home, so I applied to the Colonel, and obtaining the free use of a house which had long lain empty, I had the family come to live there with me. The house was large and dry, though we all lay upon straw on the floors. My eldest brother had obtained a situation at a very small remuneration, and another brother, finding it impossible to get employment, enlisted in the army, fighting for Queen and country all through the Indian Mutiny. My poor father was now thoroughly broken down, and could do nothing. He soon died, after a painful and distressing illness: I trust, in the mercy of God, safe for the future.

Owing to the gardener leaving the Colonel's employ, I left soon after. On the following Sunday, being greatly cast down, I did not go to church, but somehow strayed into the Methodist Chapel in Carlow, where I felt comforted. After the service was over, a man sitting behind me touched me, saying, ' Can I speak to you for a moment ? ' to which I assented. He remarked : ' I was struck with your singing in the service. You are a stranger, I think.' To which I said : ' Yes.' ' May I ask if you are in want of a situation ? ' ' Well, indeed I am.' Then he said : ' It was only yesterday, on paying my rent, my landlord asked me if I knew of a man who would take a temporary clerkship at ten shillings a week. Now, he continued, ' I think I can get it for you if you wish.' I thanked him heartily, assuring him I should be most grateful for it. ' Well,' he replied, ' meet me to-morrow; I will introduce you to him.' I did so, and was at once appointed. Oh God, Thou art a faithful and merciful God !

This work having come to an end, I heard of, and obtained, a situation as gardener at six pounds per annum, with full board, as a first step in that line. There were now only two little ones with mother, who had to leave the house, as it was then let. She took a cottage in Carlow. I feel I cannot adequately describe the ways in which my darling mother honestly and cheerfully set herself to keep up the little home for herself and the two small children, with no help but three pounds per annum, out of the six pounds I was getting. Oh, what will not a loving mother do for her children ! Can they ever forget her ? In the light thereof we can all the more appreciate the words of our heavenly Father : ' Can a woman forget her sucking child ? . . . Yea, they may forget, yet will I not forget Thee.' Hallelujah ! Praise the Lord !

I was happy in my new position, though the wages were so small, and the food, while sufficient, very plain. It was a truly Christian household, consisting of the master and his two sisters, with four domestics, and there was family prayer twice a day, at which all had to be present. This was a joy to me. I soon found a place in the Bible-class of the rector of the parish, in the church choir, and, as was my privileged custom, at the Lord's Table. The rector was more of a student than a pastor. He wrote ' The Dark Deeds of the Papacy.' He was an able, faithful preacher of the true Gospel, contrasting it with error, specially with the errors of the Church of Rome. From him I had really my first lessons in the Romish controversy, which gave me a new inspiration of pity for my Romanist fellow-countrymen, together with an ardent desire to show them God's way of salvation; but there were no signs of any opening in that direction.

I have reason to know that I gave satisfaction as a gardener; but that, or indeed anything else, was nothing in my estimation compared with being able to carry in the humblest form the message of God's Gospel to Romanists. I thought, I prayed, I waited, if perchance a way to that end might be pointed out to me; when I saw a notice in the Carlow *Sentinel* of a disturbance in Carlow, consequent upon the labours of two agents of the Irish Church Missions to Roman Catholics. I made inquiry how I could see those agents, and found that one of them was a distant relative of my own. I called on them several times, by appointment, and they saw how interested I was in their work, even though it was often exposed to risk and danger. One day my relative asked me: ' How would you like to be employed by the Irish Church Missions, as we are ? ' ' Oh dear ! ' I nervously replied : ' why, that would be the joy of my heart ! I have been praying and waiting for such an opening. I can get you testimonials.' ' Well,' he said, ' I am going up to Dublin in a couple of days, and will put your name before the Reverend Superintendent of the Missions.' I was much exercised in prayer until the answer came, which was, ' Let him come up to Dublin.' I went up, passed the examination, and was there and then appointed at thirty pounds per annum, with the promise of an increase. The first to share my joy was my darling mother, who wept, and, with kisses and prayers, blessed her son. My master seemed rather proud that the heart of his young gardener was in such a good work.

About a year after, I succeeded in getting the coachman appointed on the Irish Church Missions' staff. He proved to be a most thorough and successful agent for over forty years, until he was called to his rest.

When I entered upon this new sphere of work, to which I felt sure God the Holy Spirit had called me, I had reached my twenty-first year; and, having a

few days to make ready, my heart and memory were
filled with the recollection of the first two decades of
my life, of all the way my heavenly Father had led
me ; that His eye was ever upon me for good ; that
through all He had kept me in constant use of the
means of grace, and in touch with His ministering
servants wherever I had been. I recalled how He
had enabled me to form, and how He had taken care
of, my character, when, like young folk, I felt the
force of temptation and a tendency which, if not re-
strained, might have been my ruin ; and, although
my knowledge was very small, still, I felt sure I could
and would tell to Romanists what I knew of the blessedness of justification by faith only—that Jesus is a
whole Saviour, that there is none other.

While I have thus far narrated the way my
heavenly Father brought me in my early life, doubtless
fitting me for His service, I think I ought to state,
to His praise and glory, that He has been graciously
pleased to give my immediate branch of the family
a thousandfold more in the end than in the beginning.

I feel it is due to the Hobson family generally to
record that one of them married into the 'upper ten,'
that five qualified for the medical profession, that two
entered the ministry of the Church of God, and that two
of them are barristers-at-law. But infinitely beyond
that, many of them are in living, loving, union with
the Lord Jesus, and are walking in His holy ways.
Hallelujah !

> ' What am I, oh Thou glorious God,
> Or what my father's house to Thee ?
> That Thou such blessings shouldest bestow
> On me, the vilest reptile, me ?
> I take the blessings from above,
> And wonder at Thy boundless love.'

PART II.

AGENT OF THE IRISH CHURCH MISSIONS.

Irish Church Missions work—Preparation—Romanist brutality at Drogheda—Riots at Ardee—Agrarian attack—Rector's daughter—Fatal result of riot—Appointed head of Louth Mission—Study of Latin and Greek—Visit to High Mass—Savagely attacked—' Rosy ' and Irish Church Missions' texts—' Hard nut ' for Popish priests—Perversions to Popery — Attack on Mission school — McConvill's conversion—His will—Rev. M. Rainsford—Popish priest's arrogance —Treatment of Romanists—' War Hawk '—Questions and answers—Bill-posting—House visitation—' Salting '—Tribute to Irish Church Missions — Dr. McCarthy — Sister's marriage — Wrongly addressed letter—Testimonial.

THE ' Irish Church Missions to the Roman Catholics of Ireland,' founded by the Rev. Alexander R. C. Dallas, rector of Wonston, Micheldever, Hants, was at this time in its infancy. It had an office in Dublin, at 6, Bachelors' Walk, and the local work was heartily and zealously carried on in St. Michan's Church and Schoolroom, by the then rector, the Rev. C. S. Stanford, D.D.—a Father in Israel—and his curate, the Rev. Charles F. (afterwards the renowned Dr.) MacCarthy, in prayer and faith, with much learning, devotion, and success. I entered on the work at once, full of zeal and love, determined to give myself to it body, soul, and spirit : being placed under the lead and care of a senior lay agent, and, for controversial instruction, under the teaching of Mr. MacCarthy, who had the sole training of all the society's agents. I found the reading and visiting very trying, yet most congenial. I drank in like a thirsty soul the doctrines of grace, as set forth in the Thirty-nine Articles and expounded by my teacher, who excelled all other teachers I have ever known. The first book for study was Stanford's ' Handbook to the Romish Controversy,' and the following are some of the points which were pressed home as to the best method of dealing with a Romanist : —

Try to feel his pulse as to education, piety, prejudice, adapting your words accordingly.

Never thrust controversy at him.

Try to show the points on which you and he agree, where the divergence comes in, and why.

Try to convince him that you love his soul, and would have him share in the common salvation.

Never lose your temper.

Realize that to convince of sin (error) is the work of the Holy Spirit.

Be much in prayer, etc.

Mr. MacCarthy's Tuesday evening Controversial Inquiry Class for Romanists, in St. Michan's School-room, was crowded. Several of those present put smart questions, and at times gave sharp answers to questions from the chair, on the creed of Pope Pius IV. ; but Mr. MacCarthy always angled his opponent until he landed him. The Romish priests were highly indignant at the Irish Church Missions attempting to convert their people. About this time the learned Dr. Salmon, of Trinity College, Dublin, brought out the *Catholic Layman,* a monthly journal, which rendered invaluable service in upholding the doctrines of the Irish Church, as opposed to those of Rome.

The Louth Mission, with stations at Drogheda and Ardee, under the superintendence of the Rev. Charles Miller, incumbent of Ballymakenny, Drogheda, had been recently opened, and the agents were suffering great persecution, owing to denunciation by the Romish priests from their altars. One agent lay in Drogheda for months, apparently at the point of death, the result of brutal kickings by Romanists, and others had been

severely wounded. Extra police were ordered into
the town, the Romanists having threatened to pull
down the mission-house, where the agents lived and
held their inquiry class, and to wreck their schools.
Bishop Ryle, of Liverpool, used to say : ' As you tread
on the devil's tail he squeals.' As in our Lord's time,
the priests hounded on their dupes, who would otherwise have received the Gospel ; yet great good was
undoubtedly being done amongst the Romanists in
Drogheda at that time.

The house-to-house visitation of Romanists went on
most hopefully in Ardee, until the senior Romish
curate held forth from the chapel altar against the
society's agents, after which no one would continue
to lodge them, or even to sell them food. It was deemed
prudent to withdraw two of them from Drogheda, and,
although having been only a year in Dublin, I was
despatched, with another, to take their place at the
seat of war in Louth.

As we travelled thither we thought, ' What can we
do in face of an infuriated populace ? ' But we were
encouraged by a conviction that the cause was God's,
and that He was with us. It is no small honour to be
placed in the front of the battle. I found there were
many inquiring Romanists in Drogheda, coming on
the quiet to the agents, but directly the latter appeared
in the streets they were followed by a hooting crowd.
There is, however, a good deal of generous feeling even
in an Irish mob.

I was soon sent on to Ardee, with food for the agents,
and, if possible, to obtain lodgings, in which I was
successful, afterwards even procuring a mission-house.
There I remained for two years, during which time the
agents certainly had to endure ' a great fight of affliction.' One day, as I was passing along a country road
with my colleague—a dear man of God—a large stone
whizzed over my left shoulder, grazing the chin of my
companion, and making quite a hole in the road.
Turning round, and seeing the man who threw it,
running off, I pursued him to the farmhouse where he

was employed. His master, also a Romanist, seemed ashamed when I identified the fellow, who shook like a leaf. After sorrowfully saying a few kindly words, my fellow-worker and I came away. Thank God, the very man who threw that murderous missile used subsequently to visit the mission-house as an inquirer after the truth, which, however, was the cause of his being obliged to fly the country for his life.

Another day, as we were passing through Ardee, there was an unusually violent outburst of feeling against us. We were followed by a crowd, who threw stones and mud, and then, closing up round us, seemed determined to use their sticks ; when a daughter of the rector passing by, and seeing we were in great danger, came to our rescue. Throwing her arms around me, she cried out : ' If you strike these men, you must strike me ;' and then, pointing at the more violent, she said : ' I know you.' Happily the remonstrance and influence of that brave lady quelled the violence of the people ; but, I grieve to state, not before my companion had been struck over his right ear by a stone, which, cutting through his hat, raised a lump on his head, though without breaking the skin. On reaching the mission-house, however, he spat blood, and from the effects of that blow he never recovered.

The *Drogheda Conservative*, a Protestant newspaper, was requisitioned, as an aid of the work ; whilst the *Drogheda Argus*, a Romish journal, wrote bitterly against the mission. Many of the Church of Ireland clergy kept entirely aloof, and some were even opposed to the mission ; but ' there was no small stir ' among the people.

I was recalled to Drogheda, where the work was being vigorously carried on ; and some time afterwards, on changes being made in the staff, I was appointed by the Clerical Superintendent—with the sanction of the Committee in London—to the oversight, under him, of the Louth Mission, with an increase of salary. About this time I got a Latin and a Greek grammar, which I studied with the aid of a tutor at intervals, as I could

afford to pay for one. On acquainting the good vicar
of St. Peter's with my intention to take up classics, he
remarked : ' I hear you have some idea of the ministry ;
if so, any book in my library is at your disposal.'

A well-known characteristic of the Irish is that,
though disapproving, and even resenting, some particular course of action, they appreciate and admire daring ;
but they have a great contempt for the ' white feather.'
In the course of events a synod of Romish Bishops
was announced to be held in their principal chapel at
Drogheda. The editor of the *Conservative*, a champion
for the truth, and I—having paid for admission—
attended High Mass there, though, of course, we took
no part in the service. We were amongst the last to
leave, and as we passed along a rather narrow yard
leading through the main gate into the street, we
noticed a number of men on each side, evidently waiting
for us. In a sudden stampede of one lot, my friend
and I got separated, when the other lot made a rush
at me, and why I was not thrown down I never could
understand, unless because the Lord graciously inter-
posed. On passing through the gate I received a kick
in the back, which almost doubled me up, and I nearly
fell ; when, in God's good providence, the Mayor
happened to pass, and seeing the danger I was in, he
put his hands on my shoulders, and called out : ' As
Mayor of Drogheda, I charge you to do this man no
harm ' ; at which my assailants drew back, and he
most kindly took me to the mission-house, they yelling
like demons on the way. I was soon on my knees in
thankfulness to God for deliverance from those mis-
guided and mistaken men. The editor escaped safely.

If it be asked, ' Why did you go there ? ' the answer
is : ' Because, when Romanists are spoken to about the
Mass, they often reply, " What do you know about
it ? Have you ever heard Mass ? If you had, you
would think differently." ' We decided, therefore,
to be present at a Mass, especially on such an occasion.

The agents were going on with their labours, notwithstanding, in the strength of faith, gaining access here

and there to the homes of the Romanists ; the inquiry
class was well attended ; and in the school the ' Hundred
Texts '—the importance of which cannot be over-
estimated—were carefully taught.   I remember one
day meeting a woman who formerly attended the
mission-school, but had left through fear.   She seemed
pleased to see me.   I said : ' Well, Rosy, I am glad to
see you ; I have been missing you.'   ' Ah, sure,' she
replied ; ' it's the priest.'   ' Well, Rosy, he cannot
take from you what you have learned of God's Word
in the mission-house.'   ' No, indeed.'   ' Well, Rosy,
I want you to repeat one of the hundred texts.'   ' Ah,
I have a bad memory.'   ' Come now, let me hear.'
' Well '—after thinking a little—' I'll repeat John iii.
16 ' ; and on she went, doing it correctly.   ' Thank
you, Rosy ; now another.'   ' Well, Jesus says, " Come
unto Me . . ." ' finishing the text.   ' Now another.'
She thought awhile, and then said, smiling : ' There's
John xiv. 6, " Jesus saith unto him, I am the Way." '
Here she stopped.   ' Go on, Rosy."   ' And the Life.'
' Well done, though not in order.'   Looking puzzled, she
added, very feelingly : ' And that's the thruth.'   ' Well
done, Rosy.   The priest may frighten you away from
the school, but he cannot take those blessed words out of
your mind and heart.'   ' Ah, no ; I'll keep them to my
dying day.   Jesus '—making a curtsey—' is my priest ;
I'll always go to Him.'   And she burst into tears.
Thank God, His Word is not bound !   The love and
zeal of that little band of Irish Church Mission men
was of the Lord's giving and sustaining, which alone
enabled them successfully to battle with the waves of
Romish opposition.

The Romanists of Louth, and especially those of
Drogheda, were particularly hard to reach, the latter
having had impressed upon their memories the tradi-
tions of Cromwell's and William III.'s visits to their
town and its neighbourhood ; and the priests knew
right well how to turn them to account for the
unholy purposes of their Church.   God was, nevertheless, enabling a great work to be done there

at that time, many receiving Christ and also confessing Him.

Amongst other difficult questions for Romanists to answer is this : ' What does the priest break when he breaks the host ? ' If the answer be, ' He breaks bread, the wafer,' as the wafer is broken after its ' elevation ' and adoration, it follows as a logical sequence that both priest and people have worshipped a wafer ; which is idolatry : whilst, if the answer be, ' He breaks the body of Christ,' that is falsified by the Word of God, which says, ' A bone of Him shall not be broken.' So that from the dilemma there is no escape.

When on the banks of the Boyne one day, there came along a nice young fellow whom I recognised as a Romish priest, so I determined to put that question to him. Accordingly, when we met I bowed, and he did the same. As I halted, he halted too, when I accosted him thus : ' Seeing you coming, it occurred to me to ask you a question, if I may.' He answered kindly : ' Yes, by all means.' ' Well, then, may I ask what you break when you break the host ? ' ' I break the accidents,' he replied. ' Can accidents exist apart from substance ? ' ' No.' ' When, therefore, you break the accidents, do you not break the substance ? ' He thought for a moment, and then said : ' Christ says, " This is My Body." ' ' True ; but do you admit that when you break the accidents of the host, that is, the wafer, you break the host, that is, the body of Christ ? ' His only reply was the repetition of Christ's words, as quoted, which he said he took literally. I answered : ' Well, then, I limit you to those very words, and ask you to explain them without the context, if you can. May I ask you what body did Christ mean ? ' ' He meant His natural body.' ' But Christ did not say, " This is My natural body." I hold you to the words of Christ.' Then he asked ' What other body has Christ except His natural body ? ' I replied : ' He has three bodies, His natural body, His body the Church, and His sacramental body.' ' Well, then, which body did Christ mean ? ' ' His sacramental or figurative body.'

'But Christ did not say, "This is My sacramental body,"' he rejoined. I answered : 'True ; we must therefore go to the context. In Luke xxii. 20, Christ says, of the cup. "This cup is the New Testament in my blood," where he uses a double figure, putting the cup for what was in it, and what was in it for the blood of Christ.' He replied : 'These are not in the words of institution,' quoting Matthew's version. I answered : 'Not in Matthew, but these words are given by Luke.' 'I have not seen those words,' he replied. 'Have you not a Douay Testament ?' I inquired. 'Yes, and when I return to my rooms I will look for myself.' And, bowing, he went on his way. I went on mine, with a prayer in my heart that the Holy Spirit might enlighten the dear young man.

Having heard that Protestant lads were admitted to Sir Rasmus Smith's institution in Dundalk, by examination, I brought my youngest brother to Drogheda, and had him coached up for the next examination, which he not only passed, but did so with credit. It is a joy to know that he has been as successful in business, has the comfort of being surrounded by a large family, is a communicant member of the Church of Ireland, and, best of all, is a true Christian.

On being appointed rector of Dundalk, the Rev. Marcus Rainsford invited the Irish Church Missions to send agents who would assist him in his parochial duties. I was despatched to open the mission there, with instructions to make it headquarters, visiting Drogheda and Ardee in turn. The late rector, a married man with no family, had two curates, gave all his income away to the needy, without any distinction as to denomination, and died a poor man, though his stipend was said to have amounted to sixteen hundred pounds a year. Yet from a spiritual point of view his ministry was a failure. His congregation had been gradually melting away. I actually made a list of seventy-six persons then living in the parish who were perverts from Protestantism to Romanism.

Before long, however, not only was this terrible

leakage stopped, there were also several conversions from Popery to Christ; besides which, the mission gained strength and influence, by drawing to itself many friends and helpers of high social position and Christian character. With much prayer to God on its behalf, the work was soon being carried on with efficient zeal. The school was attended by seventy-one Romanists, old and young; a controversial class was held in the parish church school; and Romanists were being visited at their homes. Suddenly an attack on the mission was made from the altar of the Romish chapel; the town was in a blaze, the agents were hooted up and down, visiting became impossible. The worst attack was that on the mission Sunday-school. One of the Popish priests sent a young man who ' served ' at Mass, to take down, and report to him, the names of all Romanists who attended. I now became special door-keeper, and saw the young man challenge each one of the scholars entering. He had with him a crowd consisting of the scum of the town, who threw mud and stones in abundance. The next Sunday there were but twenty-one Romanists at the school; soon we had not one, only a few Protestants. The teachers, however, met for prayer each Sunday, and I was still door-keeper, in face of an infuriated mob, led on by the same young man, with whom I tried to get into conversation. After several Sundays I succeeded in quoting 1 Tim. ii. 5, from the Douay Testament, putting it thus, after a few words of kindly remonstrance : ' Now, my friend, Paul says, " There is one God, and one Mediator." I will give you five pounds if you will show me a text in your own Bible saying there is one God and two mediators.' I kept him to that one point : his only reply was : ' There is no such text in the Douay Testament.' The crowd listened, but at times renewed their yelling, so that no good seemed to come of it ; but, to my amazement, that young man called at my house, next morning, and asked whether the above-mentioned text was actually in the Douay Testament, which, at his request, I lent him for a week. After only three

days, however, he came, and declared that he would
never again pray to either the Virgin Mary or the saints.
He continued to call, secretly, as an earnest seeker after
truth ; which, happily, soon ended in his receiving the
Lord Jesus as his full and only Saviour, followed by his
openly going to the very school he had been the means
of crushing, attending the parish church, and becoming
' valiant for the truth.'   This created a great stir ;
indeed, it made the common people wild, and there
seemed to be a doubt as to whether the agents could
hold the station.   A volume might be written about
what that young fellow had to go through, of which the
following may suffice as an illustration.   He was
surrounded one day in a street of Dundalk, lifted on
to a jaunting-car, his mouth was bound up, and, with
two men holding him, he was driven off in a certain
direction amidst the shouts and jeers of the mob.
Hearing of this a few hours afterwards, I reported it to
the senior magistrate, a true friend to the mission.
In his trap, with a man-servant, he pursued the party
to a town nine miles off, reported the case to the head-
constable, and had two policemen told off to search the
town for the poor fellow.   On being found, to the disgust
of his late captors, he was taken by the police back to
Dundalk.   The next day he applied to the magistrates
for protection, which was at once accorded, and I
walked with him from the court-house to my home,
guarded by six policemen.   The town was again in an
uproar.   The mob seemed determined to get possession
of him, keeping up their threatenings until past one
o'clock in the morning.   Not having a spare bed, I
gave him a pillow at the foot of my own, and he soon
fell asleep ; but from me sleep had departed.

On the evening of the day on which the dear fellow
was carried off, a few friends met in my house for special
prayer on his behalf.   As one of them was pleading
with the good Lord to bless the rescue search, a gentle
tap at the room window was heard, and on the door
being opened, in walked the magistrate, who in a
joyful tone said, ' Your prayers are answered,' telling

us all that had happened. We knelt again, and gave praise to God. Ultimately our young friend was advised to enlist, as the only means of escape, for nine attempts were made on his life ; and, let it be told to the praise and glory of God, in India he was made the means of bringing six comrades out from Romanism. On returning to England he lived in my parish, died there, and was buried by me. His simple faith was unshakable, his joy in Christ was constant, his life was without a flaw. For a copy of his Will see Appendix A.

He was very dear to me in the Lord.

Rome is a relentless persecutor of God's saints, especially of those who have left her in order to become such. In England those who ' vert ' to that system receive no such treatment, however grieved their relatives and others may be.

Having now, thank God ! a house of my own, I had darling mother and my youngest sister to live with me, sending the latter to the best girl's school in the town. Oh, what indescribable delight it was to both my beloved parent and myself, that she should be living with her son, no more to struggle for mere bread, freed from toil and care—though not to live in ease and idleness, for such she could not endure—with time and opportunity to give herself still further to the Lord she trusted and served !

I feel constrained to record that in this great conflict I was spiritually fed, nourished, and greatly sustained, by the faithful ministry of the rector, the Rev. Marcus Rainsford, subsequently of Belgrave Chapel, London. Often, after hearing him preach, especially sermons on John xvii., have I had in my heart and on my tongue the acclaim, ' Bless the Lord ! Glory ! Hallelujah ! ' Greatly was I encouraged, also, by two of the best men in the Church of Ireland, residents in Dundalk— the late Mr. John Murphy, J.P., and Mr. James Barton, who were ' not ashamed of my chain '—as well as by the late Miss S. A. Shekleton.

One day I met in the street a certain Romish priest,

who, as he passed, turned to me and said, in a flustered
tone of voice : ' I have been wanting to speak to you.
I have a message for you.' ' Thank you,' I replied.
He continued : ' The message is that you leave the
town.' As I only smiled, he went on : ' Remember,
I have given you the message to leave Dundalk.' I
answered : ' I am one of Her Majesty's subjects ; I
will not leave the town. And, more than that, as you
have in effect threatened me, I will hold you responsible
if anything should happen to me, and I shall make
your threat known.' Off he went, but turning again,
said : ' I shall go and let the stipendiary magistrate
know.' Having reported this episode to friends, I
was advised myself to inform the stipendiary, which
I did, applying for the priest to be bound over to keep
the peace. My application was granted ; the priest
was summoned, appeared in Court—trembling like an
aspen leaf—and was bound over. Evidently our
decided action had a most salutary effect upon the
Popish population, and, humanly speaking, saved the
mission. Strangely enough, there was no apparent
notice taken of this by the people, though it was considered quite likely that the Romanist mob would set
the town ablaze again. How God works and overrules
for our good ! Is it not evidently necessary to be
firm when dealing with Irish Romanists ? When they
see a man timid and yielding, they become bold and
imperious, and there is no limit to their insolent demands. There is truth in those well-known lines :

> ' Tender-handed touch a nettle,
>   And it stings you for your pains ;
> Press it like a man of mettle,
>   And it soft as silk remains.'

So there is also in the paraphrase :

> ' Weakly take for *truth* Rome's teaching,
>   By its speciousness you're caught ;
> Sift it deeply, God beseeching,
>   He will bring it all to naught.'

If the nation only realized this, and would compel the

Government to legislate accordingly, I am certain almost all the Irish problems would soon be solved.

The *Dundalk Democrat*, a weekly newspaper, was ' down ' on the mission and its sympathizers in the town. The editor christened poor me ' War Hawk,' by which supposedly opprobrious cognomen, I became generally known ; but finding that I gloried in it—if I were, indeed, such an one for God and His people—he substituted ' Ware Hawk,' which, however, did not ' catch on.'

After a prayer-meeting, I had a conversation with a fine intelligent young man, a draper's assistant, who had been present, and, telling him of the mission work, he said : ' Ah, go on, God is with you. I was a Romanist, now I am a saved man ! It came about in this way. Whilst serving my time at Drogheda, I heard a controversial sermon on Purgatory, which led me to get a Douay Testament, in order to see whether the preacher's quotations, which I had taken down, were in it ; and seeing they were, I went on reading, until God opened my eyes, and I left Romanism with my wife and two children. Since then I have brought my sister out of that fatal system.' How God works !

One of the agents, when on the quay at Drogheda, was recognised by a man who, with his wife and family, was just going off to America. He said : ' It is hard to leave one's country and friends, but, I tell you, in secret, I am really going to America that I may read my Bible and worship God as I ought. If it were known here that I have become a Protestant, I'd be kilt.' And I have no doubt there were many such cases. Ah, in spite of all the opposition, that was a blessed and glorious time of winning souls for Christ.

In due time the violent antagonism toned down, and the work was carried on as usual with prayer, faith, and vigour. Each winter there was a course of controversial sermons in the parish churches of Drogheda and Ardee, each one putting the Gospel in juxtaposition with some error or errors of the Church of Rome so plainly and clearly that none—not even the

Romanists who attended—could fail to understand. This was also a most effective way of instructing our own people, by building them up in the faith of Christ Jesus, and so enabling them intelligently to meet the dangerously aggressive, because plausible, proselytizing efforts of the Romanists, who are taught, if nothing else, to misapply James v. 20, for which they consider Protestants to be fair game.

The inquiry classes for Romanists afforded good opportunities for them to put, or reply to, questions relative to the differences in teaching between the Church of Ireland and Rome ; giving occasion, also, for setting forth the way of salvation ; and many Romanists attended, especially in Dundalk. There was a mission school at each of these stations, which was well attended by adults of both sexes, as well as by children. There the main effort was to teach, and catechize on, the ' Hundred Texts ' bearing on Sin, the Saviour, the Holy Spirit, Godly Living, and the Controversy, in such a way that the scholars could understand them. I have long been convinced that Sunday-school teaching is, in the main, lamentably deficient. It is seldom that a child, even after having attended a Sunday-school for years, knows the way of salvation !

Another mode of instruction was by Scripture placards, such as :

Question : From how much sin are true believers cleansed by the blood of Jesus Christ ?

Answer : ' From all sin.'

Question : What is the way by which God can be approached ?

Answer : Jesus said : ' I am the Way, the Truth, and the life ; no man cometh unto the Father, but by Me.'

Or with the words of such texts as John iii. 16, and Heb. vii. 25, in large plain letters, not fancifully formed ones.

At times, through fear of the priests' displeasure, no one could be got, for love or money, to post a placard on the walls of any of the stations. It is a fact that at

such times, even if I could find a man brave enough
only to accompany me, I had to mount the ladder and
post the bills ; and, what is more, when I could find
no one to go, I went out alone, and posted them myself.
Since then I have often wondered at my temerity ;
it would have been so easy for one or more to cripple
me for life, or even to take my life there and then.
However, though I was often the object of jeers and
scornful laughter, which I used to pass off by some
humorous or racy remark, no one ever really interfered
with me on those occasions. Bless the Lord !

But the best of all our efforts was house-to-house
visitation. This was most trying work, and more
calculated than any other kind of mission work to cast
the worker back upon God. There was always the
disconcertingly unpleasant uncertainty as to the reception wherever a visit was paid. For those who boasted
of the certainty that their Church, and it only, was the
true Church of God, and that they were therefore,
as their phrase has it, ' in the way of salvation,' to
have overtures made to them—even with the undeniably
kind motive of saving their souls—which, perhaps,
with as much plainness as tenderness showed their
Church to be a false one, and they themselves ' out of
the way,' was sure to raise resentment in many cases,
and to engender suspicion in most. Hence the strain
upon the agents was often very severe.

The mission dealt largely in the free distribution of
admirably written handbills addressed to Romanists.
They were left at all the houses if possible, dropped in
the streets and roads, placed in the railway cars—in
fact, were put everywhere. That we used to call
' salting.'

There were generally twelve agents of the society
working at the three stations, and it was my business
to visit those stations, and to encourage those dear,
though despised, men of God. It is with unfeigned
thankfulness to the Lord, I am able to state that,
during the eleven years I was permitted to labour for
Him in the Louth Mission, nearly four hundred souls

were converted from Romanism ! In addition to that, there were the preventive results in enabling Protestants to withstand Papal aggression. The Gospel of Christ is the best, indeed the only, antidote to the poison of Popery for my dear countrymen. If the Irish were brought to the knowledge of the truth, they would be England's right arm, and second to none in the whole world.

I bless God for even the small share I had in working for the Irish Church Missions as a layman. I consider there is no mission to surpass them in their doctrinal teaching, so full and so sound in the truth as it is in Christ Jesus ; whilst their methods are the outcome of prayer, faith, and love. That God has blessed them abundantly, by owning their work, goes without saying. The work is still carried on, and blessings still attend it, but, owing to a large reduction of income, the sphere of operations is more restricted than in my time. I wish my means would allow of me filling the society's coffers, and I am thankful that, during my incumbency of St. Nathaniel's, Liverpool, I gave it two collections in aid each year. On one occasion Dr. MacCarthy came as deputation, and in the vestry he said, warmly shaking my hands : ' Well, Hobson, I am glad to get under your roof.' Most of the first workers and friends of the society have now gone to ' be with Christ, which is far better.'

Meantime my eldest sister had married one of Drogheda's wealthiest business men, of good standing ; and my youngest sister was in the Irish Church Missions Training School, Dublin. With the cordial approval of my darling mother, who had for several years lived with me, I arranged for her to reside with her oldest daughter, but still to be under my loving care. The time seemed, therefore, to have arrived for me to make a move towards taking Orders in the Church of Ireland. In this I was encouraged by my brother-in-law, who lent me one hundred and fifty pounds, which I was in due time enabled to pay back, most grateful for the loan, as it, with what I had, enabled me to get through. I had

decided to enter St. Bees' College, and wrote for its
curriculum ; but I addressed the envelope wrongly,
putting ' Birkenhead ' instead of ' Cumberland.' The
letter went to St. Aidan's Theological College, Birkenhead, and the Principal, Dr. Baylee, thinking it was
really meant for him, sent me his curriculum, which
led me to enter at St. Aidan's. This was of the Lord,
as was afterwards evident. Thank God, for the fact
stated by the Lord Jesus Christ, ' One of them (sparrows)
shall not fall on the ground without your Father.'

The intimation of my intended resignation, and
proposed plans, came as a great surprise to my Clerical
Superintendent. On finding my mind was quite made
up, he very kindly and generously said that if I were
then, or later on, in want of money to help me through,
he was prepared to assist me. On my thanking him
heartily, and saying that my way was clear in that
respect, he expressed the hope that I would return to
Ireland for ordination, remarking that he felt sure the
Irish Church Missions would gladly avail themselves
of my experience and services, in a higher capacity.
He was the first to sign the address which accompanied
the presentation made to me on leaving. I had his love
to the last. It was my intention to return to my native
land, but the Lord showed me otherwise, and I followed
His leading. Since then I have constantly been brought
to see how clearly it was His will that I should take
Orders in England, and work for Him there.

The way was now open to realize the great idea of my
life. My darling mother was made quite comfortable,
my brothers and sisters were all grown up and occupying
good positions, and my dear father's soul was, I believed,
with Christ. Therefore my heart was filled, and overflowed, with gratitude to the Lord for all the blessings
He had bestowed upon me, and all the mercies
He had shown towards me. For though the iron had
entered into my soul, I felt sure God had led me in the
right way. He is too wise to err, and too loving to be
unkind. Just before leaving the Irish Church Missions'
work for St. Aidan's, a testimonial was presented to

me (see Appendix B) ; for which I did and do thank God. Though in work for Him it should be His approval that we seek, it is encouraging to have the approval of His faithful people.

PART III.

STUDENT AT ST. AIDAN'S COLLEGE, BIRKENHEAD.

Life at St. Aidan's—Principal's misleading teaching—Cross wearing
—Controversial discussion—Dr. Blakeney's offer accepted—After-
intercourse with opponent — Offer from Irish Church Missions —
Testimonial from fellow-students—Interviews with Bishop—Ordination.

EARLY [in January, 1863, I entered St. Aidan's
Theological College, Birkenhead, as an indoor
student; a perfect stranger, having the acquaintance of only one person in the whole of England.
But I knew the Lord was with me, and that sufficed. I
resolved to devote myself assiduously to study, and
therefore read hard—fourteen hours a day in term time,
and five hours during vacation—which was in a measure
rewarded, as I never fell below a good place in the
second class, and finished by tumbling into the first,
an event that had not occurred for several years.

Like some of my fellow-students, I found the study of
mere theology, as I had found the Romish controversy,
not conducive to spiritual-mindedness; we therefore
met weekly, for devotion and waiting upon God about
this matter.

The Principal of the College, the Rev. Joseph Baylee,
D.D., had the reputation of being a great linguist, an
able anti-Theistic and anti-Romish controversialist, and
thoroughly evangelical; he was also a leading clergyman of the Church of England. The college was full:
some of the students were ritualistically inclined,
others were nondescript, only a few were decidedly

Protestant. The Principal rather encouraged us to ask him questions, and professed not to mind our differing from him. I often tackled the ritualists, whom I found feeble in argument, my knowledge of the Romish controversy standing me in good stead on such occasions.

It was not long before I caught, in the Principal's teaching, accents which grated on my ears, and seemed to have a disturbing effect on some of my class-fellows. Waiting until I had really got hold of the subjects to which his remarks referred, I then, in the Lord's strength, began to ask him questions in class, and even to differ from him openly, but, of course, with the greatest courtesy. The following are specimens of his more than doubtful teaching :

Apostolic Succession—*i.e.*, ' hand-over-hand grace.'

Grace, though not life, given in baptism *per se.*

The Holy Spirit given in confirmation by the imposition of hands.

The germ of the resurrection body communicated in the Lord's Supper.

The absolution in the morning service more than a declaration.

The blessing given by the priest more than a prayer.

The cross a Christian symbol.

As Holy Scripture and the standards of the Church alike teach that faith—loving trust which is itself ' the gift of God,' unites to Christ, purifies the heart, works by love ; that it is the channel through which the life of Christ flows into the soul, the only way by which the soul, at all times, in all places, under all circumstances, has access to God through Christ, by the Spirit, apart from, and altogether without, either angel, saint, bishop, or priest ; and, also, that the Lord's Supper and other means of grace are full of blessing when used by that same divine gift, faith : all other teaching is consequently contrary to Holy Scripture, opposed to the standards of the Church, and a breaking of ordination vows by those who are thus guilty of imperilling souls ' for whom Christ died.'

Apostolic Succession, as taught by Rome, and by
her imitators in the Church of England, well-nigh
limits the flow of Divine grace to ordinances performed
by men episcopally ordained, thus making those
ordinances absolutely essential; the logical sequence
of which is to cut off all non-episcopal Churches from
Salvation, and to constitute the episcopally ordained
man a mediator. Happily, some of those holding
these unscriptural doctrines illogically fear to face
their tremendous consequences. That was the Principal
of St. Aidan's case.

I well remember a man there who was so sensitive,
that, seeing his cousin, already one of the students,
wearing a cross, he remonstrated with him, and it
was given up. Yet that tender-conscienced young
fellow, having confidence in the Principal, apparently
became unsettled by his teaching, consorted with the
ritualistic students, and, after ordination, seceded to
Rome, in which he remained for some years. I was
not a little touched by seeing in the press, long after,
a statement of his main reason for returning to the
Church, which was ' I could not allow anyone to take
precedence of the Lord Jesus in my heart.' One day
I received a heavy blow from the Principal. When
in conversation with him, I said how sorry I was he
had told a dear friend of mine, concerning me, that
my ' mind was beautifully opening.' He replied :
' Yes, I did say that ; and is it not true ? ' I answered :
' Well, if I know my own mind, not an iota.' ' I am
sorry to hear it ; and,' he continued, ' now, let me
tell you that when I am twenty years in the clay you
will have burned your fingers.' I said : ' I trust not.
The God who has so watched over and kept me up
to the present will keep me to the end.' I confess
I felt these remarks very much, seeing they came
from one whose power to make or mar a student's
prospects was a current tradition in the college.

A student who had a large Bible-class for men, in
Birkenhead, returned one Sunday afternoon a little
excited, stating that a member of the class took exception

to his instruction on Article VI., and challenged him, or any student in St. Aidan's, to prove that the Bible was a sufficient rule of faith. Looking at me, he said : ' I want you to meet him.' I declined. A deputation of students waited on me with the same request, to which I said, ' No ' : subsequently, however, under great pressure, I consented.

The Principal promised to preside, and all the preliminary arrangements were made. On the afternoon of the very day on which the discussion was to take place Dr. Baylee had an unexpected and imperative call to one of the Midland counties, which obliged him to leave by an early evening train. At that short notice the Rev. Dr. Blakeney, vicar of Christ Church, Claughton, near to the college, kindly consented to act for him. The place of meeting was filled, and nearly all the students were present. I allowed my opponent to lead off, but, after my rejoinder, he could say no more, and the discussion was closed. Dr. Blakeney then, offering me his hand, asked me how soon I would be ready for ordination, adding that for a year and a half he had been looking for a curate, and that he would be happy to give me a title for Deacon's Orders. Thanking him, and saying that I had only one more term to get through, I went on to tell him that I could not think of commencing my ministerial work amongst a rich and highly-educated congregation such as his was. He rejoined : ' Well, come to my house to tea to-morrow evening, and we will talk over the matter.' I went ; we had the proposed talk ; and, as the result, I hesitatingly, yet in faith, accepted his offer. Little did I think, when twice refusing to take up that discussion, that on it was to depend, humanly speaking, the trend of my future ministerial life. As I left the house to return to college, my mind was filled with the thought of God's faithfulness and love. Only a few weeks afterwards I had an offer from the Irish Church Missions of a title in the Diocese of Tuam as their missionary. It was not altogether unexpected, but it came too late. The Lord had work for me to do in

England, although I had no idea of the ministry there.

In order that God may be glorified, I feel constrained to record that, though I do not know whether my opponent in that discussion was then a Romanist, or a Ritualist, or only a wobbling Protestant; or whether that discussion was a factor in shaping his subsequent spiritual life: I do know that, through the years since, we have been as brothers in Christ; that he has been an earnest worker for Christ; that he has, on occasions, come over from his residence in Birkenhead to my parish in Liverpool, to speak in the open air for Christ; that God has prospered him in business; and that though we are still in close fellowship in the Lord, with the exception of perhaps a very occasional passing allusion we have never spoken about that memorable discussion.

On leaving St. Aidan's, a testimonial, which accompanied sundry volumes, was presented to me by some of my fellow-students (see Appendix C).

The Bishop of Chester, Dr. Graham, said to me, on my interview with him, that I might come to his next examination of candidates for ordination, which would be about three months from then. During that time I gave myself to much prayer; to much introspection as to my spiritual state, as to my motives for the step I was about to take, as to whether I was indeed moved by the Holy Spirit to seek the office of a minister in the Church of God. I sought to carry all the past, with my own poor self, to the fountain of Christ's most precious blood, for washing and acceptance afresh by God, my Father, in Christ Jesus; and to the Holy Spirit for the blessedness of sanctification. I felt overwhelmed, as I recalled God's loving kindness and care; how He had kept me from falling, had 'covered my head in the day of battle,' had led me on step by step; and looking to Him for guidance, I felt that He would still use me, as a minister of His Gospel.

According to notice, I attended at the Palace, Chester, for examination, which I passed, with the Bishop's commendation of my Greek viva voce; and, in the good providence of God, on Sunday, March 12, 1865, I was ordained, in Chester Cathedral, a Deacon of the Church of England. That was Dr. Graham's last ordination : shortly afterwards he was called into the presence of the Great Bishop of souls. Though others wore the surplice, I was ordained in the gown ; and I did not turn to the east in the Creed.

At this time much prayer for me was offered to God by many dear friends who took an interest in my welfare, especially by my darling mother, my old Sunday-school teachers, my Irish Church Missions fellow-workers, and my incumbent ; hence, doubtless, the conscious blessing which the Lord vouchsafed to grant me in the ordination itself, manifested as the Bishop, on handing me the New Testament, said : ' Take thou authority to read the Gospel in the Church of God, and to preach the same if thou thereto be licensed by the Bishop himself ' ; when my heart leaped for joy at its being the Gospel I was given authority to read and preach—the Gospel, good news to lost sinners, the glorious Gospel of the blessed God. From the depth of my soul there went up the silent prayer : ' O God, help me to read the Gospel as Thy Gospel, and to preach the Gospel as Thy Gospel, now and always, in its purity and fulness. I thank Thee that I am not sent to preach my own vapourings, or Church authority, but that my commission from Thee this day is to preach Thy Gospel as it is in Thy Holy Word.' My heart overflowed, and I do thank Him that tears rolled down my cheeks, falling on the chancel steps where I stood and knelt. I thank God for having received, there and then, a glorious commission, which it has ever been the desire of my heart, ' in season, out of season,' to discharge, by proclaiming that Gospel which is the ' power of God unto salvation,' the one thing men need. They want a living, loving, personal God, an all-sufficient Saviour, a sanctifying Comforter. ' Oh, sing praises, sing praises,' that God, in His great grace, not only made me His own, by regeneration and adoption, when a child, but hath counted me faithful, putting me into the ministry. I knew I did not bring into it qualifications in the matter of academical degree, or a high order of intellect, as did others; but I had no doubt as to the Divine call. To me had been granted a very practical experience in the school of adversity, of grace, and in the home mission-field; I therefore felt humbly confident that I was not running without having been sent, and that the Holy Spirit would use me as an ambassador for Christ to glorify God in the salvation of souls. I thought of myself as being in a sense somewhat like David, taken by God from the sheepfold, and, after severe discipline and bitter trials, ultimately made leader of the Lord's chosen people.

PART IV.

CURATE OF CHRIST CHURCH, BIRKENHEAD.

Curacy at Claughton—First sermon—Congregation visiting—New work started—Ordained presbyter at Liverpool—Matriculation at Trinity College, Dublin—First-class prizeman—Social invitations—Dancing — Cards — Church Association — English Church Union — Conditional offer of new district accepted—Sermon on 1 Tim. iv. 8 requested—Cattle epidemic—Presentation on leaving Claughton—Tribute to Dr. Blakeney.

ON the day of my ordination, Dr. Blakeney announced in church that (D.V.) I would preach on the following Wednesday evening. On that occasion, when in the vestry before service, my heart began to palpitate, and I said : ' Doctor, I cannot preach to-night, I feel too nervous.' Looking at me, he merely remarked : ' Let us kneel, and ask God to give you composure.' On rising, I said : ' Doctor, the answer has not come ; do take my place this evening. Again he prayed, and again I pleaded to be excused. He then proposed that he should take all the prayers, and that I should sit in the inner chancel ; assuring me that he was certain the answer would come, and that as I went into the pulpit he would be praying for me. During the service his holy fervour set me all aglow, and there came an answer to the prayers which had been specially offered up for me, in that I felt calm and composed. Whilst I was ascending the pulpit stairs it seemed as if the good man's prayers were like arms underneath me, lifting me up. The text was John iv. 49, ' Sir, come down ere my child die ' ; and the Lord gave me great liberty in preaching. As my incumbent considered it advisable for a beginner to use notes only, I did not read my sermon.

So soon as I was settled, the good Doctor kindly introduced me each week to the various families forming the congregation, which was really eclectic, there being practically no parish at that time. Accompanying him for the purpose, I found he was a devoted pastor, and I noticed that those who lived in ceiled houses looked for and appreciated his visits. When we had finished our visitation, he expressed a wish that I should visit the whole congregation systematically.

A glimpse had now been afforded me of social life, to which I was until then a total stranger ; and how to comply with the requirements for successful pastoral visitation of such people seemed a task too formidable for me to achieve. I therefore cast myself upon the Lord, claiming from Him the needed faith, wisdom, and grace ; and on the strength of my commission to read and preach the Gospel I went forward, to find that the stone of difficulty was rolled away : for I was kindly received by all, was cordially received by most, and by some was welcomed as a minister of Christ. Amongst them were many of God's own children, who became my true and fast friends in the Lord.

It was laid upon me to initiate the following, for congregational, and ultimately for parochial benefit, each being with the entire concurrence and approval of my incumbent, and all being largely attended.

A Bible-class on Thursday morning ; amongst the members was Mrs. Codner, the authoress of ' Lord, I hear of showers of blessing.'

A weekly class for study of the Prayer-Book, principally for men.

A class for the cultivation of sacred music.

The Literary Society kindly elected me one of its vice-presidents.

The church seated 1,300. The number of communicants was very large. The congregation contributed about two thousand pounds a year for outside objects. I felt deeply the privilege of being curate to such an incumbent, and of such a congregation ; and I was ever looking up to the Lord for wisdom and power, praying that the Holy Spirit might make use of me amongst that people for Christ's sake. In 1866 I was ordained Presbyter in St. Luke's Church, Liverpool, by Dr. Jacobson, Bishop of Chester.

At the suggestion of Dr. Blakeney I matriculated at Trinity College, Dublin, carrying off two first-class prizes in the catechetical divinity examination. I had the privilege of reading with my incumbent some of the proofs of his great work on ' The Book of Common Prayer, in its History and Interpretation.'

In the Doctor's absence I visited several of the many young ladies' schools attending the church. I also helped to train young men in the Romish controversy, for the Protestant Reformation Society ; two of them I influenced to study for the ministry, which in due time they entered, and are both faithful and successful pastors. One is now an Hon. Canon ; the other an Hon. Canon and a Rural Dean. Thank God !

Not long after I was ordained I accepted an invitation to a wedding breakfast at the house of one of the rich families in the congregation, and, amidst all the display, there was nothing to offend the conscience. For the same evening I had a supper invitation, and on reaching the house I found it filled with people, mostly members of the congregation, in evening dress. When dancing began I felt that was not the place for me, so making my way, as soon as I could, out of the drawing-room into the hall, I asked a servant for my hat and coat, and off I slipped. On passing my vicar's house, seeing a light in it, I rang. He opened the door, and I told him what I had done, when he said : ' Oh, is there a dance ? Thank God you have escaped.' My next thought was whether the host and hostess, or their company, would have taken offence ; but they had not, continuing to be my friends. I know there is a difference of opinion about this matter ; but I felt I could not stand up before the congregation and deliver the Lord's message if I had compromised myself by remaining.

At a quiet tea one evening a lady asked me if I danced. On my replying 'No,' she said: 'Well, the other night I had a clergyman as my partner.' I rejoined, 'I dare say'; when she continued: 'He said he was going to preach on the following Sunday in a church near to my house. I said I should go to hear him. His reply was: "Oh no, do not come to hear me, for I am a dry stick."' I then put to her, very solemnly, this question: 'Tell me, if you were dying, would you send for that clergyman?' She answered: 'Oh dear no; I would take care he should not visit me then.' 'Exactly; he may have been a very pleasant partner in the giddy dance, but you would not like to see him on your death-bed.'

On another occasion, after tea, cards were introduced, and I was asked to play. I refused. Again I was invited to make one at the card-table, when I gave the same answer. Soon the hostess came to me, and said: 'Oh, do join us; there is no harm in them.' I answered solemnly: 'I do not play cards'; and after a little while, wishing her and her husband good-night, I left. These incidents occurred during the first year of my ministry, and, account for it as one may, though I accepted several kindly-given invitations from many members of the congregation, I was never again placed in positions such as those described.

Those who have been distinguished 'fishers of men,' fathers of many spiritual sons and daughters, were not known as dancers or card-players. But oh, how difficult it is to preserve one's influence as an ambassador of Christ!

One day Dr. Blakeney asked me to have a walk with him, as he had something special to say; it was this: 'What do you think? I believe the time has come for the formation of an association in the Church of England to maintain its doctrine and discipline against the inroads of semi-Romanism now being made by that disloyal body the "English Church Union." I propose writing a letter to the *Record*, suggesting such, and to wait three months to see if anyone will take it up.' He wrote, but no one took the hint. Later on he came to me, saying that he had been much in prayer as to his letter to the *Record*, and that he had decided to write a hundred letters to as many well-known clergymen and laymen, inviting them to meet him in London for conference on the subject. He did so, and over eighty attended. After prayer and conference, it was unanimously decided to form a society as suggested, to be called ' the Church Association,' appointing the convener honorary secretary *pro tem*. I have been a member of that organization from the beginning.

The Council subsequently accepted, and hung on its office wall, No. 14, Buckingham Street, Strand, London, Dr. Blakeney's life-size portrait, presented by the late John Hope, Esq., of Edinburgh, bearing the following inscription : ' R. P. Blakeney, D.D., LL.D., Founder of the Church Association.'

The history of that association, as to its aims, methods and achievements, is well known. I shall therefore only say that if its findings in test cases set forth by the Privy Council, had been enforced by the Bishops as a body, the English Church Union would not to-day be able to print and publish to the world, in ' The Tourists' Guide,' the names and addresses of over nine thousand clergymen more or less advanced on the way to Rome. What the end of it all will be who can tell ? Of this we may be sure : ' The Lord reigneth.' His ' counsel shall stand.' He will do all His pleasure. Meantime He tells His faithful ones, ' Ye are my witnesses.' Oh, to be found amongst the ' called and chosen and faithful ' !

I had just passed my third year in this ' land of Goshen,' when the Rev. Herbert Woodward, incumbent of St. Clement's, Toxteth Park, Liverpool—afterwards Canon Woodward, D.D.—called upon me, though a total stranger, to say that he was forming a new parish out of his own, that a church was being built, that he wanted for it a man of truly evangelical missionary spirit, that there were sixty-five candidates, including a

D.D., but that, from what Dr. Blakeney had said to him about me, he had called to offer me the appointment, saddled with one condition that I would withdraw from Trinity College, Dublin. About ten days afterwards he called again, and kindly said he was willing to modify the condition accompanying his offer of a week or so ago, by proposing that I should only suspend my course in Dublin University. I agreed to consider that, and promised to let him know my decision. After much thought, prayer, and conference with trusted friends, especially with my dear incumbent, I accepted this conditional offer, as from the Lord.

I had been shown over the proposed new sphere of labour, which certainly was dismal and gloomy indeed. As I stood, looking round, I had a distinct impression as of a voice saying, ' This is the place for you.' I never had a doubt about it. I have always felt that there I was in the place that God had prepared for me, in which to ' spend and be spent ' for Him.

I have reason to know that the Lord did use me in Claughton, not only by assisting the incumbent in his ministrations to that rich and educated congregation, but in leading some to decide for Christ, and in building up some who were His already. What a mercy !

One evening a gentleman called to tell me that my sermons had led him to think and to give himself to God, and to ask if I would preach from 1 Tim. iv. 8, ' Godliness is profitable unto all things.' He remarked : ' I see I shall never be a rich man. I cannot in my business do that which is necessary to make money. But I do not doubt having enough.' About a year afterwards he took typhoid fever, and whilst he lay ill I constantly visited him. One morning I was called to him very early, and on reaching his bedside I found him dying, but quite conscious. Grasping my hand tightly, he said : ' All is right.' As, with his hand in mine, I committed him to God, his mother, sisters, and brothers kneeling just outside the room door, his hand dropped, and his spirit departed, to be ' for ever with the Lord.'

A dear sister in the Lord called upon me to ask if I

would join her and her husband, at twelve o'clock that day, in prayer to God that He would be pleased to keep their cattle free from the disease which was carrying off those on the next farm, or, if it attacked them, to bless remedies for their cure. I went back with her to the farmhouse, where she and her husband knelt with me and we spread the whole matter before the Lord, as we did every week-day for nearly a month. And, let it be told to His praise and glory, God was gracious to hear our cry and grant our petition, inasmuch as not one of those dear people's cattle was even smitten, though the disease attacked and killed many of those on the neighbouring farms. It would be difficult to explain this otherwise than as being an answer to prayer. I may add that two members of that family are now in the ministry, and nearly all are on the Lord's side, mainly due, under God, to the beautiful life and holy influence of a truly Christian mother. I have often heard her petition to the Throne of Grace : ' Lord, I do pray that every one of my children may be Thine.'

Whilst at Claughton I was presented with a set of robes and a purse of money, accompanied by an address (see Appendix D).

On my leaving, the Sunday-school teachers gave me a silver pocket Communion Service and an address (see Appendix D).

From the gentlemen of the congregation I received a valuable gold watch ; and from the Literary Society a time-piece and an address (see Appendix D).

The time having now come for my departure from Claughton to enter upon a new sphere of labour for the Lord, which I then little thought was to be the main work of my life, I found it difficult to part from valued friends with whom I had been associated in God's work since my ordination. Especially was that the case with regard to dear Dr. Blakeney and his family. I have a thousand times blessed and thanked God for the privilege of being curate to him. He took me into his confidence, and I saw into, and felt the holy influence of, his inner life. I am free to say of him that I never knew any other man as well as I knew him, who seemed to me so like our blessed Lord. Thank God, I had his Christian love until he was called hence to his eternal home.

How gracious God has been to me! My life is a clear proof of His tender loving care. He is the same God and Lord still. May any who are finding God's leading different from what they wish, trust, wait, and hope on to the end. Amen.

PART V.

VICAR OF ST. NATHANIEL'S, WINDSOR, LIVERPOOL, 1868-1901.

' Sixteen acres of sin '—Service in cellar—First service in ragged school—First confirmation class—Conversions—Band of Hope restarted —Cellar readings—An unauthorized ' cross '—An ' Altar ' Table— Church named—Designation of district—Consecration.

1868-69.

THE proposed new district, sixteen acres in extent, with a population of 4,500, was in the ecclesiastical parish of St. Clements, Toxteth Park, but in the civil parish of West Derby, and was locally known as Windsor. Its area was, socially and morally, the lowest in all the south-east portion of Liverpool. The houses were small and badly built, and narrow courts and inhabited cellars abounded, causing the place to be a hotbed of fever and other deadly diseases. One street was unfit, and even unsafe, for the passage of ladies. Another was wholly given over to the ' social evil,' and was known as ' the little hell.' The inhabitants generally were styled ' the roughs of Windsor,' and advertisements for labourers constantly, indeed usually, bore the ominous warning, ' Windsor men need not apply.' Sixteen public-houses and two beer-shops pandered to the drinking propensities of the population. Though the famous Milner's Safe Works were situated there, very few of their employeès lived near them. A sprinkling of respectable artisans and small shop-keepers, together with a few families who even kept a servant, were redeeming features in the otherwise disreputable neighbourhood.

The incumbent of St. Clement's had come to the conclusion that the only way by which those sixteen acres of sin could be won for God was to plant a church in their midst, and to provide them with a clerical missionary. He began by establishing a ragged school, to work which he assigned a curate, who, however, lost heart after a time, and departed. His place was taken by another, who soon filled the schoolroom on Sunday evenings, but with people for whom the service was not intended, which caused friction, and led to the incumbent parting with him. He obtained a curacy in an adjoining parish, and, having enlisted the sympathy of the people he swept the deck of the little mission. It was under such unfavourable conditions that I accepted the curacy of this new district (being subsequently appointed incumbent), and entered upon the work November 14, 1868.

I felt it would be wise to ignore the recent disagreeables, and also to take up a position which, by its neutrality, would render me entirely independent of them. My first effort, therefore, was made in Cellar 6, Oliver Street, on the day of my arrival, when there were present three women, one man, and a little fellow who sat on a creepy stool. I sang ' Rock of Ages ' and ' There is a Fountain,' read the parable of the Lost Sheep, and prayed twice. What it was that went home to him I know not, but oh, wondrous grace ! that one man was quickened by the Holy Spirit : ' the first drop of the coming shower. I never had evidence of any of those three women having been then or afterwards ' born again ' ; but that little lad was in after-years led to the Lord, was confirmed, became a communicant, now fills a responsible post in Liverpool, and, with a wife and family, is living in the fear and love of God.

On the Sunday following there were, including children, about thirty present in the schoolroom. I preached from Matt. x. 3, viz., ' Matthew the publican.'

I gave myself entirely to visitation from house to house, and, by God's grace, I found favour in the eyes of the inhabitants, whether Church people, Nonconformists, or Romanists. Then I got the addresses of the ragged children, and visited their parents, with excellent results. It was not long before the room, which held 250, used to be filled to overflowing by the people near about. The first administration of the Lord's Supper was to eight communicants, one of them still living.

That winter I formed a confirmation class, and in the following summer sent through the mother church forty candidates of whose new birth I felt assured. That was a cause of great joy, alike to myself and to the incumbent of St. Clement's, which was then well filled, the congregation including many truly Christian people. I was specially interested in one of the candidates, the son—and sole survivor out of eleven children—of pious Wesleyan parents, who, as their boy was not the Lord's, rejoiced at his coming under the good influence of the confirmation class. In the personal interview I had with him, as with all the other candidates, just before the day appointed for the rite, amongst the questions I put to him was this one : ' Are you born again ? ' He first looked at me, and then, looking down, said, with much feeling : ' I should like to be.' We knelt down at an old box which stood in the anteroom of the ragged school, and the lad, with his hands covering his face, rested it upon the box, whilst I lifted my heart in audible prayer to the Holy Spirit, that he would be pleased to beget this boy anew in Christ Jesus. I then rose, but he remained motionless. Waiting a little, I again knelt, and pleaded for the gift of a new heart to the dear fellow. Again I stood, but he made no movement. Feeling almost as if my heart would break, after another slight pause I went on my knees the third time, in earnest supplication for the blessing, and then got up, feeling I could do no more. Almost directly he also rose, quite calmly, and, reaching out his hand for mine, said, in an assuring tone: 'The blessing has come.' We at once knelt together and gave God the glory. In due time he became, and is still, a church-worker; and, by God's grace, though he has had his trials, he has never tripped. I married him to a Christian girl, baptized their children, and solemnized the marriage of the eldest, whose firstborn was also baptized in the church. The dear fellow's parents had the joy of knowing that their only child was the Lord's and was engaged in His work. I had the pleasure of presenting the aged couple with a cake on the occasion of their golden wedding, and when they died, first the mother and then the father, I was present at the burial of each.

I will name two other instances of Divine blessing on the mission-room work. A gentleman by education, living on the border of our new district, finding out somehow, that I knew some of his rich relatives in Cheshire, attended our simple service, when the Holy Spirit arrested him. He made himself known to me, and, walking in the ways of the Lord, became an active, devoted, prominent helper in the church. It is outside my purpose to describe all he has been, and has done for God, in well-nigh every department of work by turn, all along, ever since. The Keeper of Israel not only kept him safely, but used him greatly. Thank God, on my resignation I left him in the work, as true as steel, after thirty-three years unbroken, loyal, efficient service, a trusted fellow-labourer in Christ Jesus.

A sweet, ladylike little girl found her way to the mission service, and so interested her Christian mother by the description of what she heard there that she came also, was one of the first seat-holders in the new church, and a most efficient and successful worker, bringing into the service education, culture, and perseverance, as well as prayer, faith, and love. She, too, continued with me to the end of my ministry. I could record many other such instances. The Lord always finds instruments with which to do His work.

That winter I made a special point of winning, by

sundry ways, the hearts of the ragged little ones. It is something to gain the love even of poor children ; often it is the door of their parents' hearts. I found it so. I had, and have, a never-to-be forgotten recollection of my own childhood and boyhood days ; hence my sympathies were deeply moved for the poor, and specially for their children ; and when the bitterly cold weather came, I felt my soul stirred by the destitute and lost condition of a large number of the people in my charge.

The communicants increased, the mothers' meeting was resuscitated, and the ragged children's Band of Hope was restarted. I continued the cellar readings. There were sometimes two on the same evening, each lasting three-quarters of an hour, with a breathing interval of about twenty minutes in the open air, for even in winter it was very stuffy in the cellars.

Though I had no official voice in the matter, I kept my eye upon the church building, and so made two discoveries. The one was that a stone erection looking like a cross appeared on the west gable, to which I called Mr. Woodward's attention. We went at once to the architect and persuaded him to amputate the arms, as its erection was contrary to the intended meaning of the sealed design for the building. The other discovery was that against the east wall a raised platform was being erected, on which the Communion Table would be placed. To that also we took very serious objection, desiring to have the Table stand right away from the wall ; and after considerable hesitation the architect gave way, agreeing to have it as we wished, provided the intended platform space on the floor was marked by different tiling.

It was now summer, and the school-room being very crowded, we were longing to occupy the church. One day I met a well-known Liverpool clergyman, who made inquiries as to the mission work, and, after speaking about the approaching consecration of the church, remarked : ' Well, you have got the poor to the

room, but will they go to the church?' Greatly
surprised, I answered, 'Oh, surely yes!' He then
stated he had known cases where it was not so. I
asked, and obtained, his leave to mention that in the
mission service; which I did, expressing a confident
hope that all would go to church: and all went. The
consecration was fixed for July 17th. In God's good
providence I had already been duly nominated incumbent. The church was to be called after Nathaniel,
whose name, though not in the 'Calendar,' is written
in the 'Book of Life'; for was it not of him the Saviour
spoke those words of high commendation, 'Behold
an Israelite indeed, in whom is no guile'? There are
in the 'Calendar' many so-called 'Saints,' whose
sole claim to the title is based upon the worthless
authority of some not too reputable Pope!

The description 'Windsor, West Derby,' arose from
the deed conveying the site of the church, describing
it as 'situated in a place called Windsor,' and that being
in West Derby, caused the twofold designation by
which it is styled in legal and ecclesiastical docu-
ments.

By 'consecration' is simply meant the setting apart
for ever of the newly-erected building for Divine worship
according to the rites and ceremonies of the English
Church; in which, as a feat, there is no legal warrant
for any specific form of consecration, that depending
to a great extent upon the discretion of the Bishop;
but the custom of using a form of prayer and praise,
with the reading of psalms, which has grown to be
quite common, is not out of harmony with our Church
standards. The idea of 'exorcism' is thoroughly
Popish and superstitious.

As the date drew near, we devised many little ways
of creating and increasing, throughout the new district,
an interest in the occasion. Much constant prayer
had been offered for God's blessing upon the building
of His house, and in the same way was sought a similar
blessing upon its consecration to the service of His
great name.

1870.

Church consecrated — Plan of work — Church described — Broken windows—' Little Bobbies '—Men's Bible-class—' Roughs in church ' —Christmas generosity—Chairs in inner chancel—Bishop's offer of tablets—Rectorial fees—Runcorn vicarage offered and declined— Girl's gratitude—Children's Bible-classes—Diocesan Society grant— Distressed family — Confirmation — Designs for tablets — 'Cities of Refuge '—Business workers for God—Small-pox epidemic—Revolting case—Testimonial from Men's Bible-class.

THE Church was consecrated July 17, 1869, by the Bishop of Chester, Dr. Jacobson, who preached from 1 Cor. vii. 35, ' Attend upon the Lord without distraction.' It seemed a strange text for such an occasion ; but in after years I found it ' a word in season.' There was a fairly large attendance. Then followed an octave of services, with sermons by special preachers, including the rector of West Derby, and the incumbent of St. Clement's. My induction and reading myself in caused me to feel more than ever the weight of the work, and I was well nigh overcome by contemplating the awful degradation, and the terrible poverty, in which a large proportion of the people were living, or rather existing. I realized that an iron will, and the strength of a lion, would be needed to do, and to continue doing, that which must be done, if those people were to be won for the dear Lord.

Knowing there are many ways of working a parish, I had long thought deeply and earnestly as to the best method. I was greatly encouraged by the tokens of blessings upon my labours already vouchsafed, and I hoped that my past experience might prove helpful to me in the future. I could not but realize that if the people were to be evangelized, it would not be any haphazard kind of administration, but by working systematically, and that I must not merely feel my way. Over and over again I had recourse to the Throne of Grace for guidance, direction, and strength.

There was no doubt in my mind as to either the attractive power of an uplifted, blessed, personal Saviour, or the accompanying power of the Holy Spirit to arrest, convince, and save the lost; and I thanked God for it. My heart's desire was accepted, and my soul's petitions were answered; for I am persuaded that the following general plan of work came to me from ' the good hand of my God ' :

That for sin, poverty, and dirt, in evidence on all sides, even under the very shadow of God's house, the Gospel of His free grace is the first and chief remedy.

That in every department of work for God, the Holy Spirit shall occupy a prominent place.

That all teaching, whether in the pulpit or outside it, shall be on distinctly Evangelical Protestant lines.

That the services shall be plain, warm, and hearty, and such as can be joined in by all.

That the one great aim in all church work shall be the spiritual regeneration of souls, and their sanctification, as seen in the life of faith, and of its outcome, good works.

That loving sympathy and adaptation shall be the lever in constant use.

That the work shall be missionary as well as congregational and pastoral; and that the Lord Jesus shall be made known in the homes of the people, whether church, chapel, or Romish.

That only communicants shall be eligible as wardens, sidesmen, teachers, singers, visitors, or for any regular church work.

That to prevent there being drones in the church hive, the pastor shall not do work which might be done by others.

That the pastor shall be always willing to receive any who call upon him, whether members of the congregation or not.

That no prizes shall be given in the Sunday-school.

That the ragged school shall be carried on, if transferred from St. Clement's to St. Nathaniel's.

That the church shall not get into debt.

That before baptism, words of explanation and counsel shall be spoken to parents and sponsors.

That much time and prayer shall be bestowed upon Confirmation classes.

That baptism shall have its due place ; and that the Lord's Supper shall be administered in the evening at least once a month, as well as at other times.

That at the solemnization of matrimony the church shall be open to all, and that the exhortation shall never be omitted.

That extempore prayer shall be freely used in the pulpit.

That after a funeral all the mourners shall be affectionately urged to attend the next service in church, when there shall be some seasonable words spoken from the pulpit, or a special prayer, or an appropriate hymn, or the Dead March shall be played.

That the people shall be taught to regard the church as God's house, placed by him in their midst for their use.

We were now in a brand-new church, full of thankfulness to God for providing it, and of hope that by its means, directly and indirectly, He would do great things for us. It was a marvel of cheapness, considering the beauty of design, the materials used, and the workmanship. Built of plain grey brick inside and out, having a nave, two aisles, an apsidal chancel brightened by a seven-lights window, an organ-chamber on one side, and a vestry on the other, with clerestory windows, a lofty, boarded roof, and accommodation for 750 worshippers ; the cost was £6,000, £1,000 for the site, £1,000 for endowment, and under £4,000 for the building, of which amount nearly £4,000 was obtained from the Liverpool Church and School Extension Society.

The situation was unfavourable, the church standing back, and being scarcely in sight, hemmed in on three sides by poor streets of wretched houses, with bad approaches. The Building Committee did their best, and everything essential had been provided previous to the consecration; but much remained to be done before the church was completed. There was no money in hand, as the twenty pounds collected at the consecration had been already appropriated by the committee. A member of that body told me some time previously that they would not be able to wire the windows. When I replied that I did not think it was needed, he answered, ' You do not know this place as I do.' And it looked as if he were right, for, from the glazing of the windows until the consecration—nine days—no less than seventy-six panes were broken.

Nevertheless, remembering the promise, ' My God shall supply all your need,' we did not lose heart. Whilst we were using the ragged school sufficient had been raised, in small sums, to provide communion plate for the church; the harmonium hired for the consecration was retained for the church services; and I had decided on having a collection for church expenses and unsupplied requirements, every Sunday evening at least. I at once called together a few of my more active helpers, for conference as to the best way of carrying on, and providing for, the work before us. All were of one mind; all were full of hopefulness and fixedness of purpose; and it was decided to raise money at once for the erection of a temporary fence round the church, and for the paving of contiguous pathways : happily, the latter was done by the Corporation, free. These were our first financial efforts.

Whilst yet in the consecration octave I was naturally thinking of the windows. I resolved to try the power of love on the poor children who swarmed around the church, since they were the offenders in the matter of the broken panes. On seeing me approach they flocked around. After saying that I was pleased to see them enjoying their play; that I knew many of their faces as having been in the ragged school; and that I was sorry to hear of the church windows having been broken; I pointed to the building, and asked : ' Whose house is that ? ' They looked at each other as if they expected to be caught in some way, and there was no answer. I

then told them that big building was God's house, but
that it was their house as well ; and inquiring whether
they would like to break the windows of their own
houses, they all said ' No.' To my question whether
they would like to break the windows in God's house,
there came the same answer. ' Well, then, I wish you
not to break them. I want you to become my " little
bobbies," to take care of the church windows.' At
that they laughed outright, being quite tickled at the
idea of becoming ' bobbies,' knowing only too well what
a ' bobby ' was ; and they all cried out : ' Yes, teacher ;
we will, we will ! ' This little expedient of love was
occasionally resorted to by me during the whole of my
ministry, and I can truly say that though the church
windows were unwired, the breaking of glass in them
was a rare occurrence indeed. Is there a greater power
than loving kindness ?

The sights of child destitution round about were such
as to make on hide one's face in shame that they could
be possible in a highly civilized and professedly Christian
city. They suggested, instead of the too usual question,
' Am I my brother's keeper ? ' another : ' Can I do
anything towards helping to put an end to such a fright-
ful state of things ? ' I need hardly say the poor children
had ever a very tender place in my heart.

On the second Sunday I commenced an afternoon
men's Bible class in the church. Only two came, but
that small beginning grew into a large and very important gathering, yielding many candidates for confirmation,
producing helpers in church work and adding to the
number of regular attendants at the Lord's Supper.

My strength and time were now devoted chiefly to the
church services and house-to-house visitation : to the
latter I gave six hours for five days in the week, and
three hours on Saturdays. My reception was most
cordial. It was soon found that even the ' roughs '
of the place were beginning to attend the church
services, and, as a rule, they behaved themselves
quite properly. One Sunday evening, however, two
big fellows fell out before the service began, and went

on ' nagging,' until one of them opened a clasp-knife, declaring he would stab the other ! Feeling how difficult it is to get such within the walls of a church, and still more to keep them, our task was to retain them by influencing them ; in a great measure we did that, by some of our helpers sitting amongst them, and by gentleness and kindness, to which the spirit of irreverence yielded.

It was now near our first Christmas, with its joyous associations. It was a time of special interest to us all, but to me of great anxiety as well ; for the number of sick, which was usually about sixty, had now risen to eighty, and the fund from which such cases were assisted was nearly exhausted. Early on Christmas morning, as I was going to church for the eight o'clock administration of the Holy Communion, a man in livery stepped out from a doorway, and handed me a letter, which, on being opened, I found to contain a cheque for fifty pounds, from Mr. W. Milner, Founder of the Phœnix Safe Works situated close by, and one of the Church Trustees, to be devoted to the needs of the parish as I might think fit. Truly from my heart did I offer God thanks, with prayer for that generous donor. My spirit revived ; I took courage from the thought that the Lord would ever provide for His work in His own time and way. That day some of us caught the meaning of Bethlehem's strains, ' Glory to God in the Highest,' and ' worshipped the King.'

The Church rapidly filled on Sunday evenings, largely with the poor. I had forty chairs placed in the inner chancel, which rather shocked one of the late Building Committee. From this flow of attendance resulted many cases of real spiritual blessing.

In the early part of the New Year, at the house of a neighbouring clerical brother I met the Bishop, who, taking me aside, remarked that, whilst there was in St. Nathaniel's everything necessary for consecration, he would like to see the tablets replaced by more suitable ones, and, if I had no objection, he would be very pleased to present such to the church. I thanked him for his generous offer. Looking at me, with a half-smile, he said : ' I won't ask you to have anything ritualistic.' Smiling in return, I replied : ' I hope not.' The Bishop then added : ' I shall be going up to London soon and will order them.'

But for the moral certainty that the Ecclesiastical Commissioners would endow it, the church would probably never have been built, on account of the extreme poverty and degradation of the district in which it was erected. Since the purchase of the site, however, the Commissioners had introduced a new rule, making their grants conditional upon the rector, or vicar out of whose parish a new district was carved, giving up his right to a third of the fees arising from it. In the case of St. Nathaniel's, that right, which would be affected to the extent of some five pounds, or so, per annum, rested with the rector of West Derby. A deputation waited upon him, to state the case and seek his concurrence ; but he firmly refused their request. That was disappointing, as my stipend for the first short financial year amounted to only seventy-five pounds, derived from pew rents.

Just as this critical moment two elderly gentlemen, strangers, were noticed in church on two consecutive Sunday mornings. They afterwards called on me, there and then offering me the vicarage of Holy Trinity, Runcorn, of which they were the sole patrons. It was a completed church, together with schools, a curate, and a house, with three hundred pounds a year. This I confess was a very tempting offer, for it would be the merest affectation and the grossest hypocrisy to pretend that ways and means are nothing. There are people who seem to think a clergyman ought to live almost on air ; yet those same individuals look very carefully after their own bread-and-butter, though they are highly spiritual persons. This offer soon got wind, and I think it was as well for those two good men that they did not pay a third visit to St. Nathaniel's church.

I took two weeks to consider the offer, which, meantime, my friends were urging me to accept, saying that having been quite unsought, it looked like a Divine call. Ultimately I took a sheet of paper, put down the pros and cons, and then knelt and asked the Lord for direction. It was vouchsafed, and I rose from my knees with the determination to sink or swim with St. Nathaniel's. The following Sunday I made the announcement, from the pulpit; and I have never regretted it.

The next morning a girl was shown into my study Her manner evinced pleasure and nervousness. She said how glad she was to hear in church my decision to stay; and then, handing me her savings-bank book, she added, in an entreating voice : ' As a thank-offering to God I wish you to take for your use what is in that book : it is not much, but it is all I have.' I refused even to take the book into my hand ; whereupon she wept, and apologized for having made the offer. I warmly assured her I quite understood and appreciated her kind motive, and that I accepted the will for the deed. I inquired whether she had any particular reason for calling and making her generous offer : to which she replied : ' Oh yes, I have ; it is only two months ago that I went to St. Nathaniel's for the first time, when I was led to think as I had not done before. I felt I must go again, and I have continued to do so. I am now, I believe, a true child of God ; that is why I brought you my savings-bank book, because you have decided to remain at St. Nathaniel's.' This was better than a big cheque !

It was now necessary to form other Bible classes on Sunday afternoons, as there were already those competent to take them ; and classes for children were added. All had to be held in the church, which was the only available place.

Easter Day arrived, and had a very uplifting effect upon us, especially upon the little band of earnest workers who had gathered round me. Oh ! how I longed for yet more of the power of our risen Lord, to keep and fit me, and those working with me, for His service. Our first Easter Vestry was a happy gathering, partaking more of a spiritual than of a merely parochial character.

I had another surprise, in the form of a cheque for fifty pounds for my own use, sent to me by post from the Chester Diocesan Society for helping ill-paid Incumbents; though I was unaware even of its existence. The Lord is a rich provider!

Hearing of a distressed family in one of the courts, I at once went to visit it, and found the place bare and filthy. On an old sofa lay a dead child; near it was another child, ill. There was no fire, no food, and no one else in the room. Upstairs I found the father on a wretched bed, suffering from typhoid fever, but quite conscious. Knowing me, he groaned, ' Oh! God bless you for coming, sir.' Looking at something stirring in a corner, on the floor, I saw the hair and the black, distorted features of a woman. The man managed to say, as well as he was able, ' That's my poor wife. She has just been confined. The nurse gave her rum, and see the look of her.' And he began to cry. I at once took charge of the family, had the parents removed to hospitals, the sick child cared for, the dead one buried. I visited husband and wife regularly in the hospitals. They both recovered, but she lost three toes and two fingers. He began to attend church.

Some time after, I met him accidentally in the street, when he caught me warmly by the hand, and looking me joyfully in the face, said : ' I have good news to tell you. I was born again last Sunday morning, in church, praise God.' For twenty-five years he lived a consistent Christian life, and was then called home. It was pleasant to hear him at times testifying, at open-air services, what God had done for his soul. His wife remained as she had been, a slatternly tippling creature. How he could have lived with her was a wonder, and yet he loved her, and, to his great joy, some two years before he died she showed signs that gave hope in her death, which took place some months before his. ' Oh! to grace how great a debtor!'

The Bishop of Chester had a confirmation in the

church, when, out of one hundred and forty-one candidates, one hundred and six were confirmed, all, thank God, professing to have passed from death unto life, and to have received from God, through Christ, the pardon of their sins ; this being the Church's standard as set forth in the confirmation service. The church was packed. The singing and responses were heart-stirring. The Bishop took the north side of the Table, and I the south. There were before him two hymn papers. Whilst singing the second hymn on the list, I noticed tears trickling down his face, and, whether unconsciously or not I cannot say, he folded one of the papers and put it in his pocket. After the service, he asked me if I would give him the tunes of two of the hymns, adding : ' Give the people the old hymns and tunes, give them over and over again. I do not think there is anything, out of heaven, like a whole congregation praising God.'

The roll of believers now numbered nearly two hundred ; for though, during the first half-year of my ministry, forty were presented for confirmation through the mother church, they all continued with us. ' This is the Lord's doing, and it is marvellous in our eyes.' Our joy in the Lord was almost unbounded. Bless His holy Name !

I must not omit to record that on entering the vestry before the service, the Bishop laid on the table two little scrolls, with the remark, ' Those are designs for the chancel tablets which I promised you for the church ; tell me which of them you prefer.' On opening the scrolls I found one to be just a couple of unconnected plain tablets, and the other very pretty, but with the drawback of having a Latin cross. I liked the latter, but, to avoid having the cross—an emblem of Pagan origin— I said, ' I prefer the former ' ; when the Bishop rejoined, ' I will see you later.' After the confirmation he again asked me which I preferred. I adhered to my previous choice, but seeing how the land seemed to lie, added : ' Please come into the chancel, where we can perhaps see which design seems suitable.' The Bishop took in his hand the one with the cross, I took the other, and we went into the chancel. Going to the Holy Table, he opened out his scroll, and pointing with a finger to the cross, said looking at me : ' Tell me, have you any objection to that ? ' I answered : ' Pardon me ; I would rather not have it.' ' Do you like it minus the cross ? ' he inquired. ' Minus the cross it is beautiful,' I replied. ' Then,' said he, ' you shall have it minus the cross.' ' I am very grateful for the gift, but specially for your great kindness and considera-tion,' was my rejoinder. The position was rather trying, and could well have become a very awkward one ; for, being Bishop, and donor, he might have pressed his own choice on me, with the alternative of withdrawing the offer.

A course of sermons on the Six Cities of Refuge was much blessed. In that course it was shown that instead of those six cities being regarded as one type of Christ, each of the six was a picture of our dear Lord, as indicated by their names (Josh. xx. 7-9).

Kedesh, Appointed ; Christ—the sent one (John x. 36).
Shechem, Shoulders ; Christ—' the government shall be upon His
  shoulder ' (Isa. ix. 6).
Hebron, Fellowship ; Christ—' truly our fellowship ' (1 John i. 3).
Bezer, Rock ; Christ—the Rock (1 Cor. x. 4).
Ramoth, Exalted ; Christ—exalted (Phil. ii. 9).
Golan, Joy ; Christ—our Joy (John xv. 11).

During their delivery, a respectable intelligent young man called, and asked for something to do for Christ, giving as his reason the following : ' On seeing the placard announcing sermons on the Six Cities of Refuge, I resolved to hear them, and—with emotion—by God's grace I have fled for refuge to Jesus in whom I find safety and rest ; so I want to do something for Him.' Thank God he still not only abides in the Refuge. but is also an active, efficient, and successful preacher of Christ, as the Refuge for sinners, to a large congregation, with Sunday-school and other like agencies ; and that, too, free of charge : as he continues to pursue his calling, that of a commercial traveller.

Early this year, a small-pox epidemic breaking out in Liverpool found a congenial soil in the parish, where it spread with rapidity, and gripped its victims with a tenacity simply awful. This was a testing time. Shall I visit such cases, and risk infection, or shall I not ? I came to the conclusion that I ought to do so. For if medical men visit them, why not the messenger of the Lord ? Is not the soul of more importance than the body ? If Romish priests will visit such cases, why should not Protestant pastors be equally ready to save, console, and comfort ? The people take careful note, not only of what is done, but also of what is not done ! I am fully alive to the need and the propriety of adopting measures of precaution, both for one's own preservation, and for the prevention of infection.

I visited all such cases in the parish, most of them having been removed in due time to the hospital. Never, either before or since, was work so trying, and so loathsome, as visiting these small-pox sufferers in their filthy fœtid homes. I took no precautions against infection, in the way of consuming spirits or using scents ; but I dieted myself more liberally than usual, in the way of extra meat. If able to manage it, I did not visit until after an early dinner, and, if possible, I afterwards either went down to the river, outside an omnibus, or had a bath. I was anxious about my landlady's little children, but, thank God, not one of them was smitten !

One case nearly took me off my feet. It was that of a sweet Christian girl, recently confirmed, an only daughter. In the room where she lay I found father, mother, and five women ! How foolish ! how wrong ! I saw the poor girl, looking as black as a negress, stayed up in bed, with her arms outside the bed-clothes, quite uncovered, and the virus running down to her hands. ' Oh, M——, I am sorry,' I said, when she reached out her right hand. For a moment I thought : ' Shall I take it ? if I refuse what will the poor girl think ? ' I took it, when she squeezed mine in hers and the virus oozed between my fingers. I certainly felt an awful shock. I was stunned. She still held my hand tightly. I did not well know what either to say or do. I remember saying ' Let us pray,' and their kneeling down with me ; yet I cannot remember what I tried to ask the dear Lord for. But He knew what I meant. The girl held my hand till I rose, when, from sheer exhaustion, she let it drop. I at once wiped it well with my handkerchief, and got out as soon as I could without seeming to hurry.

The next thing I remember was waking up from a most refreshing sleep on the grass in Sefton Park—which was then being made—where I must have been lying some three hours or more. I have not the least recollection how I got there. Calling on my doctor, and telling him what had happened, he examined me carefully, and then informed me that in all probability that sleep in the open air had saved me. The poor girl died shortly after I left. The young man to whom she was engaged, who had seen her when ill, and attended the funeral, took the disease, and died too. I buried both. It is a joy to record that the father, mother, and eldest brother of dear M—— were afterwards brought to God.

I will venture to say that during my thirty-three years' ministry in Windsor nothing so won the confidence, and secured the goodwill, of the people, as my ministrations during that terrible visitation. It greatly helped to bridge over the chasm separating the church from the people ; for the latter felt that I had done my duty to them in the time of their sore need ; and none are quicker than those of that class to appreciate thoroughly whoever will not satisfy himself with mere words, but will give effect to those words in deeds for their benefit.

This year I began to expound on Sunday mornings the Letter to the Hebrews, taking it seriatim : I much value expository preaching.

The men's Bible-class members had, within eighteen

months, risen to one hundred and eleven. In the enthusiasm of their appreciation they presented me with a handsome study table, and an address, which touched me deeply (see Apendix E).

As yet the Ecclesiastical Commissioners had not endowed the church. This was very serious, not only for me, but also for the people, as, although the church was consecrated, there was no district assigned to it legally. Hence the Church Pastoral Aid Society could not make me a grant for a curate; my only paid helper was a Scripture Reader, from the Liverpool Church of England Scripture Readers' Society.

I found even those who were spiritually minded very shy in coming to the Lord's Table, owing probably to insufficient instruction as to its nature and privilege. I therefore preached frequently on this subject, showing that as the Lord's Table supplies the children's bread, and is meant for the children of God, it is their duty, as well as their privilege, to partake thereof.

A goodly number of the sittings in the church were now taken.

The first year closed with a full church on Sunday evenings.

The money raised during the year amounted to two hundred and seventy-six pounds.

1871.

First Watch-night service—Evangelical Alliance prayer week—Laymen's rights and place in Church work—Bishop's reredos—Gallery erected—The tablets described—Present-day Church treatment of God's Commandments—Conversion—Open - air work—Cottage and cellar readings—'Windsor in the Streets.'

' Come thou with us, and we will do thee good : for the Lord hath spoken good concerning Israel ' (Num. x. 29).

ONE milestone, with all its intervening weaknesses, failings, faults, sins, mercies, and blessings, had been passed. The old year was closed, and the new year opened, in church, by a service beginning at 11 p.m. and ending at 12.30 a.m. ; the text and motto for the year being as above. A service at such an hour and on such an occasion, was not usual at that time in Liverpool, but with us it was the first of a series ; and the church was crowded, chiefly by the lost and the degraded ; men in their working clothes, and unwashed ; women in dirty aprons and with unkempt hair ; there were present also some of the regular congregation. We had the Litany, some hymns, and the sermon, with extempore prayer before and after. As I glanced round that motley assembly I cried, from the depths of my heart, ' Lord, save this people ; Lord, bless Thine own word to-night. Make bare Thine arm to save these lost ones.'

This beginning was followed during the first week of the new year, by meetings for special prayer, as arranged by the Evangelical Alliance. Meeting in church each evening at eight o'clock, the Vicar presiding, we began with a hymn, had some of the Prayer-book collects, and then read a portion of Scripture ; there followed prayers by laymen, interspersed by hymns. Truly it was good to be there. Thus was the first week of each year observed during the whole of my ministry.

This occasion was the first really organized effort to utilize the services of laymen, who, in my opinion, ought—after New Testament example—to have their proper place in the Church, and that place a more prominent one than the mere serving of tables. I always sought, up to the straining point, to give them as much spiritual work as I could, within the limits of Church order. Surely they are entitled to be entrusted with duties more important to the congregation, and more helpful to its minister, than passing round the plates, and counting their contents. Often have I wished that our Bishops would follow the example of their Canadian brethren, by licensing suitably qualified laymen to read the entire morning and evening service—with perhaps a reservation, or even without—and to preach, in church. I do not see how, otherwise, the work of the Church is to be done, at all events in large, populous, and poor parishes ; though some of the villages are, by having only one clergyman, quite as badly off.

It may be that to bring about so desirable a state of things, the laity would need more encouragement, direction, and training, than at present ; which, however, should not be a difficulty : for I rejoice to state that on my resignation I left over fifty men fit and ready to lead in prayer and give addresses ; whilst some were far more competent than many young curates, who, until they were made brand new parsons, were probably without any such experience. It cannot be denied that in these respects the training of candidates for ordination in our Church is lamentably deficient.

In proportion to the number of communicants there were few at the Lord's Table on either of the two past Christmas Days, chiefly owing to their custom of celebrating the day by feasting, which they considered not quite in harmony with that holy ordinance. The week of prayer, however, fitted in with the New Year Sunday evening administration ; hence on that occasion we had the largest attendance in the year. The Passion Week services were most helpful in regard to the great

Festival of our Blessed Lord's triumphant rising from the tomb.

The seating accommodation of the church, even including the forty chairs placed in the inner chancel, was now insufficient for the Sunday evening congregation. Therefore we decided to erect a gallery at the west end, and set to work all those whose hearts the Lord made willing, to collect the necessary amount, which the architect estimated at two hundred and fifty pounds. The plans were approved, a faculty was obtained, and in a few months the gallery was put up, paid for, and filled. Out of the multitude there were being added to the Lord many of ' such as should be saved.'

The tablets promised by the Bishop arrived and were duly placed on the east wall. They contained Alpha, and Omega ; the Ten Commandments ; the Lord's Prayer, and the Apostles' Creed ; with ' I.H.S.' in the centre ; and the memorial words ' Do this in remembrance of Me ' underneath. There was no cross. The tablets were in keeping with the place, and worthy of the generous donor. I heard they cost forty pounds. I cannot refrain from expressing the opinion that one of the deplorable signs of the times is the frequent removal of God's Commandments, the Creed, and the Lord's Prayer, from their proper place at the east end of the church, and their relegation to either the belfry or cellar, when an old church is renovated or restored ; whilst in most new churches, the Commandments, the Creed, and the Lord's Prayer, are ' conspicuous by their absence,' and would be left out of the Communion Service, if some ' Anglicans '—as they term themselves—could have their way, auricular confession being substituted, as, forsooth, more ' Catholic,' whatever that may mean.

Up to this time the ragged school had been under the care of the mother church, which was a great help to our poor parish. I was asked to purchase the school building for four hundred pounds, which I declined to do ; as it seemed only reasonable that St. Clement's, having formed the parish, and built the church, should transfer the ragged schoolroom thereto : instead of which it was afterwards conveyed to the Charity Commissioners. That meant our accepting grave monetary liability if the school was to be carried on ; as its cost was about two hundred and fifty pounds a year, the raising of which depended entirely upon voluntary subscriptions : and that did not commend itself to some of my helpers. However, loving the poor children, and feeling the work was really required, I resolved myself to take it up, in full reliance on the promise, ' My God shall supply all your need.' That resolve I never regretted ; for I believe that school has enriched St. Nathaniel's church and parish.

Amongst many remarkable evidences of the Holy Spirit's power in our midst, was the following : A lady, quite a stranger, called upon me to say that through the preaching of the Gospel in our church she had been brought to the Lord. For more than a year she had been passing near the building, always under the impression that it was a Romish chapel. On one occasion, seeing so many people going in, she followed them, when, through the sermon, God sent her His message. On coming into the light herself, she got distressed about two of her children then being educated, free, in a Liverpool convent, mainly by the persuasion of her sister, who, marrying a Romanist, had ' verted.' With tears, she asked what I would advise her to do. I said, ' Take them away immediately, at all cost. God will provide. Trust Him and do the right thing.' She did so. Becoming subsequently one of my most devoted helpers, often in weakness of body, but in the strength of faith, her rare gentleness and spirituality were used by the Master in His service, until He called her to Himself. Others, too, who knew the Lord, some of a good social standing, joined us in worship and in work, about this time. I am quite at a loss to express my feelings of thankfulness for the abounding goodness of our God in owning and blessing the work. I am thoroughly convinced that it was because we humbly gave the people a full Gospel, in a plain way,

without any meretricious adjuncts, whether of doctrine
or of ritual, pointing to the one Mediator as the only
way by which in simple faith, a seeking soul can find
acceptance with God.

The open-air work was gradually prospering ; it
takes time to educate workers, for in this, as in every
kind of service for the King, those who are willing
require guidance and instruction. This kind of work
is a great test of sincerity and courage, from which
many shrink ; yet the Master was an open-air Preacher,
and so was each Apostle. Up to this time I attended
all our open-air services. It is one thing to say ' Go,'
it is quite another to say ' Come.' The pastor should
lead the way in the first instance, as an encouragement,
and an example to those who in time ought to, and will,
take his place. If men will follow an earthly leader,
and fight their country's battles, though that may
involve fearful hardships, and the loss of health, limbs,
or even life ; should not those who profess to be
Christians follow the Great Captain of their Salvation,
and fight His battles against irreligion, error and sin,
though that may bring upon them sneers, contempt,
persecution, ill-treatment, or even worse ? Oh, for
more of that holy courage which will deliberately
choose, rather than avoid, the most trying kind of
work for God, not only for the work's sake, but also as an
incentive to others !

Another form of work took definite shape at this
time ; that of cottage and cellar ' readings ' in the
winter, as a sort of addendum to open-air work in the
summer. One such reading means a little band of, say,
four men, with a leader, taking a street, visiting the
houses in it—probably thereby finding out the most
ungodly families—getting leave to hold a meeting
in one of them each week, at a suitable hour in the
evening, reading the Bible intelligibly and explaining
it quite simply in the plainest of language, singing
hymns and having prayer, without giving any remuneration for the room, light, or fuel.

In after-years it was no uncommon thing to have had

twelve such gatherings in a week. Sometimes the place
was full, at other times there were only one or two.
The godly poor were allowed to come, but they were
not sought after, it being considered that they were
well provided for by the ordinary means of grace. The
object of this work was to reach the unreached, and,
as many can testify, it was used by God for His glory
in the salvation of souls. Our endeavour was to keep
steadily before those engaged in any of the agencies
the need that each should do a distinct work.

The confirmation this year was at a neighbouring
church. Our candidates, of which there were a goodly
number, walked thither; which drew into the streets the
admiring population of Windsor, in all their unwashed,
sad, wretched condition. The sight made one's heart
ache, and one's courage fail, so apparently impossible
did it seem to reach and raise such specimens of
humanity. Seeing it in the aggregate, prompted me
to give notice of a sermon, entitled ' Windsor in the
Streets,' for the following Sunday evening. The church
was packed. I have always found the masses ready to
hear plain speaking, and to have their faults pointed out.
In fact, they like a minister to hit out straight from the
shoulder, provided he shows no animus. Therefore
whilst I sympathized with them, and sought to woo
and win them to God through Christ, I did not hesitate
to tell them of their sinful lives, and to warn them of the
consequences, dealing with the different forms of vice
and evil to be seen in the various streets of the parish.

The amount raised this year was four hundred and
seventy-three pounds.

1872.

New organ—' A cheerful giver '—The Church endowed—Curates and Vicars—Orange Lodge—' Jelly-fish spirituality '—The vicar of St. Clement's—Young men's Literary Society—' Ragged School day '—Parochial visiting.

' Yea, the Lord hath done great things for us already, whereof we rejoice ' (Ps. cxxvi. 3).

A SECOND milestone is passed, and another year's labour is entered upon with faith in our Covenant God, with hope for still greater success in winning souls to Him, and with love for feeding the sheep and lambs of the fold.

By the addition of ' draw out ' seats in three of the aisles, the church can now accomodate 1,010, which is the utmost extent of its capacity. To see the building crammed on Sunday evenings, and to hear the roll of the responses, and the volume of singing, might well set on fire the heart of any minister. The hired harmonium being of insufficient power to guide the congregation, we held a conference, according to our custom ; at which it was resolved to make an effort this year towards obtaining an organ.

Whilst readily allowing that instrumental music may be helpful if kept in its right place, that is, entirely subservient to congregational singing, I was fully convinced that organs and choirs are in very many cases real hindrances to spiritual worship. I had long felt the present day parson and choir duet to be far less conducive to it than the parson and clerk of olden time. We, however, would have neither, but taught the people to take their part in the service, just as the minister took his. In due course donations were invited and collecting-cards were issued ; the result being that before the year closed we had an effective organ, at the cost of three hundred and fifty pounds.

The details of one donation may be recorded. On

Wednesday evening, a poor woman came into the Vestry, before the service began, and handed me an envelope, saying : ' I wish you to accept what is in that, towards the new organ.' On opening it I found thirty shillings, and, looking at her, I said : ' This is too much for you to give.' ' No sir, it is not.' ' Take back twenty shillings of it.' She refused, remarking : ' My poor afflicted daughter and myself are only too thankful to give that thirty shillings, because of the good we have got in this church.' ' But how did you manage to get together so much money ? ' ' Well, we live by washing, and we have saved a little each week for a good while.' ' Do you mean that this money comes out of the wash-tub ? ' ' Yes, sir.' ' Out of the suds ? ' ' Yes, sir ; we have no other means of getting it.' ' Do, then, take back twenty shillings.' ' No, sir ; if I did, my daughter would be angry.' And, as she was leaving, she added : ' I hope I may live to hear the new organ.' That desire was granted ; she heard it once, and was delighted, poor soul. She died soon after, a true, simple, believer in Jesus. What will not gratitude and love do ?

At last the Ecclesiastical Commissioners endowed the church with two hundred pounds a year, constituting the district of sixteen acres a new parish, and the incumbent vicar thereof. The Church Pastoral Aid Society made me a grant of ninety pounds a year towards the stipend of a curate. God is good !

It is much to be regretted that the then rector of West Derby, having a large clerical income, should have caused a loss of six hundred pounds to a needy brother minister, the incumbent of a wretchedly poor and demoralized district, with a population of over four thousand, for both the bodies and the souls of whom so much remained to be done.

In one sense what did it really matter ? I had bread and cheese. Yet few are so exalted ' in the heavenlies ' as not to feel the loss of six hundred pounds. I do not believe that, ordinarily at least, God will allow one of His ambassadors, who seeks to do His will in His way, to starve ; but if He should, that one will win a martyr's crown.*

Perhaps at no time in the history of St. Nathaniel's Church was the gracious rain of Heavenly blessing falling in such abundance, with quickening and edifying results ; our hearts were well-nigh day by day full of new-born joy in the Lord.

As yet, I had no regular clerical help : I was alone. In a sense I often thanked God for it, though my strength was tried to the uttermost. Just after having advertised for a curate, I met a Liverpool vicar, who, referring thereto, said : ' Now your trouble begins.' ' Oh, pray do not say so,' I replied. He shook his head, and passed on. I could not forget this remark ; and I regret having to admit that my experience has shown me there was some truth in it. Vicars, however, make mistakes as well as curates. The relation in which a vicar and his curate stand to each other is a tender and a delicate one. It may be made very helpful to the cause of God, or the reverse. Some of my curates were most efficient, and some were a trial : my first one was certainly most disappointing.

A deputation waited on me to know whether I would allow an Orange Lodge to be formed in the parish? Whether I would join it ? And whether it might be called St. Nathaniel's Orange Lodge ? To the first and last I cordially replied in the affirmative, but to the

---

* The issue of a Second Edition probably presents a seemingly suitable opportunity for correcting an unintentionally erroneous statement which appeared in the Liverpool Diocesan Gazette for April, 1904, that ' Some months later ' (*i.e.*, than the consecration, on July 17th, 1869), ' after a tedious correspondence and a personal interview ' in London with the Earl of Harrowby and the Ecclesiastical Com- ' missioners, Mr. Woodward obtained from that body an endowment ' for St. Nathaniel's of £200 per annum.'

As a matter of fact, although Canon Woodward's energetic efforts were well backed up by both the late Bishop Jacobson and the late Dean McNeile, the endowment grant was not obtained until July, 1872, just *three years* after the consecration (a clerical error on page 72 of the First Edition dating it in 1871), as shown by a document included in the archives of St. Nathaniel's Church, handed by me to the Rev. D. H. C. Bartlett, M.A., on his becoming my successor in 1901.—R. H.

second in the negative. Continuing, I said, that, though my preaching was, as they knew, often contro-versial, I did not see my way to become a member, but that I would help them by all means in my power, on the Protestant side of their programme.

I do think the Evangelical clergy make a great mistake in not utilizing, by appeal, instruction, and direction, the latent Protestantism of the masses ; and in not taking Orangeism under their wing, which upholds the Bible and the Protestant Constitutional Settlement of 1688. Though this particular lodge did not, as a fact, come up to my standard, it was a factor in the success of the church.

There is a jelly-fish spirituality, which does not ap-prove of this line of action, holding the entirely erroneous opinion that controversy must mean ' bad blood.' Of course it may, but it need not : all depends upon those engaged therein. I fear such objectors would take exception to the work of missions to the Jews, the heathen, Romanists, and others, if they happened to be where the agents of those societies operate. There is a special burden to be borne in all such work, and that is the real difficulty.

It is truly to be deplored that so many deeply taught Christians, rather than run the risk of having their spiritual life ruffled, by their silence condone the introduction of almost all the God-dishonouring and soul-destroying doctrines of Romanism into our Church.

It now occurred to me that as well-nigh all those concerned in the mission disruption before I came to Windsor, who had vowed they would never enter the new church, had been led to see that it was a blessing to the neighbourhood in many ways, and were fre-quently at the services amongst the general congrega-tion, it would not be amiss to call them together. I did so, and, without going into the past, I asked if they were not now quite persuaded that the incumbent of St. Clement's had always been, and was still, their real friend. They admitted it. I then asked whether they would like to present him with a short address, setting forth that fact. They quite approved, and requested me to draw up, frame, and present it on their behalf ; which I did gladly. It was well merited ; for his whole ministry had gone to show how he yearned over the poor of his parish.

I was asked for the use of the schoolroom in starting a friendly society or tontine, and was invited to become a trustee. As the proposed society was to be worked by the members, and to be undenominational, I at once assented. The organization was a combination of working men, paying a small sum weekly, to provide aid in case of sickness, or accident, and a death payment ; making, also, a ' divide ' amongst its members once a year. Surely that is a good thing. Is it not our duty to encourage thrift and independence amongst all classes ? I am thankful to say it has proved a great success, having ordinarily not less than one hundred and eighty members.

Another most useful agency was set on foot—viz., a penny bank, of which I became trustee and treasurer, open every Saturday evening, in the ragged school. That also succeeded, and, thanks to the workers' good management, my duties were so light, that I really think they took hardly an hour in any one year of the many during which I was connected with it. I delight to recall the efficient voluntary service rendered by a few members of the congregation in carrying on this useful agency. Truly God is glorified in work done for the good of men's bodies, no less than in that for the benefit of their souls ! Did not the blessed Master care for the people's temporal well-being as well as for their spiritual ?

This year also saw the foundation of a Young Men's Literary Society, on distinctive Christian principles. Its motto was ' Give attendance to reading.' To carry on such a parochial agency as this, in such a parish, almost under the shadow of the great Young Men's Christian Association, Mount Pleasant, which derives large and liberal monetary support from our fellow-citizens, was indeed a formidable undertaking. But

we found our Society had a place, and answered a
purpose, of its own, notwithstanding ; contributing
to the parish its quota of good work. It made only
slight calls upon my time and strength, a most worthy,
and thoroughly qualified member of the congregation
representing me, as chairman, for twenty-four years !
The membership scarcely ever fell below a hundred,
and it was self-supporting. Not often does such a
society continuously prosper for thirty years. Only
once in all that time did anything happen which caused
me sorrow, in connection with the society ; and that,
thank God, was set right.

Though we took over the working of the Ragged
School with diffidence, yet we had trust in the Mighty
One ; and I am thankful to record that even during
the first year there was an improvement in every way.
It was a happy thought to have the ragged children in
church on the occasion of our annual appeal for funds
to carry on their school. The chancel was filled to
overflowing with those poor waifs and strays, who sang
special hymns in a style peculiarly their own, which,
by its rough rattling ' swing,' touched the hearts
and opened the purses, of the congregation.

Whoever heard of ragged children being placed in a
chancel ! Why not ? I do not think there could have
been on that day, in any church in England, a more
beautiful looking chancel than ours, crammed with
three hundred poor children !

Were they not living images, made in God's likeness,
and for whom Christ died ? It was a sight that, I feel
sure, moved the Divinely tender and loving heart of
Him who said ' Feed My lambs.' Some, I fear, would
rather see in a chancel images of wood or stone, things
forbidden by God's own commandment, such as were
cast out of our chancels at the glorious Reformation.
The collections amounted to £85. We repeated the
experiment each year, with very satisfactory results.

The preaching of these annual sermons for the little
ones was to me a pleasure and a privilege which I was
unwilling to forego. On only three occasions, and then

but once in the day, during the whole period of my vicariate, were the sermons preached by another minister; so that for thirty-three years I pleaded annually on behalf of our dear children : and I never pleaded in vain ! There was no need to bring ' great guns ' from afar on these occasions. I am satisfied that, for such objects, if the vicar be not as able in his own pulpit as a stranger, there is something wrong, something wanting.

We now felt that there was need for a Sunday evening service in the ragged school, for those in its immediate neighbourhood. Accordingly such was started, and has been continued ever since, on each Sunday evening, at the same hour as the service in church. I put it into the hands of a layman to conduct, and though the ordinary attendance may not have been very large, by God's blessing it has been found helpful. Latterly it was changed into a short service for men only, which resulted in some real tokens for good. Many tributaries are needed to make the flowing river.

This year is remarkable for the formation of five agencies in the parish. It is one thing to start such, but quite another thing to sustain them. By ' the good hand of our God upon us,' all those departments of parochial work were successful, and I left them in a healthy condition ; probably because not one was established until there was an evident need for it.

There were no less than a hundred and thirty-six church-helpers, and they were fired with that freshness and glow, which is so characteristic of young converts : it seemed as if nothing could damp their ardour. What a privilege and honour to be the minister and leader of such a body.

At the end of this year I began a course of instruction on the Psalms.

The average number of communicants on Sunday evenings was a hundred and eleven.

Up to now no less than £1,400 had been expended upon the church, including fittings : but there still remained much to be done.

I felt utterly unable to have a confirmation class this year, finding it necessary to husband my strength in order to bear the burden of every-day parochial work which pressed so heavily upon me. Up to this time I had not taken any holiday, which was perhaps a mistake ; but it is not always easy to do what one would like. In this instance it did not seem possible.

I still systematically visited from house to house, attaching great value to that form of ministration, which I took good care to make something more than a simple how-do-you-do call. My visits were of a teaching character, in the sense of always utilizing any opportunity—and one was almost sure to occur—for dropping appropriate words, which, like good seed, might germinate, and bring forth fruit ; just following the example of Paul, who taught ' from house to house,' as well as in public.

There is visiting, *and* visiting. It needs a prayerful heart, and a discerning mind, always to say the right word, at the right time, in the right way. Though it is not always possible to read the Word, or to have prayer, in the homes of the poor, it is always possible at least to leave on the peoples' minds the impression that one is a heaven-sent messenger, seeking their good in every way. Such work taxes the energies, tries the patience, and tests the love, of the visitor. It will be given up with many apparently justifying reasons, unless there be a daily supply of Divine grace, for nothing can make up for the absence of that. There is truth in the saying, ' A house-going parson makes a a church-going people.' For, strange to say, no matter who else visits them, they look for, and will not be satisfied without having, the vicar to visit them too.

I often cried to our Heavenly Father for grace to be kept humble, tender, loving, diligent, and faithful. It is so easy to grow tired, and even weary, in the Lord's work.

There was no lessening of activity in any of the agencies.

The amount raised this year was seven hundred and twenty-three pounds.

1873.

Special Mission — Lady district visitors — Growing disregard of authority—The expression ' Church '—Ridicule—Conversion—Conscience-stricken correspondent—Dublin Degree—Parochial agencies.

' And I, if I be lifted up, . . . will draw all men unto Me ' (John xii. 32).

THIS was the New Year watchword, from which I preached on the last night of the old year, when numbers could not find even standing room in church. The pulpit prayer, immediately after twelve tolls of the bell had announced the New Year, was that the Holy Spirit might move over that miscellaneous gathering, imparting His light and life to those spiritually dark and dead. The prayer was answered, for His power was truly felt that night. At 2 a.m. I laid my head down on the pillow, saying, ' Lord, I am weary. I have done my little best. Accept it, and me Thy servant. Give me sweet sleep. For Christ's sake.'

The opening week of the New Year was kept as usual, and on the first Sunday evening there was a blessed gathering around the Lord's Table. This was soon followed by a special mission, when seventeen souls professed to have been born again. Bless the Lord ! I am a believer in special missions, and in my time have conducted several ; yet in my own parish I have looked for souls not so much to them, as to— what every pastor's ministrations should really be— the all-the-year-round mission, including Bible classes, confirmation classes, and prayer-meetings, which afford grand opportunities for bringing the great truths of God's Word to bear very directly upon hearts and consciences. So far as was known, we never had many brought to God by special missions, which may have been our own fault. Still, the Lord has many ways of winning souls for Himself, as we have seen and testified.

The plan I felt directed to adopt as to Sunday sermons, was to preach to believers in the morning, to build them up, and to unbelievers in the evening, that they might through grace believe unto salvation. The week-day evening sermons were of a miscellaneous character. On the first Sunday in each month, Evening Prayer was now at 4 o'clock, in order to allow the 6.30 service to consist only of the Communion Office and sermon, as directed by the rubric.

Another agency had been started; that of lady district visitors. At the risk of being set down as ungallant, I cannot forbear stating that my experience has forced me to the conclusion that the value of lady district visitors' services, has, on the whole, been over-estimated. I cannot find words to express my indebtedness to some for their efficient spiritual help in Bible-classes and mothers' meetings; and to others for their valuable aid in occasional work, such as collecting money, sales of work, visiting special cases. But there are so many reasonable hindrances, in the way of home duties, and risks arising out of exposure to inclement weather, to their working with that regularity which is one of the secrets of successful parochial visitation, that district visiting seems to me, as a rule, outside the general scope of women's sphere.

The unpleasant subject of disobedience to parental authority forced itself upon my notice in an unexpected manner. It had always been my custom, when visiting in the parish where the family included grown-up sons or daughters, to leave with their parents messages for them, expressing the pleasure their attendance at any of the services or meetings would give me. I often wondered why it was that so many of those messages seemed to go for naught; until the explanation came one day, when a mother said to me: ' Please do not leave a message with me for my son, because if I give it to him he is sure to disregard it, as he pays no attention to me or his father.' That opened my eyes, so I changed my method, and waited for an opportunity of seeing the young people and delivering my message direct ; which, in some instances at least, was found to answer.

No one of any experience and observation can dispute the statement thatthe rising generation has an increasing disregard for parental authority ; and not for that alone, but for authority generally. So much was that felt, even in our Ragged school, that year by year the teachers found more difficulty in controlling the scholars.

One of the causes of this sad state of things is, I believe, the possession of the franchise by the masses before they had been educated to understand and appreciate its privileges and corresponding responsi-bilities ; whatever respect they formerly had for authority has been materially weakened. The remedy for all this lies largely in the hands of ministers of the Gospel, who should teach men not only to please God, but also, to recognise the authority of parents and rulers.

I found that, when inviting the people to the services, the word ' Church ' must be dropped, as it grated on the ears of non-churchgoers like an old saw, and roused many dormant objections and prejudices which prevail to an extent unimagined by any person who has not either lived amongst, or, at all events, come into close contact with, the masses. For owing, I fear, in no small measure, to unfaithfulness and worldliness in God's accredited ministers, which have a baneful effect on His professing people, religion has come to be regarded with contempt by nineteen-twentieths of the lower orders, to say nothing of the middle and upper classes. In many families, for a member to make any religious profession and act up to it, even to the extent of attend-ing a place of worship, is to bring down upon him, or her, contempt, scorn, and ridicule, which few can bear : constant chaffing by those who are fellow-hands in the factory, workshop, warehouse, shop, or office, generally proves too much for the moral cowardice which is now so prevalent in all grades of society, alike in Church and State. I have known men attending our Sunday evening services who left their homes sufficiently long before the time, to get there by a circuitous route, in order to prevent their neighbours suspecting where they had gone.

I remember saying to a member of our choir and a communicant, who was a compositor by trade, ' Now you will have opportunities of saying a word for Christ to your fellow-workmen.' Looking at me with surprise, he replied ' I dare not let anyone in my shop know I even attend church : if I did, I could not stand the place ! ' Does not this reveal an awful state of things ? How is it to be altered ? It is true that the masses wish to be married, to have their children baptized, and to be buried, by the Church ; but to attend church for worship is quite another thing, for which they have no liking, and see no need. I am satisfied that the chief causes of their suspicion, contempt, and holding aloof, are the inconsistency, the hollow sham living, of many who attend church, and the indulgence in strong drink. I am equally satisfied that one of the best ways of counteracting this general prejudice against true religion, is to re-live the Christ life among men.

There was in the parish an unskilled labourer, a terrible fellow, upon whom my eye had long rested. He would, for a wager, eat three pounds of raw steak, or lift a hundredweight by his teeth. He drank heavily, swore shockingly, beat his wife brutally ; in fact, he was about the vilest fellow in the district. One day, when he was going home to dinner, I put myself in his way. As he passed, I said, in a genial tone, ' How are you, my friend ? ' at which he frowned, and went on. We met again, on another occasion, when I hoped he would stop, but his look said What have you to do with me ? I felt, notwithstanding, that the Lord had laid him on my heart, and that I must take him in prayer and faith to the One who alone could soften his heart and save his soul.

Shortly afterwards, hearing that he was very poorly I set off at once to see him, and just as I reached his door he came out, with an emaciated infant in his arms. I said ' My friend, what a nurse you make,' to which, with a glance at the little one, he replied ' Ah, my poor babby is dying, I fear.' At that my heart leaped for joy, feeling sure that the victory was already won, in that I had got his ear. We were friends then and there ! It would take a long chapter to record all that passed between us afterwards. I shall content myself with stating that the death of the ' babby,' and then that of the wife, gave ample opportunity for putting before the poor fellow the way of life very simply, for he could neither read nor write. By grace he yielded, signed the pledge, came openly to God's house, and was the wonder of the place. In a few years his previously shattered constitution, gave way, and he died, resting in Jesus. I buried him, as I had done his child and his wife. Glory be to God for this triumph of grace.

One Tuesday morning I received a letter, dated from Warrington, bearing the signature of a person entirely unknown to me, the substance of it being that though the writer was a stranger to me, he felt constrained to write and say that he had wandered into St. Nathaniel's church on the previous Sunday evening, and was overwhelmed by the warmth of the service : that the responding and the singing of all around him felt so real, bringing vividly to his recollection how, before he came to Liverpool, he, too, used to attend church regularly with his parents, and join heartily in the services ; that his heart was filled with grief, when he realized how terribly he had fallen, in that he then lodged at the house of an ' unfortunate ' with whom he was in league ; that he resolved there and then not to return to that house, but, in order to get clear of the vile life he was leading, to quit Liverpool that night, though he must, by so doing, leave behind all his belongings, except the clothes he had on, and, too, his good situation, although he had no doubt his employers would give him a good character; and that he had some money, sufficient, he hoped, to keep him until he could feel God had pardoned him, and would allow him to meet with another situation. I replied to that letter in a suitable strain, and did not forget to pray much for the writer of it. How the Lord works out His own plans!

I had continued to entertain the hope of being able some day to resume my course in the University of Dublin, the suspension of which had been made a condition precedent to my nomination as incumbent of St. Nathaniel's church; and the time for finally settling that matter seemed now to have arrived. Therefore I made it a matter of prayer, and deep thought. On the one hand, I certainly did wish to have an Arts Degree, and as I was in a sense my own master, I could arrange for giving the time for reading necessary to procure it. On the other hand, there came to my mind all that the Lord had done, and was still doing, by His Word and Spirit, and the doubt as to whether an Arts Degree would in any way increase my power or influence in working for the Master.

I asked myself if all those who had Arts Degrees were so blessed in their labours as I at St. Nathaniel's. Then my conscience seemed to ask me whether the giving up of four hours daily for the requisite reading would not seriously interfere with my ministerial and parochial work? Would it not, under the circumstances, with soul winning in one scale, and the reading for an Arts Degree in the other, be almost to grieve the Holy Spirit? I ultimately was led to the conclusion that I should be satisfied with, and thankful for, a good degree in the Day of the Lord Jesus. And I never regretted having arrived at that conclusion.

This year was one of much real spiritual blessing. There was great love, as well as great zeal, amongst my dear workers. We were all of one mind and heart, each seeming to vie with the rest in love and labour for the Lord.

The following agencies were at work in the parish :

Bible Classes.	Children's Classes.	Domiciliary Visitation.
Band of Hope.	Children's Services.	Cottage Readings.
Penny Bank.	Open-Air Services.	Ragged School Work.
Tontine.	Mission Services.	Young Men's Society.

Truly, so great a work as this called for yet more faith and labour on our part. Whilst we rejoice to know that the dear Saviour holds the golden candlestick in His own hand, and will therefore take care of His own cause ; it still well becomes us to be more humble, earnest, diligent, and faithful, in discharging the several duties which devolve upon us, remembering that the secret of our success is the promise of the Master, taken as our watchword motto for this year, ' And I, if I be lifted up, . . . will draw all men unto Me.'

The average attendance at the Lord's Table, on Sunday evenings, during the year was a hundred and twenty-seven. The various charities received increased support.

' The Lord of Hosts is with us ! '

The amount raised this year was four hundred and eighty-six pounds.

1874.

Church Finance—Bazaar—The power of Isa. xliv. 22—More conversions—Giving ' the Glory '—Congregational picnic—' Blanket washing day '—Doctrinal preaching—' Comfort or counsel ' to an unquiet conscience.

' I will bless thee, . . . and thou shalt be a blessing ' (Gen. xii. 2).

WHILST the primary reference of this promise by God to Abraham was to the Messiah, and then to Abraham's immediate seed, it is forcibly applicable to every child of God by faith in Christ Jesus.

The old year was let out, and the new year let in, in the usual happy and profitable manner, followed by the annual week of prayer, and the gathering together round the Lord's Table.

The financial responsibility of our work was now beginning to press heavily upon me. My dear people did well, indeed some had done more than well ; yet, owing to our having to do so much to the church, in order to make it bright and comfortable in everyway, we had not sufficient for our current needs, and there seemed to be no way of obtaining the amount required. We wanted a treasurer, who, besides counting money handed to him, could and would raise whatever was necessary. But such a one was not forthcoming, therefore I had to be treasurer still, and indeed remained so up to the close of my ministry. That ought not to be : the pastor's time, thoughts, and strength should be devoted entirely to spiritual work.

Although the church was already £206 in my debt, the expenditure of a further sum on the interior had become imperative. Between the rough grey bricks of the inner walls the lime oozed, giving an unsightly appearance ; to remove which the walls were whitewashed, but the result was very unsatisfactory. They were then washed salmon colour, but that was worse still.

Evidently something very different, and of a much more thorough kind, was absolutely necessary. According to our wont on all occasions concerning the church or parish, we had a conference, the outcome of which was the resolve to get up a bazaar. I had my doubts as to the possibility of doing so strictly on Christian and ordinary business principles. The arrangements entailed an immense amount of labour on me, although I was splendidly seconded by my dear helpers and the people generally ; three other churches, where I had interest, also assisted us liberally.

It seemed to me that I made sufficiently stringent regulations as to gambling and alcohol ; but I was mistaken. When the bazaar was actually on, things were done—doubtless with the best intentions—which, though they were not in accordance with my convictions, I was powerless to prevent, and I resolved never to have another : a sale of work can be controlled, and is very different. The total receipts were £1,053, and it was decided that whatever sum remained after payment of the expenses, and the debt to me, should be expended on plastering the interior of the church, skirting the walls all round with wood, carving the capitals of the pillars, beading the two inner side roof ceilings, putting a geometrically designed stained-glass window in the chancel, raising the tower and finishing it with a spire.

This year I commenced a course of expository instruction on Paul's First Letter to the Corinthians. That the Lord was manifestly blessing His Word was evidenced by a greatly increased general interest, as seen in the larger numbers attending the various means of grace, and by other tokens.

An intelligent, respectable working man, whom I I knew to be a Christian, called at my rooms one evening with a companion, and said : ' I have failed to show my friend here how to find peace with God, which he is anxiously seeking, so I have brought him to you.' We sat round a table. Finding the friend to be in earnest about his soul, I opened my Bible at Isa. xliv., reading verse 22, ' I have blotted out as a thick cloud thy transgressions, and as a cloud thy sins'; God's own absolution, in His own blessed words. I laid special emphasis on ' have,' pointing out that it was not something that shall be, or will be, or may be, but something that has been already done; and that this great boon and blessing is to be gratefully received, and thankfully believed by simple faith, just because God Himself most graciously and lovingly says so. I showed that not to believe this absolution, not to receive it, not to bless God for it, is the greatest sin the sinner can commit; that it is, in fact, to make Him a liar. The poor fellow could not see it, though I put it to him in a variety of ways. We were thus together for an hour or more, and then we knelt in prayer.

On leaving, the man asked if he might call again that evening week. I said by all means, so he came. I took the same passage, putting the word of the living God before him; but he appeared unable to accept pardon on, as it seemed to him, such easy terms. We then prayed, and he, again asking to call a week hence, and receiving a cordial assent, presented himself for the third time. On this occasion, too, I kept to Isa. xliv., 22; and whilst I was presenting its blessed truth for his acceptance by simple faith, just because the God against whom sin is committed hath said it, he suddenly raised one of his hands, and, striking the table such a blow that I thought my landlady might be alarmed, cried out joyfully, ' I see it, I see it.' Then, looking at me, he said, in a rather reproving tone, ' How is it you have never preached like that ? ' ' Ah, my friend, I have.' ' I never heard you preach like that.' ' I know I have; but you had not the ears to hear, or faith to believe it.' I then called his attention to ver. 23, ' Sing, oh heavens, for the Lord hath done it,' and he went on his way rejoicing. Is not one such won to God of infinitely more value than £ s. d., however necessary they may be ?

I am thankful to say the dear fellow became a very ardent and enthusiastic worker. His immediate yearning was for his wife to know the Lord, and God was pleased to grant his desire, to the great joy of his soul. Oh, what wonders and triumphs of grace hath God wrought in that dear church, and in its surrounding sixteen acres of sin ! Is not this case a fair and conclusive illustration of what is intended by that passage in the Communion Service—concerning any who, of an unquiet conscience 'requireth further comfort or counsel,' 'let him come to me, or to some other discreet and learned minister of God's word, and open his grief ; that by the ministry of God's holy word he may receive the benefit of absolution, together with ghostly counsel and advice, to the quieting of his conscience ! ' That is, that by instruction from Holy Scripture, absolution, pardon, and peace, may be obtained, as God thereby bestows it, through faith in His most holy word. In this quotation from the Prayer-Book, or in its context there is not a word concerning auricular confession to a priest, or even implying that the person in special grief must be alone ; nor that the absolution or forgiveness comes from, depends on, or has anything to do with, the minister. The truth is, the Prayer-Book provides no form of absolution for such ; it is by the ministry of the word—as in the foregoing instance—that God absolves, on penitence and faith, there and then. Well may ' the heavens rejoice,' that ' God, even our own God,' thus abundantly pardons.

By the Lord's enabling grace I was never ashamed to confess Him, and to defend what I believed to be His truth, as found in Holy Scripture, and reasserted in the standards of our Church settled at the Blessed Reformation. It was my custom to preach, at times—and almost on or near July 12, and November 5—not only on the positive, but also on the negative articles of religion. I trust that I ever sought to speak in love ; feeling that the truth of God, set forth in the Holy Scriptures, was committed to my trust at my ordination, and that I must defend and maintain it by lawful means, at all costs, regardless of men's opinions or of consequences to myself. And, God being my helper this solemn duty was never shelved.

One morning, a military-looking man whom I had
noticed in church, called on me. With suppressed
emotion, he told me that he came of a Norfolk family,
and had held a commission in the army ; that he was
now living in the suburbs of Liverpool ; that his parents
were devoted Christians, his brothers and sisters also
having been brought to the Lord ; that he, the youngest,
had been the ' lost one ' in the family ; adding—
with tears in his eyes—' until the Good Shepherd found
me, two Sunday evenings ago, in St. Nathaniel's as
you were preaching from the text, " Seek ye my face ;
Thy face, Lord will I seek." ' We rejoiced together. At
my resignation I left him still a member of the church.
Though he did not take up directly spiritual work,
he rendered good service to the church in sundry
ways. Doubtless it was in answer to the earnest,
believing prayers of his parents for him. All places,
as well as times, and seasons, are in God's hands.
Oh, Thou art the faithful God, who dost say to Thy
people, ' The promise is to you and to your children.'

A man carrying on business, very respectable but
quite irreligious, had been arrested by God's grace, in St.
Nathaniel's Church, to the great joy of his sincerely
Christian wife, who belonged to the Primitive Methodists.
He called on me ; I found him an earnest convert.
His wife also called, to express her gratitude that her
husband had at length become deeply interested about
his soul, and to say that she felt she ought to support
him by attending church too, which she did. As a
Methodist she had been accustomed to give at times
what she called ' the Glory,' whilst the minister was
preaching ; and, during my sermon on the occasion
of her first attendance at church, to the amazement of
everybody she cried out ' Glory,' which almost brought
me to a standstill. Having for some years been blind,
she could not, of course, notice the surprise of the
congregation, or their looks ; but her husband did,
as he sat beside her, and it made him very uncomfortable.
He told her, in private, how nervous it had made him.

I reasoned with her on the subject, pointing out

that she could give ' the glory ' just as earnestly in her
own mind, that ' the spirits of the prophets are subject
to the prophets,' and that she should consider her
fellow-worshippers. She had a month to think over
the matter. At the end of that time she came to say she
felt so strongly that she ought to give ' the glory,'
which she was persuaded was from the Holy Spirit,
that not to give it would be to grieve Him, and that
therefore if I insisted upon her silence, she must leave
the church. I replied, ' Well, rather than leave the
church, give " the glory " ' ; she remained, but the
' glory ' grew less and less.

She was a well-educated woman. I asked her, one
day, whether she had lost anything by joining the
church. Her reply was ' No, I have gained much ;
for instance, that word " incline," in the responses to the
Commandments, always brings me a blessing ; my heart
goes out to God then specially, that He would " incline "
it to keep His law.' It was her custom, as we met at
times in the street, to accost me with ' I have a life-buoy
for you,' or ' I have a bunch of grapes for you ' ; and
then she would quote some precious promise in God's
Word. Oh, it was so refreshing ! Her husband, too,
thank God, found complete rest in Jesus. In the course
of years I laid them both, at only a short interval
between, in ' God's acre,' to rest ' until the day breathe
and the shadows flee away.' Glory !

This year there was really the first annual congregational picnic. We went to the picturesque village
of Hale ; the distance was not great, the road was
pretty, and the tickets were cheap, all which just
suited the people. There was a large party, the convey-
ance being by either rail or omnibus. This excursion
became a yearly one, and for nine years it was to that
same place. On one occasion we had no less than
twenty-seven omnibuses, filled to overflowing. All
went well, without a hitch or accident, and the people
were delighted. The weather was always so favourable
that some of the housewives used to say : ' If we want
to wash our blankets we should choose St. Nathaniel's

picnic day.' The cautions and fears of some of my clerical brethren were never realized, on any of these excursions, which went far to popularize the church in the best sense of the word. I used to ask my dear helpers to seize the opportunities these gatherings afforded them for saying a word to careless ones who might be present, but in a merely friendly non-official manner ; and good resulted from such wayside talks.

This year the various agencies were well sustained, all round. £1,490 were raised altogether! A large amount indeed. Who would have supposed it even possible, much less likely, that in one year such a sum could have been raised by a church with such beginnings and such surroundings ? Of course, ' the thing was from the Lord.' He knew what was needed for His work, and He put it into the hearts of whom He would supply it. How mistaken are those who think that any sort of a place to worship in will satisfy the working classes ! whereas they quite appreciate a handsome and a well-appointed church, but with hearty services, in which they can join and feel they are taking part.

' Worship the Lord in the beauty of holiness.'

The Lord was enabling me to observe much of His own workings in the hearts of many amongst us. Moreover, I began to realize more and more the fact that not only the unsaved and the indifferent, but also true Christians, and specially the helpers in our work, were alike looking at the pastor's life, as well as his teaching, for guidance and example. That discovery, too, caused me to fall back on the dear Lord, from whom alone I could obtain the grace necessary to be preserved myself, and to become an ensample to others, in the way of godliness ; remembering the exhortation, ' Take heed unto thyself, and unto the doctrine, . . . for, in doing this, thou shalt both save thyself and them that hear thee.'

1875.

Moody and Sankey—Church improvements ' Faculty '—Scriptural chancel—The oldest Confirmation candidate—Terrible drinking case —Confirmees collections—Object of churches, services, and pastors —Ragged school outdoor treat—Church re-opened after alterations —' Doctor, are you born again ? '—Half the congregation communicants.

' My God shall supply all your need according to His riches in glory by Christ Jesus ' (Phil. iv. 19).

THE end of another year has been reached ; with its confessed sins of commission and omission, whether in our private life or in our work for the Lord, pardoned and forgiven through Christ ; with its increased love for Him, its increased delight in His service, its stronger faith in His promises, and its greater reliance on His guidance, resulting from our experience of His gracious dealings with us in the past.

The outlook, though in one way cheering, is in another way depressing ; for whilst many have, through grace, been led to believe, and those who already believed have been built up, the great majority of these living in our parish are still unsaved.

If this work be anything it is really a spiritual one, although that in no way interferes with our doing everything we can for the bodily comfort and general welfare of our dear people.

The visit of Moody and Sankey to Liverpool was a great help to the cause of God in this parish.

Not without some hesitation did I sign the invitation sent to them ; but when they came, and I heard Moody preach the Gospel, and Sankey sing it, I recognised that the blessed Spirit of God was using them, and, too, in a manner quite new to me ; so I was thankful for having been privileged to share in the responsibility of bringing them to Liverpool.

I gathered from those gifted and honoured servants of the Most High many useful hints, as to both matter and manner in preaching to win souls.

Feeling greatly the need of more accommodation, the ragged school being occupied every evening, we rented part of a house at the corner of Aigburth Street, and there held some of our minor meetings. Application had just been made for the necessary faculty to close the church in order to make the alterations already decided on. It occurred to me that the unoccupied space round the Holy Table was unnecessarily large, and that it would be well to have the rail in front of the table shortened at each end, and joined to a semi-circular rail going behind the Table (the chancel being apsidal), placing permanent seats against the whole of the east wall, as part of the ordinary seating capacity of the church.

Through the Bishop's secretaries I asked for leave to amend the faculty application in accordance with the new design, which I showed to them. They took no exception thereto, informing me that I was then too late for the next court day ; therefore the application could not be heard for some months. On being told by me that, anticipating no difficulty in getting the faculty, the alterations had been already begun, they advised me to go on with them, and apply for a faculty confirming the work which was done.

Just previous to the day of hearing, the Chancellor came to see the proposed chancel arrangements, about which he did not make any difficulty. Therefore, when I appeared before him in his court, it surprised me to find him take exception to the rail round the Table, and to the permanent seats, the latter being actually set up. Following considerable correspondence with him, in which I very clearly stated that, as I had received quasi authority for both, I did not see my way to remove them, I received a letter from the Bishop, asking me to call upon him, with the designs. I did so ; and, after examining them for a moment, he said,

in his usual quiet tone, ' I quite approve of them.'
That settled the matter.

My beloved Bishop, Dr. Ryle, brought the famous
Canon Tristram, of Durham, to see this chancel, who,
reading aloud the words over the chancel window,
" *By our offering He hath perfected for ever them that
are sanctified.*" And underneath the window at either
side of Bishop Jacobson's reredos, described above, the
words, " *There is no more offering for sin* "; and seeing
the semi-circular seat attached to the wall for general
use ; also, the holy Table with a rail all around it,
giving kneeling accommodation to thirty-six communicants at once ; and the Table covered with a rich
crimson cloth, the fringe thereof not quite hiding the
legs of the Table, with the words on the front of the
cover in needle work, " Till He come," exclaimed,
" Well, that is the most Scriptural and Protestant
chancel I have ever seen," to which the dear Bishop
smiled assent.

I believe St. Nathaniel's to be the only Church and
Chancel in these Kingdoms where there is such an ar-
rangement. It is a return to the Plan of the Early
Church.*

This year dear old Michael Burke was called home.
He was the one man present at the first little service I
had, on my arrival in Windsor : I shall never forget it.
His new birth, as consistently witnessed to by a new
life, was, as it were, the first drop of the coming ' showers
of blessing,' which from time to time God poured down
upon the people and their pastor. When in 1870 the
Bishop noticed on the list of confirmation candidates
Burke's name, with ' aged 81 ' against it, he remarked
with surprise and interest, ' That is the oldest candidate
I have ever confirmed ; tell me about him.' And when
he heard how Burke had been over forty years a Romanist, and nearly forty years a Protestant ; how he was
the only man present at my first cellar-service, where
he was born again ; and how, leading a new life, he
desired to be confirmed, the Bishop was deeply touched.

* Notwithstanding the vexatious fire which destroyed the church
except the tower, bells, and clock, the new church has all the
characteristics of the first, with enrichments.

I heard of a family, consisting of parents and five children, in the greatest distress, owing to the father, who, when sober, could earn £5 a week in the local foundry, being out of work, through a long ' drinking bout,' and on the stool of repentance and remorse. I lost no time in going to them. There was no fire, and no food. His wife and children were in rags ; he looked quite miserable, and thoroughly ashamed of being seen by me under such circumstances. After conversing with them for a short time, I proposed that we should kneel and ask for God's blessing ; whereat the father looked amazed, but he knelt down. He showed me out, and on shaking his hand I put half-crown into it, which he took, though I could see that the touch of the coin roused mixed feelings of indignation and humiliation. But he thanked me warmly, and I believe that half-crown had more effect upon him than my prayer. Ah, we are all pretty much alike under certain conditions : the soul is often reached through the body, as, he afterwards told me, was the case in this instance. I followed him up, and with good results. The man became a total abstainer and worked regularly, the miserable place was made a comfortable home, all the family were suitably clad, the children were sent to school, and the wife attended church with her husband. The wilderness indeed blossomed as a rose. In course of time they took a house in a better street, the children were confirmed, and, with the parents, came to the Lord's Table. It was not an uncommon thing to see father, mother, and three children, kneeling there together. The one son was the last brought to God.

Let those who think differently say what they will ; I hold that there is no one more fitted to bestow temporal relief than the pastor. Did not the blessed Jesus Himself graciously feed the hungry and heal the sick, during His ministry of love ? To relieve promptly, and tactfully as well as tenderly, enhances the value of the gift. In all my experience, I have not found that my visits to the poor were in the smallest degree affected by giving occasional relief.

Each year the confirmees had very kindly made me a present, which I felt ought not to continue. I therefore resolved to suggest that in place of it, each one should take a collecting-book, and putting in it whatever he or she had intended giving towards a present for me, should ask friends to contribute, devoting whatever was raised to church expenses, as a sort of firstfruits of their recent reception into full fellowship with God's people and participation in the memorial service of the Lord's Supper. The idea found favour, and as a result, £21 were collected ! How important it is to interest the young in doing good ; and how desirable it is to take advantage of the time when their hearts are loving and tender towards God. All can do, and as a rule all are willing to do, something : what that something shall be, depends partly on the individual, and partly on the pastor ; more perhaps on the discretion of the latter, than on the feelings of the former. In that, as in every department of his work, the minister needs much sanctified common-sense.

I noticed with great pleasure the interest taken by the helpers, congregation, and parishioners generally in the alterations and improvements going on at the church ; just as if they had been taking place at their own homes. It is most desirable to get the people interested alike in the building, the services, and the officials—the ministers—of the church ; and that can only be done by showing that the building, the services and the ministers belong to them ; that the buildings were erected for them to worship in ; that the services were intended for them to take their part in ; that the ministers were appointed for them to be visited, helped and edified. But churches are being built at needless cost ; services are conducted in them which, besides being entirely contrary to the doctrines of the Church, are also quite uncongregational ; and ministers indulge in all sorts of vagaries. And as all these are without reference to the real wants or the wishes of probably more than a very small percentage of the population, it is only natural that a feeling of indifference, even if not of actual opposition, to the buildings, the services, and the ministers, should spring up, and show itself more and more.

This year we gave the first out-of-door treat to our ragged children, for whose school we raised £171, beside having always given two meals to about 150 poor little ones twice a week. I always felt that this ragged school work was one of the glories of our church, and that the Lord looked down with approval upon it : hence also our blessings.

The church was now ready to be re-opened after the alterations and additions already alluded to : and we were all struck by the improved appearance of the interior. There was the new east window in stained glass of geometrical design, and its centre light of appropriate symbols—not figures—such as : At the top an open Bible, crowned ; ' I am the Vine,' with a bunch of grapes ; ' I am the rose of Sharon,' with a bloom of that flower ; ' the lily of the valley,' with a spray thereof. Then there was the new rail round the Holy Table, at which thirty-four communicants could kneel at once ; and the bench against the apsidal wall seating thirty-six worshippers ; and there were the artistically carved capitals of the pillars. Altogether the interior looked beautiful, and we thank God for this adorning of His house, ' where prayer was wont to be made ' to Him, where the glorious Gospel of His grace was plainly set forth, and where He graciously manifested Himelf to many by His Holy Spirit. The slated spire alone failed to give satisfaction ; it was soon nicknamed ' the extinguisher.' There were large congregations at the re-opening services, and we were glad to get back to our church after the long period during which it had been closed

It was laid upon my heart at this time to put this question to a local M.D. : ' Doctor, are you born again ? ' With a thoughtful expression on his face, he replied ' I cannot say I am. I know this, I had a very pious mother, whose influence was, I am sure, the means of keeping me from excesses in my undergraduate career and is still about me.' Soon after, he joined the church, became a communicant, and seemed deeply in earnest. When his eldest child died, he wrote, and put upon the ' In Memoriam ' card (one of which was given to me), two verses beautifully breathing forth an assured hope of the little fellow's blessedness. Just then a book, written by another M.D., in which Christianity was fiercely attacked, made shipwreck of my dear friend's faith, and, being an honest man, he left the church. Though feeling his defection deeply, I thought it prudent not to discuss the subject with him, but I resolved to pray for him, and, having kept the card, I put in it my Bible, as a constant reminder. Retaining his goodwill as a neighbour, when I met him one Sunday morning with my Bible under my arm, we shook hands, he remarking ' I am going out professionally,' and I rejoined ' I am going to church.' Then drawing forth and holding up the little card, I asked if he knew that, to which he made no answer. I went on ' Doctor, I have put this card in my Bible, as a reminder of a resolution to pray for you, believing, as I do, that you will be restored to the faith of your sainted mother.' At that his face showed a piteous, hollow smile, and we parted.

Fully ten years went by, during which period whenever we happened to meet I always drew out the card, if I had it with me, to remind him of my resolution, but without bringing any remark from him, until on one occasion he said, smiling, ' Well, it will do me no harm.' Meeting him afterwards in a lonely part, I made up my mind to speak to him seriously ; so, on shaking hands, I retained his in mine, and, looking him full in the face, inquired ' Doctor, do you now believe in God ? ' ' Yes, I do,' he answered solemnly. ' Do you also believe in Jesus ? ' ' I do,' he replied in an assuring tone. Again we parted, my heart filled with joy and gratitude. His health began to decline. I got still nearer and nearer to him in visiting his home. One day, some of his family being present, he looked at me, with tears in his eyes, and asked if I would bury

him, as he felt his end was near.' I said ' As a Christian,
doctor ? ' ' Yes, as a Christian,' he answered with deep
emotion. When the time came, I committed his body
to the grave, in the blessed hope of the resurrection to
eternal life. The little ' In Memoriam ' card is still
religiously preserved. Thank God for the blessed
promise, ' I will heal their backsliding, I will love them
freely.' It is well for all of us that we are in the hands
of so merciful and gracious a God as is our God and
Father in Christ Jesus.

About one-half of the regular congregation were now
communicants, which will give greater cause for thankfulness when the Scriptural place which this Divine
ordinance has in our teaching is borne in mind : that
it is neither a repetition, continuation, presentation, nor
offering, of Calvary's sacrifice, but a blessed memorial
commemoration of that sacrifice, in accordance with the
command of Him who offered it.

The temptation, so subtle, and so often present—
specially in times of such spiritual prosperity as we
were happily experiencing—to rest on one's oars, to
take the work rather more easily, to be satisfied with
things as they are, did not fail to assail me ; but I
always sought to resist it, and to impress on my dear
helpers that we must never relax our efforts so long as
there were in the parish souls out of Christ ; swamps
to be drained, hedges to be cut, rocks to be blasted, and
plants to be watered, for the Master.

The various agencies were in vigorous operation, the
workers numbering a hundred and thirty-six. There
was a great increase in the offertories. The Sunday
services, and the two week evening services, were
well attended.

At times I stood amazed, wondering how it was, and
why it was, that the blessing of God was bestowed upon
us in such abundance. I thankfully fell back upon the
sovereign grace of God, in calling the things that be not
as though they were, ' that no flesh should glory in His
presence ' ; and rejoiced that ' of Him, and through

Him, and to Him, are all things ; to whom be glory for ever. Amen.'

The amount raised this year was four hundred and eighty pounds.

1876.

Paper read before Ruri-Decanal Chapter—Country clergy's ignorance of 'slum' work—The 'Cure of souls'—Local agencies—Sunday evening Communicants, and collections—The two Scripture-readers —Parochial elevation of tone—Antidote—Social evil—The Holy Spirit's influence.

' As for me and my house, we will serve the Lord ' (Josh. xxiv. 15).

B Y God's good hand upon us, we had come to the end of the seventh year's work for Him in the parish.

The ushering in of the new year was marked by the usual service, when hundreds could not gain admission to the church : that was followed by the week of prayer, and the New Year Sunday evening communion.

Under gentle pressure by the Rural Dean, I consented to read a paper before the Ruri-Decanal Chapter, on ' An Account of God's Work in Windsor.' In it I set forth the social, moral, and spiritual condition of the district when I began the work of evangelization in it ; the means adopted, such as house-to-house visitation, open-air and mission services, Bible and other classes for the old and young, women and men ; cellar readings ; Sunday and week-day services, in church and schoolroom ; Sunday and ragged schools ; plain church services, in which all the congregation could heartily unite ; and the preaching of a full and simple Gospel, pointing out God's offer of salvation to all who will accept it by faith in Christ Jesus ; relying upon the Holy Spirit to bless His own word and work. The paper emphasized the abundant need of sympathy and adaptability in every department of the work,

and concluding by touching, to God's glory, on some of
the blessed results ; it was afterwards published, by
request.

The Rural Dean presided, and, in winding up the
discussion which followed, said he could not well see
how such results had been achieved, as he had visited
the parish and entered a house where he saw nothing
but a family in squalor and wretchedness, whereas
he had expected at least to find tidiness and neatness ;
on which, someone interpolated the question, ' Did
you ask if the room you entered served for the drawing-
room, parlour, bedroom, kitchen, and scullery, in which
parents and children all lived ? and whether the father
was in employment ? ' The ignorance of some of the
rich country clergy as to the actual condition of a
' slum ' parish is surprising and lamentable.

To those already brought out of the awful darkness of
Romanism, and received into the Church, there was
this year added a whole family. This happy result was
more immediately due to a tract, entitled, ' Dan Carty '
—whose conversion from Romanism it described—
left in the house by one of our lady visitors. Both the
man and his wife became communicants.

I always felt that my solemn oath on induction to the
' cure of souls,' referred to those of Romanists as of all
others in the parish. I know this will be questioned, at
all events in practice. I have often been surprised, after
an appeal for funds to build a church in a parish of,
say, ten thousand souls, on perhaps meeting the vicar
and asking ' How are you getting on ? ' to be told
' Well, fairly, seeing that half of my people are Romanists.' ' But will they not receive you ? ' ' I have made
an effort, but there is no use : they would stone me.'
' Well, suppose they did : you are responsible to God
for their souls.' How many missionaries abroad have
been stoned, maimed, killed ! Oh ! for home missionary
zeal !

This year we began to have what we called a little
mission in Passion Week : by which we meant not
only to have the usual services in church, but also to

' do ' the parish every evening, in stages, sing a hymn or part of one, and give an earnest invitation to all around to join us in the house of God, to hear the story of our Lord's passion. That had a double effect for good ; it stirred up those already interested, and it gave a testimony to the passers-by. All kinds of lawful efforts are needed to arrest the attention of those who are careless and thoughtless about their soul's salvation.

This Passion Week we had, as usual, the Lord's Supper on the evening of its institution—Thursday. The next day (Good Friday) there was an additional service in church, for children, each one present having a bun on leaving. There was a large gathering, for we swept the parish, as far as possible, of every child, no matter who : I catechized them.

We also rented a room in Foundry Lane, for Sunday purposes, specially that poor lads might meet for Scriptural instruction.

Confirmation time was always one of great gladness to us all ; to me especially it brought ' joy and gladness,' the warmth and tone of those new disciples of Christ keeping my soul fresh and green. On the first Sunday evening after confirmation, the confirmees were joined at the Lord's Table by a large number of other communicants.

There was no falling off in the vicar's visiting ; it had proved too powerful a factor in the work not to be kept up, or to allow anything to prove a hindrance. The people were so ready to hear the word spoken, read, and expounded, that it was a real pleasure to go amongst them.

At this time I began the exposition of Paul's Letter to the Romans.

A survey of the Lord's doing during the seven years since I began to labour for Him in this apparently unfruitful soil brings to my mind memories of God's mercies and loving kindnesses in Christ, of the Blessed Saviour's constant companionship, and of the Holy Spirit's felt presence. From four in a cellar, the flock has now to be numbered by some thousands, old and young. The annual report contained the following :

'There are eighteen agencies at work for good and for God, all of which show signs of life, while some show great vitality, viz. : a Penny Bank, a Sick and Burial Society, a total abstainers' society, a Band of Hope, a mothers' meeting, a service for children, a service for infants, a service for women, a mission service, cellar and kitchen readings, open-air services, a prayer-meeting, a voluntary church choir, adult Bible-classes, a young men's mutual improvement society, lady district visitors, Sunday-schools with an average of 600, in which no prizes are given, a day and night Ragged School, attended by over 400 poor children. There are four services in church on Sundays, attended by over 3,000 worshippers ; and two services on week-days attended by cheering congregations : half of the regular worshippers are communicants. This great work, for great it is, and extending, is sustained by the vicar, curate, Scripture-reader, and, thank God, by no less than 185 true Christian helpers in the Lord, many of whom are full of love, glow, and zeal, for our dear Lord, and for lost ones. This is not an army on paper, but one chosen, equipped, and self-sacrificing. Hallelujah ! '

AVERAGE COMMUNICANTS ON SUNDAY EVENINGS.

1869 (half(year)	..	..	60	1873	..	..	..	127
1870	..	..	.. 75	1874	..	..	..	136
1871	..	..	.. 90	1875	..	..	..	175
1872	..	..	.. 102	1876	..	..	..	208

SUNDAY EVENING COLLECTIONS FOR CHURCH EXPENSES.

	£ s. d.			£ s d.
1869 (half-year) ..	54 7 10	1873	.. ..	112 17 6
1870	94 15 10	1874	.. ..	115 2 3
1871	107 17 3	1875	.. ..	128 18 7
1872	116 1 6	1876	.. ..	147 15 6

Though warned at first against a regular collection on Sunday evenings, which was then uncommon in

Liverpool, I felt the result would depend upon whether the people were interested or not. I never fell in with the notice ' No collection,' in announcements of services for the masses : I have always found them most willing to contribute if they have a regular opportunity for doing so. The whole thing is a matter of influence ; in fact, this is the real secret, on the human side, of success.

As two Scripture-readers were talking together, one said to the other, sadly : ' If you get hold of a man, and get him to your church, he is very likely to go again ; whereas, if I get hold of one and get him to my church, he is most likely not to come again ; and yet my vicar is considered a very learned man. I know he is a good man, and wishful to do the Master's work.' I do know that when that dear man of God was inducted he had a full church, but it soon began to decline. He thought that if the church were modernized it would be more appreciated ; so the galleries were removed : still the attendance lessened. Then the rather old-fashioned pews were cut down ; yet the congregation dwindled. Draughts were then supposed to account for the falling off ; therefore, large and suitable vestibules were erected, but without any improvement, and the attendance became invariably small. Perhaps the failure of that good vicar arose from his want of power to adapt himself, and his lack of influence over those to whom he ministered, in his presentation of the Gospel. Truly, to acquire the power of adaptation, and of influencing men for God, is worth the prayers and the study of years. This applies all round to those who desire to do work for Him.

It may, perhaps, be asked, ' What was the moral effect of all this effort on the parish generally ? ' That question is answered by the following facts. Holders of property in the parish publicly stated that the tenants were better disposed to pay their rents than formerly. Then, too, there was no longer any danger to lady pedestrians, who might now traverse well-nigh even the worse streets without fear of molestation. Nor must the very decided testimony of the police, as to the general improvement amongst the people, be overlooked. The moral tone of the people was certainly raised, inasmuch as whilst in the early days of my vicariate, the scandalous behaviour and remarks of women, even at the church door, on the occasion of a wedding, compelled me to precede the newly-wedded pair down the aisle to the entrance, to see them into their conveyances, there were now scarcely ever any immodest speeches on such occasions. Moreover, the sick-list had fallen to one-half of what it was when the work began. These were all, surely, signs of improvement due to the civilizing, elevating, Christianizing influence of the church upon the parish generally.

I do not wish to convey the impression that the sixteen acres of sin were changed into sixteen acres of holiness ; far from it. I never yet heard of any parish, no matter how highly favoured, in which every soul was really brought to God. But I do wish to say—and I thank God for being able to say it—that much, very much was done ; that some twelve hundred were baptized, that several hundreds were confirmed ; that hundreds had been brought to God, and were leading new lives ; that hundreds of poor children had partaken of tens of thousands of warm meals in the aggregate ; that numbers had died " in the Lord ' ; that eighteen agencies, representing a large staff of whole-hearted, loving Christian workers, were endeavouring to ' rescue the perishing,' to ' care for the dying,' bringing hope to many a despairing one, wiping tears away from many a sorrowing one ; that £2,500 had been raised and expended on the church ; and that two small mission-rooms were rented to meet the growing necessity for more accommodation.

I am well aware of our deficiencies ; that we did not do all we should, or perhaps could, nor did we do what we did as it might have been done. But God knows we did try to do our level best with the material at hand, and according to the light and strength given unto us. There I leave it, with the prayer to God : ' Accept what

is Thine own, and pardon what is ours.' I have often
thought that when, through God's sovereign grace, I
shall be permitted, in adoring love and gratitude, to
cast my crown at the feet of the Blessed Redeemer, I
shall love to tell Him—as if He doth not know!—
of that ' lost one,' found in No. 6 Cellar, Oliver Street ;
the first-fruit of this ingathering which He purchased
with His own blood.

The amount raised was eight hundred and eighty-two
pounds.

1877.

Phases of work—Artisan critics—Filial joy—' The little hell '—
' Unfortunates '—Corrective result of Church influence—The confirmation net—Funeral opportunities—Children's cottage sale of work.

' No condemnation ' (Rom. viii. 1). ' No separation ' (Rom. viii. 35).

THANK God for the comforting teaching contained
in these words, as the happy portion of all who
are in Christ Jesus. Whence can condemnation
come ? since it is God who justifies, acquits. And
whence separation ? since God's children are in Christ
by living, loving faith, as the branch is in the vine,
as the limb is in the body, as Noah was in the Ark ;
' safe in the arms of Jesus.'

At this time I was feeling very deeply both the
constant pressure, and the tremendous responsibility
of the work. I was in doubt as to whether my strength
would hold out, in face of all that had to be done in order
to preserve what was already won, as well as to go on
gaining victories in winning more trophies for Christ.
The demands upon my time and powers were ever
increasing. There was much pulpit preparation for my
share—naturally the lion's—of the preaching at the
Sunday and week-day services ; there was the oversight of all the agencies, and taking counsel with the
dear helpers ; there was the never-ending systematic

house-to-house visitation; there was the attendance at a meeting or meetings of some sort every evening in the week; there was a very large daily correspondence; there was the constant stream of daily callers, at almost all hours; there was the raising money to supplement the congregation's contributions towards church and parochial expenses: all which combined to leave me no opportunities for social intercourse, or for taking that rest, physically and mentally, which was becoming more and more necessary.

How I did cry to the Lord for an increase of love and power, and of a sound mind! And yet, being led to consider in detail what He had already allowed me to do, I was refreshed, and encouraged to go on in His strength, with willingness to 'spend and be spent' in His service.

I was aware that with reference to our work, some, who ought to have known better, had said, ' Any kettle of fish will do there '; but I did not find it so. On the contrary, whilst the artisan class are not book-learned, they know quite well—better, perhaps, than those who look down upon them—whether or not ' the nail is hit on the head.' And, as to a religious teacher deceiving them, they read him through and through, whether parson or layman, and seldom make a mistake about his being a real man of God, or merely a professor, a pretender!

This year I had the delight of a prolonged visit from my darling mother. She was to me above all others in this world the one around whom my heart's tendrils closely entwined themselves. There is no earthly love like that of a good Christian mother: it is so natural, so true, so unselfish, so undying. If the whole world should condemn her child, she finds, deep down in her heart, despite all else, love for her own. I had but little time to spend with my dear mother, except at meals, but we managed now and again to have brief snatches of joyful intercourse. I had been accustomed to visit her once a year, during my holiday; this year it was my privilege and pleasure to take her with me to Blackpool. On our arrival there, feeling jaded, exhausted, and rather depressed, I remained indoors ; but after a few days, taking a stroll on the shore with her, I heard the sound of singing at a distance, and as we got nearer, the wind wafted to my ears the words ' There is sweet rest in heaven.' They came to me like the voice of God, bringing comfort and cheer ; and sitting down on the beach, I wept for joy. After a little we went on, and joined the singers in their sweet service of song.

On the Government inspector examining our day ragged school, he condemned it, unless we did what was practically impossible ; for it was not to be expected that a school of its kind could be brought up to the standard required by the Government Code. Our committee therefore decided to convert it into a mission evening school on two nights in the week, when the children could have suppers instead of dinners ; leaving the adult ragged school to go on still, on the usual evenings. Since then, these schools have been mostly of a mission character, the children going to efficient day-schools ; so that in reality we lost nothing by the enforced change. The Lord still provided the means of carrying them on.

A certain street in the parish was known as ' the little hell,' on account of being inhabited by those who are called—and only too truly—'unfortunates.' That street was not overlooked by me in my visitation, but the visiting there was fearfully trying. In no instance, however, did I ever get an immodest look, or hear an immoral word, from any of the women : poor things, they seemed to know my errand, and instinctively to realize that I felt for each of them tenderly, as somebody's daughter, and somebody's sister.

From the formation of our parish my eye had been turned specially on the dwellers in that vile street, and my heart mourned over them. Recourse to the police might perhaps have resulted in their removal ; but I felt that those pitiable victims, sinners though they were against God, might be saved, just as other sinners against God were ; whilst if their conversion were not achieved, the moral tone of the neighbourhood might be so raised as to result in its resenting, and eventually putting an end to, the existence of such vice in its midst. And that is just what happened.

As we had long since hoped and expected, the up-lifting effect of our church and mission work upon the parish generally, showed itself, in the course of time, by, amongst other ways, murmurs of dissatisfaction from the people round about, and especially by those— quite a large number now—attending our mothers' meetings. There was no attack, as such, upon the ' unfortunates ' themselves, but it came to pass that if any man was seen either to enter or leave any of the houses there, it was made too hot for him : and so, as a result, all those poor creatures had now left, there not being one in that street ; nor, indeed, was there a known brothel in the whole parish.

I have no doubt what we were able to effect on a small scale could be brought about elsewhere on a larger one, if only the tone of society, whether of the upper, middle, or lower classes, were raised sufficiently to condemn this terrible, crying sin against God and human beings, male and female, which, like a cancer, is eating away the very vitals of multitudes, morally, mentally, bodily, and spiritually. In that, as in every other, crusade against vice, God's people, parsons and laymen, men and women, should lead the way.

At this time, an ' unfortunate ' who lived in a street off ' the little hell,' was rescued, by God's blessing upon the earnest prayers and untiring efforts of a devoted lady district visitor. I visited the poor girl, and heard from her lips, as she lay suffering from an illness which resulted in her death, the words of penitence and trust in God's mercy. The visitor told me that not long before, the sick one had said to her ' I want you to take away and destroy that Paisley shawl, which I know was the means of attracting many a one to sin.' She died, and I buried her. Oh, the mercy of God, who willeth not the death of a sinner, but rather that he or she should repent, find pardon, and be saved !

How awful it is to think, nay to know, that even God's house is sometimes invaded by these temptresses to evil ; for in St. Nathaniel's church I had to remonstrate with one before a service : we failed to rescue her, as she left our neighbourhood. On six subsequent occasions 'unfortunates' were discovered in other parts of the parish ; but they had to go as soon as found out : the residents would not tolerate them.

The once 'little hell' is now inhabited by very poor but moral people : occasionally there is an open-air service, or a Bible reading in that street.

The Bishop again had a confirmation in our church : out of one hundred and thirty-one in the classes, one hundred and three were confirmed. That was another red-letter day with us.

We all felt the sanctifying power of the Holy Spirit, doubtless in answer to much prayer by the candidates, the clergy, the congregation, and the Bishop. Oh, the joy of such ingatherings ! Glory be to the Father, and to the Son, and to the Holy Ghost. The confirmees included three converts from Romanism, and five adult Quakers—four brothers and a sister—belonging to the middle class, and cultured ; and what was infinitely better, professing to be the Lord's after the Church's scriptural standard of the new birth and sins forgiven. It was to me interesting in a special degree, first, to instruct them, then to baptize them, then to have them confirmed, with the joy of administering to them their first communion.

What honour God put upon poor dear St. Nathaniel's, so shut in from sight, with its wretched surroundings, and its plain services now so contemptible in the eyes of many.

Think what an addition to the spiritual life of the Church it would be if all who are confirmed were indeed born again of the Holy Spirit ; their sins forgiven, and they therefore justified in publicly taking upon themselves the responsibility of full membership in the

Church of God. Let us all ask God to show us more clearly, and to impress us more deeply with, the full meaning of John iii. 8, James i. 18, 1 Peter i. 23, Isaiah xliv. 22, for His glory and our good.

We felt that the interior of the church now needed painting, and that some other improvements were desirable, the cost altogether being £400. We set to in our usual way, the money was raised, and the work was done and paid for, bringing the expenditure on the building up to nearly £3,000. The people had already begun to say that we had only to ask for money and it came to us ; and that was the case. But it was obtained only after earnest prayer, in much faith, and with great effort in collecting it ; for we were not as some of whom we had heard, who obtained all they required, in answer to prayer and faith only, without appealing to anybody for it. I have always thought that, however catchy that statement may be, it is to an extent fallacious, seeing that the very persons by whom it is made, publish, and circulate far and wide, an elaborate and detailed account of their work, illustrated by remarkable incidents which appeal most forcibly to the hearts and purses of the charitably or religiously disposed. That mode of appeal may be more effective than charity sermons and private solicitations, but both are good.

Up to now, nearly all our dead had been buried in Toxteth Park Cemetery, and, in consequence, we were not entitled to the usual fees, as St. Nathaniel's was not within its boundary. The chaplains generally expected outside clergy burying their dead in the cemetery to take all the duty on such occasions. I did not altogether see the force of that. For it was my custom, after the last look at the lowered coffin had been taken, to offer my arm to the bereaved widow or widower, or my hands to the orphaned children, and as I led them away, to minister consolation by words of comfort which, spoken at such a moment, could not easily be forgotten. There are times and times ; and those times should never be lost, as must be the case if one had to proceed at once to officiate at other interments. Do we not read, ' He that winneth souls is wise ' ? And is it not essential to observe the times and seasons as we sow the good seed of the Kingdom ? How often we sow at random !

I had now commenced a course of sermons on the Book of Psalms, which proved very helpful to myself, and I trust not less so to the congregation.

The largest number of communicants in one day, up to this time, was 323.

The Bible-classes and Sunday-schools now numbered 1,300.

The money raised this year included £14 3s. 0½d., the proceeds of a children's voluntary sale of work in one of the cottage parlours. Little did those young folk think that it was the beginning of what became a permanent source of income for the church, and a great factor in meeting the parochial expenses. It was held annually, and in the year of my resignation reached £311.

> ' Praise God, from whom all blessings flow ;
> Praise Him, all creatures here below ;
> Praise Him above, ye heavenly host ;
> Praise Father, Son, and Holy Ghost.'

The amount raised this year was eight hundred and eighty-two pounds.

1878.

God's design in present dispensation—Needed ' Goodness '—' Father
Ignatius '—Controversial instruction—Adult baptism—School attendance—Sunday school shortcomings—Clerical and lay ' motives '—Total
abstinence *v.* the Dual Platform—Reclaimed but relapsed—' Johnny,'
a cripple—A Protestant doctor's opportunity—The Church Pastoral
Aid Society and lay help.

' I am the Rose of Sharon ' (S. of Sol. ii. 1).

I N preaching on this motto, at the Watch-night Service,
after showing that the rose of Sharon was not a
hothouse rose, which but few could procure, on
account of its rarity, but one which any passer-by
might cull, in that it covered the whole plain of Sharon ;
and that Christ was that Rose, the Rose of Sharon ;
I pressed home the thought that not only might all
take and have Him as that Rose to beautify their souls,
but that they might wear Him as people wear a ' button-
hole ' ; that by their lives they might show themselves
to an ungodly world as belonging to God in reality ;
remembering that the world scans very closely all who
profess to be Christ's, and that they are, for good or
evil, living letters, ' read of all men.' I remember
feeling deeply the force of a Salvation Army captain's
prayer, ' O Lord, make us good ! ' Yes, it is ' goodness '
that attracts the attention of the ungodly. What is
wanted, on the human side, to win the lost to God, is
' good ' Christians, rather than a profession of religion
without corresponding holiness of life.

In all our work for God it is necessary to see, and to
keep in mind, so far as it is revealed in God's Word,
what is the work He designs to do in this dispensation.
Is it not :—

To gather out ' a people for His name ' ?—Acts
xv. 14.

To build up (edify) those thus gathered out ?—
1 Cor. xiv. 3.

It may be profitable to refer to the leading doctrines of God's Holy Word, taught in St. Nathaniel's, for the accomplishment of ' that so great work ' by the operation of the Holy Spirit.

The Inspiration of Holy Scripture—2 Tim. iii. 16 ; 2 Pet. i. 21 ; Article VI.

The Trinity in Unity—Matt. xxviii. 19 ; 2 Cor. xiii. 14 ; Article I.

The total depravity of man in the Fall—Gen. vi. 5 ; Jer. xvii. 9 ; Article X.

God's electing love in Christ Jesus—Rom. viii. 28-30, ix. 11 ; Ephes. i. 4, 5, 11 ; Article XVII.

The Atonement efficacious in the elect : sufficient for all who believe—John xvii. 2, 19, 24 ; Acts xiii. 48 ; Isa. liii. 11 ; 1 John ii. 1, 2 ; Matt. xxvi. 28 ; Articles XVII., XXXI.

The absolute necessity of the new birth—John iii. 3, 5, 7, 8 ; Jas. i. 18 ; 1 Pet. i. 23 ; John i. 13 ; Articles X., XXVII.

Justification by faith only, and sanctification by the Holy Spirit—Acts xiii. 38, 39 ; Rom. iii. 28 ; John xvii. 17 ; Gal. v. 22-24 ; Heb. xii. 14 ; Articles XI., XVII.

The ministry of the Word, and Ordinances—Ephes. iv. 8-14 ; Luke xxiv. 47 ; Matt. xxviii. 19 ; 1 Cor. xi. 26 ; Articles XIX., XXV.

Eternal reward and punishment—Matt. xxv. 34-46 ; Mark ix. 43-48 ; Rev. xix. 20, xx. 10 ; Athanasian Creed.

Let us hold fast these truths, and defend them in our measure and in our place : they undoubtedly form the staple truths taught in St. Nathaniel's, which the Holy Spirit so owned and blessed.

Many of these evangelical saving truths are not taught by either the Romanists or their ritualistic imitators, being altogether opposed to, and inconveniently condemnatory of, the man-made creed common to them both ; nor by sceptics, agnostics, or latitudinarians, who find it possible to delude themselves with the idea that all the creeds will one day be

cast into a sort of smelting-pot, out of which will come
a belief in God based upon the Sermon on the Mount,
and that then the kingdom of God will appear.   We
need to beware of such unscriptural theories.   Do we
not see over and over again, in our own experience,
the changing, uplifting, purifying, ennobling, reforming,
saving influence of the ' good old gospel ' of God's
grace, turning darkness into light, sickness into health,
sin into holiness, death into life ?   Surely we do.   Have
we not daily proof—it may be in our own individual
experience—of that same glorious gospel having lost
none of its ancient power ?   Surely we have.

About this time ' Father Ignatius ' held an eight-day
mission in a neighbouring church.   Many of our people
went to hear him, and some of them told me that I was
mistaken about him, that he was a thorough evangelical,
and that he had the congregation singing on their knees
like Methodists.   That went on from Sunday to Friday,
when the ' Father ' invited the people to attend on
the following Monday and Tuesday, in Hope Hall,
where he would deliver the complement of his message
which he was not permitted to do in that church.   On
Monday some of our people went, but directly afterwards told me that they would have no more of him.
How difficult it is to shield the flock from false teachers
who pose as true shepherds : and, like many well-
known Ritualists, preach evangelical truth, up to a
certain point, in order to catch their hearers, and then
plausibly bring in deadly error.   That is neither straight-
forward, truthful, Apostolic, nor Christ-like ; but false,
deceptive, Jesuitical : it is the half-truth which is even
more dangerous than a lie.

With great pleasure I consented, at the request of a
deputation, to give, on Wednesday evenings, in church,
a course of instruction on the main doctrines in which
our Church differs from Rome.   To help the people
in following me, I bought one hundred copies of Stanford's ' Handbook to the Romish Controversy ' ; and
taking the creed of Pope Pius IV., which first saw the
light of day on December 9th, 1564, as the outcome

of the Council of Trent decrees, I got a splendid opportunity of putting the precious Gospel of Christ piecemeal before my hearers, in direct contrast with the doctrines of Rome. Error never seems so erroneous, nor truth so truthful, as when the two are placed in juxtaposition : just as black and white contrast most strongly when seen side by side : there cannot be, there is not, a more effective way of teaching and conveying the truth than by collating it with its own antithesis, error, either Romish, Ritualistic, or of any other kind.

I do not hesitate to say that if this were done in our pulpits—whether rural, urban, or cathedral—neither Romanism, Ritualism, nor Broad Churchism, would have much chance of making ' verts ' in dear old England. But the enemy of souls has many devices, and one of them is to delude good, well-meaning, and especially spiritually-minded, people into regarding controversy— which, be it noted, is only the proving by truth that error is error—as contrary to holy living. Such is not the mind of many godly ministers in our own time, nor was it that of the Reformers, or of the Apostles, or of the Master. The experience of thirty-three years as a parochial minister enables me to affirm that controversial preaching and teaching is a fulcrum for the lever of rousing and uplifting apathetic careless, sin-stricken souls. Of course controversy of all kinds, whether by preaching, teaching, or disputation, should be in love. We should love the erring one whilst hating the error, and earnestly seek to lead all such into the right path, that they may be saved in the day of the Lord Jesus.

The annual appeal for our ragged schools was, as it ever had been, very touching. The poor children lined the chancel, and the infants sang their own little hymn ' I will sing for Jesus.' Notwithstanding the grave financial responsibility it involved, I think we all felt thankful that God had cast these children into the lap of our love.

Early in the following week a man called upon me, and after apologizing for having done so, said ' I called

to ask you to baptize me.' ' Were you not baptized
as an infant ? ' ' No. My parents were Baptists,
and when I grew up I did not care to go through the
ceremony. My wife attends your church, and I have
never hindered her, though I would much rather have
had her go for a walk with me. Last Sunday evening
she persuaded me to go with her and hear the ragged
school children sing. We sat in the gallery at the very
back. The children's singing touched me at once,
and when the infants began the hymn " I will sing for
Jesus," the thought that I could not do that went
through me. The next thought I had, What has
Jesus done for me ? filled my eyes with tears, and I was
afraid lest they might be seen rolling down. We went
home, and sat by the fire till 2 o'clock in the morning,
my wife pointing out what Jesus had done for me, if I
would only take it. I did so, and I want you to baptize
me.' We praised God together.

When at the Font, on the occasion of his baptism, as
I poured the water on his head in the name of the Blessed
Trinity, he still held my left hand in his right for a few
seconds ; and if one soul ever flowed into another, I
think our two souls did then, feeling one in Christ
Jesus. He became a communicant, lived a truly
Christian life, helped the church in certain ways, resigned
his position in Liverpool as a police cab inspector,
retired on a handsome pension, returned to his native
village in Yorkshire, became a Justice of the Peace,
had his life spared for a few years, and died in the faith
and hope of the resurrection. Ah, my God, Thou art
wonderful in working. ' Thine is the kingdom, and the
power, and the glory.' Amen.

There was a thorough canvass of the parish for more
Sunday-school scholars, specially between the ages of 4
and 20. It was found that, compared with the three
Nonconformist schools, the church school was attended
by a vast majority, whilst a very small percentage did
not attend any school. Efforts to reach these last were
put forth with good results. That return showed the
hold which the church schools had upon the children
and the people of the parish.

By special request, I read before the East Liverpool
Church School Sunday Association, a paper—which was
afterwards published—on ' Reminiscences of my Sunday
School.' I pointed out that the elder scholars are not
retained ; that the instruction is usually too general
and therefore too shallow ; that the way of salvation,
and the need of the new birth, are not sufficiently
dwelt upon ; that the children are not encouraged to
learn texts so thoroughly, nor is the explanation of
them so clear, that the words and their meaning are
never quite forgotten. I suggested separate adult
classes in church, with the Litany service, as in our
experience the best means of retaining the elder scholars;
more concrete teaching ; and use of the Irish Church
Missions' Hundred Texts. It is deplorable to find that
of those who have attended Sunday-schools say from
five to even ten years, so few have any true idea as to
how their souls are to be saved. I feel certain that one
text—say, for instance, John iii. 16, thoroughly learned
and properly explained, is far better, will do far more
good, than fifty-two lessons such as those ordinarily
given. But that means the teachers realizing the full
meaning of the text as regards themselves, by being
truly converted : and how many—or rather, how
few—do, or are ? Just as a converted parson will
usually be blessed with converted people, so a converted
teacher will generally be rewarded by converted
scholars : example is more powerful than precept
whether in the pulpit or the school. If men took Holy
Orders, not for social position ; or as a profession ·
or to qualify for a ' family living ' ; but because, God
having saved their souls in the new birth, they yearn
for the salvation of others in the same way : and if
young people took to Sunday-school teaching, not
because they were persuaded, indeed expected, to do
so after confirmation ; or that it seemed ' nice ' to be
amongst church-workers ; or because it was the ' right
thing to do ' ; but because they, having been brought to
God, desired to teach others how to come to Him also :
there would be many more adult souls saved in the

churches, and children's souls saved in the schools.
For preacher and teacher alike would then realize the
awful responsibility and blessedness of those solemn
half-hours of glorious opportunity, every Lord's Day,
in the pulpit and in the class. That some change from
the present state of things is imperatively called for,
and that without further delay, none who have at
heart the welfare of this nation, the interest of its
Church, and, above either, the honour of its God, can
for a single second doubt.

The Total Abstinence cause had now many adherents,
the number enrolled exceeding a thousand. As a
pledged abstainer I gave it my hearty support, realizing
that in every philanthropic or Christian work, and
specially in this one, it must be ' Come, not go, do as
I do.' And whilst for some, ' temperance ' may be
good, because sufficient : for the vast majority, ' total
abstinence ' is better, because necessary. It is so difficult to convince the ' masses,' and even their ' betters '
of the ' classes,' that one glass need not lead to a second.
We tried the dual platform of the C.E.T.S., but it well-
nigh killed our society ; so we reverted to our old total
abstinence basis and again prospered.

One evening a carter, who lived in one of the lowest
courts, came in to one of the meetings, and with trembling hand signed the pledge. He was terribly addicted to
drink, and so was his wife, who would even pull out
the fire-grate and pledge it, to gratify her craving.
There was only one child, a boy, who attended our
ragged school, and belonged to our Band of Hope.
The wife was induced to sign the pledge, and they both
went on well. The home, which had been destitute,
was soon made comfortable and before long they moved
into a well-to-do street. They were constant attendants
at church, took seats, and became communicants.
One Christmas Eve the wife brought me fifty-two
garments which she herself had made for our poor
ragged children. When I said it was too much, she
replied, with tears in her eyes ' Not too much for the
school where my boy had the hunger taken off him.'

That ' boy ' had grown to be a fine young fellow, had been confirmed, and was a communicant. He was also a great help to his parents, who had first one horse and cart for hire, then a second, and afterwards a third. Then came an awful relapse. The mother took to secret drinking, the father followed, and the end was, if possible, worse than the beginning. We did all we could, but we failed to reclaim them. Thank God there was hope in the poor father's death. The son emigrated, and is prospering, leading a respectable and Christian life in Brooklyn.

Who dare speak a single word in defence of the drink traffic, since such cases can be numbered by hundreds, if not thousands, every year ?

When going to church one Sunday morning I overtook poor old ' Johnny,' a cripple, who on his crutches was getting along very slowly. A heavy shower was evidently about to fall, which would have drenched him ; so I proposed to carry him to church. He, laughing, said ' No, no, vicar ' ; but without a moment's delay I took him on my back, and his crutches in my hands, telling him to hang on with his arms round my neck. He was soon in his seat at church, to the wonder, and I dare say the amusement, of those going there too. My action was entirely unpremeditated, but I honestly believe it did our church and work much good. It certainly brought down upon me, from certain quarters, censure and scorn, as being *infra dig.*, and unbecoming ' the cloth ' ! I ought to add that it became the custom for two of our dear church workers to call for ' Johnny ' at his lodgings, in turn, to carry him on their backs to God's house every Sunday. To carry on one's back a fellow-worshipper, or indeed to do for another anything in our power, is as nothing by comparison with even the smallest portion of what has been done for each of us by Him who gave His back to the smiters and His face to them that plucked off the hair. What a blessing it would be to ourselves as well as to others if we could only be moved to do the right thing, in the right way, at the right time.

I knew a young medical man, in the North of Ireland, a Protestant, whose practice was small. One day he was called in to attend the parish priest, other physicians having failed. His treatment proving successful, his fame spread, his practice rapidly increased, and he made a fortune. Why are not the Lord's people as keen to take advantage of any opportunity for ministering spiritually to sin-sick souls ? God gives at least one to each, and to some He grants several. As that young doctor's special skill cured the Romish priest, and reaped a rich reward ; so let us see to it that we, lay as well as clerical, use our God-given talents so skilfully in His service that we may have many souls to our hire, and many seals to our ministry, our ' exceeding great reward,' after this life, to enter into the joy of the Lord.

The confirmees were not so numerous this year as last ; but we were able to rejoice over them as usual.

I readily record how much I owed to our band of devoted helpers for the success which crowned our work, but my indebtedness cannot be adequately expressed in mere words : I doubt not that is the case with many, indeed all, evangelical parochial pastors similarly situated.

The work to be done is so vast and so varied, that it can only be fully done by every true Christian man or woman lovingly taking his or her share thereof. Yet not so very long ago it was thought, and by some is to this day deemed, almost sacrilege for any of God's work to be touched by lay hands, though it neither was nor is considered wrong for the cost to come out of lay pockets !

It is not as well known as it ought to be, that the admission of the laity to a share in their church's work for souls, was due to the often opposed, but eventually successful, efforts of the Church Pastoral Aid Society.

The amount raised was six hundred and sixty-nine pounds.

1879.

Composition of the Congregation—Separate *v.* General Mission in Liverpool—Unitarian teaching—A ' missing link '—Women drunkards —Loathsome case—Quarrelsome neighbours—A sad slip—Choir boy and the Confessional—Effect of Isa. liii. on an aroused soul—Disparaging the work.

' All Scripture is given by inspiration of God, and is profitable for doctrine, for reproof, for correction, for instruction in righteousness; that the man of God may be perfect, throughly furnished unto all good works ' (2 Tim. iii. 16, 17).

THIS year's motto was circulated as usual amongst the congregation at the Watch-night Service, when the church was literally packed. We also had our usual New Year week of prayer.

The working classes, and the very poor, made up the great majority of those who usually attended the church; but from the very commencement there were some of the middle class, a few of whom lived in the one small portion of the parish where alone such would, or indeed could, live; whilst others came from the near surroundings; and there were those who joined us from a laudable desire to help in the work which they saw was being carried on in our parish. For that I was grateful to them, but still more grateful to God for putting into their hearts the desire to do so, for their appreciating love of the pure Gospel, and for being myself enabled to proclaim that Gospel to them plainly and fully. Some of those dear helpers brought not only piety, zeal, and heartiness, but education and refinement into the work, which had a wholesome and beneficial influence upon it in many ways. For pastor and people alike it is well that a congregation should not consist solely of either the rich and the educated, or of the poor and the illiterate. I often had cause for regret that from the inception of the parish it was constantly stated that our church was for the poor. In the main that was no doubt the case, but it was not exclusively for them, it was for all; and the statement created a sort of 'caste' feeling, which it was neither wise nor fair to foster; for the masses did not like the idea of being labelled, and for a time we suffered in consequence. However, there was, notwithstanding—thanks be to God—no lack of people to fill the church.

At the end of the preceding year there was a general mission in the Liverpool churches. In consequence, however, of it including those wherein ritualistic practices were carried on, fifteen evangelical incumbents, knowing that what the ritualists preach is not the pure Gospel, refused to unite with them, but had in their churches at the same time a separate mission, to which I was appointed secretary. At its close, the various preachers, meeting for conference, had good accounts to give of apparent results. One incumbent stated that in his church 400 were led to God; in our own we could not report many such. We were, however, thankful for the mission, in that it had brought numbers to hear the way of life—including several Romanists—who seldom, if ever, had heard it; and it had also greatly refreshed and encouraged those of the Lord's servants who were perhaps sometimes inclined to faint by the way as they journeyed on towards the Celestial City.

For the first time—and, happily, it was the last—I had to discharge the extremely painful duty of silencing one of our most prominent helpers, who had been enunciating false doctrine in the direction of Unitarianism. The thought of that rendered me almost sleepless for more than a week; but I felt it must be done, as the erring brother was a teacher, and one who often spoke in our meetings. On afterwards telling this to a neighbouring incumbent, he looked at me with wonder, and said: 'Quite right; you are a strong man to have done it: that man might have split your congregation in two.' I trust it was done in love, and in fidelity to the truth. I was thankful that, in spite of certain literature circulated by him on his departure from the church, he had only one follower ; and I rejoiced that though he never rejoined, he was now and again to be found with us at the Lord's Table. Thank God !

The missing link needed to complete our parochial machinery was now supplied, in that we saw our way to employ one of our lady visitors as our own Bible-woman. Through a period of sixteen years she proved a real help to us in the cause of God, as only one who was a lady as well as a Christian could do.

I am confident that, however many voluntary helpers there may be in a parish, it needs also official agents ; not only to take the lead in the various departments of parochial activity when occasion offers, but to supplement the labours of the honorary workers : with the advantage of their ministrations being capable of greater method than is possible for those who have only the leisure of ' between whiles ' or of ' after business ' hours to place at their pastor's disposal.

Drunkenness amongst married women had long proved an awful evil. It broke up homes, blighted the lives of husbands and children, was a fruitful cause of untold misery, and seriously hindered Christian work in the parish. Our lady district visitors, therefore, decided to form a Total Abstinence Society for Women, with a committee of its own to manage its affairs. This agency, the outcome of faith and prayer, entailed great labour upon its promoters. There were of course many failures to keep the pledge, but there were also many cases of real permanent reformation, each of which was great gain. May God have pity upon our drunken land ; may He open the eyes of its inhabitants to the shocking results of drunkenness, to flesh and blood as well as to soul and spirit ; may He inspire all His true children, for the three-fold sake of Him, of their neighbours, and of their own selves, to unite in a life-long consistent crusade against the liquor traffic, beginning by themselves becoming total abstainers, to influence others. If the followers of the false prophet,

Mahomet, have done that for centuries, cannot the servants and subjects of the true ' Prophet, Priest, and King,' the Blessed Jesus, do so too ?

The sights and sounds, the poverty and dirt, to be met with amongst so large a proportion of our population, are enough to overwhelm one with despair and to break one's heart, to make some touch the work very lightly because almost hopeless, and to drive others to give it up in sheer despair. Yet, are Christians to stand aside and let philanthropists do the work ? For the work has to be done, and will be done ; but by whom ? By those who seek only to elevate socially, or by those who strive to do that, and to save spiritually as well ? That is one of God's questions, to all the members of His church : and from each He will require an answer ! Is it surprising that I often came out of houses with a feeling of loathing, and yet of deep pity for those who have to live or exist in such places, when the following was no uncommon experience ? On visiting a poor old woman lying ill in bed, I found an obliging neighbour just finishing the floor sweeping, the ' fluff ' being near the grate, actually alive with unmentionable undesirables. Saying ' Please, sir, wait a moment,' she shovelled the sweepings into the fire, when the crackling was like volley-firing. I tried, but unsuccessfully, to persuade the poor old sufferer to go into the workhouse ; so giving her what I could for both body and soul, I left, sick at heart that such a state of things should be possible in Christian Liverpool. If only the nation could be brought to realize the absolutely awful state of degradation to which so many have sunk, and in which they are grovelling, seemingly powerless to rise, there would be such a general demand for reform, that righteous laws would be enacted for properly bettering the condition of the poor, and God's people would be inspired by such zeal for missions to the home heathen as is now shown for those in the ' regions beyond.'

Two women were quarrelling in the street : one, I was in a way sorry to hear, for she occasionally came to church, and the other went at times to a Dissenting chapel near by. They had seemingly exhausted their vocabulary of vituperation, when one flung at the other ' Begone, you——, you go to St. Nathaniel's church, where the blackguards of Windsor go ; I would not go to such a place, no, not I.' There was consolation in the accusation being true, in that some of ' the blackguards of Windsor ' were attending church, and that by God's blessing some of them at least had learned to know Christ thereby. I have always felt that the church ought to be the spiritual and moral hospital for all sorts of sin-diseased people, whether the degraded poor, or the profligate rich : as well as the place for building up the saints of God in their ' most holy faith,' that they may abound in such good works as God calls on them to do for His name.

A working man communicant, living in a court, removed to another house on the opposite side. He fretted so at being obliged to leave the house in which he had lived so long, that he broke his pledge, gave way to the old habit, beat his wife—also a communicant— got into prison, was visited there, on his release again lived happily with his wife, accompanied her to God's house, and after some years died in the faith of Jesus ; as did she.

That shows how little it sometimes takes to cause even a child of God to fall : and how great is the value of following up such cases with brotherly pastoral tenderness and sympathy.

I missed one of the choir, an orphan youth. Meeting him, and finding he was in the choir of an extremely Ritualistic church, I remonstrated with him, but in vain. ' I like the choir surplice,' he said, and off he went. I was greatly exercised in mind about him. A year or so afterwards, to my joy I noticed him in our church. When the service was over he asked if he could see me privately during the week, which was arranged. At that interview he told me why he had returned. A certain ' Father '——had just had a mission in that Ritualistic church, and he expected even the choir boys to go to confession. My young friend hesitated, yet went. On entering the inner vestry he saw the 'Father' seated, with a stool at his feet. Being motioned to kneel on it he did so. His blood almost boiled at certain questions put to him by the 'Father,' who at the same time assured him that he knew well of certain sins youths sometimes commit. He could bear it no longer, and, standing up, said 'Sir, you are teaching me sin,' and walked out. Taking hold of my hand, he said 'In the presence of God I declare to you that "Father" —— questioned me about sins of which I knew nothing, though I do not profess to be an angel. I have done with Ritualism.' How I did thank God for His recovery! Think of it! Think of this vile confessional! the cesspool of the immorality of the parish! the 'picklock of the conscience!' going on in the Church of England, polluting our youths, our sons and daughters, and the wives of too confiding husbands! Is there, in the inspired history of the Apostolic Church for eight-and-twenty years, as recorded in the Acts, a single instance of auricular confession? When Simon fell into sin after baptism, did Peter exhort him to have recourse to the confessional for pardon of his sin? which he would have done if he had understood John xx. 21-23 as Romanists and Ritualists do. He did nothing of the sort, but, instead, he did exactly what a truly Protestant minister of Christ would do under the same conditions, he admonished him 'repent therefore of this thy wickedness.' Indeed even in Rome itself the 'I absolve thee' was not obligatory till the twelfth century, previous to which period the form had been precatory, 'The Lord forgive thee.' But then Rome, whether Pagan or Papal, was not built in a day.

At the invitation of the Church Association local committee I delivered in Hope Hall, Liverpool, to a crowded and enthusiastic audience, a lecture on 'Shall we go back to Rome?' It was afterwards published.

In compliance with the request of a carter who attended the church I preached on Isa. lvii. 21 : 'There is no peace saith my God, to the wicked.' After the sermon he came into the vestry, deeply affected, and, with emotion, said to me ' I want to have peace with God.' I was so thoroughly exhausted by the whole Sunday's work, that, feeling quite unable to speak to him as I would wish to do, I replied ' Let me have that Bible in your hand,' and marking Isaiah liii., said ' Go home, see what God says to you in that chapter, and let me know the result.' The next day I met this man in the street, black with coal-dust, standing in his waggon, driving. Saluting me, he pulled up, jumped out, and rushing up to me, cried out ' I'm a new man : God showed me last night that my sins were laid on the " Man of Sorrows," and I'm at peace with Him. And everything seems new to me, the sky, my horse and cart, you. Praise God.' He took both my hands, and I thought he would have embraced me : if he had I would have responded with the glow of my soul's love in the Lord. The dear man joined the Carters' Association, but he never left the church, nor did he ever trip, bless the Lord. Indeed he was the means of his wife being brought to Jesus, and, in due time, their two daughters ' were added to the church ' through the confirmation class : it was touching to see the four kneeling together at the Lord's Table.

How strange it seems, yet how true it is, that of Paul's two injunctions, it is easier to ' weep with them that weep,' than to ' rejoice with them that do rejoice.' The work of God in dear St. Nathaniel's parish brought down upon it disparaging remarks by those who should rather have rejoiced. To account for the success thereof, the following reasons were assigned ; some of which were partially untrue, some entirely.

The vicar is unmarried.

He is one of the people.

He waits on the people like a counter-jumper.

Every new church succeeds for a time.

The congregation is made up of one class.

The church is in the midst of the people.

The vicar's power is a sort of mesmerism.

He is a strong Protestant.

He is generous with his purse.

A full church is no good sign of fidelity to the truth, since the sheep are a ' little flock.'

I shall not reply as I might to such miserable sayings. The real truth is, it is the work of God, through the labours of a large staff of His devoted, zealous, soul-quickened servants. It is still true that the disciple is not above his master. He had carping critics of His matchless work.

There was no flagging amongst the dear brethren and sisters in Christ who were with me in harness ; and if any little difficulty arose amongst them from ' over-lapping ' through zeal, ' the oiled feather ' was brought into use with good effect ; for where all is founded on love, anything wrong soon gets set right.

The amount raised was six hundred and twenty-one pounds.

1880.

Cottage readings—Tardy ' light '—The female Romanist's text card—The ' Hundred Texts '—Romish converts—Bishops and Ritualism—Pusey's dictum—History repeating itself—The first Bishop of Liver-pool—Bishop Jacobson—Parish Hall or Vicarage ?—Trusting God for money.

' Casting all your care upon Him ; for He careth for you ' (1 Peter v. 7).

NO one had greater need of this comforting exhorta-tion than I. Standing in the breach made by the inroads of sin, or leading the attack upon the enemy's strong entrenchments throughout the parish ; realizing the awful issues at stake, depressed by contemplation of what had still to be done, as compared with what had already been achieved at the cost of much time, thought, prayer, and money, with incessant labour trenching sometimes upon intervals for rest on even for meals ; it was well to know and feel that there stood on record the dear Lord's gracious command to cast all our care upon Him, for the loving assurance's sake that He careth for us ! How often we ' cast ' it, but do not ' leave ' it, there ; as it were, rolling it upon Him for the time being, but taking it away from Him, and bearing it again just as before.

In all our activities it is well to remember that the work is the Lord's, not ours ; and that ' the battle is the Lord's ' too.

The following, sent in to me without any thought of publication, will help to give an idea of our cottage and cellar readings :

' 24, M—— P——,

" April 16, 1880

' He that winneth souls is wise.'

' REV. AND DEAR SIR,

' I closed my cottage readings on Tuesday evening last for the season, and I am very happy to state that they have been very pleasant meetings, and profitable to many souls. I have noticed changes in the right direction in many families, and also that there are some who did not attend any place of worship come now to our mission service on Sunday evenings in the schoolroom I have also been welcome, and never found any difficulty in finding rooms or cellars for our meetings, for which I am very thankful. On one occasion after the meeting three signed the pledge who had been indulging in drink very much, two of whom have kept it.

' My dear pastor, I trust God has been pleased to bless all the cottage meetings which have been held this past winter.

' Yours in Jesus,

' ——

' P.S.—The following are the totals for the last seven

years. Have I now served my apprenticeship " for
God and for good ? " '

Year.	Readings.	Adults.	Children.	Total.
1873–74	23	148	63	211
1874–75	44	241	136	377
1875–76	26	193	120	313
1876–77	44	345	200	..545
1877–78	43	434	184	618
1878–79	51	404	110	514
1879–80	44	454	182	636

What a blessing to have had from eight to twelve such
little gatherings every week in winter, mainly made up
of those who did not go to any place of worship !

A poor old dying man expressed a wish to partake of
the Lord's Supper. I found him in a blessed state of
mind. He said to me ' I was quite ignorant of God until
about a couple of months ago, when two of your young
men came to hold a meeting here ; they were the men
who opened my eyes, God bless them. I wish I had had
the light I now have forty years ago.' He partook of
the Lord's Supper, and a few weeks afterwards he
passed away. Only a couple of nights before his decease,
at his own request those two young men had their
usual reading in his room, greatly to his delight and
comfort.

One of our ragged children was passing the door of a
Romanist, who, seeing the child with a nice-looking
card, asked if she might look at it. He handed it to
her, and she, having read the words thereon, ' Come
unto Me, all ye that labour and are heavy laden, and I
will give you rest,' begged the little fellow to let her
keep it, as he could get another. It was given to her ;
and when, some few years after, she was found dead
in bed, that little text-card was in a small bag lying on
her breast. Let us hope the meaning of the text had
been laid up in her heart, and that she had responded
to its loving invitation ' Come unto Me.'

When visiting the senior ragged school to catechize
on the ' Hundred Texts,' it was very gratifying to find

in one large class thirteen Romanists, and to hear that there were several in the other classes too. The answering was fairly satisfactory. These schools were the sowing-ground for the good seed that in due time brought forth abundant fruit, even amongst Romanists. Efforts were constantly being made to get such away from the school, and occasionally with success, but those who were induced to leave generally came back again after a time.

I had the joy of receiving into the Church an entire Romish family, making the third. The father had been in the army serving in India, and the first beam of light that shone into his dark mind came from hearing some of his Protestant comrades, as they lay in camp on Sunday evenings, sing that soul-inspiring hymn, ' Glory to Thee, my God, this night.' He was now a very ardent convert, and wished to be received, with his wife, and three children, into the Church. I admitted them by hypothetically baptizing them, to remove any scruples they might have had : in other cases I only ' received.' It is necessary to have some form of reception, otherwise such converts would scarcely consider themselves actually Protestant. I may say here, that neither I nor our visitors ever neglected to call at the houses of Romanists as well as at those of Protestants, and we were almost always well received. They probably had no idea of becoming Protestants, but they were not unwilling to hear about the true way of salvation. It requires great tact, if not even special training, to deal successfully with Romanists.

They must not be allowed to feel that we are in any way afraid of them.

We ought not to begin by offering tracts, particularly to Irish Romanists, as they have a strong prejudice against them.

We should take common ground with them, on, say the immortality of the soul, heaven, hell, the Trinity, etc.

We must treat them tenderly, but clearly, in a manly way, racily, perhaps even wittily, but without levity, and being careful to make no mistake, on the various points of divergence, or on essential differences, which are sure to come up.

We should realize that Romanists generally have a very inadequate sense of sin, though having—at all events the pious ones—a deep sense of unworthiness, with an entirely erroneous idea of the tender-hearted Jesus, whom they regard as an austere Judge, which causes them to resort to Mary, as being supposedly more sympathetic. It tells effectively to allow their unworthiness, and then to show them Jesus as their Brother, Friend, Saviour, able and ready to save them: I have often found that the avenue to their hearts.

At this time we conducted an inquiry which resulted in our discovering that there was not a known infidel in the parish. That there were those who were leading infidel lives was painfully evident, but there was not even one who openly opposed the truth of God: it had not always been so.

The exposition, on Sunday mornings, of the Gospel by Matthew was now begun.

The Church Association Council having appealed for funds with which to take legal proceedings towards ascertaining the law on various points of Ritualism, our branch guaranteed £47.

If, instead of failing to keep their consecration vow ' to banish and drive away all erroneous and strange doctrine,' by winking at Ritualism in their clergy, and in some instances being guilty of it themselves, the Bishops as a whole had kept that vow, and had put in force against those clergy the findings of the Privy Council as to its illegality, that ' Brummagem ' Popery would have been checked, if not stamped out altogether. It is idle to say that ' Ritual ' means nothing very serious, in face of what that arch-conspirator against Protestantism, the late Dr. Pusey, has left on record : ' Ritualism is children's play, unless it enshrines doctrine.' Ritualists have openly declared that their intention is to Catholicize—Romanize —the Church of England. Shall we allow this ? Shall we not war against it, no matter what it costs us individually, not alone in money, but in other ways also ?

The conspiracy of Charles I. and Laud to attempt the same thing brought down both Church and Throne. History often repeats itself. The Church worshipping images contrary to the first commandment, or worshipping the Lord through images, contrary to the second commandment, will surely incur, as of old, the hot displeasure of God. And what is the worship of the wafer in the Mass, or of the Christ through the wafer, but idolatry of the grossest kind ? From idolatry, good Lord deliver the Church of England.

This year witnessed the consecration of the Rev. Canon J. C. Ryle, as first Bishop of Liverpool, the new diocese having been taken out of the See of Chester ; an appointment which was hailed with delight by every evangelical churchman throughout the world. For alike by his telling Gospel tracts, his controversial books, and his convincing sermons, Dr. Ryle had long since vindicated the evangelical character of the Church in England as settled at the Reformation ; and by his consistent godly life had both commended to others the religion which he himself professed, and accentuated the great Gospel truths which he had so striven to set before the whole Church of God. Whilst much was expected from him generally, in which our parish might proportionately share, we of course did not indulge the idea of his proving such a blessing as he actually became to us.

I record with pleasure my sense of deep obligation to my late diocesan, Dr. Jacobson, who ordained me to presbyter's orders ; under whose episcopal jurisdiction I lived officially for fourteen years ; and from whom I received, both as an individual, and as one of his clergy, much kindness and consideration. It must have been well known to him that I was one of the eleven evangelical incumbents in Liverpool who ignored his charge against evening Communion, and that I was a decided Protestant ; yet as Bishop, he treated me not only with toleration, but with special marks of favour and goodwill. He was not a propagandist of his moderately ' high ' opinions on certain Church subjects. He could, and did, appreciate work done by evangelicals, whose *locus standi* in the Church he fully and cordially acknowledged. I shall ever hold his memory in grateful remembrance.

In the autumn I felt the time had arrived for making a great effort to raise funds for the erection of a suitable parochial hall ; for the church was fairly finished. Our great congregational gatherings had to take place in Hope Hall, as the only accommodation we had for meetings of any kind consisted of the ragged school, and two small mission rooms which were rented. Some of my dear friends and helpers thought that our next effort should be to buy or build a vicarage ; but I was unable to agree with them, considering that a large commodious parish hall was a matter of primary importance, whereas the housing of the vicar was of secondary consideration. The expense was estimated at £2,500, which caused many friends to regard the raising of such a sum as impossible. But there was, belonging to the church, and close to it, a strip of land, unoccupied, sufficient for the purpose ; and I felt convinced that if it were utilized, as the project was neither fad nor a fancy, but a provision for a real need in His work, our Heavenly Father would bestow His blessing upon it.

We conferred and prayed about the matter, as to whether it should be carried out, and if so, how. Having an objection to another bazaar, I invited seventy male members of the congregation to meet me, and submitted to them the following scheme which I had devised :

		£	s.		£
10	Guarantors of	20	0	each equal	200
20	,,	10	0	,,	200
70	,,	5	0	,,	350
80	,,	2	10	,,	200
300	,,	1	0	,,	300
480					£1,250

I did not then, nor do I now, see that faith in God, and prayer to Him, preclude the most strenuous efforts being made when ' the King's business ' is concerned, as strenuous as in a merely worldly matter. I made it quite clear that if, after earnest prayerful effort, anyone who had become a guarantor failed to obtain the sum he had promised to get, no legal proceedings would be resorted to against him.

The readiness with which the scheme was approved and taken up more than equalled my expectations. It assured me that, in effect, the money was already raised ; and the result showed I was not mistaken. For though we did not get quite the full number of guarantors, many of those who put down their names raised more than the sum for which they became responsible : one collected £1,300, and his Bible-class £300. Thus the strong helped the weak.

A true Christian once asked me if I could trust God for money, adding that he had not known any who did so, though they undoubtedly trusted Him for everything else. My reply was that I did trust our Heavenly Father for money, just as for all other things. Indeed I could fill a folio with answers to 'prayer and faith concerning money : let one instance suffice. It was our custom to make gifts in kind to about three hundred poor widows, and to certain poor families, in their homes for Christmas. One year our coffers were very low, and on a Sunday morning before I went into the pulpit with the intention of naming the fact to the congregation, it occurred to me to tell the Lord in extempore prayer before the sermon, that the congregation hearing it might answer Amen. I did so, and then in my sermon gave particulars. On going into the vestry after service, I saw lying on the table, a letter addressed to me. It contained four £5 notes, from an anonymous donor, ' for the poor of the parish, as the vicar thinks fit ' : it was dated two days previously. The sexton told me a man left it with him to be given to me, just after I had gone out of the vestry to begin the service. Thus that gift was already in store before our prayers were

offered, fulfilling the promise ' Before they call I will
answer.' Yes, I have trusted God for money ; to be
used, however, for His glory, in His service, not on the
things of the flesh.

The annual sale of work produced £72. My own men's
gallery Bible-class now numbered two hundred and
twenty-one. Praise the Lord !

By God's help the general work had been well sustained. The dear brethren had a mind to labour, and
each one worked on the wall as it was appointed him,
with the trowel in one hand and the sword in the other.
Those who build without defending, or defend without
building, are alike deficient : they fail to do the Lord's
work fully in the Lord's way.

Some dear helpers think all they have to do is simply
and lovingly to teach the truth positively, leaving the
result with God : was that the way of the great Teacher ?
Others lean unduly to the side of defence, and to a
degree neglect teaching sufficiently the positive truth
as it is in Christ Jesus : was that the way of Him about
Whom it is recorded that they ' wondered at the gracious
words which proceeded out of His mouth ' ? The need
is for due proportion, as found in the Word, which
should be our guide in all things.

This year six hundred and seventy-two pounds were
raised.

1881.

Constant high-pressure—The *Porcupine*—A Jesuit's challenge—The Jesuit challenged—Monetary offer—Introduction to the Bishop—Bishop's sermon for Irish Church Missions—' I make much of hands '—Bishop joins the congregation—Census of church and chapel attendances—Parochial Hall foundation-stone laid—Answers to believing prayer — Faith healing — Daily prayer at one o'clock gun-fire — Insomnia.

' God is our refuge and strength, a very present help in trouble ' (Ps. xlvi. 1).

OFTEN, when wending my way to or through the parish, have I asked, ' Lord, will it always be necessary for thy servant to press on at this rate ? ' And I seemed ever to have had the answer, ' Yes, until the fulness of the Gentiles be come in, through the preaching of the everlasting Gospel : then shall the end be.' I therefore ever sought to make it clear that the work of this dispensation is to gather God's people out of ' this naughty world,' and that therefore the urgency of the work will continue until this has been done. That assurance seemed to revive one's courage and renew one's strength ; and God was praised for having placed one right in front of the battle against the great enemy of souls, and for the year's motto of comfort and cheer in the conflict.

Hitherto I have been setting forth the work which the Master has allowed His servants to do for Him ; it may be well to give the view which one of the Liverpool papers took of our parish, and, indirectly, of the work there.

For so doing there is the example of the Blessed Saviour Himself, who laid under tribute external testimony as to His person and ministry. ' Had ye believed Moses, ye would have believed Me ; for he wrote of Me.' ' Ye sent unto John, and he bore witness unto the truth.'

⌐ I may just premise that the publication from whose columns I quote regards things more from a social than from a religious standpoint (see Appendix F).

' Father ' —— of the St. Francis Xavier Jesuit Chapel, Liverpool, openly challenged the Bishop of Liverpool to substantiate some statements—reported in the Press as having been made by him when preaching in one of the city churches on the words ' Son, behold Thy mother ; woman behold thy son '—showing the entire absence from Holy Scripture of any foundation for the unwarrantably alleged intercession of the virgin Mary. Naturally no notice of the challenge was taken by the Bishop ; but I rather thought some of the diocesan dignitaries would have dealt with it. As, after nine days' waiting, there was neither sound nor sign, I had the hardihood, following David's example, to make it publicly known that I would meet the Jesuit Goliath, with only the sling and stone of God's Holy Word. He, however, evidently thought ' discretion is the better part of valour,' for he did not respond ; so I took my revenge by announcing a course of sermons, on Sunday evenings, upon ' The so-called intercession of the virgin Mary.' The church was filled to overflowing.

To make the matter more clear to the masses, and to give the challenge a distinctly practical character, I openly offered to pay down £300 to any institution ' Father ' —— might name, if, to the satisfaction of competent judges, chosen by both sides, he proved the following :

1. That the Blessed God, the Blessed Jesus, or the virgin Mary herself, had given a command to ask her intercession.

2. That there is an instance in Holy Scripture of anyone ever having asked her intercession.

I said very emphatically that if it were fairly claimed, I would pay the £300 even if I had to sell my books. That offer told well with the masses.

Some time after, I was at a public lunch, sitting not far from the Bishop, who, reaching over towards me, inquired in a pleasant tone ' Hobson, have you sold your books yet ? ' Rather startled by the question, I replied in the negative, the challenge not having been taken up ; at which he shook with laughter, and after telling the matter to those more immediately around him, said to me ' I know all about it.' Thus I made the acquaintance of the good Bishop, who had already won my heart.

Dr. Ryle's first visit to St. Nathaniel's was to preach for the Irish Church Missions, on Sunday evening, March 13, after which nearly four hundred partook of the Lord's Supper. That was an evening never to be forgotten in the history of the parish ; for truly we felt the Saviour's presence, in answer to much prayer, and in fulfilment of His own promise. The service began at 6.30 o'clock, and it was past 10 o'clock when the Bishop left. In the vestry he said ' I make much of hands, and I conclude that five out of every six of your communicants are working people. St. Nathaniel's is an answer to those who say the Church of England is not suited for working people.' He added ' I wish to preach in this church every six months, only give me sufficient notice.' Happily he exceeded his own proposal, by dispensing the Lord's Supper on two other Sunday evenings during that year.

Finding that at my Diocesan's request two pews had been assigned for his servants' use, I offered my own pew in the outer chancel for himself and his family : which he accepted.

The only attractions to be found by Dr. Ryle in St. Nathaniel's were the pure Gospel, a simple hearty service, and the manifest power of the Holy Spirit working in our midst ; I know these appealed to him strongly, and doubtless caused him to take this church under his episcopal wing, to the great encouragement of my loving toilers and myself.

It was most cheering to find the ready and satisfactory way in which soup and food were provided for those in distress, during part of this year.

A subject of special interest cropped up through the census of attendance at places of worship, taken by the

Liverpool Daily Post, on the morning of Sunday, October 16, and on the evening of Sunday, November 6. The result revealed a most deplorable and humiliating condition of things ; nor could any comfort be got from the fact of chapels being no better off than churches. The following figures as given in that census refer to St. Nathaniel's Church and parish :

In St. Nathaniel's Church, at the morning service - - -	879
In St. Nathaniel's Church and Mission-rooms at the afternoon service - - - - - - - - - -	900
In St. Nathaniel's Church, at the evening service - - -	1196
In Harding Street Mission-room, at the morning service -	174
In Harding Street Mission-room, at the evening service -	53
In Foundry Lane Mission-room, at the evening service -	131
In Upper Parliament Street Mission-room, at the evening service - - - - - - - - - - -	71
Total	3,404

According to the returns, St. Nathaniel's had the second largest attendance in Liverpool, both morning and evening. It is only right to state that on the census evening, the Bishop happened to preach in our church, and that in the last two places the numbers were given by the respective superintendents, not by the official enumerators. Truly the little one had ' become a thousand.' Praise the Lord ! Consider these figures in the light of our parochial civil census, viz., 4,255. Doubtless many attended twice ; that, however, would be more or less the case with all other churches.

The annual report for this year contained the following reference to these figures and the lesson they taught : ' What material to win for God, not only in the parish, but in the church and mission-rooms. Let us cry mightily to God, that His Holy Spirit may very abundantly water the seed of the kingdom sown amongst so great a multitude. Oh for such an increase of faith and love as will win every one of these souls for God ! Let us rejoice that so large and so effectual a door is opened to us.'

The enthusiasm with which our dear people took up the hall building proposal was truly astonishing, and the response to the appeal amongst friends outside the parish was most cheering. A committee was formed, an architect was chosen, and the foundation stone was laid by Charles Groves, Esq., in the presence of Lord Radstock, the Bishop, and a large assembly. It is worthy of remark that there were donations not only from Evangelical Churchmen, but also from Nonconformists, High Churchmen, Romanists, Americans, Greeks, and Germans.

A young father called, and asked me to visit his oldest boy, whom the doctor pronounced dying. I did so at once, and, with the parents, pleaded in prayer to God for his recovery, which, notwithstanding the doctor's statement, I felt would undoubtedly be granted. Calling shortly afterwards, the father met me with a cheerful countenance, and said : ' After you had left there was a change for the better, and it has continued.' The child did recover, and is now a fine, well-grown man. Praise God !

A lad came from his mother to ask if I would visit her husband, who was also said by his doctor to be dying, which, on reaching the house, I found to be apparently the case. Taking his hand, and kneeling down with his wife and their two children, I cried unto the Lord to spare his life. The next day, on my way to visit him I met his little son running to tell me his father was much better ; the man recovered, and lived for years. In both these cases the relatives undoubtedly attributed the recovery to prayer, and so did I. Why not ? Why should we limit God's power to hear and answer prayer ?

At the same time, I do not believe in ' faith healing ' as God's usual way of restoring sick persons to health. Two persons in our parish, well known to me, were unsuccessfully treated by faith healers. One of them, a decent woman, was suffering from dropsy, and the water certainly left one of her limbs, which gave the poor creature hope of recovery ; but it returned, and she died. There is no force in the allegation that these persons had not faith to be healed. It is true that our Lord in most instances required faith precedent to healing; but that was not so in the case of the Nain widow's son, or of the palsied man, or of Simon's mother-in-law; nor of the cripple with Peter at the Temple Gate. Of course Jas. v. 16 cannot and should not be overlooked; on the contrary, thank God for it.

I have no doubt that the little prayer, ' O God, for Jesus Christ's sake send me Thy Holy Spirit,' which by agreement, so many of our dear church members offered daily at the 1 o'clock gun fire in Liverpool, proved a source of strength and blessing. What a privilege to have had hundreds of hearts daily going up to God in prayer, simultaneously.

The blessed work of the Holy Spirit in quickening dead souls was in constant evidence amongst us.

This year, too, the confirmation brought with it a happy time; but that was the case year by year.

House-to-house visitation became ever harder to keep up. The work meant six hours of incessant mental strain and physical exertion daily. The effects thereof had already begun to tell on my constitution, never very robust; and the form it took was insomnia. The annual month's holiday was not looked for as an enjoyment, but longed for as a necessity; hitherto it had generally been the means of reinvigorating my sadly worn-out energies.

How tender of our dear Lord to say, ' Come ye yourselves apart, and rest awhile,' instead of ' Go ye.' It would not have been rest without Him !

This year five hundred and eighty pounds were raised.

1882.

Pastoral and Evangelistic work—Probing questions—Difficulties in 'holding' a congregation—The mourner 'quickened'—Opening of Windsor Mission Hall—Gospel Temperance Lay Mission—'Can they be brought in?'—No immoral house in the parish, and eight hundred communicants—Ages and autographs of communicants.

'My grace is sufficient for thee' (2 Cor. xii. 9).

THERE is no doubt much force in the late Dr. Guthrie's saying, 'No one man can do both pastoral and evangelistic work.' I think, however, one man can do it fairly well, provided he utilizes his time and opportunities methodically and wisely. Much depends upon the time devoted to pastoral work, and the nature of that work. My opinion is that many ministers spoon-feed the few, partially starve the many, and leave the rest to perish. There should be less calling upon the converted, the lion's share of time and strength being given to the godless, the indifferent, and nominal professors. Those who are 'strong in the faith' should be taught that instead of looking for the quarterly, monthly, or weekly pastoral visit, they ought themselves to be occupied in evangelistic work, assisting their minister; thus freeing him to help those who are 'weak in the faith,' or to look after the many who have no faith at all.

Following the example of the Master, throughout my ministry I have always sought to deal with souls not only collectively by preaching, but individually by visiting, and even by casual interviews. It can be done in many ways, most frequently, and perhaps most effectively, by utilizing favourable opportunities for quietly putting such questions as, Are you all right? Are you born again? Are you fit to die? Is God often in your thoughts? Do you have intercourse with God

by prayer ?   Do you feel yourself growing in grace ?
Have you delight in serving God ?   I never found such
inquiries resented, if made in a tactful way.

The difficulties attendant on ' holding ' a congregation
are ever on the increase ; and especially is that the case
in thickly populated districts, where sin abounds in its
most vicious forms, and by a sort of spontaneous
generation spreads with a rapidity which is altogether
astonishing, and attains a power which is actually
awful. Yet the explanation is not far to seek. When one
considers the heresies in the Church ; the disturbing
influences which denominational controversies exercise
over God's own people ; the startling increase of
atheism, deism, spiritualism, Mormonism, scepticism,
indifferentism ; the quasi instruction misnamed education, affecting ' all sorts and conditions of men ' from
the lowest of ' the masses ' to the highest of ' the classes '
the inconsistency of so many professedly Christian
people in frequenting, or at all events tolerating, the
concert of frivolous if not vulgar vocal music, the
theatre, with its plays of often more than questionable
morality, the music-hall variety entertainment, and
kindred places of amusement ; the direct disobedience
to the Saviour's great command to all His people —
or as the clergy erroneously consider it the great commission to themselves alone — ' Take my Church into the
world,' by taking the world into His Church ; and the
Satanic hypnotism of Jeremiah's time, — ' My people
love to have it so ' — which is leavening the lump of
professing Christianity ; the minister of Christ finds
it indeed uphill work to make head against or to withstand, such obstacles to the carrying on of his work,
even if he be a man of great ability in preaching ;
whilst if he be below the average there is but small
chance of his getting a hearing.

Still, in his intercourse with his flock, as well as in his
preaching, he can, by giving ' line upon line,' by finding
and apportioning work for all connected with the congregation, and above all, by himself living out the great
truths of God's Word, apply these truths, and drive them

home, to the building up of believers, and the gathering in of those who are still out of Christ. Oh, the persuading, convincing, holding power of a holy life ! Surely it should be sought ; for truly it shall be found. It is the pastor's great need ; and for its supply, as for that of every other need, there are the dual promise-texts, ' My strength is made perfect in weakness,' and ' My Grace is sufficient for thee.'

During this year I took the Acts of the Apostles for exposition on Sunday mornings.

On attending a funeral—having had, as usual, prayer before the body was placed in the hearse—after the interment I went back with the mourners to the house, and whilst waiting for tea, I read a portion of Scripture, and offered another prayer. There was present, amongst the deceased's relatives, a man of good character, but not spiritual, and it pleased the Lord then and there to quicken his dead soul. He became a communicant, and though he did not take up any definitely spiritual work, his sweet, kind, beautiful, Christian life was a bright example to others : he raised £41 for the Windsor Mission Hall, and annually collected a stated sum for our ragged schools. Long after, his wife also was made ' alive unto God.' I buried them both, strangely enough, at the same time in the same grave, in assured hope of their future life in the glory land. The Lord does His work ' in season, out of season.'

One of the great events of this year was the opening of the ' Windsor Mission Hall ' by the Bishop, who had taken the deepest interest in its erection, and, on account of his frequent visits while it was being built, was quietly styled ' clerk of the works.' God so favoured our efforts to build that house for Him, that we were able to open it free of debt, without a grant from any Church Building Society, a bazaar, or even a collection on the occasion, though the actual cost exclusive of the site was £2,104. What a cause for devout thankfulness to the Giver of all good !

There was great enthusiasm at the ceremony. The *Protestant Standard* reported the Bishop to have said

' they were gathered together upon a very interesting occasion : that night they used, for the first time, their new Mission Hall, which at length, by the zeal of Mr. Hobson, had been erected as an assistant to St. Nathaniel's Church, Windsor. He regarded the opening meeting with the greatest possible interest. They wanted many more in the diocese, and as long as the pulpit of the church was rightly lined, a good work for the Master would be done. He hoped they would bear that in mind, if they had anything to do with the building of a church. The architecture might be very beautiful, the windows might be very grand, the seats might be splendidly carved, but after all, the grand point was the pulpit lining. Don't forget the lining of the pulpit : the pulpit of St. Nathaniel's is well lined.'

The following extract is from an editorial in the *Protestant Standard* : —

WINDSOR MISSION HALL.—The labours of the Rev. R. Hobson in connection with the parish of Windsor are being signally owned and blessed by God. From strength to strength, and from achievements to still greater achievements, the pastor and congregation of St. Nathaniel's have gone on, hand in hand, lovingly and harmoniously, in the work of the Lord. That a rich harvest has attended the preaching of the Gospel by Mr. Hobson in multitudinous ways, is evident in the parish of Windsor. A church filled to overflowing : Bible-classes numerous, and attended by hundreds of intelligent students of God's Word ; Sunday-schools crowded with scholars ; outdoor and indoor mission work, and other prosperous and Christian efforts of various kinds and character. Now we believe the cause of all this glorious success has been the right exercise of faith in a faithful God, and energetic working with a singleness of eye to His glory. Faith in God, energized, if we may so express it ; and as a consequent result, it has happened to the Pastor and congregation of St. Nathaniel's church according to their faith, in conformity with the Saviour's promise. Such sweet and precious experiences in the past cannot fail to stir up bright hopes for the future.'

The opening of the hall was at once followed by a Gospel Temperance Mission, under the management of laymen, at which four hundred and ninety-six persons signed the pledge and donned the blue ribbon, whilst one hundred and fifteen professed to have received spiritual blessings. Thank God !

I well remember that though there was joy in spiritual births through the agencies and the ministry of the Word, this year was, outside the seventy-four confirmees, one of much less than the usual manifest ingathering savingly to God in the Church itself. Perhaps it was due to our being too much occupied with the building and opening of the hall ; for it is quite possible to be so taken up with the secular side of work for God, as partially to neglect the spiritual. We are not ignorant of the devices of the tempter, who will strive to divert the attention of those labouring for the Master from the great objects of their labours, to other objects of secondary importance, should he be unsuccessful in his endeavours to turn them altogether aside from their work. And this is specially so when it looks to be more than usually prosperous.

I must not omit to mention the Bishop of Liverpool's testimony—in a paper he read on ' Can they be brought in ? ' at the Derby Church Congress this year—to the Lord's cause in our church and parish (see Appendix G).

Two assertions in that statement were privately questioned in Liverpool, viz. : That there were eight hundred communicants ; and that there was not a house of ill fame in the parish. The Bishop told me, with an assurance that he had not the slightest doubt as to the absolute accuracy of what he had stated.

At my suggestion, and under pressure on my part, steps were taken to draw up a table containing the name, age, address, occupation, and autograph, of the communicants. When accomplished, an exact copy was made and entered, together with the following official declaration, in a small book which I handed to the Bishop :

' We, the undersigned, do hereby declare that we have seen the autograph of each communicant contained in this book, which are deposited amongst the records of St. Nathaniel's Church, Windsor, West Derby, Liverpool; and we further declare that a large proportion of them have or do live within the parish of St. Nathaniel, and that they are *bona-fide* communicants.'

' (Signed) ⎰JOHN A. SHORT, *Minister's Warden.*
　　　　　 ⎱TIMOTHY WEBSTER, *Peoples' Warden.*

Communicants' age analysis, as given to the Bishop in the book referred to :

From 15 years old to	20 years old	-	-	118
,,　20	,,	30	,,	-	-	219
,,　30	,,	40	,,	-	-	139
,,　40	,,	50	,,	-	-	117
,,　50	,,	60	,,	-	-	90
,,　60	,,	70	,,	-	-	49
,,　70	,,	80	,,	-	-	14
,,　80	,,	90	,,	-	-	3
Age not given	-	-	-	-	-	-	53

　　　　　　　　　　　　　　　　　 802

Thank God.

As to there being no house of ill fame in our midst, we applied to the Detective Department of the Liverpool Police, who are supposed to have information about all such in the city, and their statement was as follows, ' We know of none in St. Nathaniel's parish.'

When the Bishop received the book he said, pleasantly, ' You know I never doubted the correctness of my statement. I will keep this book amongst my special papers.' On thanking him for his kind reference to our parish work, and expressing an opinion that though it had done us much good, it had created jealousy in certain quarters, the Bishop replied, ' I knew it would ;

you must live it down.' That balm was not by any means new to me ; it had been in use during well nigh the whole of my life ; and I find it necessary still.

The last day of this year fell on a Sunday, and a busy day it was ; for there were no less than fifteen separate means of grace provided by the following services :

> Church, 11 a.m. ; 2.30, 6.30, and 11 p.m.
> Mission Hall, 11 a.m. ; 2.30, 6.30, and 11 p.m.
> Harding Street Room, 11 a.m. ; 2.30, 6, 8, and 11 p.m.
> Foundry Lane Room, 2.30 and 6 p.m.

The overflow from the church filled the Windsor Mission Hall, and the Harding Street schoolroom at 11 p.m. The same hymns were used at the three midnight services ; and as the church clock struck twelve the three congregations arose from their knees, and sang ' All hail the power of Jesus' name.'

Who can doubt that the waiting thus upon God brought down more and more of that ' power ' which alone can make church work real and lasting ?

The amount raised this year was two thousand eight hundred and eighty-two pounds.

1883.

The real under-shepherd—The flock's needs—Popish anathemas—
Thomas Rendell—The 'little maidens of Windsor'—Open-air work—
Church service unsuited to the masses—Converted working men's
addresses — Tardy Communicants — Financial 'false pretences' of
ritualistic parsons—Garston Vicarage offered and accepted—Congregation a deputation—Acceptance withdrawn—Deputation's visit to
Bishop.

' He shall feed His flock like a shepherd : He shall gather the lambs
with His arm, and carry them in His bosom ' (Isa. xl. 11).

HOW truly, and fully, was this prophetic promise
fulfilled in the Lord Jesus Christ, the veritable
Good Shepherd, when on earth.

As the days of my ministry multiplied, I, an under-
shepherd, saw more and more clearly the need of such
tender-heartedness, such loving kindness, such true
sympathy, as would enable me, in my life, to reproduce
or reflect, in those respects, something more of the Great
Shepherd and Bishop of souls.

The fact is ' babes in Christ,' whether they be converts
from Romanism or from nominal Protestanism, require
a spiritual nurse, to care for and to feed them, to build
up and to strengthen them. Too much is expected from,
too little allowance is made for, them in the early days
of their conversion, when they not unfrequently become
disappointed, depressed, disheartened ; needing a loving
tender heart to comfort, cheer, revive, and a loving
hand held out to strengthen, sustain, restore ; whereas
in too many cases, if they do not come up to a certain
expected standard, they are left in the cold shade of
neglect, or it may be, are regarded as hypocrites.

How many-sided is the work of a faithful minister
of Christ, a real under-shepherd, not a mere ' hireling,
whose own the sheep are not.' The true pastor

must be like a nursing mother to his flock, and especially
to the ' lambs.' They need, and to grow up ' strong in
the Lord ' they must have, an abundant supply of ' the
sincere milk of the Word,' the ' Water of Life,' the
' Honey out of the Rock ' ; to be tended in the ' green
pastures ' and by the ' still waters ' of God's Love. A
shepherd being once asked how it was that his sheep
were so fine, replied at once ' Because I take care of the
lambs.' I fear, so far as we are concerned, many a lamb
is lost for want of this under-shepherding.

Whilst a conductor of Cottage Readings was, with
his assistants, in the kitchen of a poor Romanist widow,
a priest called, and, looking at the woman, said, ' Who
are these you have here ? ' She trembled, but said
nothing. He then asked, ' Are they bidding you go to
confession ? ' She replied, ' Oh, Father, they are not
saying anything bad.' The conductor, recovering from
his surprise, said to the priest, ' I have been to
confession.' ' You have been to confession, and you are
here now proselytizing this old woman : you are doubly
damned ! ' Then he said to the old woman, in a very
peremptory tone of voice, ' Turn them out ' ; and away
he went. The poor old creature said to them nervously
' I do not like to turn you out, but if you will go out
you can come in again ' : they did so, and finished
their reading !

The dear brother in Christ who conducted those
readings had been the Lord's for over fourteen years,
during the whole of which period he had worked in the
parish and elsewhere with great devotion. As I write
there is before me the following cutting from the
Liverpool Daily Courier of December 28, 1901, a well-
deserved tribute to him, whom I loved so well ' in the
Lord,' dear Thomas Rendell :

' THE RAILWAY MISSION AND THE DINGLE
CALAMITY.

' On Thursday evening the Walton branch of the
Railway Mission held their annual reunion

'The chairman, in an interesting address, paid a tribute to the valour of the gallant fellows who lost their lives in the Overhead Railway disaster. The late Thomas Rendell, foreman, was, he said, a bright Christian, and possessed a remarkably genial disposition, and to know him was to admire him. He was never tired of toiling for the Master in every department of Christian labour, and as a member of the Railway Mission he was an enthusiastic worker for the cause. As a true Christian, and a valiant man, he sacrificed his own life in endeavouring to save others. Miss T——, in a capital discourse upon " The Christian Life," spoke in glowing terms of the Christian character of Mr. Rendell and his brave comrades. Miss A—— made a touching reference to Mr. Rendell, who, she said, always bore a bright smile when and wherever you met him, and his genial countenance will be missed at the annual conference of the Railway Mission, where his cheery face and pleasing voice was a feature of the gathering.'

Our Sales of Work on behalf of the Parochial Mission Fund have been an unqualified success in helping to raise money for our needs. They are always opened with prayer and closed with praise. Neither alcohol, gambling, lottery, palmistry, nor dancing, has even been allowed. They have been simple honest Sales of Work at fair prices, held in our own parish rooms from year to year ; affording our people opportunities for meeting socially : and so far from having had any reason for regret, we have had every cause for thankfulness.

For many years they were carried out by 'the little maidens of Windsor,' under the direction of two or three ladies. No work stands more in need of ' common-sense ' than does work for the Lord : but the common-sense must be ' sanctified ' !

The open-air work had attained great growth : our plan was as follows. We had, say, twenty men : these were formed into four groups of five each, one being the leader. Each group undertook to have a service every

week, thus insuring one on four evenings. The usual
time was eight o'clock, and the services lasted for about
an hour and a half, less or more, according to circumstances. There was a portable pulpit, a harmonium,
and a flag bearing the name of the church on both sides ;
' God is Love ' being on one, and ' Jesus Only ' on the
other. Sankey's hymns were used, and it often happened
that we had as many as eight of them, with the same
number of short Gospel addrsesses, and prayer at the
opening and close. All the helpers were welcome at
any of the services ; some were bound to attend :
all who were present, whether it was their evening or
not, were expected to have, if called on, ' a shot in the
locker,' in the form of a thought-out message from God's
Word. The clergy attended only one evening each week.
I had meetings of the workers from time to time, to give
hints as to the most suitable style of addresses, and for
correction where desirable.

This going out to ' compel them to come in,' made the
people understand that the church was alive ; it gave
work to earnest-minded young men, and women too, who
if not employed by the church would drift away from it,
and either find use for their zeal amongst other
denominations, or, failing that, might lapse altogether :
it also tended to remove from the minds of the people
that not unfounded, and therefore not unnatural,
conviction which so many non-church goers have, that
a large proportion of the clergy do not really believe
what they preach, or they would be more in earnest than
they are.

The Church of England has lost most seriously and
lamentably in not having long ago adapted itself to
change of circumstances by providing adequate ways and
means for getting and retaining a hold upon the masses.
The church services are far too inelastic : suited to the
times in which they were settled, they are in many ways
unsuited to present-day requirements.

I have been condemned in some quarters for thus
encouraging what have been styled ' ignorant spouters.'
It is, I am convinced, one of the best ways to touch the

thoughtless, many, nay most, of whom would not enter
a church even if the parson could pray and preach like
an angel. The common people will listen to a converted
working man, one of themselves, whose language is,
though often faulty in both grammar and pronunciation,
that of his hearers, as he stands in the open air, and says,
as I have often heard, ' Come along, chaps, you know
me, I was born and grew up in Windsor, and I will tell
you how it is I have a good coat ' ; or ' Come along,
I'll tell you why I believe in God.' Such a man may not
quote Holy Scripture altogether accurately, but he will
give the true sense and meaning.

Of course there are working men who sometimes say
strange things in open-air addresses ; perhaps if those
men had enjoyed the advantage of proper training they
would not do so : though what shall we say of those
men, educated and trained for the ministry, who speak
not only strange but actually blasphemous things, in the
very pulpits of the Church ?

Do we not want all the help we can get in our
endeavours to reach the masses ? Why not seek such
in our churches, and train both men and women to go
and work, and speak for God, each in his or her own
place ? I am certain the Master would own and bless
those servants. It has been my firm conviction that
all that is really good in Dissent should be found in the
Church.

The Bishop had a confirmation at St. Nathaniel's on
Whit-Sunday, and in answer to much humble, earnest,
faithful prayer, both before and at the time, it was
again a season of refreshing ' from the presence of the
Lord,' not only to those confirmed, but to the congregation, and to the clergy. It was my custom to get all
unconfirmed converts, from whatever ' ism,' to attend
the confirmation classes, leaving them to decide whether
they would be presented

Missing two of the seatholders from their pew for a
few Sundays, I called on them, and was greeted with
' Oh, we are so glad to see you, and were just wishing

you might call ; for we were offended at your saying in the last sermon we heard you preach, " How can persons sing ' This will I do, my dying Lord, I will remember Thee,' when they have no intention of doing so ? " That came home to us, for we never intended to go to the Lord's Supper. But we have been talking over it and have come to a different mind. See here, we were just looking through the Communion Service, and we now want some instruction.' They became communicants, which they should have been long before.

Severity in preaching is one thing, plain speaking is another. ' The fear of man bringeth a snare,' hence God says, ' Be not afraid of their faces.' Whether men will hear, or whether they will forbear, I have never hesitated to ' call a spade a spade.'

The urgent need of instruction about the errors of Ritualism, specially in the interests of our young people, caused us to arrange for a Church Association Eight Day Mission in our parish. It was opened in the church by the Rev. Dr. Taylor, afterwards the Ven. Archdeacon of Liverpool, being carried on during the week in our great hall, mainly by laymen. The interest created, and I believe also the good done, thereby was considerable.

The contrasting of truth with error by the exposure of what is practically veiled Romanism in the Protestant Church of England ; the putting people, especially the young, on their guard against the seductive subtleties of men who are not ashamed either to break their ordination vows daily, or to receive the pay of one church whilst they are doing the work of another ; surely these are amongst the best methods for preserving God's truth in our midst, and no reasonable person can fairly take exception to them.

The strain of the work to which I had now for a long time been devoting myself, body, soul, and spirit, was making itself felt more and more, developing insomnia, and causing me to feel very weary. I was thoroughly happy in my labours, and the dear Lord had seen fit

graciously to bless them ; therefore the insistence of
my medical adviser on partial rest as the only possible
means of obtaining restoration to health, came to me
as an unpleasant surprise, and in the face of so much
work, on which there was so much blessing, it seemed
scarcely possible to act upon his advice.

At this juncture the appointment to the then vacant
vicarage of Garston lapsed to the Bishop, who offered it
to me, giving me eleven days to decide, and in that
time writing me four long letters stating reasons why
I should accept it. He allowed me to consult my
relatives, but not to let even one of my parishioners
know of the offer. My family agreed with the Bishop,
and the upshot of it all was that I accepted his offer.
The matter got wind at once, and the consternation
and distress in the congregation and the parish were
such as to make me feel intensely unhappy. Yet, as I
thought the thing over, there seemed many advantages.
The parish was partly rural and partly urban, the
population was double that of Windsor, the income was
much larger than my present one, the change to pure
air and a fresh congregation would be a great relief,
the offer had come to me without being sought, the
present state of my health needed consideration. All
these had their weight.

Thus things remained for a few days, when, quite
unexpectedly, a large deputation consisting of male
members of the church, came to ask me to reconsider
the matter.

As I listened to what they said, and saw their sorrowful and loving looks, accompanied in the case of some
by tears, I felt not only as if I must accede to their
request, but also as if I could lay down my life for them.
I was quite overcome, and when they had finished,
I said, out of a very full heart, ' Friends, I shall withdraw,
if the Bishop will allow it.' They then asked me to
write a note to him to that effect, for them to go in a
body and deliver it, there and then. I did so. They
went to the Palace and saw the Bishop, who rather
reluctantly acceded to the request in my letter. They

then came back with the answer, and I wrote a formal letter of withdrawal, which one of them delievered at the Palace.

When I saw the Bishop afterwards, referring to the deputation he smilingly said : ' When I heard there was a number of men at my door waiting to see me, I suspected what they were about. I saw and heard them, and I think if I had not agreed to your withdrawal they would have knocked my head off.'

Thank God I never regretted that decision : it was of the Lord. I often thanked Him that it fell to my lot, in His kind providence, to be able to make such a sacrifice for the dear people of St. Nathaniel's. ' A man's life consisteth not in the abundance of the things which he possesseth.' To have gained such a wealth of love from that dear people is infinitely more than fine gold.

Amount raised, eight hundred and four pounds.

> ' Oh to be nothing, nothing !
> Only to lie at His feet.
> A broken and emptied vessel,
> For the Master's use made meet.'

1884.

Breakdown—Language of baptismal service—' Election '—' I'd as soon shake hands with Judas '—The working man's Bishop—Sunday-school attendance—Window gardening—Consolation in flowers—Presentation.

' We have this treasure in earthen vessels, that the excellency of the power may be of God ' (2 Cor. iv. 7).

I WAS now suffering seriously from insomnia, and felt as if it were impossible to go on. My doctor distinctly declared that there was no remedy but absolute rest and change. I therefore managed to take a long holiday, which certainly relieved me to a great extent, but did not fully restore sleep. Brain and heart, and the body generally, will not for ever stand such strain, and though the work was increasingly delightful, I felt the necessity of drawing in ; but how to do so was the question, and a difficult one to answer. It is very easy for kind-hearted and well-meaning people to say, ' Cut your work down ; it will strengthen you for the future.' And there is doubtless a good deal in such counsel : but the one concerned, while longing for rest, cannot always see it right to come to that conclusion. In due time the Lord opened a way which, though then scarcely discerned, proved helpful.

The work of the parish was going on well, and I began to feel that the workers might safely be left for a longer period than hitherto.

We had again abundant evidence of blessing upon the confirmation candidates, who were—especially some of them—so wonderfully clear and bright as to their spiritual standing, that it was a season of great rejoicing to us as well as to them.

The language of the baptismal service is that of faith, hope, and love. In faith the child's spiritual regeneration is prayed for, and thanksgiving is offered at the end, on the supposition that the petition has been granted. But it is not the language of assurance and certainty ; nor indeed can it be : for if in due time the child does not give evidence of a holy life, it is idle, nay, it is untrue, to say such an one was ' born again in baptism ' ! The Saviour says, ' By their fruits ye shall know them.' If those who have been baptized bear evil fruits, how can we honestly say they were ' born again in baptism ' ? There is no getting over this.

In the Christmas Day collect, prayer is offered for regeneration, ' that we, being regenerate, etc.,' which of course means that we may be regenerated, etc. ; just as in the service for use in time of storm at sea, the prayer ' that we being delivered out of this distress ' means that we may be delivered. To any fairly intelligent mind that is clear. If the Church taught that spiritual regeneration necessarily takes place in baptism, would she (as in the collect named) put into the mouths of her adult baptized members a prayer for that blessing ?

The theory of baptismal regeneration containing ' the germ of life ' is utterly devoid of foundation in Holy Scripture, or even in the Prayer-Book.

Simon was baptized, but certainly not regenerated : whilst Cornelius and his companions were regenerated before they were baptized. I have always made the ' new birth ' the great test for confirmation, casting on the candidates the examination of themselves in their own consciences, at the same time tenderly and gently indicating the marks in Holy Scripture of being ' born again.' It is manifest that in the confirmation service the Bishop does not pray for either the regeneration of the candidates, or the forgiveness of their sins, but assumes that they have given evidence of the former, and have received the latter. Confirmation administered and accepted with that meaning becomes a blessed reality, a strengthening of the faith, provided the assumption is justified ; but not otherwise !

To my grief and loss I found that incapacity and disproportion in presentation of a great truth may do much harm. An official in the parish, a real man of God, and most useful, asked and obtained permission to hold at his own house a Bible-class for truly Christian men, and some fifteen or so of my spiritual sons joined it. I knew the good man held and taught, in accordance with Article XVII., ' election unto life,' which has ever been a resting-place for my own heart, the assurance that God's purpose would stand and that He would do all His pleasure being a great encouragement to me in my work.

On making inquiries as to how the class was going on, I had a favourable account of it. But after a while I missed some of the dear fellows from church, and to my surprise the leader called, and referring to the class said, ' Those fellows are like wild beasts, I cannot control them.' ' Why ? ' I asked. He replied, ' They cannot bear any subject but election. They have gone further than I can see. I fear I have led them on too far.' That I learned to be the case. I soon found they were dissatisfied with my teaching, which included responsibility as well as sovereignty. They were openly disaffected, and, alas, alas, these my own sons in Christ actually became my enemies, charging me with unfaithfulness in my ministrations. Some left the church and joined the Particular Baptists ; some met on the Sundays in their houses, for the reading of God's Word and prayer ; while several, recovering themselves, found their places in God's house again. Meeting one of those who permanently left us, I held out my hand. He drew back, saying, ' I'd as soon shake hands with Judas ! ' I remarked, ' Well, I think you will at all events allow that I did one good thing in my life.' ' What was that ? ' he rather doubtingly inquired. ' I solemnized your marriage.' ' Yes, that was a good work,' he smilingly answered, and turned away. Did not some of Paul's spiritual sons amongst the Galatians treat him in a somewhat similar way ? There is nothing new under the sun. Are there not sorrows, as well as joys, in the ministry ?

In the spring of this year a tea was given to all the men employed in the coal-yards near the parish—in which some of them lived—and they filled our great hall. The Bishop had been invited to come and address them, and they cheered him lustily on both arrival and departure ; for he had already made his mark amongst the working people of the city by his terse, homely style of speaking, and the practical nature of his strong, sound, common-sense utterances : indeed, he might well have been styled the working man's Bishop.

It was gratifying and encouraging to us, conducting our services in a plain, hearty, congregational manner, with the gown in the pulpit, the psalms read, and the people warmly taking their part in the responses and in the hymns, to know that we had not only our diocesan's full approval thereof, but that he showed it by, when not engaged elsewhere, preaching or attending as a worshipper in our church.

The returns made to the Liverpool Sunday-school Association by the various parochial Sunday-school and Bible-class superintendents showed that in our parish there were no less than two thousand and fifty on the rolls, about eight hundred being adults ; which was nearly, if not quite, the largest number of any Sunday-school in the diocese. It was the more remarkable in that, whilst all the neighbouring schools gave prizes, we gave none. This satisfactory result was due to the combined influence of our teachers, who themselves sought influence from above !

Truly it is a blessing and a privilege for a minister to be surrounded and aided by such a staff of teachers. Ours numbered ninety-five, more than half being men ; in the main they were the outcome of numerous adult Bible-classes, the more capable members of which were, in due time, drafted out to become, in their turn, teachers of others. A missionary spirit was thus fostered in each class.

We did a great deal in providing flowers for those who were sick or infirm, which were much appreciated, and benefited both givers and receivers. There are many ways of serving God.

The Liverpool Window Gardening Association was cordially supported in our parish, with excellent results. The providing boxes of flowers for cultivating and training, with prizes for those who were most successful in decorating the window-sills of upper storey rooms, proved very successful, and many of the rewards fell to our share.

One day a poor sufferer said, as I entered the room, ' See that rose, left here just now by a young lady ! Did not God make the world for our use ? But did He not make flowers to delight us ? As I look on that rose I feel how good God is, and it partly reconciles me to bear my lot.'

Is it not Godlike to cheer and comfort the poor, and especially when they are sick ? Pain is bad enough to

bear when anything that can alleviate it is obtainable ;
how much worse must it be when the very necessaries
of life are wanting ? Truly to visit the sick is to visit
Christ ; and He will recognise it.

Amount raised, eight hundred and twenty-six pounds.

For the account of an address and an accompanying
presentation, together with my reply in acknowledgment
of the dear people's loving generosity, see Appendix H.

1885.

Spiritual ' prescription '—Comparing notes on baptisms—The Gospel's
power—Sunday cycling—Challenge to ' Father Ignatius '—Evangelical
apathy and ignorance of the ritualistic controversy — Prophetic
warnings—Christmastide service for poor widows—' Worthy ' and
' unworthy '—Four months' furlough—American millionaire—' Golden
gates of the West '—Pierpont Morgan—Niagara's soporific influences—
The ' Union Jack '—The ' Stars and Stripes '—Visits in America and
Canada—St. Nathaniel's ' supply.'

' All things work together for good to them that love God, to them
who are the called according to His purpose ' (Rom. viii. 28).

THIS is one of the best-known and most comforting
passages in God's Word. The word ' together '
suggests a doctor's prescription, composed of
various drugs mixed together, in order, by their individual action upon each other, and their general action
when combined, to produce a medicine which shall prove
beneficial to the patient.

Thus it is in God's providential dealings with us.
Our lives are made up of sunshine and shadow, mirth
and sadness, success and failure, health and sickness,
riches and poverty. In the life of all God's children
there are some of those ingredients working for good,
because prepared and prescribed by the great Physician
of souls.

Strangely enough, few people quote the latter part of

Richard Hobson
at the age of 19

Patrick William McConvill

Dr R. P. Blakeney

The Cellar at 6 Oliver Street, Windsor

St Nathaniel's Ragged School

The interior of St Nathaniel's Church

The 'Little Hell'

Mrs Catharine Hobson,
the author's mother

J. C. Ryle, first Bishop
of Liverpool

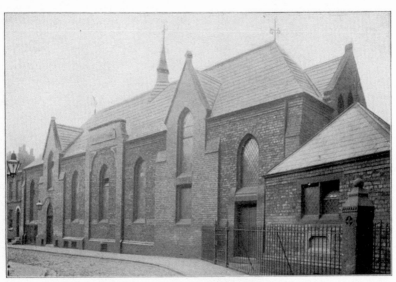

The Windsor Mission Hall

The Jubilee
Memorial Hall

St Nathaniel's
Vicarage

F. C. Chavasse, second
Bishop of Liverpool

Alfred Butterworth, J.P.

Officers of St Nathaniel's Church in 1901

Richard Hobson in 1893

this text : which may arise either from taking it for granted that the two are practically synonymous, or from an unwillingness to admit the limitation it declares. It can hardly be due to a shrinking back from the idea of God having a plan in His infinite mind. For just think of a God without one ! How blessed and consoling is it for God's children to be able, ' amidst all the changes and chances of this mortal life,' to rest on the gracious promise of this text in its entirety.

The annual administration of the Lord's Supper, on the first Sunday evening in the New Year, had now grown into one of the great spiritual privileges to which we looked forward. This year the Bishop preached, and afterwards officiated at the Lord's Table, which had become his regular custom. It was truly a season of heart-feeding, by faith, on Christ, not only at the time of Communion, but also as we listened to the Bishop's sermon, pregnant with those glorious Gospel truths which some of us had happily known from our childhood, proclaimed with a freshness and a power that sent us on our way rejoicing. No less than four hundred and nine partook of the Lord's Supper that evening.

I well remember a former college class-fellow of mine calling to see me, and, as we compared notes about our respective work, saying how it distressed him that, in the parish wherein he was curate, of the children baptized in church more than sixty-five per cent. were illegitimate. He could scarcely believe that of the infants baptized in St. Nathaniel's, the illegitimates numbered less than four per cent. !

Let those who will, declare that the pure Gospel, as evidenced in Evangelical religion, is effete : I deny it. If it has power to check and banish sin in all forms, to lift up the fallen, to purify the immoral, to make the thief honest, the liar truthful, the drunkard temperate, to heal the soul-sick, and convert the sinner, it cannot be effete. It is a vital force, as it ever has been, when presented in its living power and purity to the multitude ; as by the Master Himself, by His Apostles, and by His true servants through all the succeeding ages, right up to our own time.

One Monday morning a man carrying on business in the parish called, and as he sat down, said, ' I'll never ride my bicycle on Sunday again.' ' I did not know you had a bicycle.' ' Oh yes, I have.' ' Why do you say so ? ' ' I was at church last night, and heard you preach on " Now, if any man have not the Spirit of Christ, he is none of His." I felt I had not the Spirit of Christ ; I prayed for it, and I believe I have it now. My eyes have been enlightened. I am a new man.' We rejoiced together. ' Sing, O ye heavens ; for the Lord hath done it ! '

For one year this man kept, on Sundays, the principal door of the church, and getting hold of ninety-two persons who were either loitering about it, or had come there but were ashamed to enter, actually brought them in. He is still in the way to Zion. There are many ways of catching fish. Oh, to be indeed ' fishers of men ' !

' Father Ignatius ' failing to obtain the Bishop's permission to hold a mission, on behalf of his monastery, in any church of the Liverpool Diocese, took a hall in the city, and there held forth for a fortnight. Some of his discourses—as reported in one of the local papers—on the intercession of the Virgin Mary, were so entirely unscriptural and misleading, that I ventured upon challenging him to prove his allegations from Holy Scripture or the standards of our Church.

As he took no notice, I delivered in St. Nathaniel's Church on Sunday evenings a course of lectures in refutation of his erroneous teaching : which created no little stir, and about which he complained bitterly to the Bishop. Before leaving, he said he would return and reply to my statements, which had appeared in the paper that reported his. He did return, and had two meetings, attended by a mere handful of people : the wind had been taken out of his sails. He never attempted another mission in Liverpool.

If, instead of fighting shy of it, the Evangelical clergy would only acquaint themselves more with the Romish

and Ritualistic controversy, and take steps to instruct
their flocks in the true nature thereof, their people would
not, as in so many instances they do, wander from the
right path ; nor would so many even of their own children be led astray from the truth as it is in Christ Jesus !

The present sad state of things in our Church proceeds
principally from the timidity, and the apathy, of the
Evangelical clergy as a body, with regard to the Romish
and Ritualistic raids upon the Protestantism of the
nation. Wherever the clergy are loyally leading, there
the laity are faithfully following. Let the Evangelical
clergy take warning before it be too late. There is
thunder in the air, already its murmurings may be
heard ; there is a storm brewing, already its approach
may be discerned. Not only is the ' Establishment ' in
danger, the influence of its ministers is threatened. The
tomfooleries of the Ritualists, the ribaldry of the Broad
Church, the worldliness of so many Evangelicals, are
alienating the people.

In common with all similarly situated parishes we
have long had brought before us the changing character
of the masses. And this year we felt it more than
usual, owing to the erection, on our different borders,
of thousands of small houses, the freshness, cleanliness,
and other advantages of which naturally attracted
many of our people to them. Some continued to
attend our church, but most of those who moved away
became, as was only to be expected, attached to churches
in their new neighbourhoods. In one way that was
well, the natural tendency of the Gospel being to elevate
socially and morally, as well as spiritually ; so that our
labour, as regards those who left us to better themselves, had not been ' in vain in the Lord.' This made
our task of keeping up numerically the attendance at
church and at the mission halls all the more difficult.

This year I went through the Gospel by John on
Sunday mornings.

On visiting two persons owning several small houses in
the parish, our conversation turned on the poor seeking
better homes. One said to the other, ' Did we not often

remark that after our tenants " got agate " of going to
St. Nathaniel's we were sure to lose them, because they
soon sought better houses ? '

Most of our agencies had long since become strong
and vigorous. This was true also of the effort we had
been making to render the poor widows in the parish
special objects of our care : to which we in a measure
gave effect every Christmas, when they were all invited
to attend church on a week-day just previous to the
great Festival. On those occasions we sometimes had
over two hundred and fifty. Altogether, including
Romanists and Dissenters, we usually mustered about
three hundred. The question of being ' worthy ' was
not raised ; we included all, because we wanted to gain
all for Christ. It is true we took special care of the
known deserving poor, but all had a place at Christmastide ; and it told, for some ignorant, thoughtless ones
were by it won to better ways, if not to Christ.

I rather think it would fare badly with some who are
so extremely critical in discriminating between the
' worthy ' and the ' unworthy ' on such occasions, if
their own special fitness for many, if not for most, of
the blessings they enjoy, were to be as carefully ap-
praised by the One who bestows them. It is true God
does especially bless those who are His own and seek to
do His will ; but He also causes the sun to shine, and
the rain to descend, upon both the just and the unjust,
the evil and the good. And ' the goodness of God
leadeth men to repentance ' : let us therefore try to do
as He does, in this respect as in every other.

I have always felt a sort of pardonable pride in it
having fallen to my lot to provide for so many poor
widows. It was very touching to pray with, and to
speak to, them as a congregation, though only once each
year ; to see their sad faces, their dejected manner,
their worn-out clothes, their appearance of loneliness ;
and to realize that many of them knew nothing about
loving God, or His loving them. He has small sympathy
in his composition, and can therefore have but little

love for God in his heart, who is able to look on such a sight unmoved.

It was a real pleasure to put into the hand of each one, as she left the church, an envelope containing tickets for provisions and fuel, that none might want, at least on Christmas Day ; like one of old who ' caused the widow's heart to sing for joy.' To care for widows as a class is Apostolic.

The lost of any class will not be won for Christ by throwing stones at them, scorning them, or neglecting them ; but they may be got hold of by sympathy and efforts to benefit them temporally, which will pave the way for leading them to higher things.

To love, and to show it to, those who are ' out of the way,' without respect of persons, is Christlike. Neither John iii. 16, nor 1 Tim. i. 15, makes any distinction between ' worthy ' and ' unworthy.' Nor must we.

I could adduce numerous instances of aid given to apparently the most unworthy, being the very first coal that kindled in their hitherto cold hearts the fire of love to God. Praise the Lord !

Under medical advice I started for a four months' respite from the heavy strain of my much-loved labours, leaving Liverpool in the s.s. *Germanic* for New York. On the evening before my departure, three hundred and sixty-two of my dear flock had partaken with me of the Lord's Supper. Life on board the liner was a new experience. The state room opposite to mine was occupied by a well-known American millionaire, who lay coughing, through the night, in a way that told his days were numbered. I felt for him, thinking how gladly he would give his gold if that could purchase health, and how utterly useless was his wealth for the purpose. Little did he think there was within a few feet of him a sleepless one who was nightly praying that the Lord might touch his heart, and prepare him for the event which was so soon to happen. Shortly after my arrival in the States I read of his sudden death.

As we anchored off Sandy Hook the sky was all aglow with the glories of the setting sun. I expressed my admiration to an American gentleman, who, waving his hand as he spoke, replied with evident pride and pleasure, ' Yes, the golden gates of the West ! '

Whilst on board I made in a casual way the acquaintance of a New Yorker ; a quiet, calm, dignified, evidently cultured man, having, I felt, a deep sense of true religion. We spent much of the time together on deck, and during our intercourse it transpired that the rector of the church in New York City, where my companion was churchwarden, had been known to me from boyhood. My stranger friend was none other than the now famous Mr. Pierpont Morgan, well known as one of the greatest financiers in the world.

My first special visit in the New World was to a dear sister of mine, whom I had not seen since she was taken out to Canada from Ireland by an uncle, with his own family, in 1848, as previously mentioned.

The Lord was gracious to her. She married a worthy Englishman in Canada, afterwards settling in Fulton, Oswego Co., N.Y., where I found them and their olive-branches. As I was locked in her embrace chords vibrated which I did not know existed.

It was delightful to me to find that from under their roof, family prayer went up to God three times a day. The happy restfulness, peace, and joy of that sanctified home, following on a voyage, brought back to me a measure of sleep.

I then went on a visit to Niagara Falls, the spray of which fell on the windows of my bedroom in the hotel, on the Canadian side. I retired at 11 p.m., and did not wake till 6 o'clock the next morning ! Thus seven hours of sweet, unbroken, refreshing sleep, such as I had not known for many, many months, made me feel as if I could leap over a five-barred gate. The sound of Niagara's wondrous waterfalls had lulled me to sleep. Thank God.

As I looked at, and contemplated, those marvellous Falls, I felt almost spell-bound : never before, perhaps, had I so fully realized the mighty power of God ! Strolling on the Canadian side as far as the Cantilever

Bridge, I turned to cross over by it, and on looking down I unexpectedly saw a new Union Jack floating majestically. I felt touched and inspired by the sight of my country's flag, and I exclaimed, ' Oh, England, England, are you keeping watch thus ? ' I was as happy as a child. On reaching the other side I, also unexpectedly, saw another new flag, the Stars and Stripes, doing a like duty for the States. And I offered a silent, heart-felt prayer that the two greatest nations of the world, Mother and Daughter, might always thus dwell side by side in peace, emulating each other in works of peaceful enterprise, of philanthropy, and of service for God.

England and America thoroughly united would be the van of civilization and pure religion ; and should the awful arbitrament of war be resorted to, they would together prove victorious over an opposing world.

I afterwards visited relatives in Michigan, and in Canada at Hamilton and Whitby. All this was, as it were, life from the dead ; more blessed still, I found many of them were alive unto God through Jesus Christ our Lord.

I thank God for the good which this happy voyage to, and sojourn in, America did me, just at the very time when I was so sorely needing it.

I found the good cause did not suffer through my enforced absence ; owing to the valuable pulpit help of the Bishop, Archdeacon Taylor, and many of my clerical brethren ; to the devotion of my faithful curate ; and to the zealous and loyal efforts of all the dear workers in the parish. How gracious God has ever been to His poor servant.

Amount raised, seven hundred and ninety pounds.

1886.

Love's ' holding ' power over workers—Brands plucked from the
burning '—Rejoicing restoration—The ' submerged tenth '—Romish
priest's trickery—Relations to Nonconformists—Bishop Ryle's advice
as to unity—Romanist wife's treachery—Christian Church government
—Visiting an Infidel—Topical sermons.

' He that dwelleth in love dwelleth in God, and God in him ' (1 John
iv. 16).

LOVE is God's unique attribute. It does not, however, interfere with His other attributes, Justice,
Truth, Holiness. The greatest proof we have of
God's love for us is the wonderful gift of His own and
only Son, Who, by magnifying the law and making it
honourable, so harmonized those attributes, that God
can be just, and yet the Justifier of him who believeth in
Jesus ; hence God's love, flowing in and through Christ,
is the mighty power which wins lost ones for Himself.

Then to dwell in love is to dwell in God. What a
dwelling-place ! Is not this the great need in all our
work—indeed, our life need ? Yet, how few dwell
there ; which accounts for so large a part of the lives
of even truly Christian people being unloving and
unlovable, and for there being so little real love—
though plenty of zeal which is mistaken for it—in the
work of those who labour for the Lord.

A well-known, and highly honoured, toiler in God's
vineyard once said to me, ' I do not wonder so much at
the number of workers in your parish, as at how they
are all held together.' I was able to answer, ' We seek
to have only workers who personally know, and therefore believe in, the love that God hath to us ; we
endeavour to fan and intensify that Divine spark ; and
we realize that whatever may be the shortcomings of
such workers, their dwelling together in that love holds

them to each other and to the work, and either pre-
vents or removes any of the misunderstandings which
occasionally arise from overlapping through zeal.' And
to that I attribute the fact that so many of the workers
I left at St. Nathaniel's had been there ten, twenty, and
some even thirty years ; for there was no potent spell,
beyond that of love, either to enlist or to retain them.

Truly the basis of work there was love : all its reality
was the outcome of the principle to dwell and to labour
in love.

Again it needed the church and the two halls to
accommodate the congregations on New Year's Eve.
The usual week of prayer ensued, and the following
were the attendances at eight o'clock p.m. : Monday,
47 ; Tuesday, 113 ; Wednesday, 141 ; Thursday, 120 ;
Friday, 98.

It was something to get such a company of one's own
people together evening after evening for prayer. I
believe the best and the right place for such gatherings
is the church. I sought as far as possible, without wishing to do anything contrary to law and order, to use the
body of the church in that way, which I believe is quite
legal. These annual New Year prayer-meetings were
greatly blessed. On the first Sunday evening three
hundred and ninety-six partook of the Lord's Supper,
the Bishop officiating. Thank God !

A Christian young man called to ask me for a testimonial, which I gave with much pleasure, recalling the
day when I found him and his two brothers, with their
mother, in a cold cellar. I rejoiced at recollecting
also that the children attended our ragged school, and
were brought to the Lord ; that their mother became
His also, and thenceforth lived a thoroughly Christian
life ; and that later on she was supported by her three
sons, who have all grown up to be men of God.

Trying to lift up an individual, a family, a nation, by
education, civilization, social science, philanthropy,
without Christianity, is to begin at the wrong end.
That is to work from the outside, whereas God's plan

is to work from the inside. His Gospel, ministered by the Holy Ghost, purifies the soul, enlightens the conscience, changes the heart, raises the individual, who is thereby impelled to become industrious, to rise in the social scale, to lift up the head, to call God Father, to seek for ways of serving Him, stimulated, encouraged, energized, by the mighty motive-power of love to God, and therefore love to men.

A lady called on me—constrained to do so, she said—and made the following statement : For a long time she had lost the joy of salvation which she had formerly known. In our church on the previous Sunday morning, she heard me preach on ' Restore unto me the joy of Thy salvation,' and felt the sermon was for her, it seeming as if her exact case had been well known to me. And God's smile again beamed upon her soul, so that she could again, from her heart, call Him ' Abba Father.' We knelt, and rejoiced together before the Lord. Casting in her lot with us, she lived in the enjoyment of God's love, until He called her into His own bright presence. She left me her Bible, which was to her the greatest treasure on earth. Another trophy !

Our Passion Week Mission, conducted entirely by ourselves, was now well established, and most encouraging. It is always well for people to hear the Word of God, wheresoever, or by whomsoever, it may be spoken. Our congregations, counted, were :

Monday.	*Tuesday.*	*Wednesday.*	*Thursday.*
11 a.m. - 30	11 a.m. - 30	11 a.m. - 42	11 a.m. - 30
2.30 p.m. - 87	8 p.m. - 154	8 p.m. - 180	8 p.m. - 158

Good Friday. 11 a.m., Sunday morning congregation ; 4 p.m., children's service.

There were three hundred and seventy-eight communicants on Easter Day.

The services that day were inspiring, and full of glorying in our Risen Lord.

I had long been led to believe that the best way to reach the ' submerged tenth,' is for those in charge of a parish containing such—and where is the parish that does not ?—to seek a deeper spiritual life, first for themselves and afterwards for the congregation ; then, in the strength of increased spiritual power, vigorously to tackle the great problem, trusting the Lord to point out the way in which He would have it solved. Doubtless, as in a mission, a fresh face, a strange voice, a different manner, a new way of putting things, may be useful in some instances, if its possessor be full of love to God ; but the flock needs, and—if he be a true one—prefers, its own shepherd, who is the one best able to reach, nurse, and train the ' submerged,' and, with his well-tried agencies, to form in them, and build up, a strong moral character, which is not accomplished by merely spasmodic efforts.

A communicant, who had lived for many years as lady's maid in a family of high position, lying very ill, was constantly visited by a fellow-servant, a Romanist. One day, after she had left the room, the sick one being unconscious, there was a knock at the street-door, and, on the landlady opening it, a person looking like a clergyman inquired if he could see the sufferer. Being shown into the room, he asked for a lighted candle, and, after remaining alone with the unconscious woman for about twenty minutes, left, saying, ' Thank you.'

The landlady began to suspect something was wrong, which was confirmed by the Romanist maid calling soon after, and asking if Father —— had been. She ' gave her a piece of her mind ' about the matter, to which the girl replied, ' Oh, it is all right now,' and went away. The priest also called next day, but quickly took his departure from the door. The sick woman recovered, and, on being told what had happened, bitterly complained to me, with tears, of her fellow-servant's cruel falseness, declaring that she scorned the priest's ' extreme unction.' When well, she again found her place at the Lord's Table as usual. She died after a few years, and I interred her.

Another case was that of an Orangeman, married to a

Romanist, who actually knelt as I prayed, from time to time, by the bedside of her sick husband, and blessed me as I left. Calling one day as usual, when she opened the door I asked ' How is your husband ? ' to which she replied ' Dying ; unconscious ; the priest has been, and you are not wanted.' As she closed the door, I replied ' Oh, you traitor ! ' The poor fellow utterly abhorred Popish priests and all their soul-destroying teaching. I have good reason to hope that his soul was cleansed in the blood of the Lamb, which all the priest's oil-rubbing could not touch !

I dare say, if the truth were known, many of the paraded ' Popish perverts ' are of this sort !

My relation to orthodox Dissenters, by which I mean all who hold the Head—Christ—and the doctrine of justification by faith alone, through the atonement of Christ once for all, had always been of a very cordial character. With two Dissenting bodies, however, I could have nothing to do : Unitarians and Romanists. The former remove the very basis of all my hope for time and for eternity, the latter corrupt the truth of God ; the one is like a cup of undisguised poison, the other resembles a cup of pure milk with a deadly drug in it. It matters little to me which I take ; both are poisonous, and I have but one life to lose. Politically and socially there is a vast difference between Unitarians and Romanists. As citizens the former are loyal to the Throne and to the Constitution, and are characterized by benevolence and philanthropy ; the latter yield primary allegiance to Rome, the Pope coming first and the Sovereign of their country second, whilst socially the advancement of their own interests at the expense of all others is their ' great and chief concern.'

I earnestly desire, and devoutly pray, that all Evangelical churches may be drawn closer together : that is the only unity I believe in or dare advocate. As to the various branches of God's Church, whether episcopal or non-episcopal, I fully agree with the saying of good J. C. Bishop Ryle, ' If we cannot remove

the hedges which separate us, let us keep them as low
as we can, and shake hands over them.'

' The Bidding Prayer ' in our Church's 55th canon
directs us to pray for the Church of Scotland, which
when the canons were published, was, and is still,
non-episcopal. Nowhere in its standards does the
English Church declare that episcopacy is the *esse*
of a Church. They certainly provide that none shall
minister as clergy without having been episcopally
ordained : and a Church has in such things a right to
decide for itself. I prefer the triple order because it
seems to me more agreeable than any other form of
Church government to what is found in the New
Testament Scripture ; which, however, contains no
set of regulations as to the government of the Christian
Church, such as we find were in the Old Testament
given by God for the government of the Jewish Church.
In fact the only thing absolutely essential to real and
acceptable worship is set forth in the words of God's
own dear Son, ' God is a Spirit, and they that worship
Him must worship Him in spirit and in truth.'

I was now feeling almost as vigorous as ever, which
enabled me to resume my full parochial visitation. All
our hearts were rejoiced too, by the great manifestation
of the Holy Spirit amongst the newly confirmed. On
the evening of confirmation day, two hundred and
thirty-seven, including all the confirmees, were at the
Lord's Table.

On calling at a house to visit a sick man, his wife,
trembling, and with tears, said ' I fear my husband will
insult you if you go into his room. He is what is called
an infidel. I wish he would receive you.' I replied, ' Go,
and say I have called.' She soon returned, smiling,
and said ' He will see you.' As I entered the room he
raised himself in bed, and, reaching out his hand, said
' I am glad to see you because you are kind to the poor
children.' That was the avenue to his heart. Thank
God ! Sometimes it is not so much what we say, as what
we do, that the Lord makes use of for reaching souls.

Blessed Father, we want Thy way, not our own, in this thing also ; only be graciously pleased to save the lost, if not through us, through whom Thou wilt.

It was my wont on some Sunday evenings to preach on topics suggested by passing events. Though it rather taxed one's mental powers to treat such special subjects in suitable style and language, I always found the plan to succeed. For instance, when I preached on the royal supremacy in connection with the Queen's visit to the City ; the Gunpowder Plot ; the Accession of William III. ; the opening of Parliament : or, taking Scripture subjects, on Eve, Lamech, Light Bread, The Ark in Jordan, Unholy Alliances, The Queen of Sheba.

There was no decay in the work ; we were strong ' in the strength of the Lord,' unto Whom be the glory for ever, Amen.

Amount raised, eight hundred and twenty-six pounds.

1887.

Jubilee Memerial Hall—Welsh Mission Church—Four simultaneous Sunday services—An invaluable sexton—A mourning mother's rescue from intemperance—A model choir—An ignorant organist—Preaching against drink—Withdrawal of publican seat-holders—' Our people die well.'

' What hast thou that thou didst not receive ? ' (1 Cor. iv. 7).

IS not this true, physically, morally, mentally, and spiritually ? There is nothing inherently good in any ; ' all things are of God.' God is a Sovereign : we must not dare to call Him to account. We are debtors to His bounty, in both providence and grace.

Besides sending us blessings, He daily teaches us, if we be only willing to learn, how to use them, and if there be any failure, the fault is ours, not His. Specially should we now call to mind the temporal blessings we have for so long been receiving as a nation, and the spiritual blessings that have been showered upon us as His people ; but with the recollection there must come the consciousness of how little we have deserved, and what an insignificant use we have in the main made of, either the one or the other.

Our parishioners shared in the national joy and thanksgiving that the ' King of Kings ' should have spared our gracious and beloved Queen to attain her Jubilee as Sovereign : and they showed themselves to be as loyal as any of Her Majesty's subjects, in celebrating the happy event, and in marking this year as a truly memorable one, by purchasing and opening a ' Jubilee Memorial Hall,' under the following circumstances.

The Bishop, and others, had been struck by the want of spiritual provision for members of the Welsh Church residing in Liverpool ; and the historic title of the Queen's eldest son suggested the idea of associating benefit to natives of the Principality which gave him that title, with loyal devotion to his venerable and venerated mother.

Our plan for carrying out the proposed undertaking was somewhat similar to that adopted for the Windsor Mission Hall, with the satisfactory result that, though the entire cost was over £1,100, we had, after paying it, a balance of £102. Thus again was the promise fulfilled, ' My God shall supply all your need.'

On Jubilee Day the hall, which was intended for parochial purposes, as well as for carrying on the proposed Welsh Mission, was opened by the Bishop of Liverpool, with whom were present Dr. Hughes, Bishop of St. Asaph, and Dr. Bardsley, then Bishop-elect of Sodor and Man.

Welsh-speaking people filled it in the evening, when a sermon in their native tongue was preached by Dr. Hughes, who, on leaving, squeezed my arm, and said ' God bless you for your kindness to my countrymen ! '

I knew that the imposing on my dear people and

myself the originating and sustaining of this new and separate agency meant an additional financial responsibility, for the Welsh curate's stipend and other necessary expenses; therefore it would bring no grist to my mill: but, feeling there existed a need for it, and that an opportune occasion had occurred for supplying that need, I took no heed to warnings from friends as to whether it would work at all, or how.

The mission was therefore begun, nursed, fed, and sustained by us.

It was in charge of two Welsh curates, consecutively, and, on the appointments of a third, there were about four hundred adherents, and one hundred and twenty-one communicants. Of course, the latter belonged to us, so that our communicants' roll at St. Nathaniel's now numbered over one thousand!

Alas! there came a blight upon the mission, which nearly died; but it survived and recovered. I shall not describe either the blight, or how I suffered by misrepresentation, as both are now well known.

I rejoice that St. Nathaniel's Welsh Mission is now firmly rooted, and worships in a building of its own, recently erected, at the top of Upper Parliament Street, after having been fourteen years under our care. I do trust it may ever have the pure Gospel, and a service in which all can join; and that the new church may be the spiritual birthplace of precious souls in ever increasing numbers. Amen.

One dark Sunday evening, having conducted Divine Service up to the hymn before the sermon, I left, on my way to the Jubilee Hall to administer the Sacrament to the Welsh people for the first time. Passing our great Windsor Mission Hall, a well-known hymn was being sung by a large gathering of children, and on going by Harding Street School I heard the tones of a familiar voice giving a Gospel address. Reaching the Jubilee Hall as the general congregation was leaving, I administered the Sacrament. None can realize what were my thoughts and yearning desires, or how I was almost overwhelmed¡with mingled feelings of wonder, gratitude, and joy, as my prayers went up to God for a blessing on those four congregations which had been that evening as usual simultaneously worshipping Him.

On Sunday mornings the church was well attended, and in the evenings it was entirely filled, insomuch that the wardens were wishing they had more seats.

We were, and had long been, greatly indebted to our indefatigable sexton, dear K——, for his valuable help in all sorts of ways. He was the Lord's own before he came to us. His tact was remarkable ; his influence over young and old astonishing. Wherever he went his topic was the church and its agencies for God ; his very look attracted even strangers on entering the building. Each year he collected £10 in his box for the ragged schools ; and there were many additions to the yearly confirmation classes through him. He visited the sick in the way of friendly calls, and was welcomed by all our people. Through his means eighteen seats in church were taken one half-year ; his house was a centre for the church in many small but useful ways. In fact, that dear, simple, faithful, Christ-like man was, in certain respects, of more value in the parish than any other helper I ever had, either voluntary or official. How God uses even the weak ones in His service !

The temperance work was being well sustained, especially the women's branch of it. It has constantly been asserted that if a woman falls altogether into drunkenness she cannot be reclaimed : my own personal experience as a parochial minister leads me to an entirely different conclusion. I could quote several cases of women who had become drunkards being thoroughly reformed. The following case will suffice :

The wife of a merchant, a lady by birth and education, both she and her husband regular in attendance at the Lord's Table, and having family prayer, lost a child, whose death so affected the poor mother that she gave way to secret drinking, which all the loving efforts of relatives and friends failed to stop. Her husband went down also, and within a few years everything had gone. One day I met her, wretchedly clad, her dress draggling in the gutter, but still looking the lady. Opening her purse, she said : ' There is the last halfpenny I have.' I was quite overcome.

It was the lowest depth. A dear Christian relative took a small house at a distance, had the whole family removed to it, and lived with them there. That was the turning-point : the poor soul gave up drinking, and became quite herself again ; the children were cared for ; the husband died. Fifteen years have now gone by since the time of rescue ; and the record is that that dear sister has been fully restored, and kept, enjoying again communion with the God she loved and served in former days.

Amongst the many church agencies, the choir merits an honourable place, and deserves special mention ; it has never given any real trouble, as so many, if not most choirs do. By singing, not to its own glory, as is so frequently the case with choirs, but to the glory of God, it has proved a blessing in leading the songs of the sanctuary. I am thankful to record that our endeavours to impress the members with a sense of the privileges and responsibilities belonging to their share in the services of God's house were not in vain.

Congregations owe much to such choirs, for it means no little self-denial in various ways, to attend regularly twice every Sunday, and for rehearsal once each week. We not only never sought, but never would have, singers who did not belong to the congregation, no matter how good their voices might be.

Our choir was a mixed and voluntary one, numbering generally not less than thirty-five : with a strong and telling volume of harmony they led the congregation heartily and well. We had nothing sung but hymns, the canticles being chanted ; occasionally we had an anthem. The psalms were read. I reserved absolute control of the chants and tunes. The older members were communicants. The choir seldom had a treat or an excursion such as is usually given.

My own warden called on a neighbouring clergyman one day, and found him in conversation with his organist about the musical part of his service. The vicar asked ' How do you manage in your church as to the choice of chants and tunes ? ' The reply was ' Our vicar controls both ; he will not have any tunes or chants which the congregation cannot easily follow.' Thereupon the organist broke in with ' I consider the singing of a congregation like the braying of asses ! ' Comment is needless.

At one time we had some six publicans' families as seat-holders ; but they took offence, and one by one gave up their sittings, for which I was sorry. Still, on principle, and in view of my awful experiences of the distress and ruin resulting to my parishioners from drink ; of the fearful inroads which the love of, and craving for, intoxicating liquor was making upon everyday social life in all classes of the community ; and of my individual duty as a total abstainer ; I felt bound and constrained from time to time, both in the pulpit and out of it, to deliver my soul of the responsibility resting upon me as one of God's ambassadors, to expose the evils of drink and the drink traffic, to warn people against the possible, if not probable, results to both body and soul, alike in this world and in the next.

One of those who left the church on account of my plain speaking moved out of the parish, and took another licensed house a good way off : he, poor fellow ! was exceedingly angry with me. Yet when he was seized by an illness, which ultimately carried him off, he would have nobody but myself to visit him. That I did, and, at his own request, when he died I buried him, with good hope, too, of the better life. I was sorry to have been obliged thus to give my warning against the dangers of strong drink, but it was my duty, and I did it regardless of consequences to myself, amongst which was the lessening of my income through those publicans' families ceasing to be seat-holders. It is not always easy to be faithful when one's bread-and-butter are thereby jeopardized.

I have always felt sorry for those in what is known as ' the trade,' especially for such of them as would gladly get out of it if they could only see their way to do so ; for I have known both brewers and publicans of whose real piety I could not have a moment's doubt.

John Wesley said : ' Our people die well.' When I think of the vast number of those dear people in our parish and congregation who have died well, my heart is joyful ; but when, better still, I think of those who live well, that is the crowning joy of joys. The names of the many dear ones I laid to rest in God's acre ' until the day breathe and the shadows flee away ' are not to be mentioned here ; but they are in the ' Book of Life,' and often fill my memory.

It makes me feel that when, in God's good time, we who still remain cross the Jordan, we shall have joyous greetings with the ' loved ones gone before,' next in delight to that from our Elder Brother, the blessed Jesus Himself.

Amount raised, one thousand eight hundred and thirty-nine pounds.

1888.

Advice to a curate—The aim of most modern preaching—A stranger's impressions of eleven Liverpool sermons—' Who could resist love ? '—A ritualistic Baronet's short sojourn—Paper on the Church and working people—The dying Ragged School scholar—Fifteen thousand free meals for children—Training evangelists—Bishop Ryle's annual presbyters' gathering—Ragged School boy's honesty—Death of the Author's mother—Apostrophe—Gift of a Church safe and a Jubilee Hall clock.

' For Thou hast been a strength to the poor, a strength to the needy in his distress, a refuge from the storm, a shadow from the heat, when the blast of the terrible ones is as a storm against the wall ' (Isa. xxv. 4).

IS not our God all this, and more ?
Is not our Jesus all this, and more ?
Is not the Holy Spirit all this, and more ?

Should it not be the yearning desire of every true under-shepherd likewise to be in a sense, all this, though of course falling infinitely short of such a standard ?

A poor parish is by some considered a reproach, whilst a rich one is regarded as a recommendation. Why ? they both alike contain souls to be either saved or lost.

A curate once asked me what book I would specially recommend him to read, after the Bible. My answer was ' Read the people in your parish. Study them. Mark well their habits of thought, their special needs, and learn to adapt your ministry to meet those needs.' He looked rather taken aback.

An intelligent, attentive lady said to her minister, ' I wish you would not give us such very long and difficult sermons. I can and do follow you about half-way, and could carry away what you have said, if you would stop then ; but the next half wearies, if not puzzles me.' His reply was ' Well, I am sorry to hear you say so ; but I have a character to maintain as a preacher. I preach to please myself. I shall probably not be in this church always.'

Exactly ; that, I fear, is more or less the aim of modern preaching ; preachers want to be thought learned ; they must all be, or seem to be, mighty clever. They say the critics, or the would-be critics, will not listen to anything else. To aim at being ' a strength to the poor, a strength to the needy in his distress, a refuge from the storm, a shadow from the heat,' is beneath such preachers. Yet that is what Father, Son, and Holy Spirit, so graciously are to those who are poor in spirit as well as in this world's goods ; and the servant should not be ' above his Master.'

One day I had a talk on an omnibus with a gentleman, apparently a Christian, who said ' I am only a stranger in Liverpool ; but I have been to eleven churches, and have heard eleven sermons by eleven different preachers ; and with one exception, I could not quite gather that they actually believed what they were preaching ! '

I remember hearing during a holiday in the North, ten sermons ; each one of them well composed, fairly if not well delivered, useful discourses up to a point : but I felt—and it saddened me—that if a poor sorrowful seeker after Christ heard those sermons such an one would in vain seek for Him in any of them. Is it surprising that with such preachings, so few conversions to God are heard of in these days ?

The Gospel is still ' the power of God unto salvation.' ' By the foolishness of preaching to save them that believe ' ; that is, by the method of preaching, which is a very different thing from foolish preaching. But if the Gospel be not preached in its purity, and in a tender loving spirit, it is frustrated, on the human side.

I once said to an intelligent Christian Scotchman, ' Tell me how you hard-headed Scotchmen could listen to Moody.' His answer was ' Who could resist love ? ' That is it. I knew a true minister of Christ who emptied

a church, because ' he seemed cased in ice ' : so his
people said, and they seemed right. Does not Paul urge
' speaking the truth in love ' ? Mark, ' the truth ' :
but the truth in loving tones.

Sir Baldwyn Leighton, Bart., a member of St. Alban's,
Holborn, London, a well-known Ritualistic church,
was one of the chosen speakers at the Church Congress
in Manchester this year ; his subject being ' Lay Help.'
Having heard of the work in our parish, he wrote expressing a wish to visit it, and stay from Saturday to Monday,
in order to see for himself what was done, by whom it
was done, and how it was done. As he was a well-
known Ritualist, his testimony, found in the official
report of the Congress proceedings, is specially valuable.
I therefore append an extract (see Appendix I).

This year I read a paper in Wycliffe Hall, Oxford,
before a large gathering of clergy and laity, on the
subject selected and formulated for me, ' How can the
Church of England win the Confidence of Working
People ? ' The paper was afterwards published. Little
did I think that on being introduced to the Rev. F.
J. Chavasse, then a rector in Oxford, I was shaking
hands with my future diocesan, one who, as Bishop of
Liverpool, has been so kind and good to me. O Lord,
how gracious thou hast ever been, and art still.

The following will illustrate the work of our ragged
schools in two different ways :

A mother called, in great distress, for me to pray with
her little boy, who was dying. Wringing her hands,
she said, ' My boy asked me this morning to pray for
him. I said, " My child, I do not known how." Again
he said, " Mother, pray for me." I thought my heart
would burst. I would do anything in this world for
my child, but I was obliged to say again, " My boy,
I don't know how." I afterwards asked him what
I should say if I did pray. He answered, " Say ' God
save a poor sick child.' " I knelt down by his bed, and
cried over and over again " God save a poor sick child."
I thought I should have died. After I had finished,

he said, " Go for Mr. Hobson." " Oh my boy," I
said, " he might not like to come to a child so young
as you are." He answered, " Yes he will, if you tell
him I am one of the ragged school lads." '

I was soon at his bedside, when he reached out two
little hands, with a smile on his wan face. God heard
the prayer of the dear little fellow, and answered it ;
but it was by taking him home to glory. It is something
to have won the loving confidence of even a ragged
child.

In the street I was accosted by a lady, a stranger,
with this exclamation, ' May God bless St. Nathaniel's
ragged schools ! ' To which I said ' Amen.' ' You will
be glad to know,' she continued, ' that after one of your
ragged school children had sold some chips at my house
for a penny, the servant, on answering another ring at
the bell, found at the door the same little fellow, who
said to her " Please you gave me this half-crown instead
of a penny, so I have brought it back to you " : and
that very child, having had pieces of bread and meat
given him by my cook, brought back a silver spoon
which he found amongst them.'

This year we were able to give fifteen thousand
warm meals to our poor dear little ones. What a
mercy, what a comfort to them : and what a privilege,
what a joy to us !

Early in the year I had formally organized a band of
young men to be trained by myself as evangelists, the
result of which gave me cause for great thankfulness.
I had always felt that, in order to make our helpers a
power in work for the Master, they must be trained as
well as taught ; and, moreover, that they should
be drawn from the congregation, an outside supply
being difficult to obtain, and when obtained, often
unsatisfactory.

At the annual gathering of the clergy who had been
ordained presbyters by the Bishop of Liverpool, those
who took part in the proceedings assembled at St.
Nathaniel's Church, where, in the morning, there was a

celebration of the Holy Communion, at which about one hundred clergymen were present. The Bishop himself administered the Sacrament, assisted by the vicar.

An adjournment was afterwards made to St. Nathaniel's Jubilee Hall. The Bishop took the chair, and opened the meeting ; but as those annual meetings were designed purely to encourage those clergy in their work, the proceedings were not of a public character.

A discourse was delivered by the Rev. Canon Girdleston, Principal of Wycliffe Hall, Oxford, upon ' The Bearing of Modern Studies on Pastoral Work.' Those present subsequently lunched with the Bishop at the Windsor Mission Hall, and in the afternoon an address was given by the Rev. H. Webb-Peploe, incumbent of St. Paul's, Onslow Square, London, on ' The Secret Life of Believers, as Supported and Fed by the Lord.'

This gathering was held yearly until 1899, inclusive, when the last took place just previous to Bishop Ryle's resignation of the See.

As it was my privilege to be present on these interesting occasions, I am able to testify to their value in keeping the young presbyters on evangelical lines, and in building them up in the true faith. Nothing could be more delightful than the genial, loving manner of the Bishop, or more helpful than his wise, fatherly counsel.

It was also an incidental object-lesson for those young ministers to find their way into, and pass through, that very poor parish, amongst a people upon whom God was showing forth the power of His word in saving so many shipwrecked souls from eternal death, to the glory of His great name.

The greatest trial of my life befell me this year, by the ' calling home ' of my darling mother, the well-beloved of all her children.

That I might be with her at the last was her great desire, and it was granted ; for four days I stayed by her bedside, and then prayed her spirit home !

She had a due estimate of herself and her family, though, except for the last thirty years, her path through life had been a rough one. Her wants were few and sweetly simple ; her disposition cheerful, and encouraging to others ; her hope was ever high, she was ' saved by hope ' ; she always had a deep reverence for religion, and an unshaken, unshakable, faith in God her Saviour ; when providential circumstances had set her free from hard work and wearying care, she gave herself fully to the Lord ; and having ripened for glory, she was ready for God's angel reaper to thrust in the sickle.

As I sat alone in the room where she reposed in death, and looked stedfastly on her dear face, oh, what memories filled my heart ! That form, now so still, had given me life, had nourished me, cared for me, tended me. Those eyes, now closed, had looked on me in untellable love ; those lips, now sealed, had kissed away my tears, and commended me to God in prayer ; those hands, now motionless, had worked for me ; that heart, now pulseless, had beat with affection such as only a mother can feel ! Never was human love greater or deeper than thine, so tender, so unselfish, God's aptest illustration of His love to His children ! Oh, my darling mother, thou hast done well : the Master will have said so to thee already, and that will infinitely more than make up for all thou hast gone through. With Him I leave thee until He comes, bringing thee and all His other Saints with Him ! Her precious remains were lovingly laid in the churchyard of Drummully, co. Monaghan, Ireland, of which parish her youngest daughter's husband was the rector. And there her children, who ' rise up and call her blessed,' erected a suitable monument to her memory.

Hearing that the contents of our mission-boxes in the church had been stolen, the Bishop most kindly gave us a safe, in which his own plate was formerly kept ; he also presented a clock for the Jubilee Hall.

The ' little maidens' ' Sale of Work brought £138 into the Lord's treasury.

Queen Elizabeth's reign was rendered illustrious mainly by the celebrated statesmen, warriors, philosophers, theologians, and poets who then flourished ; the equal of which is not to be found in the history of any other English Sovereign.

There are few ministers, if indeed any, surrounded and helped by so large a number of such loving, willing, devoted, efficient, whole-hearted, truly converted workers in the Lord, as was the vicar of St. Nathaniel's ! I knew it, I felt it, and I was deeply thankful to God and to them for it.

There were four hundred and six communicants this Eastertide.

Amount raised, eight hundred and sixty-eight pounds.

1889.

Wall posters—' Feed My lambs '—The cornered hairdresser—Saturday night parochial perambulations — A tender-hearted pastor — Southport vicar's generosity—Lord Mayor's state visit to the church — A trophy — The Scotch policeman — ' I have received Christ ' — Writing to the Guardians on behalf of a Romanist widow—Summary of collections.

' Thy people shall be willing in the day of Thy power ' (Ps. cx. 3).

' Compel them to come in ' (Luke xiv. 23).

THESE two texts may be said to dovetail the Sovereignty of God, and human responsibility, as to the ingathering of precious souls. How truly blended both are in the ministry of the Great Missionary, our Blessed Saviour. How they are illustrated also in the life of Paul, ' the Grace Apostle,' whose writing of Romans viii., ix., x., xi. did not cause his efforts to lessen.

Divine Spirit, breathe Thy life and love all around that a great army may stand up for God. And give Thy servants grace and power to ' compel ' sinners to ' come in ' to the Gospel feast.

In many little ways we, too, strove to ' compel them to come in.' By way of illustration : I failed to reach a rough hairdresser, whose wife loved the Lord ; if he saw me enter his shop he bolted. One day he could not get away. I said to him, ' I want you to cut my hair.' ' Oh, the wife will do it.' ' No, no, you shall do it. Come now, I am in a hurry.' So he cut my hair, the ice was broken, he got friendly, and although he did not become all I could wish, he was a very different man, and a better one : there was hope in his death.

We found boards on the walls very useful for posters : twenty-five were as effective as a hundred. On the first occasion, I mounted the ladder, to teach the man employed to post the bills how to do it. There is an art in drawing up posters : unless the announcement is put into brief words which can be taken in at a mere glance, few will trouble to stop and read it. We used a great deal of printer's ink : it is most difficult to advertise anything thoroughly in a crowded parish. I have often wondered why evangelicals do not use the Press and the ink more than they do.

A man called on me, and said that he was in great mental trouble, and did not know where to turn for advice ; that he saw my name on an old placard, with the words ' Feed My Lambs ' ; and that he at once thought the man who cared for children might be able to help him. I told him to ' open his grief,' so that by the ministry of God's word I might be of use to him. He did so, and left bright and hopeful. Is not this too, in principle, such a case as is contemplated by those who framed the communion service ?

I made a custom of going out late on Saturday night for a stroll through the parish, to see how the land lay ; and it was not at all unusual to meet from ten to thirty persons—many of them men—with whom I shook hands, and dropped a precious seed, that it might grow. The difficulty of getting at men is so great ; with many I knew it was that or nothing. I found it paid.

It was a great pleasure to me to preach annually at the Anniversary Mission Service in Harding Street schoolroom : this year my heart was rejoiced by the attendance of two hundred and twenty-five poor persons. The service was conducted for nearly twenty-four years by one of my right-hand lay members ; in fact, until failing health compelled him to give it up.

I often bought lollypops in a court in the parish, and gave them to the little children around ; to their, and still more to their mothers' delight. ' Scatter seeds of kindness.' All the tradesmen—butcher, baker, grocer, tailor, etc.—with whom I dealt, either lived in the parish, or belonged to the congregation ; and I encouraged our people to follow my example, though I did not inculcate exclusive dealing.

If a young man set up in business I gave him an order if I could ; and I always paid at the time of purchase. In these ways I was, as it were, speaking a word for the Master.

If a father fail to show love for his children in many trifling ways, will he not run the risk of, in all probability, losing the love of those children ? Should not the relation of the shepherd to the lambs and sheep of his flock be similar ? Often have I cried to the Lord to keep me tender, bright, and cheerful ; for a sharp, morose, unsympathetic minister is a sad object to behold ; beside which he can have little real influence upon those committed to his care.

This year there was quite a special exodus from our parish, by reason of several streets of small houses having been recently built just outside the boundary : that so reduced our population that it numbered scarcely the four thousand required by the Church Pastoral Aid Society to secure its grant in aid for a curate. By the active help of the Bishop, however, our parochial borders on the north were considerably extended, adding to our charge some two thousand five hundred souls, and so raising the population to over six thousand. The hand of God was there.

The congregation now decided to provide an official residence for their pastor, in loving appreciation of his ministrations, and to celebrate the church's coming of age next year. That touched me deeply.

The vicar of All Saints' Church, Southport, the Rev. C. T. Porter, D.D., most kindly and generously affiliated our parish to his, for the sole object of assisting us financially, without guaranteeing any specific sum, or binding himself to any particular period. Moreover, a member of his congregation was good enough to send us three hundred volumes towards a library : we had long possessed a suitable room for such, but were without books for it.

There were one hundred and nineteen in the confirmation classes this year, but only sixty-seven were presented : their average ages were, men twenty-two years, women twenty-one years. It was a cause of regret and disappointment that in consequence of the sifting and testing nature of my teaching in the classes, towards the close so many came to the conclusion that they were not fit, and therefore ought not to be confirmed ; but I dared not, by pressing them, be the means of their making what might have been an unreal profession. On the other hand, what a source of joy to add sixty-seven to those already in Christ ! From time to time many of those who had drawn back came up again. Amongst the newly confirmed were seven converts from Romanism. Of those confirmed, four brothers were baptized together hypothetically on the previous evening, the youngest being seventeen years old ; their father had been baptized at the same font four years previously.

This year the Bishop preached in our church twice, and worshipped with us three times as one of the congregation. On Easter Day he and his family partook of the Lord's Supper after the morning service; he was with us seven times this year.

The Church Pastoral Aid Society made a grant of £50 for the Welsh curate.

The Lord Mayor of Liverpool, E. H. Cookson, Esq., attended our church in state on the annual Ragged School appeal day.

My main subject on Sunday mornings this year was Paul's Letter to the Ephesians.

A woman was shown into my study. On being seated she began to cry, and then, with a sigh of relief, exclaimed, ' Thank God I have got in; three times I had my hand on the bell, but my heart failed me. I have called to tell you what the Lord has done for me. I always loved my church in the South of England, where I was brought up. Against my will I had to come to Liverpool, to live with my son. I was told St. Nathaniel's was High Church; that would not suit me at all, so I did not go to it. In the Cemetery Chapel, Smithdown Road, I heard an address which went right down into my heart. I found out that the minister who gave it was the vicar of St. Nathaniel's; and I made up my mind that, whether High Church or Low Church, that was the minister for me. I have been attending for a short while, and have come to tell you all this. Now I see why God brought me to Liverpool against my will.' We knelt together, and gave God all the glory. Another trophy!

One day a policeman saluted me on the landing-stage. I shook hands with him, when he said, ' I have been wishing for an opportunity of speaking with you. Last New Year's Eve I was at the service in your church, and your salutation after the clock chimed twelve, " I wish you all a holy, happy New Year," struck me strangely, and made me think very seriously. As a Scotchman I was quite familiar with the salutation " A happy New Year," but I never before heard it put as a " holy,

happy New Year." I felt at once I was not holy, therefore how could I have such a New Year as you wished ?
I tried to get rid of the word " holy," feeling more and
more how unholy I was in God's sight. I tried also to
banish all thought about it, but I could not. Then,
remembering how I had been taught that Christ came
into the world to save sinners, I went as one to Him, got
pardon for my sins, and am happy.' We shook hands
as brothers in Christ, giving glory to God.

As I stood by a dying woman's bed, she said, ' I am
pleased to see you. I know you will comfort me. The
other day a young curate stood where you are now, and
his first inquiry was, " Have you received the Sacrament ? " I made no answer, and he repeated his
question. I then answered, " I have received Christ."
He left, and has not been again.'

In the *Liverpool Daily Courier* of December 7th was
the following :

' The good people of Windsor are about to mark their
appreciation of their vicar by providing a vicarage, of
which he would be the first occupant, feeling as they do
that he had made great sacrifices for them, ministering
to their needs undeterred by small-pox, vice, misery, or
dirt ; prompted by an ambition to serve them, though
it were by pulling them out of the fire.'

In a cellar there lived a poor but respectable widow,
a Romanist, whom I knew well, who used to maintain
herself by hawking, but was now no longer able to get
about. As I was passing one day, she called me in,
saying, ' I have something to tell you. God bless you
for the note you gave me to the Guardians. They
have made me an allowance. But what do you think
the relieving officer said when he visited me before the
grant was made ?—" Are you a Roman Catholic ? " I
said, " To be sure I am," for I could not deny my
religion. " Do you mean to tell me that if you are a
Roman Catholic, the Rev. Mr. Hobson would write for
you to the Guardians as he has done ? " I answered,

"Ah! sure you would not say that if you knew him."'

Although that poor, worthy creature never left the Romish Church, her ears were open to hear words pointing out the way of life ; and I believe that through Christ she reached the better land. We had many such cases. Oh, the abounding grace of God !

SUMMARY OF COLLECTIONS FOR 1889.

	£	s.	d.
Church Expenses - - - - - -	113	11	2
Poor Fund - - - - - -	6	6	3
Parochial Mission Fund - - -	124	18	4
General Repair Fund - - - -	40	10	5
Windsor Mission - - - - -	18	18	0
Foundry Lane Mission - - - -	17	7	6
Ragged Schools - - - - -	139	1	3
School's Treat - - - - - -	23	2	1
Vicarage Building Fund - - -	750	0	0
Welsh Church - - - - - -	112	4	4
Total Abstinence Society - - -	25	19	6½
Church Association - - - -	9	10	4
Church Missionary Society - - -	26	17	7
Church Pastoral Aid Society - -	42	6	0
Church Diocesan Trust - - - -	2	4	0
Zenana Mission - - - - -	9	0	0
Church of England Temperance Society -	2	13	0
Irish Church Missions - - - -	10	13	6
Scripture Readers Society - - -	28	9	3
Jews' Society - - - - - -	2	19	6
Hospital Sunday - - - - -	8	15	3
	£1,515	7	1½

' But who am I, and what is my people, that we should be able to offer so willingly after this sort ? For all things come of Thee, and of Thine own have we given Thee ' (1 Chron. xxix. 14).

This year the average number of communicants on the fourteen occasions of the Lord's Supper in the evening was two hundred and twenty-two. If there be one time more suitable than another for this ordinance, surely that time is the evening.   It was instituted in the evening ; therefore the quiet evening hour is most in accord with its institution ; and, happily, the English Church has no rubric against it.

1890.

Stumbling-block of Christian peoples' inconsistency—The parish's ' coming of age '—Demonstration in Sefton Park—' Darkest England ' —A ' Hallelujah wedding '—The Parochial system in theory and in practice—Foundry weekly service—A vicarage purchased—Another visit to the United States—Collision—Captain converted.

' The Scripture cannot be broken ' (John x. 35).

'THERE is nothing new under the sun.' Certain wise (?) men—higher critics—following in the wake of the Sadducees of old and others since, are trying to do—whether conscientiously or otherwise matters little—what the Great Teacher, the Son of God, says cannot be done.   But there are also men—quite as learned as, and more reliable than, these critics—who champion the immutability and absolute trustworthiness of Holy Scripture.   It goes without saying, that here the word ' Scripture ' refers to the Old Testament as received by the Jews in the days of our Lord.   That He received and upheld those sacred writings in their entirety, as the Word of God, and therefore binding on the conscience, who can doubt ?   If He is not to be followed as an infallible Teacher, the Socinians are right in holding that Christ was a sinner like other men ; which is too awful to contemplate, much less to believe. But in that case we had better become agnostics out and out.   This is a trial to both reason and faith ; but as I write, I remember those words of blessed assurance, ' The grass withereth, the flower fadeth, but the word of our God shall stand for ever.' The Scriptures hang together ; they ' cannot be broken.'

On the whole, this destructive teaching has not yet found its way down amongst the working classes, who happily still revere the whole Bible ; and they would not only revere it yet more, but would also take it as their standard, and endeavour to live up to it, and accept the salvation which God offers them in it, if professing Christians, especially those who preach and teach, clergy as well as laity, led less worldly, and more consistently Christlike lives.

I have sometimes wished the higher critics saw the rescuing, uplifting, ennobling results of having received into the heart, through the Scripture written by men inspired with the Holy Spirit, Him who is the Incarnate Word. I think their hands would tremble to touch the Ark of God.

The Son of God lived His earthly life by faith in His Father's covenant with Him, as revealed in Holy Scripture (Matt. xxvii. 43). Oh, that my life may be thus characterized. And He died in the faith of Psalm xvi. 9-11. Oh, that I may die in that faith too, in the same sure and certain hope of a blessed resurrection.

The Lord's Supper, at which our dear Bishop officiated, on the first Sunday evening of the New Year as usual, was largely attended, being the commencement of a sixteen days' special mission in the parish church.

The lapse of time has not greatly modified my former estimate of professed ' conversions ' resulting from special missions : it was something to know there were such. Perhaps where the mission told most was in the strength imparted to the spiritual life of the Lord's own people. The preacher gave us most liberally of his best ; and those who know him know what that is. It may be that the meagreness of the ingathering was owing to some fault on our part.

I have had some little personal experience in conducting missions myself ; and from all that I have both seen and heard, I am still of the opinion that the best mission is the all-the-year-round mission of constant uninterrupted preaching and teaching the Word of Life, in the pulpit, at the lectern, on the platform, in cottage readings, in the homes of the people, in the open-air, lovingly, persuasively, practically, impressively; and, to give the powerful influence of reality to it all, to live it out daily by God's grace in the sight of all, of those who are the Lord's, and of those who are not.

By the grace of God, we, as a church and parish, attained our majority this year. The event was marked in various ways. We secured special preachers at a course of services in church; wherein we truly and heartily thanked and blessed God for all the way by which He had led us, with its many mercies; for all the wondrous love displayed to us, and the rich blessings vouchsafed; for large numbers of dead souls quickened by the Holy Spirit, and given a place amongst God's children; for the many who had crossed the Jordan and entered the heavenly Canaan; for the bountiful supply of all our financial needs in carrying on the Master's work; for the deepening of spiritual life in our workers; and for the vast numbers who had flocked to share in the means of grace provided for them. Our cup of blessing was indeed full to overflowing.

We had an open-air demonstration in Sefton Park. It rained on both the preceding and the following days, but our day was fine and beautifully bright. The Bishop and the Lord Mayor drove through the park to the great platform at which I was officially called to preside; helpful speeches being delivered by the head of the diocese, and the head of the municipality, representing the Church and State, and by other speakers. The Press had kindly given notice of the novel and interesting event, and although a small charge was made for admission, over four thousand persons, of all classes, were present. The whole thing was carried out without a single hitch of any kind, and the day was one never to be forgotten by our dear people. Thank God!

Just at this time there was published General Booth's book, ' Darkest England ' ; from which it might be thought that the Church was entirely dead to the claims of the ' submerged tenth,' and that the Salvation Army's methods were alone able to empty the workhouses, asylums, and gaols. I failed to take that view. That the movement has done great good I thankfully admit : but has it touched even the fringe of the ' submerged tenth ' ? To my thinking, its net has many holes. The Salvation Army laboured in our parish on a Sunday morning for years, and I know of only one case in which real good resulted therefrom. There may, however, have been others : but thank God for even one.

On the walls appeared an immense placard announcing a ' Hallelujah Wedding ' in one of the Army barracks, on a Good Friday ; when two people, who, whilst living together in sin, had been reached by that organization, were brought before the audience and married as reported. Many of those present went away saying, ' See that, the Army is reaching a class which neither churches nor chapels can get hold of.' But is that so ? It is true we did not, for shame's sake, exhibit, or even speak of, such cases : but many of them in this parish were reached, and at the present time there is but one remaining.

In my opinion, there is no system equal in theory to the parochial system of the English Church, which is 'A fold for every sheep, and a shepherd for every fold.' What is needed to carry it out is that those shepherds be converted men : men of missionary spirit and zeal, who will give themselves, spirit, soul, and body, to ' rescue the perishing,' on strictly evangelical lines. Meantime, God bless all who are endeavouring to do so.

I have always held that the English Church, with its vast resources, should do all kinds of Christian philanthropic work. Let us pray for a great revival of true spirituality in all its members, specially in its ministers, that their cold apathy may be cast out, that the Holy Spirit may dwell in them, and work by them. Let us pray also that with this revival of those who are His ministers officially, He may be pleased to touch the hearts of the laity, who are just as much His ministers, only unofficially, and make them, godly men and women, willing to devote their lives to that true home mission work, that real labour of love, the seeking and saving the lost millions at home in their own land.

For several summers we had been endeavouring to get at those employed at the foundry in our parish, by holding on the premises a short service during the last half of the dinner-hour, once a week ; but as we were unable to accomplish that, the next best thing was to have it outside. Accordingly we met at the entrance gate, where, as the men sat down, or lolled about, for their smoke, we had a hymn, a prayer, another hymn, and a short address. It was working under great difficulties ; but it was that or nothing. And the men, though a rough, or at all events a very mixed lot, never raised any objection, or offered any opposition.

' In season, out of season.' ' My word shall not return unto Me void.'

This year saw the actual purchase of a suitable house as a vicarage. Though situated outside the parish—to which the Bishop had given his sanction—it was within ten minutes' walk of the church, and was sufficient for the requirements of a modest vicar of a modest church with a modest income.

The Lord never failed us in the matter of money : the effort in simple faith to raise a sum sufficient to purchase a vicarage was crowned with such success that it produced £160 more than the required amount—£835. One member collected over half of it.

This was my first experience of having a place which I could rightly call ' home,' all my ministerial years, for over a quarter of a century, having been lived in lodgings.

For my ordinary holiday this year I took a trip to the United States, via Boston. The steamer left on a Saturday, and the next morning, when off Wicklow Head, we ran into a dense fog. Suddenly we were all alarmed by a terrible shock as of a collision, and at once there was a call : ' All hands on deck ! ' Some of the passengers rushed up. I turned out of my berth and remained still. The thought filled my heart that I might soon see the Lord, and I thanked Him that all was well, that I was safe in Jesus. It transpired that a barque was about crashing into us amidship, but by promptitude in reversing the engines, she only collided with us, carrying away some of our bulwarks. The danger being over, our fears were allayed, and on the fog lifting we sped on our voyage as usual. Being Sunday, there was service on board, which the captain asked me to conduct. In the address, on ' The Precious Blood of Christ,' there was a message from the Lord to the heart of the captain, which he, thank God, through grace received : in the evening, to the surprise of the officers, he was with us, on the deck, singing hymns. He sent me word that, as he had heard I was very weary, I might have one of his two state-cabins. How ' mindful ' the Lord has ever been of His servant !

I had a most delightful companion on board, a truly Christian man. He was a professor at Harvard University, and, though descended, in the eighth generation, from one of the Pilgrim Fathers, had become a member of the English Church in Boston. On our arrival there he showed me no little kindness.

The voyages out and home, and the restful little visit to my dear sister and her family, in Fulton, revived me much.

The average attendance at the fourteen evening communions this year was two hundred and thirty-six.

Amount raised, one thousand one hundred and forty-three pounds.

1891.

The parochial minister's duty—'God forsaken and demoralized '—
Church tower replaces spire—Individual influence in money-raising—
Spiritualists—Attendances at church and chapel—'My friend, give up
considering '—Congregational trouble—The pastor closely watched
and correctly criticised—Good Friday children's service—Injudicious
attentions.

'As soon as Zion travailed, she brought forth her children ' (Isa.
lxvi. 8).

A LL true revival is of God, who, having filled His
own people to overflowing, through them begets
anew in Christ Jesus, by His Spirit. To travail
for souls is of God. It is a part of the true minister's
and evangelist's work which is not seen of men, being
that which, in the privacy of God's presence, engages
the mind and the heart.

It is to hope, long, yearn, watch, wait, pray, agonize
for, and to expect, the ' new birth ' of souls through
the Word : for ' of His own will begat He us with the
Word of Truth.'

In this, God is sovereign ; He works as, and by whom,
and when, and where, He pleases.

That is a very different thing from what is called
' Catholic revival,' which is a stir about rites and
ceremonies enshrining deadly error.

It is something more, too, than merely filling a church,
even though the Gospel is preached. This ' new birth '
is followed by ' conversion,' a new course of life : ' Old
things are passed away ; behold all things have become
new.' ' By their fruits ye shall know them.' These
quotations also entirely disprove the statement that this
new life is given *per se* in baptism.

From Rom. vi. 23 we see that this life is eternal : it
is for this that the real man of God travaileth.

There are many kinds of life, such as social, official, local, with all which the parochial minister should be in sympathy so far as he can consistently be. But the spiritual life of others should be his great and chief concern : for that it is his duty and privilege to travail. Having experienced the Holy Spirit's ' cure ' of his own soul, he should strive for the spiritual in those of whose souls he by solemn oath undertook ' the cure ' at his induction to a benefice.

But those who make travail for souls their first and chief object, are often charged with Congregationalism, individualism, and other ' isms,' and are looked down upon, and regarded with pity bordering on contempt : to many this is disconcerting and discouraging.

In all large cities and towns there is a great tendency on the part of the clergy to busy themselves with matters that, though good in principle, cannot compare in importance with the immortal interests of the souls committed to their care. I am of opinion that men with ' cures ' of even a thousand souls should refuse to undertake well-nigh any external work, lest it should trench upon their time, to the neglect of parochial duties. From long experience, I hold that nothing can take the place of constant and almost never-ending house-to-house visitation. The Saviour's ' Wist ye not that I must be about My Father's business ? ' and Paul's ' This one thing I do,' should be the great examples to follow, for God's glory, the welfare of souls, and one's own spiritual benefit.

One of the priests belonging to a Romish chapel near to us spoke publicly of our parish as ' God-forsaken and demoralized.' I felt sure few Romanists in the parish, or even in the city, would agree with that remark. Anyhow, some members of our church wrote spirited replies, which appeared in one of the Liverpool dailies : they were very pleasant reading.

We quite understood the priests' annoyance and anger at seeing so many of their people in our parish turn their backs upon them, by turning their faces to Jesus.

I was asked what proportion of our confirmees continue communicants, and I was able to answer a large proportion of those who remain in the parish or neighbourhood. And, too, that the means by which they have been retained are threefold, viz. : getting them to continue in, or become members of, adult Bible-classes, held in the church ; giving them some work to do for the church or parish ; and carefully and lovingly shepherding them. Of course, the migratory character of our people told against us all round, and, therefore, rendered the adoption of those means all the more necessary.

The Corporation gave our wardens notice that the church spire was unsafe, which was a great relief to us. For it had been, from its erection, an offence in the eyes of almost everyone, although designed by the church architect, being generally termed ' the extinguisher ' ; and we were now provided with an opportunity of doing away with the eyesore.

A conference which was held decided on its removal, and the raising of the tower to its present handsome proportions. The cost, £460, was soon obtained, and the work was at once done and paid for. This was for the glory of God and the adornment of His sanctuary : a monument of prayer, love, and self-denial, in the midst of poor surroundings.

> ' These temples of Thy grace,
>   How beautiful they stand !
> The honours of our native place,
>   The bulwarks of our land.'

I took Mark's Gospel for exposition on Sunday mornings during this year.

The following incident will show what one individual can do in raising money :

A seamstress, hearing me plead for our ragged schools, became filled with zeal for the poor children. She interested first the servants of the house in which she was working, then the mistress, and then the master. The latter sent me a cheque for £15, and from that family there had been received, at the time of my resignation, no less than £190.

One of our helpers, a working man, who came into contact with many merchants, so interested one of them, that he sent through him a message to me promising £10 a year for the parish, because I ' not only worked, but made others work also ' ! From that generous man I received, up to my resignation, cheques amounting in all to £170.

Is it any wonder that we blessed the Lord ?

A member of the mother church, a working man, who actually raised £40 for the building of St. Nathaniel's, became a spiritualist, deserted his lawful Christian wife, and disappeared, with another female. Where they went no one has ever found out. A sad case indeed.

One of our teachers also became a spiritualist, but by God's blessing on frequent visitation, she was rescued, to our great joy, and specially to that of her Christian mother. However, we had not many professors of that delusion in our midst.

This year a branch of the National Protestant League was formed, with the object of binding together the working classes for resistance to the designs of those who are leagued together to Romanize the Protestant Church of England.

The parochial annual report for this year contained the following : ' From the second decennial census of persons present in places of worship on a particular Sunday morning and evening, taken by the *Liverpool Daily Post*, it was found that out of four hundred and ten places of worship of all denominations, in Liverpool, St. Nathaniel's had in the evening the fifth largest number, viz., in church, 982 ; and in mission-rooms, 514 ; total, 1,496.'

This is specially encouraging, when it is taken into consideration that since St. Nathaniel's was consecrated, no less than eleven places of worship have been opened around it.

I know mere numbers are not a sure sign of real success ; but is a small attendance in a church, mission-hall, or Bible-class, an evidence of God's approval ?

Did our blessed Lord rebuke the multitudes when they flocked to hear Him ?

I have always been more encouraged by ministering to large congregations than by preaching to only half-filled seats.

Our first people's warden was always ready to excuse, or account for, a small attendance. It was ' Well, the congregation was very good to-day, considering the wet '; or ' Well, the congregation was not so bad to-day considering the heat.' This he repeated so constantly— I suppose to encourage me—that at last I said to him ' My dear friend, give up considering. We must get the people ; therefore, let us ask that God will enable us so to preach His word, and to make the services so interesting, that the people shall feel compelled to come.'

A helper was one day speaking about the number of communicants at St. Nathaniel's to a clergyman, who, in a doubtful manner which rather surprised his inform-ant, asked ' How many of them are born again ? ' The other replied, ' Our vicar, at all events, makes it clear that the Lord's Supper is the children's bread ; and that none should partake thereof who have not passed from death unto life : he cannot read the com-municants' hearts.'

I happened to know that the said dear clergyman had very few communicants ; and even about them the same question might be asked.

It is sad to notice the strange ideas which get a grip on the conscience of even some really good men, and so paralyze their influence for good.

The annual report also had : ' While we long to know of a greater number of spiritual sons and daughters born into the family of God, and of a higher and holier standard of attainment to the likeness of Christ, we are not still without such tokens of the Holy Spirit's life-giving and sanctifying power in our midst. This is the

only work that will stand, for the fire shall try every
man's work of what sort it is. Let us remember the
promise, " If any man's work abide, he shall receive
a reward." At the same time let us also remember that
the work of saving grace cannot be counted by heads,
nor measured by tape, for " The kingdom of God cometh
not with observation." '

At this time I was again feeling the strain of the work
very much. I found myself again asking, ' Dear Lord,
will it be necessary to go on for ever like this ? ' The
temptation to draw in was very strong, but I thought
of the old saw, ' It is better to wear out than to rust
out.' It is one thing to begin in the gutter, it is another
thing to remain there.

I always avoided asking others to do work which I
was not prepared to do myself. It was for me to lead
if others were to follow. To say ' Come ' is always
more encouraging than to say ' Go.' And few would
work in the gutters if the vicar himself kept clear of
them. But I did really feel that neither mind nor body
could continue working at present pressure for long.

At the end of the year I was called upon to endure a
great trial in the work, which was in no way due to or
caused by myself ; under which I was greatly sustained
by having the full sympathy of the Bishop. I shall
make no further reference to the unhappy circumstance,
beyond saying that if I had not, in the providence of
God been so strong in the affections of my dear people
as to enable me to steer the vessel of the church through
the stormy waters of that troublous time, it must have
been totally wrecked. The hand of God was there.

The privilege of preaching the pure Gospel is the
greatest pleasure of the true pastor ; though its constant
exercise for many years before a congregation consisting
in large measure of those who have long been attending
the same church demands anxious thought, thorough
preparation, and deep devotion ; entailing upon him, too,
an ever increasing strain, physical, mental, and spiritual ;
but I am bound to say the experience of many years has
convinced me that even more trying to the pastor is

having sometimes to meet and deal with the idiosyncrasies and imperfections of his colleagues, of his dear fellow-workers, and, though to a lesser degree, of his congregation, even where love is known to exist on both sides.

Of course the pastor is no more infallible than are his people : and if he be a truly converted man, he feels this so keenly, that he almost trembles lest, by any error in judgment, his influence, which should be, and may be, all-powerful for good amongst his people, becomes impaired. He cannot do what others may. For him in particular, though it may be that ' all things are lawful,' it is certain that ' all things are not expedient.'

For no man is more closely read, or more carefully weighed, than he. His private and his public life are equally well known : his littlenesses in the pulpit and out of it are alike made matter for comment and judgment.

Many good men, not realising this, are surprised at finding after only a few years a falling off in their churches, and they assign all sorts of reasons but, perhaps, the real one, which not unlikely is the continued waning of their influence upon the people personally. That is one of the arguments in favour of ministers of the Church being moved after a certain period, say of ten years or so, in one place.

For many years we in St. Nathaniel's were obsolutely as one family ; though towards the end of my vicariate there appeared to be a tendency towards parties in the church : against which I had always stedfastly set my face, perhaps more by example even than by precept. A congregation as such ought to be one ; and it is a cruel wrong to the cause of God for either vicar or curate to create a party in it.

To have our own private circles is another thing. Out of His many disciples the Saviour chose twelve ; of that number three were taken by Him into closer relationship ; whilst of those, only one lay on His bosom.

It had now for years been our custom on Good Friday afternoon to have a gathering of children in the church and Windsor mission hall. On some occasions they numbered a thousand ; for we did not mind who or what they were provided they lived in the parish ; and we gave to each a bun on leaving. This won golden opinions for the church amongst the poor.

By diligent visiting, and lifting up of the Saviour in faith, with earnest prayer, a wife, and mother, died in the Lord, and her husband was at the same time much impressed. He was a powerfully built man, and used to earn from £8 to £10 a week at piece work in the foundry. He became a total abstainer, and kept his pledge ; there were also certain important improvements in his character.

He had a difficulty about attending church, being unable to follow the service in the Prayer-Book. I offered to get him over that, but he did not accept the proposal. He took sittings for his children, and himself attended occasionally. One Sunday evening, in the early part of the service, a man offered him a Prayer-Book, to which he bowed a refusal. Another man did the same thing, and with the same result. A third offer was made, when the poor fellow felt so uncomfortable, that the perspiration ran down his face. He never entered the church again. Our liturgy, admirable though it be, is not very suitable for non-church goers, or for the masses generally.

This man, however, went on well ; he became a reformed person and was thoughtful about things which made for his soul's salvation. I have good hope of his reaching the Father's home. He was devoted to me, and at the works collected money for our ragged schools. When we wanted another safe for the church, he offered, if we would purchase the material from his employer, to make it, charging nothing for his labour. I accepted his generous offer, and he made the safe for us, presenting it in due course.

There are no two cases exactly alike. Some obtain

the assurance of salvation at once ; to others it comes by degrees.

Amount raised, one thousand three hundred and eighty pounds.

1892.

Another breakdown—Visit to the East—Joppa and ' one Simon, a tanner '—Sharon's Rose—Jerusalem—A sprained ankle—Bethlehem— Gethsemane—Calvary—Golgotha—Joseph's tomb—Olivet—Bethany —Jericho—The 'little duckses '—Dead Sea—Jordan—Apples of Sodom —Pyramids—Cairo—Sermons on Palestine—Pleasant Saturday Evening Brotherhood—Harding Street—' Babsy — Training Protestant Reformation Society agents.

' The Lord will not forsake His people for His great name's sake ; because it hath pleased the Lord to make you His people ' (1 Sam. xii. 22).

HOW reassuring to Israel must have been these words addressed to them when under a cloud. God had made them His people by Divine right of His Sovereign pleasure, and He willed that they should remain so. And the words should be equally reassuring to the true members of His elect Church now, as fore-shadowed in Romans viii. 28-39.

In the early part of this year the dear Lord permitted me to break down sadly. Indeed, it was even rumoured that I was dead ; but God ordained otherwise, and I bless Him for it. Not that I had any fear of dying, for I possessed the blessed assurance that all was right. Nor had I any great wish to live. My happy feeling was that I could safely leave the issue to that Lord, ' whose I am, and whom I serve.' On becoming convalescent, and it being winter, I was ordered away to the East, for warmth ; to Egypt and Palestine.

The Bishop approved of my choice, and oh, what a prayer he offered for me, when I went to take leave of him ! I left London on March 1st, in a P. and O. steamer for Alexandria, and on arrival there I decided to start the following morning for Jaffa. Egypt and Palestine teach different lessons : the former, antiquity ; the latter, devotion.

Palestine, O Palestine ! the land of the prophets, the land of the Apostles, the land of Jesus.

> ' Those holy fields,
> Over whose acres walked those blessed feet
> Which, eighteen hundred years ago, were nailed,
> For our redemption, to the bitter cross.'

The country in the south, and the Holy City, are woefully desolate : in fact Southern Palestine is like a land of stones, with a funeral pile raised on it, the soil having, in parts, actually perished. It is treeless, barren, wild, and depressing. Once the ' land flowing with milk and honey,' it is now under the curse ; though there certainly are signs of returning vitality. But its hills, valleys, plains, and rivers, nay, even its very stones, spoke to me with an eloquence which was unique. Memory recalled, and imagination reproduced, scene after scene of the inspired narrative, making God and His Christ more real than ever, and the Bible as it were almost a new book to me. I landed at Jáffa and set foot on the Holy Land, with a feeling of solemnity. I visited the house of ' one Simon a tanner,' which is situated on the very margin of the sea, the odours of a tannery being still actually in evidence. As I went up on the roof I enjoyed quiet communion with that God who there made known to Peter His gracious Will as to the calling in of us Gentiles. Outside the village there are the famous orange groves, covering four hundred acres.

As we crossed the plain of Sharon on our way to the Holy City, I noticed small groups of animals, which my

dragoman told me were foxes : they were so tame, that
not until we threw stones at them did they run from
us. I remembered that the plain of Sharon was formerly
the land of the Philistines, where Samson caught the
three hundred foxes : they are there is abundance at
this day.

It was dark before we reached Ramleh, where the
Crusaders built strong fortifications—the remains of
which still stand—to command the approach to Jerusalem. I put up at the little inn, and, getting up the
next morning at four, when the sun shone gloriously,
the first objects I saw were nine lepers asking for
' backshish.'

I noticed on the greensward of the plain a flower of a
deep blue, which was pointed out to me as the rose of
Sharon, recalling the Saviour's words, ' I am the Rose
of Sharon,' and filling my heart with gratitude to Him
for showing by that figure how anyone may appropriate
salvation by faith, just as anyone may pluck and
possess the flower.

I gathered enough to wear in my hat and my button-
holes, and to fill my hands, asking the Saviour that in
like manner my heart might be filled by Him, and that
I might wear Him before men, to His praise and glory.

Several places of interest were pointed out on the way
to Jerusalem, specially the valley of Elah, where
David slew Goliath. The brook flowing through it was
dry, so I walked along its bed, gathering some of the
smooth stones, and I asked the Lord for strength and
skill so to sling the stone of Gospel truth, as to slay
sin, in all its giant forms, and triumph over Satan for
God. O, for power thus to reach the hearts of the
Lord's enemies ! The shepherds in those parts are
said to be able, with a sling and stone, to kill a bird
flying.

I reached Jerusalem on a Saturday evening, and felt
unworthy to enter the Holy City. Once inside, it was
almost too much for me to find myself actually there,
and in my room I wept for joy.

The next day, Sunday, I set out for Christ Church,

Mount Zion, and on my way I sprained one of my ankles ; but I went on, though in pain, enjoyed the plain, hearty service, and partook of the Lord's Supper, which, as I realized how near was the spot where it was instituted, was doubly blessed to me. On returning to the hotel, I had to call in a doctor, who applied leeches ; my dragoman, seeing the blood, looked at me, and said, in a tone of great significance : ' Sir, you have shed blood in Jerusalem.'

I visited all the principal places, such as the Jewish Christian schools and hospital, the Church Missionary Society's church and schools, the American House, the Tower of David, the pools of Hezekiah, Bethesda, and Siloam, the mosque of Omar, the Jews' Wailing-place, the tombs of the kings, the so-called Holy Sepulchre. There were then more Jews in Jerusalem than at any time since Titus destroyed the city, A.D. 70. The traditional holy sepulchre is in the custody of Latins, Greeks, Copts, Syrians, and Armenians ; and the Pasha of Jerusalem, a Mohammedan, finds it necessary to have a hundred soldiers on duty in the church every Sunday to keep order ; so that the custodians and their partisans can scarcely be considered a happy family.

My first visit outside Jerusalem was to Bethlehem. At the first glimpse of it I went flat down on the ground. On regaining control over my feelings, I was moved to cry out : ' O God, was it in yonder village, on the slope of that rising ground, that Thy Son, my Saviour, as man, drew his first breath ? Not in Rome, nor Athens, nor Corinth, nor even in Jerusalem, but up there in that hill village of Judea. O my God, Thy ways are so unlike man's ways. I cannot understand, but I see it was so, and that is enough.' All this greatly puzzled my dragoman, an intelligent native Christian, recommended by ' Cook.'

Bethlehem is a poor village : its inhabitants, especially the women, are the best-looking in Palestine. The church of the Nativity is said to cover the khan in the manger of which our Saviour was born. It has a very plain exterior : inside there are two aisles and a nave, with idolatrous altars. Steps lead down to a candelabra-lighted compartment, on the floor of which is a star, marking the supposed spot on which the birth took place. The inner ceiling, reconstructed by the Crusaders, is of English oak. The plains of Bethlehem are well covered with grass. I stretched myself at full length thereon, and, closing my eyes, I gave myself up to realization of the revelation given there nineteen centuries ago. I seemed almost able to hear the very tones of the heavenly harmonies, and my soul was fully attuned thereto. In the distance I saw Hebron, with its huge mosque, which actually covers the Cave of Machpelah. This is said to be the oldest city in the world.

And then Gethsemane! The Garden of the Agony! The old gnarled olive-trees there may have sprung from the very roots of those under which our Saviour sat, and taught, and prayed, and agonized; but they cannot be the very ones, as the monks in possession say; all the trees surrounding Jerusalem having been cut down when Titus besieged the city. I contrasted the overflowings of my heart, salt tear-drops, with the outpourings of my Saviour's agony, sweating blood-drops.

The fraudulent tradition that the church of the holy sepulchre within the city covers the Calvary where our Saviour was crucified has been exposed. The Bible itself refutes it, by this definite statement: ' For the place where Jesus was crucified was nigh to the city ' (John xix. 20). The real Calvary, the skull-place, so called because of its skull-shape, is outside the walls; a steep, rocky mound, about fifty feet high, covering four acres, with a Mohammedan cemetery on one part of it. There is a hewn sepulchre therein, that may possibly be Joseph's new tomb. The angular piece of ground controlling the approach to the sepulchre has recently been purchased by British Protestants, and I had the privilege of being permitted to contribute to the cost. Was it a dream that the possession by English Christians of this place of solemn interest, coupled with the fact of the ceiling in the church of the Nativity being of English oak, is but the initial step towards our dear country assuming, and exercising the duties of, a protectorate over the whole of that land ?

As I ascended the mound from the rear—the Golgotha —there came over me a deep feeling of solemnity at the sacred surroundings, and of trembling at the awful associations of the place. Then I, as it were, became entranced, and, feeling as if I could not come down from that holy mount to earthly things, I committed myself more definitely than ever to the dear Lord, and in my desire to be with Him, asked if it were His Divine will to take me to Himself.

After much hesitation, as if I hardly dare do so, I entered the sepulchre. It is about twelve feet long, nine feet high, and seven feet wide, cut in solid rock, with one raised platform, having a niche for the head. Neither tongue nor pen could describe my emotions as the events of the burial and resurrection passed before me. I exclaimed : ' O my Saviour, was it there Thy sacrificed body lay ? And didst Thou thence rise from death for me ? O Lord, I am wholly Thine for ever ! '

Later on, my doctor, learning that I had not yet been to Bethany, offered me the loan of his ass, which he said was the finest in Jerusalem. I rode on it, accompanied by his servant, round the spur of Mount Olivet, then to Bethphage, and back to Bethany. As I realized that it was from Bethphage the Saviour rode, up through Bethany, on to Olivet, down and up into Jerusalem, and that I was riding along these very bridle-paths, I felt as if my soul would melt away. On reaching the point where probably Jesus beheld the city, and wept over it, tears ran down my cheeks, and I cried : ' Oh that I could not only love the lost, but weep over them, too ! ' For the minister of Christ has a special need of such feelings towards perishing souls.

Going down from Jerusalem to Jericho we came to the reputed ' Samaritans Inn,' where we had refreshments, and further on my dragoman, directing me to look down a very steep ravine, said ' See, it was down there the prophet Elijah was hid when he drank of the brook Cherith, and the—' here he paused, evidently for a word—' and the oh yes, I have it, where he was fed by the little duckses ! ' Seeing me smile, he inquired why ? ' You mean the ravens.' ' Yes, that is the word, excuse me.'

On arriving at Jericho I was very tired, and went to bed early, but my sleep was thrice disturbed by what I thought must be barkings from a kennel. Next morning I expressed to the hotel proprietor my surprise at his having a kennel there, mentioning my experiences during the night. ' Oh, what you heard was not the barking of dogs, but the howling of hyenas and jackals from the hills of Judea. I thought of our Blessed Saviour during His temptation, when, as Mark i. 13 says, He ' was with the wild beasts.' How did he escape ? Did they feel His power ? Did they lie down at His feet ?

I visited the Dead Sea, with its waters—containing many chemical properties—so clear to look at, so horrid to taste, so buoyant that none can dive in them, so deadly that nothing can live in them. I, however, saw birds flying over it.

I rode to that part of the Jordan where the Israelites must have crossed, and then to the reputed place of Jesus' baptism, the Scripture records of both events coming to my memory with a vividness which enabled me in fancy to behold each, but especially the latter. Though so very insignificant in itself, no other river in the world possesses for all true Christians such hallowed and awe-inspiring associations as the Jordan. But it is deplorable to behold its plains, once well watered and fertile, now without vegetation, destitute even of grass : and Jericho, once the city of palm-trees, now without even the trace of one. Elisha's fountain is still there, the stream flowing therefrom nourishing on either bank, as does the Jordan, a narrow strip of vegetation. Near by, I gathered ' apples of Sodom,' which, though looking rosy and beautiful, on being pressed, gave forth nothing but dust. The district is practically uninhabited, there being, beside a convent, only a few fellaheen who live, or rather exist, in abject poverty. Is there not a cause? Is it not God's response to that awful ejaculation, ' His blood be on us, and on our children ' ?

In consequence of not being strong enough to journey through mid and North Palestine, I spent three weeks in Jerusalem, which enabled me to visit thoroughly the various sacred places there and in South Palestine, without distraction, and at leisure.

Now that I have been to the Holy Land I would not have missed it on any account. Oh, how kind and good my Heavenly Father has been to His poor servant.

Turning my steps homeward, on the return journey, I took Egypt, staying for ten days in Alexandria and Cairo. I happened to be in the latter city when the Khedive was proclaimed. On that occasion the concourse of people was large, and the Oriental costumes were a marvel. I visited the Great Pyramid, the Sphinx, the Sakkara pyramids, and the tombs of the sacred bulls covered with hieroglyphics. Having been that day under a very hot sun, I was seized in the evening, at the hotel, with an attack which, the doctor told me, would have developed into cholera if nature had not righted itself. Truly, ' the very hairs of your head are all numbered.'

The head waiter sat up with me. Opening my eyes during the night, I saw him reading a book, and was astonished to find it was the New Testament in English. To my inquiry ' Where did you get it ? ' he answered, ' From Dr. H——, a missionary in Old Cairo.' ' What do you think of him ? ' ' Why, he would not tell a lie for the world.' ' Why do you make so much of that ? ' ' Because no one can believe a word people say in this country.' I found he had attended a Church Missionary Society's mission school in Old Cairo, and that on the death of his mother, a Mohammedan, he intended to confess Christ in baptism. Anyhow, there he was, at dead of night, reading God's Word. That cheered and comforted me in my weakness. How true is Ecclesiastes xi. 1.

I afterwards visited the Boulac Museum ; the site of Heliopolis, where probably Moses was educated ; and the reputed spot where Pharaoh's daughter found him.

I was intensely delighted with Miss Whately's mission school in Cairo, consisting of over four hundred scholars, most of whom were Mohammedans. On examining an elder class I found they knew a great deal about the facts and saving truths of the New Testament.

In God's kind providence I returned in safety to my dear people, refreshed and strengthened ; deeply indebted, too, to the Bishop, and to twenty-seven of my clerical brethren, who occupied the pulpit in my absence. I was enabled to give in church, on seventeen consecutive Sunday evenings, to overflowing congregations, descriptive discourses on my visit to Palestine ; using them as so many pegs on which to hang and exhibit the blessed Gospel of God's free and sovereign grace. Thus my illness, brought about mainly by the special strain of many months' great anxiety, and severe trial, costing me much suffering, exertion, and expense, was made the means of furthering God's cause in the parish.

I had long been anything but satisfied with the efforts made to bind working men together, apart from the tontine, the Young Men's Society, the Orange Lodge, or the National Protestant League ; nor could I find anyone both willing and competent to take up that work as it had shaped itself in my own mind. My first idea was a Pleasant Sunday Afternoon in the church ; but that I found would interfere with twenty-two adult Bible-classes meeting there at three o'clock. I am, however, fully persuaded that it would have been the best realization of what was in my mind.

After much thought, I inaugurated a ' Pleasant Saturday Evening,' in the Mission Hall, which left more freedom than on the Lord's Day. The order of procedure was the Lord's Prayer, by a member, Sankey's hymns, short addresses on the Gospel, temperance, biography, history, with a large choir and orchestra to render good music, anthems, part-songs, etc. Prizes were given, and a voluntary benevolent society was attached, to help sick members. It was considered that if a working man made himself nice, and came to this meeting, he was not likely to tumble into a public-house, even though his wages were in his pocket.

This proved to be the best movement ever made in the parish to get men together. As I write, ten years after its start, numerous incidents could be adduced showing the good results of which it was the cause. I left it in full swing, though scarcely so strong as a short while ago, owing to my failing strength.

A herbalist in the parish said, ' Since the formation of the Pleasant Saturday Evening Brotherhood, I find men's throats are not so dry on a Sunday morning as they used to be.'

A young Romanist left that soul-destroying system through it ; Sankey's hymns were the immediate cause.

We thought of having a cocoa-room and a labour bureau ; but there were difficulties in the way of both. The cocoa-room would have been a boon, but no person competent to manage it could be found amongst our voluntary helpers, and for me to undertake additional work was quite out of the question. The labour bureau, too, would have been an excellent thing, but the conditions necessary for its efficient management were still less easy to fulfil. In addition to that, we always shrank from starting anything fresh, without feeling that it had a fair prospect of succeeding. To that I partly attribute the well-known fact that hardly anything we took in hand failed.

We also thankfully availed ourselves of any well-established emigration scheme, of the *Indefatigable* training-ship, of the Blue-Coat School, and of the various orphanages for our poor lads and girls, by means of which many of them were given a good start in life, and have got on well.

Whilst not neglecting to help on the social side, we

made the spiritual side our chief concern, being convinced that to reform from within is the truest and surest ; is, in fact, the only real reformation.

After many previous efforts, we this year succeeded in getting the Corporation to demolish one side of Harding Street. It was an awful rookery, unfit for human habitation ; for three months in the year no ray of sunshine ever entered its courts. On the site small, neat cottages were built by the Corporation.

It is impossible for men, women, and children, fathers, mothers, and grown-up sons and daughters, to live, nay, rather let me say to herd, together in such vile places, without all sense of decency being destroyed, and all feeling of self-respect blunted ; even though there may happen to be no actual immorality practised in its most repulsive form : so that body and soul alike suffer, are alike exposed to fatal results.

About this time the Lord touched with His saving power the heart of a man in whose house my worthy curate had been holding cottage readings. Though a respectable man, he had not been to a place of worship for fifteen years. He professed the new birth, and came to church and to the Lord's Table ; the reality of his new life being manifested in his brightness, humility, and deep earnestness as a worker for the Lord. I found that his feelings, opinions, and new life were shared by his wife, whom I knew as having formerly been in our Sunday-school, and concerning whom the following circumstance had happened at that time. Missing her and an older sister from school, I called to know the cause of their absence, and found that some female connected with a Ritualistic Sunday-school had induced them to attend it, by giving them each a hat. Taking the younger one, known as ' Babsy,' on my knee, I asked her to show me her hat. On seeing it I said, ' It is not a new one, is it ? ' The sisters looked a little abashed. I then said, ' My dear children, won't you come back to your own parish Sunday-school ? Your teacher will be so glad to see you.' They hesitated. So I went on : ' Now come with me to a shop, and you shall each choose a really new hat, with pretty ribbons, and you will look so nice at your own school next Sunday.' That secured them, to the great pleasure and amusementof their mother, who had heard all ; they never left the school until their parents left the parish. Therefore, it gave me intense delight now, after many years, to see ' Babsy ' with her husband, and, in due time, three of their children, at the Lord's Table.

This year there was again great cause for gratitude to the Lord on account of the confirmation candidates affording such evidence of the Holy Spirit's saving and sanctifying power in their hearts. Oh, these blessed confirmation classes !

At this time I undertook for the Protestant Reformation Society the training of their agents in the Bible and the Romish controversy, which extended over some years. It is quite as necessary to train men as missionaries to Romanists as it is to train them for missionary work amongst the heathen or amongst the Jews.

I felt it not only a good work, but an honour, inasmuch as I was thereby succeeding my former vicar, dear Dr. Blakeney, who had for many years assisted the Protestant Reformation Society in that way.

The amount raised this year was one thousand one hundred and eighty-one pounds. Thank God !

1893.

Twenty-fifth year of ministry—Church's Silver Wedding—Gift of eight bells for tower—' At Homes ' for communicants and friends—Sale of work—Church clock given by extra-parochial friends—Set of robes—£43,000 raised in a quarter of a century—The Pope's audacity—Two sermons about it—Romish priest's call concerning them—Controversy —Visitor's belief shaken—Protestant treatment of converted priests —*Porcupine's* tribute—Defective Sunday-school teaching—Mission Hall congregations—An afflicted man's prayer—Philanthropy of Spirituality ?—A vicar's mistake—Visit to Ireland—Hacketstown Church—Christian itinerant hawker—Boots and Missionaries—Children's contribution to Church Pastoral Aid Society.

' Ye are complete in Him ' (Col. ii. 10).

THIS blessed fact was one of the great fundamental truths taught and realized in St. Nathaniel's from the very commencement. For, as there was complete alienation from God's favour, in Adam, by his fall (Rom. v. 12), so there is complete restoration in Christ, by the Father's love (1 Cor. i. 30), by the new creation (2 Cor. v. 17), by living, loving faith (Ephes. iii. 17), by fruitfulness in good works (Ephes. ii. 10), by power in prayer (John xv. 7), by right judgment (Phil. iii. 7), by dwelling hereafter eternally with Him (John xvii. 24).

This precious truth roots up all erroneous teaching of human merit and self-righteousness ; it defines the present standing of all God's people, whether they realize it or not. And they ought to do so ; for only by realizing its possession can they be so really happy as to ' rejoice in the Lord alway ' ; or find themselves able to do, from the highest motive, great things for Him, who delights in, and desires, their willing, loving, joyous service.

We passed through the joyous season of Christmas in our usual happy way, endeavouring to cheer the homes of the poor, and striving to repeat, in spirit as well as in word, both in church and all round, the angels' song on Bethlehem's plains. We prayed, and preached, and sang the old year out and the new year in ; we had our special week of prayer ; and the Bishop officiated at the Lord's Table on the first Sunday evening. Having completed my twenty-fifth year as minister in Windsor, we celebrated it as the silver wedding of the church.

It was our custom to lay hold of, and utilize, any circumstance connected with the work, in order to promote the good cause of God's truth amongst us.

We therefore marked this interesting occasion as follows :

By the congregation accepting from me, as a thank-offering, a peal of eight -tubular bells for the church tower.

By ' At Homes ' to the communicants and their friends, amongst them being the Bishop, whose arrival was greeted by the ringing of the bells for the first time.

By a Sale of Work to raise funds for putting up a suitable fence round the church, asphalting the church-yard, and renovating the interior of the church ; which proved so successful that it realized the handsome net sum of £329.

By placing in the church tower an excellent clock, costing £150, paid for by kind friends outside the parish, our good Bishop contributing £50.

By the congregation presenting me with a set of rich Irish poplin robes, including the time-honoured gown, which I consider the legal preaching vestment.

This was, therefore, a year of joy to the workers and myself : it was also a year of thankfulness, by reason of our remembering all that the Lord had done for us in the past. The cause of true religion in the parish was never stronger, nor in a more healthy condition, than now, at the end of twenty-five years, despite the inevitable comings and goings, approvals and fault-findings, weaknesses and infirmities—perhaps even sins —with which we have to contend in our present mixed condition.

No less than £43,000 had been raised : which was indeed wonderful. We had, including those in our Welsh mission church, *more than a thousand communicants, of whom over two hundred were church workers.* Neither a known infidel nor a house of ill fame was now to be found in the parish. The moral tone of the place had therefore greatly improved ; the sick-list had fallen to one-fourth ; and if only the drink shops—those traps for men, women, and children— were put down, Windsor would have been in a measure a little paradise.

I need hardly state that the one and only cause of such a result after a quarter of a century's labour was our having made known, in the pulpit and in the mission-rooms, from house to house and in the open-air, the simple story of the pure Gospel of God's grace, through faith only, in language ' understanded of the people,' and in having endeavoured to live that Gospel in their midst.

Could anything therefore be more fittingly emblematical of the Lord's trophies in the parish than the simple palms beautifully painted this year on the interior walls of the church, telling of victory ? They are reminders of many a hard-fought battle of faith, prayer, patience, with sin in its most repulsive forms, with ignorance and indifference. They recall, too, memories of consecrating and sanctifying grace ; of spiritual travailing for souls born into the family of God ; of loved ones whose *Te Deum,* alike during life and at the hour of death, was ' Thanks be to God which giveth us the victory through our Lord Jesus Christ.'

This year the Pope, through his henchman, Cardinal Vaughan, had the audacity to give England as a dower to Peter and the Virgin : and I dared to call in question his right to do so, by preaching upon the subject on two Sunday evenings. The day before the second one, on my return home from the usual visiting, a card was handed to me, and the person whose name it bore was shown into my study. He was gentlemanly looking, with a peculiarly pensive expression on his face, and introduced himself as a mission priest then at work in Liverpool, and sent by the Romish Bishop to ask me ' whether my sermons were to be considered as the answer of the Church of England to Cardinal Vaughan ? ' ' No.' ' Are they, then, to be regarded as the answer of the diocese ? ' ' No.' ' Or Bishop Ryle's answer ? ' ' No, they are my own answer, and I alone am responsible for them.' Looking rather severely at me, he said, ' Is it not, then, great presumption on your part to attempt to answer Cardinal Vaughan ? ' ' Oh dear no, I would answer the Pope himself.' He was about taking his departure, when I gently detained him, and we were at it ' hammer and tongs,' on infallibility and the Mass, in a good-natured way, for over an hour. On leaving, he said, ' If I can get away may I come to hear your sermon to-morrow evening ? ' ' By all means.' He came. The church was crowded. There was a number of men who sat through the whole service ; evidently Romanists, as they were without books, and would not take any. My text was Matt. xvi. 18, ' Thou art Peter, and upon this Rock I will build My Church.' The sermon lasted an hour, and in the vestry, afterwards, I told the wardens that I felt sure good would come of it.

The next morning the priest again called, and I could see he was extremely nervous. His first words were, ' I was at church last night.' I replied smilingly, ' I know you were.' Then looking at me most earnestly, he added, very emphatically, ' I felt God was there.' ' Praise the Lord,' I rejoined. We then had a long talk and prayer together. With a deep sigh he exclaimed, ' How can I ever say Mass again ? If I come out I shall be doubted. What am I to do ? ' I answered, ' Come out at all costs. God is not dead. Trust Him. He will take care of you.' He afterwards wrote me many letters, but I ultimately lost sight of him. I dare not doubt either his sincerity or disinterestedness ; so I leave the case, knowing that God can complete His own work, and that if this was of Him, it will be found to the glory and praise of His great name in the day of the Lord Jesus.

Subsequently I found that there was real reason for this priest's fears that if he came out of the Romish Church he would be doubted. That is too bad ; it is neither reasonable, consistent, nor fair to those who become converts from Rome. They are blamed if they do not see their errors, and so remain : yet when they do see them, and come out, they are regarded with suspicion. It is more than a pity, it is a shame, that there is in England no provision for such men when they renounce Romanism. They need taking by the hand, establishing in the truth, building up in the faith. It is true some such converts have proved unsatisfactory ; but is not this true of converts from any ' ism ' ? And the cause, and therefore the fault, may not have been with them alone. All converts need to be treated considerately, tenderly, tactfully, and with fatherly affection.

A representative of the *Porcupine* called to say the editor proposed to describe St. Nathaniel's parish and the work done there, if I would supply him with details, by the loan of annual reports or other parochial papers, and would afford facilities for showing the church, mission-rooms, and the parish generally. I at once consented, as there was never any secrecy in our work. As a result, there appeared a series of descriptive articles, seven in number—of course, from his standpoint—which were afterwards published as a booklet ; all the statements in which are true, being matters of fact. The following is a quotation from it :

' From the commencement of his ministry Mr. Hobson has been very distinctively Evangelical and Protestant ; and it may also be added with safety that during the past twenty-five years he has not altered in either doctrine or practice. The gown is worn in the pulpit, and the psalms are read ; but, all the same, there is a swell of response and singing which is intensely real.

' The vicar's style of preaching is simple, earnest, and practical. His Sunday morning expositions are instructive, and bear the marks of study and research ; while the evening discourses partake more of the Evangelistic.

' His freedom from affectation adds greatly to the power he wields over the vast congregations which are drawn to St. Nathaniel's on Sunday evenings.

' In all his work, at every turn, it is evident that his dependence for success is on the Gospel ministered in the power of the Holy Ghost.'

Having for some years now had mission-rooms for all parochial purposes other than regular full church services, on looking back I feel thankful that for thirteen years, while the parish contained no room adequate for our needs, we were compelled to use the church in every legitimate way, which, of course, all the more had my strength and efforts; much of which would have been given to a hall had the parish possessed one, and in all probability, as a consequence, the church would not have gained the popularity it possesses in the true sense of that word.

It is my conviction that unless halls, and rooms, and even schools, are used loyally and wisely, they tend rather to weaken than to strengthen the hold of the church upon the people; though they ought, and are meant, to lead up to it as their spiritual home.

Millions of Sunday-school children have never found their places in the church; partly on account of the generally defective teaching they have had about it, and partly, though in a far lesser degree, from a disposition in those who attend mission-halls to rest there. If teachers and conductors were actively loyal, and would earnestly seek to pass on scholars and worshippers to the church, regarding their work in teaching and preaching as recruiting for it, the good they undoubtedly do would probably prove permanent.

The Workmen's Brotherhood continued to prosper, having a membership of about six hundred.

This summer, the season being fine and favourable, there were eighty-four open-air services. How essential it is, even for the workers, that the evangelistic work be kept strong and vigorous ! Many a time my own soul has been made glad by listening to addresses at such services : they were so real, direct, hearty, true, tender, and Scriptural. To hear those dear workers tell out what the Lord had done for them was indeed a privilege.

On one occasion a curate's wife noticed amongst the listeners a girl in tears. Making an opportunity for tenderly speaking a few words to the poor young creature, she went along with her, and found that she was an ' unfortunate.' Happily, as a result, she was ultimately restored to her parents.

The ambulance class progressed : it was gratifying to hear, on occasions, of its members having been able to render real service.

In thus recording year by year a little—for, after all, it is but a little—of what the Lord was pleased to do in Windsor during my ministry, I feel it a pleasant duty to recognize the good work for God done there by my Nonconforming brethren, with the limited organization at their command.

Meeting, and shaking hands with, one of our congregation, a truly pious working man, he asked me if I knew what he was praying for as we met ? I expressed a wish to be told. ' I was just saying, " Lord, leave me my affliction, but give me Thy grace." ' For a moment I made no reply, feeling very small in his presence. Whereupon he added, ' That is my prayer, because I am so afraid that if God removed my affliction I might forget Him. I would rather have it than do that.' Truly, that brother had graduated high up in the school of grace. Would that we who are the Lord's could all pray thus when under the chastening hand of our God !

One day, on meeting an honoured canon, who had wrought wonders for the benefit of poor boys and girls in Liverpool, as we were talking about spiritual work, he remarked, ' I wish I had done as you have, giving my strength to the spiritual side of the parish. A layman could do the work I am doing.'

I knew personally of much real good having resulted from his philanthropic work ; but his church was very poorly attended. The truth is, whatever else may be undertaken, it is the first and main—though it is not the only—duty and privilege of every minister of Christ to labour for the souls of his people.

As Irish Home Rule was apparently looming in the distance, I decided to spend my holidays this year in visiting my relatives in Ireland, numbering one hundred and forty-nine, to ascertain quietly if they were likely to stand fast for truth and Protestantism in the event of such an iniquitous Bill becoming law, knowing that Home Rule in that country would mean Rome Rule with a vengeance.

I was successful in seeing almost all of them, and was thankful to God for being able to conclude that by His blessing they would probably stand the fiery trial which might be at hand. I rejoice still more that I found some of them true Christians in the best sense.

In my tour I visited, amongst other places, Donard, Glen-of-Imaal, and Hacketstown.

I stayed in the Glen of Imaal with a relative, and also with the Rev. Chancellor O'Connor, who is the worthy rector of the now united parishes of Donard and Donoughmore, the latter including the Glen of Imaal.

It was a great pleasure to me to visit the old church of Donard, which for service has long since been superseded by a new one. The old church is in ruins, its east end and other parts being covered by luxuriant ivy. I entered by the doorway—still standing—through which I was carried as an infant, and there given to God in baptism, for which I devoutly thanked Him.

I also had the privilege of preaching both in Donard and Donoughmore churches. It was in the latter my darling mother was baptized, and learned to know, love, and serve God.

In Hacketstown I stayed with the hospitable rector, and preached twice in the church. Though the Protestant population is not more than one-fifth of what it used to be, the church was full, as many came from the neighbouring parishes, having, on hearing I was to preach, remembered my name.

Had not the Lord given me special help I should have broken down both in the pulpit, and, particularly, as I stood to read the Gospel in the morning service; for I at once recollected that it was at that very Holy Table, some fifty years ago, my Sunday-school teacher put the solemn question already given, viz. : ' Richard, are you born again ? '

Being permitted to fill an absent teacher's place in the Sunday-school, I took occasion to tell the lads how I, too, had been a scholar in that Sunday-school.

Near to the east window of the church are the graves of our family, and on the Monday morning as I sat alone amongst them, recalling the lives of some who lie there, but more especially as my thoughts went back to the awful famine of 1846-47, and of my gracious Lord's loving, tender care of me during the intervening period, I could only weep in adoring love and gratitude.

I did not fail to visit the very house in the town where our family distress reached its lowest depth.

I gave the rector an outline of all that was in my heart, when amongst many questions he asked me this : ' Can you tell me how it was that your Sunday-school teachers—the daughters of one of my predecessors in this parish—made so deep and lasting an impression here that it is fresh at the present hour ? '

In a very full answer I made it quite clear that those dear servants of God won the hearts of the people by distinctly Scriptural instruction of the children in the day and Sunday-schools, morning and afternoon; by constant visitation of the children in their homes; and above all by the example of their sweet, gentle, Christ-like lives.

O Lord, raise up, I humbly beseech Thee, in every parish, many consecrated like-minded and angel-like women, for the instruction of the young, for the guidance of adults, and for the edification of all.

How variously placed in life are God's own dear ones. When I was passing along one of the most fashionable and crowded streets in Liverpool, it afforded me such pleasure to recognise a certain tidily dressed man, with a basket slung over his shoulder, selling buttons, laces, and other small articles ; to know that he was a brother in Christ, a communicant member of St. Nathaniel's, a convert from Romanism, a true servant of God, and a man able, and ready too, to give, even in that fashionably frequented street, an answer to anyone who might ask him a reason for the hope that was in him as to his place in the common salvation.

Praise God ! He has His own everywhere ; aye, and takes care of them, as the foregoing shows. That dear fellow is, in himself, one of Nature's gentlemen, unlike the man who always bowed when the plate was passed to him in church, and caused the collector who had charge of it to say, at length, very softly, ' I want some of your money, and less of your manners.'

The mother of one of our Sunday-school children, who, with her husband, kept a cook-shop, one day said to her little daughter, ' Now, M——, I want you to take this old knife and cut the eyes out of these big potatoes ; and if you do it regularly and properly, every week you shall be paid wages.' The child did the work, was paid weekly, and put her wages into a little box which had been given to her. After some months her mother asked, ' Well, M——, what will you do with your wages ? ' The little girl's reply was, ' I'll buy a pair of boots with half, and give the rest to teacher for the missionaries.' ' Well done, M——, that will do.' How the Lord's treasury is at times replenished ! M—— grew up to be a good Christian woman ; I solemnized her marriage with a convert from Romanism.

Our yearly return to the Church Pastoral Aid Society always included some five or six shillings from the infants, and about thirty shillings from the older children, of the Ragged School ; both of which were noticed in the Society's Annual Report.

All, no matter how poor, should be taught to give God something, no matter how little ; and they will do so if provided with an opportunity and encouraged. There was goats' hair, as well as golden ornaments, for the tabernacle.

Few of us realize as we might and ought ' the power of the penny.' Rome understands it, and works it out : why should we not, in that respect, take a leaf from her book ?

Would that Rome, the personification of worldly wisdom, taught the true way to heaven ! Many Romanists are better than their creed ; indeed, some of them are such in name only ; and it may be hoped that God will graciously open their eyes to His truth, even ' at the eleventh hour,' so that they may not die in sin ' against light and knowledge,' but may reach the Father through the one and only Mediator and Saviour, His beloved Son, Christ Jesus.

Amount raised, one thousand five hundred and seventy-four pounds.

1894.

' A Catholic priest '—Controversy and conversion—Renunciation of Romanism—First extempore prayer—Gift of a lectern—' Ask God, and tell His people '—Children's Bible Union—Concerts—Amusements —Requests and responses.

' If ye love Me, keep My commandments ' (John xiv. 15).

T HE moral law of God, being the reflection of His nature, is as enduring as Himself. The Law of the Ten Commandments constituted the Covenant of Works, the Salvation of the Gospel of Christ comprised the Covenant of Grace. In a sense the former was abrogated by the latter ; in another sense it was accentuated thereby : if the letter killed, the spirit gives life. Perfect obedience was the absolute requirement for acceptance by the one ; eternal Salvation results from acceptance, through faith, of the other. Jesus Christ harmonized His Father's Law with His own Gospel ; for the ' new commandment ' does but crystallize the full meaning of the Ten. In Him, the moral law is the law of love, for ' love is the fulfilling of the law.'

We used to have a Sunday evening service in the church at 8.15 o'clock once a month, for the benefit of such members of the Workmen's Brotherhood as might be disposed to come, in order to draw them gradually to God's house. Generally from two to five hundred attended, which those who know the difficulty of getting men to church will agree in considering this a great gain.

On receiving a letter, signed ' D.K., a Catholic Priest,' asking for an interview, I at once answered it, naming a day and hour. At the appointed time my correspondent called, was warmly welcomed, apologized for troubling me with a call, and then added, ' I am a priest connected with a Catholic church near St. Nathaniel's. As I was walking through your parish the other evening I noticed a group of persons holding a meeting. After passing it, I asked a little girl who was that man with a tall hat on, in the centre of the group ? The child at once answered, " Oh, that is Mr. Hobson " ; and there came to my mind the thought whether you were the man to whom I dare unburden my soul. I therefore wrote to you in confidence, asking for an interview in the strictest privacy.' I replied, ' Certainly if it is about your soul ' : for it occurred to me that there might be something which the public interest would compel me to reveal. He had, he said, made known, in confession, his doubts and fears about certain doctrines of his Church, but had been told that all such were of the devil, and that he must go into ' retreat ' : his soul was not thereby satisfied, as it craved for a rest which no ' retreat ' could give. He unburdened himself freely, and, at the end of our interview, asked leave to call weekly. He did so for about five months, during which period I lent him a Bible and other books to study.

One day I strongly pressed home justification by faith only, as God's own way of saving his soul, knowing that if he received by faith the all-sufficient atonement of Christ for him, Romanism would be torn up by the roots, and his soul would have peace with God. But he could not see it.

As a month elapsed without his calling, I began to wonder whether he would ever turn up again. However, I had a note, asking leave to call as usual, when his absence would be explained. He came, and I found his mind had been greatly exercised about the all-important doctrine presented at our last interview. He was beginning to get glimpses of that saving truth, and of the inevitable result, that justification by faith in Christ only would cut away the ground on which he yet stood. The Lord then enabled me to urge his reliance on the precious blood of Christ's one atonement as his only justification in God's sight, the only cleansing for his soul, his only refuge and salvation. More light was given, the scales fell from his eyes, he became a new creature in Christ Jesus! We now knelt together in praise, as we had often done in prayer.

He decided never again to say Mass, to get his Letters Testimonial as quickly as he could, and then to leave the Clergy House without delay. But where was he to go? I resolved that, at all events, he should not want.

On Whit Sunday, May 13, 1894, after the second lesson at the eleven o'clock service in St. Nathaniel's, he stood up, as arranged, removed the ' stole ' from his neck, openly renounced the doctrines of Rome, and asked for admission into the English Protestant Church. On June 3 there was a confirmation in our church, when he was presented and confirmed. That was another very special trophy of Divine grace.

I afterwards asked the Bishop to give him letters of ' permission ' to assist me in the church services, which was done. For a year and seven months he was under my instruction, being then licensed to a curacy in the diocese. He continues a faithful minister of Christ, and has recently received preferment.

At my suggestion, on the evening of June 17, being the Brotherhood monthly service at 8.15, he gave, in St. Nathaniel's, his reasons for renouncing Romanism. In every part of it the church was literally packed by men only, including many Romanists. It was a glorious sight. The sermon was published in due course, and had a large circulation.

Amongst the many touching points of interest in this case, I shall give only the following. Mr. —— had been reading regularly with me for about a year, when I said to him, ' You will be called upon to offer extemporaneous prayer in your house-to-house visitation ; you have often heard me do so ; I should like you to begin to-day, after our reading.' He answered, ' I could not do it ; I never in my life prayed to God except by a form.' I remarked that we were alone, that in prayer we speak to our heavenly Father, who quite understands, and so makes allowances for us, His children ; and he was prevailed upon to pray. We knelt down, and there was a pause. I feared it was proving too much for him, but I waited, and silently asked God to open his lips. Suddenly there came from them, and I doubt not from his heart also, the following, which I can never forget : ' O God, I thank Thee for having brought me into the light.' Then there was a pause, followed by, ' O God, bring my mother into the true light of the Gospel.' After another pause : ' O God, show my brothers and sisters the light. For Christ's sake. Amen.'

I was overwhelmed. I may add that he has a sister a nun.

I have no doubt there are many Romish priests who have their dark misgivings as to the truth of their Church's teaching, and that many of them would ' come out of her,' and seek admission into our Church, if they felt there would be a welcome for them. I know con-

versions from Romanism to Protestantism need to be
both tested and vouched for, and there is something to
be said about the risk of our clergy being misled by the
possible plausibilities of self-styled converts ; but for
all that, I confess to feeling ashamed of the reluctance
of evangelical vicars to employ such converts as curates.
A ritualistic parson offered to take up my friend, and
warned him against allowing himself to be caught by
' the Low Church ' ; but the warning was disregarded,
and the offer was declined.   Thank God !

The Church was presented with a lectern, bearing a
suitable inscription. It seems to me only right that the
Holy Bible, the sun and centre of all our light and
truth, the Written Word, the Inspired Scripture of our
God, should have its own special place in church,
whereon it can rest, and whence it can be read, without
note or comment, to the people. Would that the clergy
were taught how to read it ; so that instead of it being
meaninglessly monotoned in cathedral or ritualistic
church, or gabbled or droned in Broad or even Low
Church, it might be really read, in such a way as to
show that the reader not only understood, and, therefore, by proper emphasis and natural intonation made
plain, the actual meaning of the words ; but also that
he had experimental knowledge of that meaning in
personal application to his own soul. The ability to
read God's Word should be made one of the qualifications
for ' Orders.' It is of far more importance than either
mathematics or classics ; the minister's sole justification
for his position being the endeavour to win souls, which
mere book learning can never do, whilst ' the Word '
can, and does.

I gave a special course of Sunday instruction upon
the Second Coming of our Lord, which I trust increased
the interest of our dear people in that great event, the
hope of all God's true children.

Some people seem to have supposed that a large
portion of my time was devoted to collecting money.
A few moments' thought about the many and varied

parochial agencies in which I had to take a more or less active part, the hours of daily visitation from house to house, the careful preparation for pulpit preaching, the many callers on matters concerning their own spiritual state or work in the parish, and the heavy official or semi-official correspondence, would suffice to show the fallacy of such an idea. As a matter of fact, I really do not believe that during the whole thirty-three years of my vicariate I made as many as a hundred calls upon people for money.

When money was specially needed, the first thing we did was to have the matter prayed over in our little prayer gathering, and God's blessing was earnestly entreated for any appeal that might be made. Then, putting the need, whatever it might be, on paper, I sent it by post, with prayer, to such friends and other people as I thought likely to help. For, somehow or other, the work in St. Nathaniel's was well known, not only round about, but also far and wide. Our faults and defects were not hidden, but neither was our social, philanthropic, spiritual work for the Lord in His name, nor the fact that He was abundantly blessing it. Our guiding motto was : ' Ask God, and tell His people ' : and it never failed us.

I dared not let anything interfere with my house-to-house visitation : for it, everything else must be given up. And by God's good hand upon me, providentially guiding and directing, the ' everything ' came in reality to be ' nothing.'

To that most valuable organization, the Bible-reading Union, there had not hitherto been assigned a proper place amongst our agencies. There had been Bible-classes and readings, but no Bible Union, as such ; we now introduced a Children's Bible Union, to which adults also could belong ; and so successful was it from the first that there were soon some four hundred members. Truly that was great gain, for there is no denying the lamentable fact, there is little Bible-reading, and even less Bible study. And how can the soul live unless it is fed and nourished by the Word of God, which is in effect to feed on Christ, the Bread of Life. For are not the Incarnate Word and the Written Word in this sense one and the same ?

At the consecration anniversary this year I had a reception for the church-workers, when one hundred and seventeen men and one hundred and seven women were present : the Bishop attended, and addressed them. I also had the pleasure of providing a dinner for one hundred and eleven poor people over sixty years of age.

Concerts did not constitute a ' vexed question ' with us : we had them, sacred, secular, and mixed. It was my constant endeavour to let the people see that the Christian life can, and ought to be, bright and joyous ; remembering that the injunction ' Rejoice evermore ' was addressed to those ' in the Lord ' ; and I sought to give practical effect to it in the matter of music, as in other ways. It no doubt needs a strong will and a right judgment, in order on the one hand to keep the tone of such entertainments sufficiently high to make them elevating and refining, as well as interesting, but not too high for the comprehension of the audience ; and on the other hand to prevent their tone being so lowered as to put them on a par with public-house ' free-and-easies.' But we were so successful in keeping our concerts just what they should be, that I have little, if anything, to complain of respecting them.

We would not allow ourselves to be concerned in anything on which we could not honestly ask and expect God's blessing ; and all our gatherings, no matter for what purpose, were opened with prayer.

I encouraged football, cricket, tennis, skating, croquet, and such-like open-air recreations ; but I steadfastly set my face against theatres, operas, music-halls, and round dancing, for which I got many a hard knock.

The various departments of our parochial work were well sustained.

On the evening of confirmation day, Sunday, June 3,

there were two hundred and eighty-three at the Lord's Table. Oh, how those communion services seemed to increase in blessedness as the years went by.

My heart used to overflow with thankfulness, as the privileged pastor of those dear people, when I saw railful after railful of the Lord's children at His Table, and remembered what some of them had been before they were won for Him ; and when, later on in the service, there came from their lips, and I believe from their hearts also, the soothing strains of that solemn hymn, ' When this passing world is done,' followed by the Lord's Prayer, ' Our Father,' the effect upon me was at times overpowering !

' An ounce of experience is better than a pound of theory.'

We read that ' The effectual fervent prayer of a right-eous man availeth much.' If rich results be promised to the faith and prayer of one, why should not those of the many be equally blessed ? If our work at St. Nathaniel's was anything, it was a work of faith and prayer.

For the glory of God I record requests made to Him in our little prayer-meetings on Sunday mornings : they are but four out of many, but they are sufficient to show the faithfulness of our God.

That God would be pleased so to bless the annual appeal for the Ragged Schools that the needed £80 might be realized. Answer, £82 15s.

That God might be graciously pleased to send us £40 to provide for the children, and specially for our poor widows at Christmas. Answer, £67 7s.

That God might be pleased to supply again, for the waifs and strays of the parish, the weekly supper throughout the year, which we had been obliged to discontinue. Answer : The good man who for eleven years had left off providing them, resumed the responsibility thereof, unasked !

That God would be pleased to supply the other weekly supper, for poor children, which had just been discontinued after twenty-five years. Answer : A brother in the Lord, on hearing from me of this want, thanked God for providing him with such an opportunity for doing good. He continued to give for the poor little ones £30 a year for six years.

Praise the Lord!

Let those who choose to think so, say these are remarkable coincidences; we felt them to be direct answers to our prayers.

God says: ' Open thy mouth wide, and I will fill it.'

Amount raised, nine hundred and thirty-nine pounds.

1895.

Ex-Redemptionist priest's admission to the Protestant Church— Honorary Canonry conferred on the Author—Three converted Romish priests conducting the service—Mission addresses to prisoners in Hull gaol—Realistic dream gives power in preaching—Influential positions of congregational members—Recurring insomnia—Small beginnings— A sudden impulse—A parochial magazine—Ragged School finances— Imperative rule not to lend money.

' Let us consider one another to provoke unto love and to good works ' (Heb. x. 24).

HOW many misunderstandings, heart - burnings, jealousies, and petty divisions, in the family and the social circle, and in work for God, too, would not have been possible, had full effect been given to this word of exhortation.

This considering sets up a high standard for God's people to attain to, for—

It is to be mutual.

It is to be with brotherly feeling.

It is to be provocative of love for doing good.

It is to be addicted to good works.

It is to be excelling in these things.

It is to be the constant habit of mind.

How altogether unworldlike!

Love is God's special attribute : it prompted Him to give us His Son. And we are told that ' love is of

God ' : so that our love for each other is either ' of God,' or it is not love at all. Tried by that test, how little of what the world is pleased to term love would be found to be such in reality !

The highest type of a Christian is a loving and a lovable one : such a one will exercise for good an influence that none other can ever possess. May the Apostolic injunction have ever-increasing weight with those who belong to the family of God and are co-workers with Him !

This year St. Nathaniel's Church saw the sequel of another conversion, one very specially interesting. The Rev. ——, an ex-Redemptionist priest of the Romish Church—who had been placed, and for a year remained, under me for instruction—read publicly, in the usual form, his abjuration of its errors, and asked to be received into the Protestant Church : he was admitted and confirmed. He gave his reasons for that important step in a sermon preached afterwards at one of the monthly Sunday evening services for the Windsor Workmen's Brotherhood, in St. Nathaniel's Church, on which occasion there were present, according to the wardens' counting, nine hundred and fifty-seven men, many of whom were Romanists. The sermon was printed and circulated, by request.

This year the Bishop offered me, by the following kind letter, an Honorary Canonry of the Cathedral :

' THE PALACE, LIVERPOOL,
' *May* 24, 1895.

' MY DEAR HOBSON,

' A Canonry of the Liverpool Cathedral is vacant to-day. . . . I write to ask if you will accept it.

' It gives me pleasure to show my deep sense of the valuable work you have done for Christ in the Church of England in Liverpool, and I shall be much pleased by your acceptance of it. . . . .

' At any rate, I should like to leave you Canon Hobson when I leave this world.

' Yours affectionately,
' J. C. LIVERPOOL.'

I felt thankful to have, in that form, the approval of my Bishop, and of such a Bishop ! Truly, it was more than I could have hoped for. How I prayed that, by God's grace, I might be made worthy of it, in being all the more humble, true, and loving, in my work for Him !

At one service in St. Nathaniel's, the preacher, and the two clergymen who took the prayers and the lessons, had been Romish priests. As I sat in the chancel, my soul was full of prayer and praise for the three, and I thought how we who had assembled were honoured by the Great Head of the Church allowing those whom He had brought out of gross darkness into bright Gospel light thus to minister for our edification and example, testifying to us of God's gracious dealing with all who truly seek Him.

There are many who, if they entered our neighbour-hood and church, would consider it ' cheap and nasty ' : there are some who would not even enter it. But grand churches and fashionable neighbourhoods do not necessarily command God's blessing.

True, the present-day rage is for costly buildings, and ornate services, by men decked out in what are really Popish vestments, conducting functions alien to the Reformed Church of England, and semi-pagan ; yet it is more than doubtful whether lost ones have ever been brought to Jesus by such means.

By all means let us have handsome churches and bright services, but with the prayers prayed, the Word of God reverently read, the singing hearty, and the pure Gospel faithfully preached. Where the parson is converted, the congregation God-fearing, and the service God-honouring, there the Holy Spirit will be graciously present, with quickening power and sanctifying grace.

When taking part in a general mission at Hull, I had to follow the Archbishop of York—at that time Dr. Thompson—in addressing the prisoners in gaol, and my mind was greatly exercised thereat. The night before, I dreamed that I myself was in prison, and was sorely troubled at what would be thought of it by my flock in Liverpool, and by my dear mother had she been alive. My agitation woke me, and, on finding it was all only a dream, I rose, knelt down, and thanked God for His protecting grace, but for which I might have been a prisoner in reality.

That dream marvellously fitted me to speak to those in the prison chapel next day, with an earnestness, a soul-pleading, which, taking me, as it were, out of myself, enabled me to cheer and encourage my hearers with the assurance—God's own blessed assurance—that though for their offences against man, punishment had to be endured for fixed periods, for their much greater sins against God there was, on true repentance, instant pardon.

Of results I could never know ; but as I heard the reverent ' Amens ' after each prayer, and marked the intensity of expression on the upturned faces of those poor captives, whilst I put before them the way of salvation in plain, simple words, as from heart to heart, there seemed to come over me a feeling of certainty that not all the spiritual seed sown that day in those human furrows could be unproductive, but that part would fall on congenial soil, and, by the vivifying influences of God's Holy Spirit, would bear heavenly fruit in the future lives of some then before me.

Our Bishop preached at one of the Sunday evening services for the members of the Windsor Workmen's Brotherhood, when the church was, as usual, well attended.

God has been pleased to use the dear people of St. Nathaniel's parish in various ways. Four have been from time to time elected members of the City Council, one is still a councillor, two have become aldermen, and the other ' is not,' the Lord he loved and served having taken him to Himself. All the four were downright staunch Evangelicals.

One of the two aldermen is a J.P., and a decidedly strong Protestant, exercising, through the many thousand members of an association over which he presides, a powerful influence, in the interest of Protestantism, upon the municipal and Parliamentary elections in Liverpool. He has more than once said publicly, ' I was taught Protestantism when, as a boy, I sat near the pulpit of St. Nathaniel's Church, Windsor.' My dear friend was married there, and his first child was baptized there. I have often felt thankful for the salutary influence of all those four former members ; but specially am I grateful to God for having permitted me to be the means, humanly speaking, of imparting the knowledge of Biblical Protestantism to one whose abilities, power, and influence, have been exercised so faithfully, fearlessly, and successfully, on behalf of the truth as revealed by Christ Jesus, and embodied in the Thirty-nine Artilces.

Oh that God would raise up many such men throughout the length and breadth of our land, to prevent His Church being betrayed into the hands of those who preach another Gospel which is not another, and so serve other gods, instead of the Lord !

The continued strain of incessant work again made itself felt, in the shape of constant fatigue, accompanied by inability to get rest in sleep. Under medical orders, I had, but with great reluctance, to reduce my daily visitation hours from six to three. It was not that parochial visiting in itself tired me, for many years' experience had made it quite natural, and therefore easy. Indeed, it was to me a privilege to be allowed a share in the joys, and even in the sorrows, of my dear people.

I had long known the power for good that true pastoral visitation may be made amongst those who, being non-churchgoers, are never, and indeed never can be, reached by the ordinary services. It is, in fact, the only means that will bridge over that great gulf which separates the masses from the church ; and though many do visiting after a fashion, according to their lights ; and some with good intentions, but more or less perfunctorily ; few realize its possibilities, privileges, and responsibilities.

Cellars, having the tops of their entrance-doors almost on a level with the street, and consisting of one apartment, or it may be two, sometimes without any opening in the rear, are not conducive to the comfort of those who visit them ; much less are they fit abodes for those who dwell in them. Yet in the poorer parts of many cities there are still such, in which human beings, made in God's own image, with souls intended for immortal happiness, live, if their state of existence be worthy of the name, and die !

There are many in Windsor, and, bless the Lord, some of them are associated with both useful and valuable undertakings.

For instance, the Ragged School, Harding Street, where an incalculable amount of good has been done to thousands of poor children, their parents, and others in Windsor, had its origin, more than forty years ago, in a very small school for very poor children, held in a cellar near by, with three young men, belonging to the mother church, as voluntary teachers. These three young men were afterwards Liverpool merchants, and two of them amassed wealth. Of those two, one not only gave liberally to Church societies during his lifetime, but also left £20,000 to them on his decease ; whilst the other still lives, and is a generous donor likewise. All three proved themselves real men of God, and a blessing to the city.

Then, too, a school for the poorest children, which a former vicar of St. Saviour's, Falkner Square, opened, by permission, in a cellar in Holden Street, Windsor, was made the basis of an appeal for funds to build schools within his parish, resulting in the erection of those handsome National Schools in Canning Street, which have for now some forty years or so ranked amongst the most successful schools in the whole of Liverpool.

My own ministrations in Windsor began in a cellar, at No. 6, Oliver Street, of which I never think but with deep thankfulness to God for having laid the foundations of the work so ' deep down.'

Some of the blessed results may yet be seen in the parish, living trophies of God's grace; and some are shown in this book; but most are known only to the Lord, and their revelation will not be until the Great Day.

It was in a cellar in our Mission Room at Aigburth Street, in this parish, on a Friday evening at 8 o'clock in September, 1879, the first meeting was held of the Liverpool Christian Police Association, which the Vicar conducted, consisting of three policemen only; soon they met in our largest room, where one of our ladies conducted it on Sunday afternoons for over a year, and it was also soon found to be too strait; when the men themselves formed a committee, built a hall, taking up the entire management thereof. The power of the Lord was manifestly present to heal and to bless. The news of this happy and blessed work rapidly spread; rumours of a similar movement were soon heard from London and elsewhere, which finally culminated in its consolidation in the Metropolis and is now known as the 'International Christian Police Association,' having branches almost everywhere. Praise God. (See Appendix J).

So that the Windsor cellars possess associations which are in their way unique.

But why wonder at these cellar results? Had not Christianity its origin in a manger?

This year our annual services on behalf of the Ragged Schools were attended by the Lord Mayor of Liverpool, who was visibly touched by the poor children's singing. He sent me the following letter:

'THE TOWN HALL, LIVERPOOL,
'*October 3,* 1895.

DEAR CANON HOBSON,
' I am exceedingly pleased to find that the collections on Sunday last were so good. I rejoice to have been able to assist you in your good cause. I was greatly interested in your statement, and I cannot but feel that the work will prosper in your hands.
Yours truly,
' W. H. WATTS, *Lord Mayor.*'

It would be difficult to describe the wretched places from which our supper children were in many cases drawn. I was always strongly of opinion that no matter how much their parents were to blame, the poor dear starving little ones must be helped, with good warm food ; and I often wished that those who differed from me could see them at their meals.

I remember one little creature peering in at the school door, evidently uncertain whether he might enter. I called to him tenderly, ' Come in, my child ; come in ' ; and in he walked, having nothing on except a dirty shirt, and torn short trousers held only by bits of cord as braces.

I noticed a poor little lad begin to cry instead of eating his supper. Asking him why, he said, ' I want to take it home to mother.' He ate heartily, on being told he should have some to take her, whom we found to be sadly in want.

I well recollect an incident which took place as I was pleading for the children on an anniversary day, when the chancel was, as usual, crowded with those poor waifs and strays, each one an object-lesson for us all.

Obeying a sudden impulse, I stepped down from the pulpit, and taking in my arms the child nearest to me, lifted him up in sight of the whole congregation, asking them whether I could give a more powerful argument than that for their support of our Ragged Schools. The collection did not suffer from my rough-and-ready mode of pleading ; we got all we required, and more.

Being asked by an interviewer, amongst many other questions, ' What is your hobby ? ' I replied, ' I am not aware of having one, unless it is hard work.' Certainly hard work seemed to fall to my lot ; perhaps, because I always had an ambition to do whatever came to hand, if I could do it at least as well as another.

Asked my reason for remaining unmarried, I said it seemed as if God had kept me single for Himself, though I did not advocate celibacy, and had always felt myself free to marry. I am strongly of opinion that a married ministry has many advantages over a celibate one ; very many, if the wife be really a helpmeet to the husband in his ministry. Unfortunately, however, the reverse is sometimes, or, rather often, the case.

For years I had wished to start a parochial magazine, but the fate of such in so many parishes had deterred me from making the attempt. The dual difficulty was securing sufficient local advertisements, and regularity in delivery.

At last I ventured, and am thankful to have succeeded, the circulation reaching seven hundred per month. Though the profit on it was small, I found the magazine a most useful parochial educator, in that it brought, and kept, those who read it in close touch with all that was going on. It was, moreover, a channel through which reliable information could be given upon many needful and interesting extra parochial subjects. By inserting all our accounts in the magazine, we saved £8, the cost of printing our annual report.

It is of the utmost importance to imbue a congregation with confidence in their minister as an organizer ; they will then follow his lead, by supporting whatever he starts. Realizing that, I was always very cautious about inaugurating any new undertaking.

Strangely enough, this confidence, which it was my proud privilege to possess, became almost a danger to us, inasmuch as when money was required for any purpose, it was currently remarked, with reference to myself, ' Oh, he will get it, and more. Is it not always so ? ' Such assurance was all very well in itself, but it might have led to a cessation of active co-operation with me on such occasions, and that would have been injurious all round.

This year I expounded Luke's Gospel on Sunday mornings.

It is remarkable that though the burden of the Ragged Schools was a very real one, as well as a loved one, we never but once had an adverse balance. The amount was just £5, and a friend of the schools sent me a cheque for that sum, in a letter chiding us for having closed the accounts without letting him know how they stood, and requesting us not to do so again ! I am thankful to say we never had occasion to utilize our dear friend's generous offer.

In a parish such as this, the minister, if easy of access, as he should be, and good-natured, as he should also be, is likely to become a prey in the matter of money-lending. Early in my ministry, applications for loans were very frequent, some even being for £50! Happily, I began with a rule not to lend money to anyone, no matter who the applicant might be. To that rule I kept, though I often wished it did not exist: but it was a wise one, for others as well as for myself. I was free to make a present if I could afford it, but to lend was out of my power. Beside which, the relationship between pastor and people makes money-lending a very unwise thing: such loans are seldom repaid, and bad feeling is sometimes engendered.

I also steadfastly refused to subscribe, or to write appeals for money, in cases of interment. The poor have an absurdly exaggerated idea as to what they call ' a comfortable funeral ': they will, in many cases, have a collection for the purpose. If the pastor has been generous to their sick, they expect him to be so in the case of death: I drew the line at the living.

Amount raised, one thousand one hundred and fifty-four pounds.

1896.

Two hundred and sixteen absolutions !—The arrow of conviction—Reading books or only having them—St. Nathaniel's trained workers—Church bells' tunes—Doctors' and pastors' visits—Pulpit preparation—A useful lantern—A third breakdown—Trip to the Canaries—St. Nathaniel's contributions to the ministry.

' The precious blood of Christ ' (1 Pet. i. 19).

I KNEW of much good resulting from a course of ten sermons preached by me on these words, which were compared to a ladder of ten rungs, reaching from earth to heaven, each rung being as usual of the same substance. So also in this wondrous ladder each rung is the precious Blood of Christ. The blood here means the life of Christ offered on Calvary as a propitiatory sacrifice for sin.

THE GOSPEL LADDER.

"THE PRECIOUS BLOOD OF CHRIST."—*I. Peter i.* 19.

HEAVEN.

INNER CIRCLE	round about the Throne of God by the BLOOD OF CHRIST.—*Rev. vii.* 14-15.
VICTORY	by the BLOOD OF CHRIST.—*Rev.xii.* 11.
FELLOWSHIP	by the BLOOD OF CHRIST.—1 *John i.* 7.
SECURITY	by the BLOOD OF CHRIST.—*Ex. xii.* 13.
FORGIVENESS	by the BLOOD OF CHRIST.—*Eph. i.* 7.
NEARNESS	by the BLOOD OF CHRIST.—*Eph. ii.* 13.
ACCESS	by the BLOOD OF CHRIST.—*Heb. x.* 19.
LIFE	by the BLOOD OF CHRIST.—*Heb. ix.* 14.
JUSTIFICATION	by the BLOOD OF CHRIST.—*Rom. v.* 9
REDEMPTION	by the BLOOD OF CHRIST.—1 *Pet. i.* 19.

EARTH (*Ascent*).

At St. Nathaniel's we always made much of ' the Blood,' knowing that without it Christianity would be but a body without a soul. The magnetic power of the Gospel is the priceless ' precious Blood ' of our dear Lord.

One day I was met by a messenger, sent in post-haste to ask me at once to visit a gentleman who was in great distress of mind, and greatly desired to see me. I had already declined to visit him, as he was neither a parishioner nor a member of the congregation; but now I resolved to go, and went at once. On asking why I had been sent for, he replied : ' I have often heard of the interest you take in the people. I have been for the last eighteen years a " monthly penitent " in St. M——'s Church, and I am not satisfied. If I sent for the vicar, he would say, " Come to confession," and that I do not care to do any more. I want you to help me. I want peace for my soul.' His wife, who was sitting by, said that she also had been to confession all those years, but not so regularly as her husband. I at once put before him God's gracious way of salvation as found in His Word, viz., simple faith in Christ's atonement ; and then had prayer with them : after which, he said, ' I have got light, and rest for my heart. I shall go no more to St. M——'s Church. Will you receive us at the Sacrament ? ' They both joined our church. Thank God !

Here was a devout man, who had received no less than two hundred and sixteen absolutions from a miserable priestling of our National Church, at last awaking to his sad state, and in God's mercy finding peace by absolution from the Great High Priest Himself, the only Absolver, the Blessed Lord Jesus.

' Thy faith hath saved thee : go in peace ' (Luke vi. 50).

' ABSOLVO TE.'

' One Priest alone can pardon me,
 And bid me go in peace ;
Can breathe the words " Absolvo Te,"
 And make these heart-throbs cease.
My soul has heard His priestly voice ;
It said, " I bore thy sins ; rejoice " (1 Pet. ii. 24).

' He showed the spear-mark in His side,
 The nail-prints in His palm ;
Said, " Look on Me, the Crucified ;
 Why tremble thus ? Be calm ;
All power is Mine. I set thee free ;
Be not afraid " ; " Absolvo Te " (Isa. xlv. 22).

' In Heaven He stands before the Throne,
    The Great High Priest above :
Melchisedeck. That name alone
    Can sin's dark stain remove.
To Him I look, on bended knee,
And hear that sweet " Absolvo Te " (Heb. ix. 24).

' A girded Levite here below,
    I willing service bring ;
And fain would tell, to all I know,
    Of Christ the Heavenly King ;
Would win all hearts from sin to flee,
And hear Him say, " Absolvo Te " (1 John ii. 1).'

A dairyman in a good way of business, supporting in
comfort a wife and a large family, had lost nearly all
his cows by disease. He was consequently in a very
disturbed and depressed state of mind. On a Sunday
evening he happened to pass by one of our open-air
meetings, and turning aside to hear what was taking
place, remained a listener to the whole of an address,
wherein the Word of the Lord came to him with such
convincing power, that he forthwith found rest for his
soul, and relief from the burden of his care.

It was the beginning of a new and better life : he
soon began to help by playing the harmonium in the
ragged children's Sunday-school. The Lord so prospered
him in business again that he is now living in the country, on a small farm, with most of his children provided
for. How good our God is !

My library was not large, but it was select. I aimed
at mastering certain books, so that I could make use of
them : books of reference are very helpful. Of course
the first and chief book was the Holy Bible. I used
Matthew Henry's Commentary, Barnes, Scott's Commentary, Wordsworth and Alford on the Greek Testament, the Reformers—by the Parker Society—the
works of some of the Puritan Divines, of Toplady,
Whitfield, Spurgeon, and Bishop Ryle, Blakeney's
writings, general history, biography, poetry. These,
together with reading on the Romish controversy, the

Council of Trent, its Canons and Decrees, the books of my theological college course, and those for the Bishop's examination, were my chief study.

It is one thing to have a vast amount of learning on book-shelves ; it is quite another thing to have such laid up in the memory, and so digested as to be able to use it. I have often wondered at men rightly reputed learned, having empty churches !

Surely much learning ought to go towards making a superior instrument for God's use in the ministry ; and in some cases it doubtless does, but they are too few.

It is a matter of thankfulness that we gave to the Liverpool Church of England Scripture Readers' Society six men, all of whom are doing well in their important work of carrying into the homes of the people the same blessed Gospel they heard when with us, the Gospel of the Grace of God : and to the Liverpool Bible and Domestic Mission three women, of whom I think most highly, on account of their Bible knowledge, their educational acquirements, their personal experience of the presence and power of the Saviour, and their zeal, devotion, and tact, as exhibited whilst workers in our parish.

God has indeed wonderfully blessed St. Nathaniel's congregation as an educational agency for fitting its members to help in His cause, and the blessing is largely owing to the true missionary spirit in which the parish has been worked, and to the workers having had pointed out to them their duty to fit themselves, by reading and study, for doing good as occasion might offer. It is well to stimulate people to educate themselves for any good work, whether sacred or secular. The Lord never fails to use who and what He pleases to do His will.

Just opposite to the church there lay a sick woman at the point of death. She was so unhappy at the thought of separation from her husband and her children, and so fearful as to her own future state, that though we visited her, talked with her, read to her, prayed with her, we were unable to comfort her.

Hymn tunes were often played on our Church bells"; amongst them were two that this poor woman had learned to sing when a girl. One was to the words ' There is a happy land, far, far away,' and the other to ' Here we suffer grief and pain.' They came home to her, speaking of that rest, peace, and resignation which she had hitherto failed to find. She died in sweet assurance of the blissful life hereafter. It rejoiced my heart that those bells were thus used by the Holy Spirit, and that I was permitted to know it.

Having a keen sense of smell, I found it very trying to visit the sick poor in their homes, especially if they were suffering from cancer, of which I remember we had five cases in one year. Cancer cases are bad enough even amidst the most favourable surroundings and conditions ; but where the sufferers are of the poorest, and do not receive necessary attention as to change of linen, and cleansings, visitation becomes extremely unpleasant and unhealthy work.

The pastor's visit and the doctor's differ in this— beside in much else—that the latter can keep his lips closed almost as much as he wishes ; whilst the former, to be of any real use, must talk, and perhaps read, and if expedient, pray, quite near, so that the sick person may hear. After visiting such cases I was often unable to take food until I had slept.

Preaching always occupied a prominent position in St. Nathaniel's services : and that needed careful pulpit preparation. For me Exod. xxxvii. 20, and 2 Sam. xxiv. 24, were full of meaning, to which I felt God was calling me to give due effect in my ministry. Yet it was with me much as it was with the Apostles, ' As ye go, preach.' The preaching, the teaching, went on not only on Sundays, but daily all the year round : and not only in church, but in mission-rooms, in the open-air, and in the homes of the people. Paul says : ' I have taught you publicly, and from house to house.'

My settled time for preparation was the forenoon of Saturday. The first thing was to fix on the texts, if possible, early in the week ; then to use every hour, or even ten minutes, for reading up the subject, taking notes, and arranging them : those I used in the pulpit for reference only.

If I had a course of expository sermons, which was usually the case, the same plan was pursued, with the addition of having on the study table special helps to be read and noted. I often found I could grasp more in half an hour when fresh than in two consecutive hours when wearied by overwork. It was no uncommon thing for me to converse upon the texts during the week when visiting, which at times I found very helpful.

Readiness to acquire, and power to adapt, grow, if rightly used ; a good memory being indispensable.

When by prayer, study of the Word, and perusal of helpful literature, I had done my little best, there constantly came to my mind a disciple's doubting question, ' What are they among so many ? ' Often have I asked the Lord that the little I had to set before His people might be so multiplied by Him in the distribution that they would be ' filled ' by His feeding.

I always sought, in prayer and faith, so to apply my sermons to myself first, that when preaching them I could speak as of things I both knew and felt personally.

It was my aim to bring forward, in turn, all the topical truths of God's Word, such as the Trinity, the Atonement, justification by faith only, salvation, the resurrection, holiness, eternal life, and eternal death ; pleading with God that His Holy Spirit might apply the Word to the peoples' needs.

We had long wished to possess a first-class lantern, and, hearing of one to be obtained on advantageous terms, we bought it. The investment was a good one, as our meetings in the halls and our evening open-air services were greatly benefited by its use : especially was that the case at the Sunday evening services for men only, in one of our rooms, when Biblical subjects were illustrated. Like most useful things, lanterns may

be put to doubtful purposes, but that does not detract
from their utility, when rightly employed, to educate,
rather than to amuse. It is often necessary to adopt
new plans for interesting people in ' the things of God.'
That, of course, supposes that the plans are not wrong
or doubtful in themselves.

This autumn my health again broke down : I could
scarcely walk, read, or even think. My doctor said that
I needed long, perfect rest, in a warm climate. I therefore went for the winter to the Grand Canary, remaining
there in a feeble condition for two months before I
began to pick up. I felt immensely improved by my
stay in that salubrious climate, thanking God for His
goodness to me. I was, however, greatly disappointed
at meeting with so few of the Lord's people : it seemed
as if they were yet only a ' little flock.'

I am thankful to record that St. Nathaniel's has given
to the Church nine ministers, all Evangelical, who are
doing good work ; and that three of her young men,
one of whom is at Trinity College, Dublin, another at
Oxford, and the third at Cambridge, are looking forward
to the ministry of the Word. Of those already ordained,
I shall refer particularly to one only, my son in Christ
Jesus. When preaching in St. Nathaniel's, he said, ' I
was born again within these walls.' Bless the Lord !
There are few clergymen more used by the Holy Spirit
than he : with that Spirit he is filled ; God has given
him ' a mouth and wisdom,' to speak of that which he
has both seen and felt, and which his hands have
handled. He, through grace, abides in Christ, and I
thank God for all that He enables him to do in the city
of Norwich. It is not too much to say that I know God
has used his ministry for the regeneration of over two
thousand souls, in his own parish and elsewhere. He is
an earnest, outspoken, Evangelical Protestant, and has
more than once written to tell me how thankful he is for
the teaching he had in our dear church on the Romish
controversy. Oh that God would be pleased thus to
fill and use all His true ministering servants, and that
He would incline and fit for the ministry thousands of

evangelical, whole-hearted, earnest, faithful, humble-minded young men, who, beside teaching and defending the truth as it is in Christ Jesus, will seek to re-live the life of Christ among men !

This year there was added to the church a vestry and a much-needed lavatory, at a cost of £90 : it was our last effort in bricks and mortar.

Amount raised, one thousand and twenty-one pounds.

1897.

Words of wisdom from Bishop Ryle—A unique welcome—St. Nathaniel's pulpit supply—Young Men's Society episode—Concerning sweeps—Southport lady's liberality—The Pope and ' Anglican Orders ' —A message of promise—A mere molehill made a mountain—Diamond Jubilee record—Ragged School collection—Child's ' cot ' at Southport —Serious symptoms.

' Come ye yourselves apart into a desert place, and rest awhile ' (Mark vi. 31).

OUR Lord's tender care for His disciples as workers with Him stands out beautifully in this gracious request. It is well the Saviour says ' Come,' not ' Go ' ; the latter would suit the body, but not the soul. Solitude and rest would not have sufficed to comfort and strengthen them for the great work which they were commissioned to do, if He had not been with them. Holiday times are proverbially times of danger, hence the greater need for the keeping power of God's presence.

Christ is not a hard Master to serve : His ' yoke is easy,' because it is the yoke of love. How often have I felt the graciousness of His consideration for me as a toiler in His service. I am able to say truly that periods of rest have been seasons of close communion with Him, such as I had need of for my own soul. It was a great delight to find myself back among my dear people after five months' absence, and to feel that they were really rejoiced at my return. It was also a subject of deep thankfulness that my health had been partially restored.

Amongst the many comforting letters I received in the Canaries were two from my Bishop. The following are extracts :

' *January* 4, 1897.—I am glad to hear from you, and also very glad to hear you are really feeling better. I think the air of the Canary Islands will really do you good, and set you up for work again at St. Nathaniel's, though it may be prudent to attempt to do less than you have been doing hitherto. God sometimes requires us to do less that we may last the longer and do more, and sometimes requires us to learn the lesson that He can do without us, and that we are not necessary for His work in the world.'

' *February* 8, 1897.—Thanks for your letter. I am glad to hear you are bettering, and trust our feeling and loving Saviour, who knows where you are, and why you are separated from St. Nathaniel's, will cheer and comfort you. He can do without us. It will do your believing people good, that they may learn to depend on Christ and not on Hobson.

' You and I, my brother, will die one day, but Christ dieth no more.'

I cannot do better than give verbatim the *Liverpool Courier's* independent report of the reception accorded me on my return home (see Appendix K).

That, however, was almost thrown into the shade by another, next evening, when going to church.

A group of our dear children playing, saw me coming, and in a moment they made a rush and gave a shout as they ran to meet me. Five got hold of a finger each, and five more of the other hand ; while four seized upon one tail of my coat, and four more had hold of the other. Thus they escorted me to the church, crying out, ' Oh, you're welcome home, welcome home.'

I do not think I was ever more honoured in my life. I did thank God for it.

It is a sad thing if a father returns to his home unlooked for and unwelcomed ; and is it not also a sad thing if a pastor returns to his people unwelcomed by them, they perhaps wishing that, instead of returning, he had found some other charge ?

It is sweet to find that ' absence makes the heart grow fonder.' After the love of God and of His dear Son, can there be anything dearer to the heart of the pastor than the real deep-rooted love of his people ? It makes him young again, giving to his ministry a fresh impetus which nothing else can provide.

It more than compensates for the things which try the pastor's heart and make it ache. It is, indeed, one of the joys of the ministry.

It was a source of comfort to me that during my long absence in the Canary Islands, the pulpit of St. Nathaniel's was honoured by the supply of my clerical brethren, beginning with the Bishop of Liverpool, Bishop Royston, the Venerable Archdeacon Taylor, four Canons, and others of the ablest men in the city. In all, no less than twenty-nine thus assisted. I said to my dear people that there was a danger of their being spoiled for me, by having had the cream of the ministry in Liverpool feeding them with the best things of the Gospel !

I had not the same thrilling accounts to give the church on my return from the Canaries as on my return from Palestine. Still, I had something to say as to the formation of the islands : their salubrious climate ; the crass ignorance of the impoverished people, only ten per cent. of whom can read ; as to how the Reformation was stamped out, burnt out, there ; as to Rome failing to elevate the masses there and everywhere else ; though in those islands she has had, for the last four hundred years, undisputed sway.

However willing the pastor may be to be gentle, even as a nurse, to the Lord's own people ; and however trustful in dear helpers ; there are times when if he will be faithful to God and His truth, and therefore anxious about the souls of those committed to his care, he must not hesitate to take the course which his own conscience and God-given sense point out to him as the right one, regardless of consequences to himself, as concerns popularity or advantage. I know policy would rather let things slide.

Having this autumn had a most favourable opportunity for taking my place as chairman of the Young Men's Society, with these high and holy motives before me, I encountered open opposition from a few of the older members, who had practically swayed the society, in such a manner as to cause me much distress ; not only by their secession, but by their endeavour to set up another and a similar society, which ultimately, however, did not succeed.

The atmosphere being now cleared, the Society took a new start, under more healthy conditions, and went on its way, doing its work satisfactorily.

There is a gentleness which may become weakness, and result in serious injury to the cause of truth.

One day I was asked if it were really true that I shook hands with sweeps. My immediate reply was, Certainly I do. There were four sweeps in the parish. A—— lived in a cellar, drank, and beat his wife, who, poor thing, was blind of one eye, and rather deaf. He signed the teetotal pledge, and broke it ; not, however, until he had saved £21, which he spent in three weeks ; he was now bad from remorse. Again he signed the pledge, and has kept it ever since. He is, for one in his station, wealthy ; drives his wife about in his own handsome trap ; and is certainly a changed man. But I cannot say he is at all spiritually minded.

B—— was a true Christian, a Methodist, but very friendly to St. Nathaniel's. As a pastor, I made no distinction between Church people and Nonconformists.

C—— was known as the whistling sweep ; he announced his presence by whistling, at which he was very clever. He was a sober, decent man, and came to church now and again ; we could not give grace !

D—— was a converted man. When little more than a mere youth, he had been found in about the poorest court of the parish by our Scripture-reader, who got him to become a teetotaler, and then was enabled to lead him to the Saviour.

One day, being very weary, I took a little turn in the suburbs. I saw, at a distance, a black man standing straight up against a newly-built red-brick wall. I felt impelled to speak to that man. On reaching him, and putting out my hand, which he took, I said, ' Well, friend, how are you ? ' ' I am well, I thank you, Mr. Hobson,' he replied. ' Oh, then, you know me ? ' ' I think I do.' ' Now, do tell me what you were thinking about.' ' Well, I have just swept a chimney, and am waiting till it is time to sweep another near by. I was just grieving over the divisions amongst Christians. Did not Christ pray, " Sanctify them through Thy truth," and "that they all may be one"? ' I replied, Certainly ; when actually tears made marks as they ran down his sooty cheeks. I did wish that I could catch those tears in my handkerchief, and put them under a glass shade ; I felt nowhere and nothing in that man's presence. After we had talked together on this topic, he asked, 'Do you really not know me ? ' ' How can I, when you are so covered with soot ? I am, however, beginning to remember you.' Then he told me who he was, and I knew that he was D——. He said he had, after leaving the parish, married, and was living in St. ——, adding, ' Won't you call ? ' That I promised to do, and asked him to come the following Tuesday evening to help at our open-air service. On that evening I noticed at the service a man who remained the whole time, and sang the hymns heartily. After the service, going to speak to the good man, I then discerned it was my friend ; causing laughter by saying, ' Excuse me, my dear friend, you are now washed.' It was delightful to hear that man expound God's Word in the open air.

Some think it lowers the dignity of ' the cloth ' for a minister to shake hands with a sweep, even though he be a brother in Christ, living in the fear and love of God. They are to be pitied.

A friend who paid for one of our Ragged School children's weekly suppers, had to discontinue doing so. We brought the matter before God at our Sunday morning prayer-meeting. I was just then about to preach for our parish in All Saints' Church, Southport ; and on that occasion I certainly did plead hard for the needed £30 a year. There was, however, no special response by the congregation. The next day the vicar took me to call upon a lady member of his church who had heard me preach the day before. We were scarcely seated, when she very brightly inquired whether I had got the £30, and on my replying in the negative, she said, ' I will give it to you, and will continue to do so while I live,' adding, ' I was struck by your remark yesterday, that when the children have had those meals they cannot be taken from them, as presents could be.' She then gave me a cheque for the £30. I was, indeed, deeply thankful, and also greatly surprised. How God sometimes uses what may be considered perhaps the least part of a sermon by which to do His will. Truly He is kind to all who trust Him. Greatly did our little gathering at the next Sunday morning prayer meeting rejoice before the Lord.

There were overflowing congregations on Sunday evenings, to hear my replies to the Pope's two letters, one on ' Unity,' and the other on ' Anglican Orders.' My reply to the one on ' Unity ' was published.

The Ritualists fondly dreamed that the Pope would allow the validity of their Orders. It was humiliating that whilst the Pope was preparing his answer Mr. W. E. Gladstone should write to him, and, as if with cap in hand, beg of him, if he did not sanction them, not to say anything against them ! In his answer, the Pope pulverized the Ritualists' claim, calling the Church of England ' a mere rabble.' He could not consistently stultify his predecessors' action in the matter : it would have been a cause of regret if he had done so. We Evangelicals knew well what the answer would be, and we cared not for either his approval or his disapproval. The validity of our Orders rests upon a sure foundation, the Word of God.

A truly Christian woman, belonging to our congregation, being left a widow, with six small children, but without any means of subsistence, started a little laundry. Early one morning, whilst at the wash-tub, she seemed to hear a voice saying, ' You shall never want chip, work, or food ' ; which she took as a message from God. Though sometimes needy, she would not apply for out-door relief. To keep her home she had to work nineteen hours a day, but the strength to do so was given. Years passed by, and five of her children were married. The remaining one, the youngest, a son, W——, was nearly blind ; but he had learned the piano, and was teaching it ; and getting his mother, now old and feeble, to give up work, by what he made as a teacher of music he supported and comforted her as long as she lived. On entering her room one evening I was greatly touched by seeing him staying his mother up in bed. The sun shone through the window right on them both. As I spoke words of comfort to her, he turned towards me, and, with big tears rolling out of his almost sightless eyes, said, ' I hope God will spare my mother to me a little longer.' His wish was granted.

When visiting her afterwards, she said it was on her mind that for a twelvemonth she had been to a Dissenting chapel instead of to church, and she asked my forgiveness. I at once set her mind at rest about such a circumstance, when the poor soul said, ' I am now satisfied.' Is not this a specimen of the cases contemplated by the absolution in the Visitation service, which has nothing to do with human absolving from sins committed against God ? I buried her, and her loving, tender son, who also died in the Lord.

This year being the Diamond Jubilee of our most

gracious Queen Victoria, we marked it by raising the largest sum we ever gathered on the Ragged School appeal day—£100 6s. That was not due to any large individual donation—for we never knew what it was to have such—but to much prayer, and to great efforts in many directions. On the Sunday night when the amount collected had been counted and handed to the treasurer, I felt quite exhausted. We knelt together in the vestry, and gave God the praise.

I am not ashamed to state that many tears of mine have often moistened the little cushion on the pulpit book-rest. How often have I knelt at it in silent prayer before giving out the text ; many times I have risen to preach weeping. But the Lord stood by me.

We had long felt the need of a ' cot ' at some seaside institution for convalescent poor children ; and after prayer and conference we decided to raise the sum necessary for procuring one at the Southport Children's Sanatorium, as a further suitable memorial of the Diamond Jubilee. The result of our efforts was an amount sufficient to maintain a ' cot ' there for ten years, which proved to be a real boon ; as three weeks each at Southport generally set the weak little ones on their feet again, to their own comfort, and to the joy of their parents. Every child in the parish was eligible, though Church children had precedence.

It was not until the end of this year that I thought it prudent to make known, even to relatives, that on my return from the Canaries, though much improved, I had consulted an eminent London specialist as to my nerve trouble. He told me that if I were to live, I must have less to do ; in fact, that I was not then—though he should suppose improved after so long a rest in the ' land of the sun '—able for more than a tenth of the work to which I was returning.

His prescriptions did me good in some respects, specially in relieving me greatly from depression, which was causing some alarm.

I found I was again working against wind and tide,

and yet I could not endure the idea of resigning, or even of exchange.

I felt at times as if I must sink, perhaps suddenly. It was not at all an uncommon thing, on awaking in the morning, after long, yet not in the least refreshing, sleep, to find that my head was immovable on the pillow ; that only when touched by my hand a little could I feel it was living ; that repeated efforts were needed to raise it, and to enable me, after a while, to rise and dress.

To do, or try to do, my work under such conditions was well-nigh impossible. At the same time I was not, thank God, all the while like this ; but very frequently. I did indeed habitually inquire of the Lord what He would have me do, and the answer came, but not then. Meantime the worst was not permitted to overtake me.

The average attendance at the Lord's Table in the evenings was two hundred and thirty-six for the whole year. The steadily increasing average of communicants despite all hindrances was pleasing.

The Sale of Work realized £201.

In mentioning these large sums raised by us year after year I have been led to remember something of the faith, prayer and effort which they denote. I feel constrained again to thank the great Giver.

Amount raised, one thousand and nine pounds.

1898.

Christmastide benefits to over four thousand—Bishop Ryle's last confirmation — Alexander Millar — Week-day services — Church insufficiently used—' But what if I died before Thursday ? '—Holy Spirit emblems—The Church must be militant.

' Fear not, little flock ; for it is your Father's good pleasure to give you the Kingdom ' (Luke xii. 32).

THESE words of comfort falling fresh from the lips of the Blessed Redeemer, go direct to the very heart of God's true servants, and become a mighty force in their lives.

God is ' Father ' of the little flock. The word means ' feeder.' This He is both able and willing to be. He finds the green pastures and still waters for them ; He makes them to lie down there ; and if they wander to other pastures, He restores their souls.

The flock is a little one. The wonder is that there is any flock at all, so tremendous are the forces arrayed against the Lord's faithful ones.

The Father is Sovereign ; and, blessed be His name, it is His good pleasure to give His little flock the Kingdom.

The Kingdom is the gift of the Father to Christ. This is our real security in this world. and our assurance for the next.

It is pleasing to note that at the Christmas Festival just past, our various agencies, some wholly self-supporting, and some partly so, touched for good over four thousand persons.

Is not the Church the real and true friend of the working classes ? Does it not proclaim the gospel of help for the body, as well as the gospel of sovereign grace for the soul ?

The number named included three hundred and three poor widows of all denominations, distressed families, and the waifs and strays in the Ragged Schools.

Does not this in some little measure reflect the loving care of the great Father, who provides for His sheep and lambs ? This, too, is the Gospel of true social science.

There is surely no need to be ashamed that the strength of the vicar and his staff went so largely in that direction. ' Ichabod ' will be written upon St. Nathaniel's should it ever be otherwise.

The church was built for the parishioners, who are, in the main, very poor ; and its great glory is that it has done its duty, by lovingly getting hold of the poor of the parish for God.

The difficulty of reaching the lowest strata of humanity is something almost incredible, and apparently even insurmountable. I remember one year having left the ordinary confirmation class mainly to the curate, that I might use all the little influence I could command to form a confirmation class of the roughest and lowest boys in the parish. I succeeded in getting sixty-seven of them into it, and had them for some time. But it was not easy to fix their attention, and I am grieved to state there was only one candidate out of the whole ! Well, I thought that one soul was worth all, and infinitely more than all, the labour bestowed. Thank God some few of them, however, came up afterwards.

I so often found that when one had apparently got to the bottom, there was a yet lower depth. Thank God for abounding, yea, superabounding, grace !

There were seventy-four persons confirmed this year, causing us again to rejoice in the Lord.

This was the dear Bishop's last confirmation in St. Nathaniel's. He was just his own self in his address, and in his usual tone. The church was not able to hold all who came to it. Thank God for all the aid rendered by Bishop Ryle to this church and congregation in confirmations on Whit-Sunday mornings !

The following are the questions whicl candidates were usually expected to answer in writing :

What is confirmation ?

Why do you wish to be confirmed ?

What is regeneration ?

Are you born again ?

Are your sins forgiven ?

Do you mean to serve the Lord ?

Will you do all, or anything, in your power for the Church of God ?

Fitness for confirmation was not determined by mere knowledge ; stress was laid rather on the indications of inward grace.

This year the Lord called up higher one of the standard-bearers of St. Nathaniel's, in the person of dear Alexander Millar, an artisan. As his pastor for nearly a quarter of a century, I can testify to his being a whole-hearted servant of God, leading a holy, blameless life, whether in his happy home, or outside it ; working, for twenty-four years, actively and successfully, for the Master, as secretary and treasurer of the Ragged School, Bible-class teacher, open-air preacher, staunch total abstainer ; constantly present at the Lord's Table, a punctual attendant at the weekly prayer and Workmen's Brotherhood meetings ; a thorough Protestant, a liberal contributor to the various parochial and congregational funds, a valued and chief counsellor in the matters of church, mission-halls, and vicarage.

In fact, where has his influence for God not been felt in our church and parish ? Thank God for his life ! By his call home heaven is richer, and we are poorer.

The first tablet in St. Nathaniel's was set up to his memory, bearing this inscription :

' This scroll was erected by the Rev. Canon Hobson, and the congregation of St. Nathaniel's, Windsor, to the glory of God, and in affectionate memory of Alexander Millar, who for twenty-four years was a devoted lay helper in the work of the Church, both spiritual and social, among the poor.'

Let me state that when our dear Bishop read it, the tears flowed down his face, and, turning to me, he said : ' You may thank God you had such a man as that for twenty-four years.'

It is sad to find how comparatively few of those who ought to attend Divine Service on week-days do so.

From the beginning we had service on Wednesday evenings, and from 1872 up to the time of my resignation there was also a regular Friday evening shortened service. The average attendance, counted and entered in the preacher's book, for this year, was, on Wednesday evenings eighty-seven, and on Friday evenings thirty-two.

It is something to have, on a Friday evening, a average of thirty-two persons all told, meeting for worship in God's house. I have a belief in small congregations as well as in large ones. I am satisfied there is not sufficient use made of the church itself, and therefore I wish there was legally more liberty in that respect : seeing the working classes will attend a mission-hall, and are blessed there ; but in so many instances they will not go to the ordinary church service.

The average attendance at the Lord's Table on Sunday evenings was two hundred and thirty-four. We never had a large number at other times ; usually from thirty to one hundred.

It is as true in sacred work as it is in secular, that ' nothing succeeds like success.' There is a sort of inspiration in the presence of the many. This is largely so in the case of the masses ; they like to see a crowd. An empty church is, therefore, likely to remain empty, and a full church is, in a similar way, likely to continue full. The warmth of response in a large and hearty congregation has considerable effect on most people. That, for instance, is one reason why I would not have three, or even two administrations of the Lord's Supper on the first Sunday in the month ; but one, and one only, in the evening, when the hundreds attended, and when the glow was inspiring.

I had a letter from a person outside Liverpool who said he was seeking the Lord, but could not find Him. He asked for an interview after business hours, which meant not before nine o'clock p.m. This was on a Monday, and I wrote at once fixing the following Thursday at nine. I had an answer thanking me, and containing the very startling words : ' But what if I died before Thursday ! ' I at once wrote naming the next evening. He kept the appointment. I received him with deep humility, and after much prayer. I found him an extremely interesting young man. He had been awakened about his soul for over two years. He read the Scriptures, prayed, and conversed with several religious people as to his state, but got no peace. I set Christ before him as the Saviour, by simple faith ; and, praise the Lord, the blessing came to him ; and in the exuberance of his soul he embraced me ! My cup of happiness overflowed : we blessed God together. That dear young man has gone on serving and working for Him. His first concern, however, was about the salvation of his wife, whom the Lord gave him in answer to faith, prayer, and the Word. Referring to that blessed circumstance, he said to her : ' We are one now, not " till death us do part," but one in Christ for eternity.'

I ought to state that all such cases were so blessed to my own soul, that I seemed never to have lost the love and glow of the new-born in Christ Jesus. Thank God !

Such sense of one's efforts being owned and blessed by God constitutes one of the greatest joys of the Gospel ministry. Oh, the happiness of having an ever-increasing family of sons and daughters in Christ, and the prospect of being enabled, through God's keeping grace, to say by-and-bye, ' I and the children which God hath given me.'

Emblems of the Holy Spirit :

' Water. Fertilizing, refreshing, abundant, freely given.

' Fire. Purifying, illuminating, searching.

' Wind. Independent, powerful in its effects, reviving.

' Oil. Healing, comforting, consecrating.

' Rain and Dew. Refreshing, imperceptible, penetrating.

' A Dove. Gentle, meek, innocent, forgiving.

' A Voice. Speaking, guiding, warning, teaching.

' A Seal. Impressing, securing, authenticating.

' Cloven tongues.'

I had still, lest it might be forgotten, to remind our people of the little prayer for the Holy Spirit at one o'clock each day, when the signal-gun goes off, viz., ' Oh God, for Jesus Christ's sake, send me Thy Holy Spirit ! ' He is, as we recite in the Nicene Creed, ' the Author and Giver of life.'

In conversation with our Bishop, the Lord's work in the parish came up. I remarked that in St. Nathaniel's we have, at least, two things—viz., the pure Word of God, and the manifested blessing of the Holy Spirit. To which he made reply : ' They are the two most powerful factors.'

Is it not evident that the Church must ever be in a militant state ? Is it not one prolonged, never-ending conflict against Satan, sin, error, poverty, and the flesh, yet remaining in God's own people ? The whole Christian armour is necessary. The enemy is not only in the field, but active.

It is not worthy the captain who leads, nor the glory and honour of our God, ever to desire it should be otherwise, even though some feel badly wounded and well-nigh worn out.

The Lord is with us ; the issue is with Him ; there can be no doubt as to what that will be : and He will recognize the services of His true, loyal, devoted soldiers in the conflict. That nerves them to go forth and fight in His name and strength.

I sometimes wondered whether it would have been better if we had had the church, halls, and vicarage, completed to begin with, with a congregation and church endowments all in apple-pie order ; than to find ourselves in the position described in these pages.

There is no doubt the flesh would choose the former, but I have long since come to the conclusion that, for both minister and people, the latter was the better.

There is just the same difference between the man who is the architect of his own fortune, and the man who inherits all that this world can give.

At all events, since we had to find so much, we endeavoured to make what some would call ' a virtue of necessity,' though it demanded, beside faith, prayer, and effort, much wear of brain, heart, and body.

It is a happy thing to be able to adapt one's self to the environments of the position in which God in His wisdom has placed one.

Amount raised, nine hundred and ninety-seven pounds.

1899.

Bishop Ryle's last sermon and gathering of presbyters—Blessed results from the Ragged School—The Church's urgent need—Intercourse with God—True meaning of confirmation—And of baptism—Church Army —The pastor the best pleader—The only protection against the ' isms ' —Bishop Ryle's last communion.

' Risen with Christ' (Col. iii. 1).

THIS is one of the most joyous resurrection notes, in the whole Word of God.

' Risen with Christ ' implies buried with Him and that implies crucified with Him ; which again implies substitution and representation. His people are therefore identified with Christ in His death, burial, and resurrection.

Christ's resurrection is the great proof of His Divine mission, and of His completed and accepted work : therefore His people are fully accepted in Him. This is why Paul says, ' Likewise reckon ye also yourselves to be dead indeed unto sin, but alive unto God through Jesus Christ our Lord.'

On Sunday, January 8, at the 6.30 o'clock service, the good Bishop preached for the last time in our church, taking as his text John xvii. 15, ' I pray not that Thou shouldest take them out of the world, but that Thou shouldest keep them from the evil.' The discourse was marked by well-nigh his usual strength and vigour. Truly whenever he came to us he brought a blessing with him.

> ' From whence this fear and unbelief ?
> Hast Thou, O Father, put to grief
> Thy spotless Son for me ?
> And will the righteous Judge of men
> Condemn me for that debt of sin
> Which, Lord, was laid on Thee ₁
>
> ' Complete atonement Thou hast made,
> And to the utmost farthing paid
> Whate'er Thy people owed.
> How then can wrath on me take place,
> If covered in Thy righteousness,
> And sprinkled by Thy blood ?
>
> ' Turn thou my soul unto thy rest ;
> The merits of thy great High Priest
> Speak peace and liberty.
> Trust in His efficacious Blood,
> Nor fear thy banishment from God,
> Since Jesus died for thee.'

This same month saw the Bishop's last ' Presbyters' Party '—of those whom he had himself ordained to the second order of the ministry,—when there were about one hundred and sixty present. He told them it might be the last time ; his words were weighty, faithful, and encouraging as ever.

It was often asked, ' Why should a poor parish like St. Nathaniel's have taken over the Ragged School of the mother church, and sustained it at a cost of nearly £300 per annum without any aid from the Government ? '

It is now twenty-seven years since the grave responsibility was incurred, and on looking back, so far from there being any reason for regret, there is, on the contrary, abundant cause for thankfulness.

I believed at the beginning that it would be, and am fully satisfied that it has been, not nearly the least of many causes resulting in so successful an issue to the work as a whole.

It has gone far to convince the working classes that our profession of religion was more than what they consider—in the absence of practical proof to the contrary—'hypocritical cant.' That was great gain.

Then there was the pleasure of doing good to the bodies of a class who could not make any return.

And marvellous are the good results which have followed from these schools. There are scores of respectable heads of families in the parish and neighbourhood who owe to them their first impressions for good and for God ; and in several instances some of them are not only true Christians, but also workers for God. Take the following :

A resident in Liverpool, a worthy man, who has acquired considerable property, and employs over sixty hands.

A commercial traveller, in receipt of a liberal salary, a communicant, and with his rented pew in a neighbouring church.

A music-teacher, residing in a good house, with a large family ; also a communicant.

Another, the superintendent of a large Sunday-school in Manchester, under an Evangelical vicar.

A captain of a merchant steamer.

Many devoted Christian husbands, wives, and mothers.

One whom I left, on my resignation, peoples' churchwarden of dear St. Nathaniel's, and superintendent of the very ragged school he himself attended for years !

Another, the truly Christian man, who, with fidelity and credit, has conducted St. Nathaniel's Penny Bank, and has been an intelligent helper in definite Christian work for the last quarter of a century.

Could anyone have thought that flowers of such elegance in form, such beauty in colour, such sweetness in scent, and fruit of such luscious ripeness, could have been grown in our original ' sixteen acres of sin ' ?

No ! Nor could they, but for the power of Divine grace ! It was the Lord's doing !

' Not unto us, O Lord, not unto us, but unto Thy name give glory.'

I estimate the cost of these schools up to the present at something like £7,000, truly a formidable sum for a very poor parish to have raised, in addition to all other necessary demands. We never had large sums given for them, except two bequests, one for £300, and another for £50 ; both which were invested at interest, as we actually did not require to use them.

One teacher, and afterwards for some years superintendent, now a comparatively wealthy man, residing in London, traces the turning of the tide in his life to the blessing of God resting upon him from the very day he put his hand to that plough ; previously to which nothing he touched had succeeded.

It is now ' an old saw ' that Evangelicalism is effete, that whatever power it may have had has gone. This comes from two sources, the Broad Churchmen and the High Churchmen. Is it so ? There is a dead Evangelicalism, I grant ; but that is not a fair specimen by which to judge. Two sayings of good Bishop Ryle admirably describe the situation : ' The people want sixteen ounces to the pound '; and, ' If you want to warm a church put a stove in the pulpit.'

Oh that God would be pleased to baptize the ministers of our Church ' with the Holy Ghost and with fire.' This is the one great, chief, urgent need, if the Church is to remain a power for good in the land.

There can be little doubt that to win souls to God is a thing of influence, aye, and of that influence which comes from on high alone. Realizing that personal intercourse and communion with God can only be obtained and enjoyed by constant private prayer, which becomes the motive power, the mainspring, of all our spiritual activities, and the source of all our peaceful rest amidst the distressing and disturbing events of daily life ; and in order that others may be helped, either by being warned or encouraged by my experience ; with diffidence and humility I make known my habits or mode of intercourse with God. I had, with others, communion with God in the church, but I never had a set time for private prayer, except by my bedside morning and evening, which from a child had always been my custom. I have also constantly cultivated habitual private communion with God ; as I went along, no matter where, when, or how, it was my wont to turn to God, through His dear Son, in prayer. Prayer was therefore to me as natural as breathing : I could not go on without it. The Saviour's command to His disciples was, ' As ye go, preach ' ; to me it was, ' As you go, pray ' ; and as I went, I prayed.

This may not be for all the most excellent way : it was, however, that for me

The following is from the *Rock's* review of ' Thirty Years' Ministry in St. Nathaniel's, Windsor ' :

' Canon Hobson has proved himself to be a model parochial clergyman, a calm, earnest, convincing preacher—in a clear, sympathetic voice—of the old, old Gospel ; in the services reverend, tender, and most devout ; and an untiring house-to-house visitor.

' An able, fair, and uncompromising controversialist, a sturdy Protestant champion, never having budged an inch from the principles of the Reformed Church, a sympathetic parson, and a friend in need, excelling beside the sick and dying.

' Such have been the leading characteristics of his thirty years' ministry, which filled a church at its outset, and has sustained it amidst changes of population, removals by death, and other hindrances.

' The services, as conducted at St. Nathaniel's, are

plain, bright, hearty, and congregational. The psalms are read, the gown is worn in the pulpit.

' There is a mixed voluntary choir, and throughout earnestness pervades this, as it does every other department of the church's work.'

There was again our annual rejoicing over the confirmees, ninety in number, for their professed individual faith in the Lord Jesus. Glory to God !

It needs to be reiterated that our Church supposes candidates for confirmation to have been born again, and to have obtained the forgiveness of their sins, so implying the gift of the Holy Ghost : a further manifestation of the same blessed Spirit is sought in the confirmation service, to strengthen the soul in answer to prayer, and not through any imagined virtue in the imposition of the Bishop's hands. In this connection, I well remember dear Bishop Ryle in one of his addresses to candidates, holding out his hands towards them, and saying : ' Do not think the Holy Ghost is going to come to you through these poor fingers of mine : ask, ask ! Let us all ask for that further gift and we shall receive it.'

I am bold to say that thousands of St. Nathaniel's people would gladly testify that after the Resurrection joy of Easter, there was none like to the blessedness of those Whit-Sunday confirmations.

Why should it not be so ? I wish our Evangelical brethren would all seek to give effect to our Evangelical services more and more : if they did, would not the results of our ministry be more fruitful in rich spiritual life ?

It always rejoiced my heart to see mothers finding their places in the church to return thanks to Almighty God for His great mercy ' lately vouchsafed unto them.' There is nothing in the service to justify the ' sneer ' that such is the survival of the Jewish doctrine of ceremonial cleansing from incidental defilement. If it be similar in the true spirit of thankfulness, it would be well if there were more of it.

The baptisms each year were in fair proportion to the births in the parish. The question frequently put in the homes was, ' Are all the children baptized ? '

All evangelicals are careful in this matter, though they do not hold that infants dying before baptism are lost.

The service is truly real, in so far as there is offered to God true and believing prayer for the spiritual regeneration of the child.

Adhering to the original principle on which our work was begun, that is of self-help and independence, I did not accept the offer of an agent from the Church Army, because there is no room for what I rather regard it to be in a parish, viz., an *imperium in imperio*. Beside which, God had given willing, loving hearts in abundance, to be trained and guided to do all that could be done in the parish, so that we were content to work on our own lines.

This will apply somewhat, too, in the matter of special preachers, though we had them occasionally. When we wanted money we tried what we could do amongst ourselves. No stranger, however superior, could get as much money from our people as their own minister. And this was not so much due to any power in his appeal, as to his having fully informed and interested the people concerning the nature and importance of the project in hand : so that they gave rather on principle, than from what might be mere passing impulse.

In working a poor parish there is the possibility of getting drawn aside to do work which, though of a kindred character, does not strictly belong to the pastor, who has all too little strength and time to do what appertains to him exclusively.

For instance, there is the work of the police, nurses, School Board visitors, relieving officers, doctors. It is the pastor's duty to be on friendly terms with all these, and to aid them ; but not to be used by them to do any of their work.

I think it is a mistake, especially in a city, for a

minister to prescribe in sick cases, even if he possess a tolerable amount of medical knowledge ; or in any way to interfere with medical professional men, in commending or condemning them as such.

If care be not taken in these relationships, the pastor may suffer in influence more than he is aware of : to suggest a simple remedy till the doctor comes is altogether different.

A most important subject is exercising the minds of all right-thinking members, both lay and clerical, of the Church in England, and finds expression in the often asked question, ' How can our people, especially the young amongst them, be best protected against the aggressions of those twin adversaries, Romanism and Ritualism ? ' That inquiry I desire to answer by a statement of facts—which, therefore, cannot be gainsaid —within the knowledge of scores, I might even say hundreds, of responsible Christian men and women.

Those facts form part of my experience as an ordained minister of the Church for nearly forty years, the major part of which was as vicar of St. Nathaniel's, Windsor, Liverpool.

That parish has a population of over six thousand, of which number fully one-third are Romanists, there being also a few Nonconformists.

There is on its northern border a large Romish presbytery, with all the usual ecclesiastical agencies of a proselytizing propaganda ; whilst on the south side there is a wealthy, well-equipped Ritualistic church, scarcely so aggressive as the other.

During the entire period of my vicariate, we had just two secessions, and two only ; one to the ' ism ' on the north, and one to the ' ism ' on the south ; whilst from the latter we received numbers of accessions, and from the former there were scores of converts

And what brought that about ? The putting—in preaching and teaching—the Truth as found in God's Word, side by side with the errors of Romanism and

Ritualism : the contrasting one with the others ; the proving from Holy Scripture that the doctrines of Protestantism are based upon and found in it, whilst the teachings of Romanism and Ritualism are founded upon perversions and corruptions of God's Word, and upon tradition, all which have been frequently exposed ; that whilst Protestantism appeals to the intellect and heart, Romanism and Ritualism pander mainly to the senses ; that *they* dishonour God by attempting to supplement His Son's Atonement, while Protestantism relies for salvation on that Atonement alone.

With all this happy experience to weight my words, I desire in humility and earnestness to press upon my brethren and fellow-labourers in the ministry and amongst the laity, especially those who are parents, the need of making known, in their several relations, the pure Gospel of God's Grace, in contrast with the teachings of error—whether Romish, Ritualistic, Socialistic, Agnostic, or Rationalistic—in faith, with prayer, and by example ; so that old and young, learned and ignorant, rich and poor, may alike have opportunities of exercising their God-given sense in choosing for this life, and therefore for the next also, whose they will be and whom they will serve now, and, therefore, with whom they will spend an endless eternity.

For some months dear Bishop Ryle was very low, but rallied towards Christmas. As we were just about to commence the 11 o'clock service on Christmas Day, a tap was heard at the vestry entrance to the church, and on the door being opened, to our utter amazement, there was the Bishop, quite bent, with his family, including his son the late Bishop of Winchester. They all sat in the vicar's pew. The Bishop, as was his custom, sat in the corner where good Mrs. Ryle used to sit. The congregation was visibly affected at seeing their dear Bishop, always so straight and commanding, now bowed down ; yet delighted to have seen him once again in the church he loved so well.

I preached from 2 Cor. viii. 9.

At the Sacrament the Bishop came to the rail, followed by his children, who knelt on either side of him. For a moment I felt almost overcome ; which he must have perceived, for, looking up at me, he said softly, ' Go on.' They remained till the congregation had gone, when I went to him. He reached out his poor hand, and drew me to him, saying, ' This is the last time ; God bless you ; we shall meet in heaven.' The big tears trickled down his furrowed cheeks.

This year there was the usual activity in all the departments of parochial work.

The sum raised amounted to nine hundred and ninety seven pounds.

1900.

Home Words—Brought to a standstill—Last interview with Bishop Ryle—The Bishop's gift—Leaves for the Canaries again—Interesting cabin companion—Bishop Taylor Smith—Liverpool lad's grave at Las Palmas—, The host '—A grateful parent—Bishop Ryle's death—Sermon at the Cathedral—The M.P. and the electric light—Bishop Chavasse—Visit to Cannes—Resignation looming large.

' Christ in you, the hope of glory ' (Col. i. 27).

THIS indwelling is by faith only : ' That Christ may dwell in your hearts by faith ' (Ephes. iii. 17) ; ' By nature Satan dwells in the heart ' (Ephes. ii. 2).

Christ is the stronger than ' the strong man.' Where He dwells, He reigns, and is supreme ; hence our souls swell with that well-grounded hope of glory hereafter (Heb. vi. 18, 19), by which we are kept from going under, amidst conflicts and trials. To this end, and for all ends, may the blessed Christ fill us, permeate us, make us ' more than conquerors.'

This year saw the introduction of *Home Words*, as our New magazine. It had a favourable reception, and the subscribers increased to eight hundred and fifty.

There was a very solemn feeling during the first week of the New Year, being the Week of Prayer. The meetings were conducted by the vicar himself, and sixteen of the brethren took part in them. On the first Sunday evening in the month two hundred and sixty-one partook of the Lord's Supper.

I felt quite unable to go on, and under medical advice resolved, though very reluctantly, to spend a couple of months in the Canaries, with the prospect of being set up again, at all events, for a little while longer.

Before leaving, I had my last interview with good Bishop Ryle, who, on account of failing health, had resigned his See.

Calling at the hour he had fixed for seeing me, I found him in his study : he was very bright, and, as was his wont, he inquired after my health and about the parish. On remarking how touched we all were by seeing him with us at St. Nathaniel's on Christmas morning, he smilingly replied, ' Yes, I said to my children, " Let us go to Nathaniel's this morning, for I am sure we shall be welcome there." '

Then he said, ' I have been thinking what memento you might like to have of me. I have thought you would like to have my Bible which I have been using on my study table for over fifty years.' I thanked him most cordially, assuring him I would value that gift beyond anything. Taking up his pen, he wrote in it :

' Given to
R. H O B S O N
by
J. C. RYLE,
First Bishop of Liverpool.
With very much Christian love.
22nd January, 1900.'

Handing the book to me, he said, ' Now let us have a

parting prayer.' I knelt by his chair, and oh, what a prayer he offered for me ! I shall never forget it !

I never saw the dear Bishop again ; but I shall see him in that land of bliss where there will be no resignations, no old-age infirmities ; where we, with all the blood-washed multitude, shall be ' for ever with the Lord.'

On more than one occasion I heard him say, referring to his well-worn little preaching Bible, that, as the sword of an officer is buried with him, so he expected his sword—the Bible he used in preaching—to be buried with him. If report speaks correctly, it was laid on his heart in his coffin !

Having secured my berth on the s.s. *Fantee* for the Grand Canary, on being shown my state-room I discovered I had as a fellow-voyager a Romish priest ; which at once set me thinking, and asking the Lord what it meant ? whether He had a message to that sickly-looking young man ? and if so, to show me what it was, and how to deliver it. My companion's berth was over mine : he retired before me. After I had prayed, though I had not been introduced to him I laid my hands on his bed and inquired if he were asleep, to which he gently said ' No.' I then said, ' Are not these words of the blessed Lord Jesus precious—" Come unto Me, all ye that labour " ? ' ' Yes,' he replied in a soft tone, ' they are comforting words.' My heart leapt for joy : I said no more. I turned in, but could not sleep for thinking of the stranger, and I cried to the God of heaven for him.

We sat at the same table in the saloon. On reaching the Grand Canary he said to me, ' Though I was going to another hotel, I would like to go with you to the Metropole. There we sat at the same table again. When he was poorly in his room, I visited him ; and on leaving him behind me at the Metropole, he refused to stand in a photographic group except beside me.

One Sunday he remarked that he had heard I preached in the Protestant Church. I said, ' Yes ; come aside.'

And I gave him the points of my sermon on the words
' The precious blood of Christ,' to which he listened
eagerly. The Lord knows I did indeed watch in love
for the dear fellow's soul. We had no controversy, as
he did not raise any ; but at the same time I put before
him the truth as to God's only way of saving the soul.
We were really knit to each other in affection. I do
not think he was likely to survive long, as he seemed
far gone in phthisis ; and as I have not heard from, or
of him, I leave him with the Lord. I cannot think that
what happened was for naught.

The voyage was enjoyable, and the destination was
reached in due time. I had some opportunities for good
on board, specially with my friend the priest.

This time the rest and the lovely climate soon told
favourably. I was able to visit the English Hospital,
and the English Sailors' Home, where I conducted service now and then. I visited sick people in their private
lodgings, and had many openings in the hotel where I
stayed, particularly with four young men.

I made the acquaintance of Bishop Taylor Smith, of
Sierra Leone, for whom the lovers of evangelical truth
have reason to thank God. He had come thither on an
Episcopal tour, the Canaries being in his diocese. He
gave me a cordial and hearty invitation to visit Sierra
Leone, promising me a warm reception from himself, and
a fever ! The latter was a damper, at which he laughed
merrily, adding ' I must put the whole truth before you.'

I laid roses on the grave of a Liverpool youth buried
on the previous Christmas Day in the British Cemetery,
Las Palmas. His distressed father made himself known
to me on board ship just as we were about to leave the
Mersey, requesting me to make inquiries concerning the
end of his darling boy. At his wish I laid my hand on
the grave, in the name of the bereaved parents, as an
indication of their undying love for the departed. Only
parents similarly stricken can understand what that
means.

Addressing the friends from the hotel who had accompanied me, I said, ' I do not pray for the soul of this youth.' I asked them to join me in thanking God, as I had it from the disconsolate father that he believed the soul of his son was with Christ.

Sitting one day under a palm-tree in Las Palmas, I heard the tinkling of a little bell ; and on looking whence the sound came, I at once perceived a procession emerging from a church close by. Preceded by a bannerette, and a bell-ringer, there were two priests in their robes, followed by a few persons. It was ' a sick call ' ; the host was being carried thither. I noticed some round about went on their knees, while all, at least, uncovered their heads. In a moment it occurred to me that not to do either might be a very serious thing : I therefore at once asked the Lord what I should do. I felt I must not—no matter what might be the consequence, I would not—in any way whatever recognize an idol of flour and water, the host, the wafer, which can neither hear, see, nor speak.

There was no notice, however, taken of my remaining seated with my hat on, and so the procession passed along. I thanked God for the result ; though it would have been an honour to suffer in protest against the idol of the great apostasy. I remembered, too, the second commandment, and that Cranmer, Ridley and Latimer went to the stake rather than cry ' Credo ' to the host.

Thank God such idolatrous processions are illegal in England.

The day before I left, the Rev. A. Duncan, M.A., presented me with an address (see Appendix L).

The welcome home from the dear people of St. Nathaniel's was a real joy and encouragement to me. There is no greater reward to the minister of Christ than the affection and love of his people. That is what neither money can purchase, nor fame secure. I cannot do better than epitomize the notice given of it in the *Liverpool Courier* (see Appendix M).

Many months after I returned from the Grand

Canary, a gentleman on the landing-stage, bowing, thus accosted me : ' You are Canon Hobson ; your name is now a household word in my home. You met our son last spring at the Metropole, Grand Canary. My wife and myself are most anxious to know how you reached his heart, for we attributed to you the thorough change in him on his return. Is he living ? ' ' No, but he died a true Christian, to the great joy of his mother and myself.' He added that before his son went to the Grand Canary as a forlorn hope, he would not allow anyone to speak to him about religion. I then told him how it all came about in the Lord's kind providence and grace. Thank God !

On five consecutive Sunday evenings I had Plain Talks upon the following subjects :

A Spring Sermon : From Death unto Life.

Voices of the Sea.

Mission Work on the West Coast.

The Sling and the Stone.

The Voices of the Stars.

The work amongst men was not overlooked, especially in later years. There is the indirect as well as the direct result in everything we do for God. The following figures show the numbers meeting in the halls, in which such subjects as the Gospel, thrift, and sobriety were set forth :

The Windsor Workmen's Brotherhood	500
The Young Men's Literary Society	100
Tontine (St. Nathaniel's)	176
Tontines (Orange)	150
Bible-classes	140
Men's Service	91
Non-Parochial Tontine	216
Total	1,373

The above figures do not include the large proportion of men who ordinarily worship in church.

It is no small thing to have so many men meeting in the parish halls ; and though some of them attend no other place of worship, they are more likely to feel kindly towards the church, which is something. If men are not drawn by kindliness they will not be drawn at all. Having had to do with vast numbers of operatives, I am bound to state I have a profound respect for them; and oh! the joy of winning them to God!

It is estimated that thirty millions in these countries are outside Church and Chapel on the Lord's Day.

If this be correct, what a problem true Christians have to solve!

Is it the will of God that this should be?

' Is there no balm in Gilead?'

' Is there no Physician there?'

Surely, Holy Scripture makes it plain that our duty and privilege lie in seeking to win all souls to Him who willeth that all should be saved. I see no likelihood of this being done, except by every true member of Christ, and especially every minister, getting back to His self-sacrificing life and that of His Apostles, being like Him and them, filled ' with the Holy Ghost and with power.' Oh! that the Holy Spirit so cleansed, purified, and filled the hearts of His people as to fit them for so great a work. This should not be too much for faith in our Covenant God and Father in Christ to plead, expect, and work for : let us all ask ourselves, ' Is it?'

The news at last reached the city, and the country, that Dr. J. C. Ryle, late Bishop of Liverpool, had passed away from the Church below to the Church above; to be with the Saviour he loved and served on earth.

There was, as usual, the general chorus of lamentation, joined in, forsooth, even by certain portions of the religious Press which had so maligned that great and good man, whose praise was in ' all the churches.' The head and front of his offending was his able championship of thorough Protestant evangelical principles. Bold as a lion for the truth, he was yet tender, even to those who could not see anything good in him, or in his work as a Bishop.

It is true he did not build a cathedral : he did more

urgent work by building forty-four churches and fifty-nine mission-halls. He set on foot the Church house ; launched an association for increasing the stipends of ill-paid incumbents ; created pensions for aged and infirm ministers ; doubled the confirmees, and the curates, of the diocese ; and gained golden opinions for the Church of England amongst Nonconformists, whom he regarded as brethren in the Lord, though never yield-his Churchmanship for a moment. Thus he set, in all these things, an example to his brother Bishops.

It was clear that towards the end of his episcopate some of those who had shown him scanty respect began to understand him. One of them, a Canon, said to me, ' Though we differ from him we have learned to love him.'

I had the privilege of preaching, in my ' turn,' at the Cathedral on the Sunday after his funeral (see Appendix N).

On July 17th, the anniversary of the consecration of the church, an open-air service was held in —— Street, which was decorated with bunting, clean door-steps, and clean faces. There was a numerous attendance. Four addresses were given, interspersed with hymns and prayer.

There is a most striking contrast between what this street is in 1900 A.D. and what it was in former years, when absolutely filled with the social evil, ' the little Hell.'

Having had the pleasure of giving the church choir a trip to the Isle of Man, I met on board the worthy and generous member for our Division, who was indeed a kind friend to our parish. In conversing with me, he, of his own accord, said that he had heard I was not strong ; and that owing to the large congregation in St. Nathaniel's on Sunday evenings I felt the heat very much. Looking at me, he added, ' If you would like it, in order to relieve you, I would gladly bear the expense of putting the electric light in the church.' I replied, ' Thank you, much, I had not thought of such a thing ; that is most generous.' He then said, ' Please go and select the fittings, have it done as you wish, and send me the bills.' The thing was done, and it cost him £180 ! This gift is all the more valuable when it is stated the donor is a Nonconformist ; though it is equally true he was baptized and confirmed in the church. Again it has come to pass : ' There is that scattereth and yet increaseth.'

We have reason to be thankful to the great Head of the Church for the appointment to the See of Liverpool of the Rev. Francis James Chavasse, sometime Principal of Wycliffe Hall, Oxford. Let us gather round him with faith, prayer, and sympathy, that he may be able not only to feed the flock of God, but to reprove, rebuke, and exhort with all long-suffering and doctrine, and to convince the gainsayer.

Soon after his arrival I called on him, asking him to preach once on our anniversary Ragged School day in St. Nathaniel's, when he replied, ' I will do any-thing for you ' ; which I felt very deeply, and humbly thanked God for thus giving me favour in the eyes of our new Diocesan.

Truly the Lord has ever been most gracious and merciful to me !

A local popular Publication paid a kindly tribute to the work and services in St. Nathaniel's (see Appendix O).

Little did I think that this was my last opportunity of pleading, as vicar, for the Ragged Schools. I have done that year by year, all along ; and almost exclusively, so great a privilege did I esteem it to be.

The general work was well sustained throughout.

As I had rest in the spring, I took no more until the autumn, when I accepted an invitation to stay with a friend in Cannes ; and having remained there a month, I returned refreshed for the winter. There came upon me, however, a growing impression that I could not hold out much longer ; I had for some years been suffering from nervous prostration, which at times was well-nigh more than I could bear.

On my return from Cannes I consulted a London specialist, who told me, as he put it, ' once for all,' that unless I had absolute rest I might ' go down ' at any moment ; but that complete rest might lengthen out my days. I dare not think what this involved : I kept it all in my own bosom.

Christmas came on with all its additional happy work amongst the Lord's poor, of which I never grew tired. I also little thought that this would be my last Christmas as the pastor of St. Nathaniel's. Late on Christmas Eve I felt as if my heart would break, as if all the ' virtue ' had gone out of me. I tried to tell the Lord all about it ; blessing Him for having filled my cup.

To preach on New Year's Eve called forth all the latent power I possessed ; the church being full of rough people, unaccustomed, as most of them evidently were, to enter a place of worship. How my soul longed to win them for God. The text was, ' As for me and my house, we will serve the Lord.'

I retired to rest at 2 o'clock a.m., feeling as if I could sleep for a week, and almost wishing my lips were closed for ever.

Oh, dear Lord, Thy poor servant specially needed rest and consolation for body and soul at that time.

The Sale of Work brought in £311 net.

The total sum raised this year was one thousand and four pounds

1901.

Struck down—The way made plain—Congregation's objection, and Bishop's offer—Resignation decided on—Incidental arrangements—Letters acknowledging spiritual good—Farewell sermon—Voyage to the United States and Canada—Second visit to Cannes and work there—St. Honorat Monastery—Conversation with a Romish priest—Return to England and sojourn at Southport—Sermons in Liverpool Cathedral and in St. Nathaniel's Church—Conclusion—Thankful strains.

' And on His head were many crowns ' (Rev. xix. 12).

PREACHING in the church, on New Year's Eve, from Josh. xxix. 15, with no distinct idea that this was the last time I, as vicar of the parish, should take part in a Watch-night service, I poured out my whole soul, to influence the vast audience in deciding for Christ.

This being the week of prayer, I gave in church a short address on Tuesday, Wednesday, Thursday, and Friday ; when, as was usual, many of the helpers led in prayer as arranged. I preached twice on Sunday, January 6, when three hundred and fifty-nine communicants gathered humbly and lovingly around the Lord's Table.

On reaching the vicarage, I laid down on the study floor, feeling as if this time without doubt I must die from sheer exhaustion. After a while I managed to get to bed, and there I lay for many weeks, prostrate. During those weary weeks of sickness and weakness, the conviction that the time had come for me to resign took shape. I besought the Lord to make it plain to me ; He did, and I felt satisfied it was His divine will. I hinted the same to two or three of my dear helpers who were allowed to see me as soon as I began to rally ; but they, in their loving attachment, would not hear of such a thing.

The Bishop visited me, and I was not a little comforted by his ministrations. On mentioning to him my intention, he expostulated, advising that I should take a year's rest, and promising that he would give me another curate to carry on the work during my absence ; for which I felt deeply grateful.

But I could not endure the thought of clinging to the emolument of my office, when I felt myself unequal to the discharge of its pressing duties, the spiritual and the temporal interests of the parish. To have done so would probably have involved the decline of the cause so dear to me, and that would be more than I could bear. I also had implicit confidence in my Heavenly Father being graciously pleased to grant to His worn-out servant rest and repose after having held aloft for a little over fifty years, though it may have been with a trembling hand, the banner of truth. I knew I had His loving smile as a son in His family. Therefore I adhered to my intention, by resigning, which I still feel certain was the right thing to do ; though it was the greatest sorrow I ever had, except the death of my darling mother.

The Bishop having promised to administer the rite of confirmation on Whit-Sunday, May 26, I thought that would be a most suitable occasion for my last Sunday as vicar of St. Nathaniel's. I decided to say my final farewell in church at the 8 o'clock service on Wednesday evening the 29th, and that my resignation should take effect the next day.

As I was now convalescent, I tried to direct the work, preaching occasionally, and making a great effort to instruct the confirmation class, as I knew it would be my last. I prayed that God's blessing might be poured down upon it very abundantly.

The ' memorial ' service on the death of our most gracious Queen was duly observed ; the church was suitably and becomingly draped. I made a desperate effort, and by God's help was able to preach on the occasion.

In order to take the congregation and parishioners into my confidence I addressed to them a circular letter (see Appendix P).

The *Liverpool Courier*, in announcing my resignation, touched upon my work during the past forty years (see Appendix Q).

The Easter Vestry was very largely attended. After the usual business had been transacted, I reviewed the work as a whole, feeling as I did very sorely indeed; and there was sadness on every face, especially when I took my leave of the wardens and sidesmen, and others present.

The whole machinery of the church and parish was kept fully ' running ' through the services of the curate and of the dear helpers : nothing was allowed to flag. I was not half myself, and the dear people were in sorrow about their pastor, sympathizing with him deeply. Many of my clerical brethren most kindly and willingly helped in the pulpit.

On Easter Day I preached twice. The Lord's Supper was administered three times, when four hundred and thirty-one partook thereof. Thank God !

As I was able week by week, I bid farewell to one agency after another ; to the lady district visitors, the mothers' meeting, the Brotherhood, the Sunday-school Teachers, etc. I set on foot the open-air work, having four groups as usual.

As I felt it would be impossible, in my weak state of health, to say farewell to the people in their homes, I sent them a farewell letter (see Appendix R).

Being desirous of having a souvenir in the handwriting of those then residing in the parish, or still members of the church, I made a request through the parish magazine two months before I resigned ; stating that I would esteem it a favour to have in writing, but not for publication without permission, testimony of spiritual blessings received through the ministry in St. Nathaniel's. That was a rather delicate request ; still I felt there were those who would comply therewith.

It is no small ground for thankfulness, that while some whom—knowing them to be my sons and daughters in

Christ—I thought would have replied took no notice, I had ninety-one letters of blessed testimony to having received the new life. I ought to state that some of the replies were from, say, a husband for himself and his wife, or *vice versa ;* sometimes from a father for himself and his children, etc. ; so that the ninety-one letters meant, in reality, many more than that number of instances. Bless the Lord for such testimony.

I could have written down the names of all those who replied, as being the Lord's, by personal knowledge.

The confirmation class numbered one hundred and seven.

It took me three weeks to see them privately : the women in couples and the men separately, at such times as they could attend. I was able to present only thirty-five men and forty-three women, seventy-eight in all. I rejoice, however, to state that I never had a set of candidates in whom the workings of God's Holy Spirit were more manifest than in that one. My cup was brimming over with joy in the Lord, as I felt the Divine pulsation of their faith and love in Christ Jesus

The service was on Whit-Sunday at 11 o'clock, when the church was crowded. There were no other candidates.

The Holy Spirit evidently inspired the service, which was one to impress itself on the memory. With a single exception, all were at the Lord's Table that evening, when three hundred and ninety-one communicated, making with those in the morning four hundred and seventy-one.

In the evening I preached on Phil. i. 21, ' To me to live is Christ, and to die is gain.' I felt greatly helped by the Divine Spirit in so doing. Can that last closing Sunday evening gathering around the Lord's Table ever be forgotten ? recalling as it did the first administration, when there were only eight !

To the praise and glory of Father, Son, and Holy Ghost, I now record that from the very commencement of my labours in Windsor to my resignation, over two thousand candidates, of whose spiritual condition I was well persuaded, were presented, confirmed, and became communicants.

God alone can read the heart, no one can give grace ; ' it is the spirit that quickeneth.'

There will ever be many differences in, and degrees of, evidence as to the new birth, and the forgiveness of sins, owing to temperament and education ; taking into consideration these and other matters, and leaning to the side of charity, I can truly state that of all that number there were none of whose spiritual condition I was not at least hopeful.

My plan was to invite any or all who wished to join the classes for instruction, viz., those who had been confirmed ; those who were desirous of being confirmed ; and those who did not wish to be confirmed ; asking them to defer till near the end of the course the decision whether or not they would be confirmed.

This arrangement prevented those whom I did not present appearing to have been rejected ; hence there was no offence taken.

The classes were held once or twice a week, and ran over six months.

The course of instruction was : — The Catechism, Articles VI., IX., X., XI., XII., XIII., XVII., XXV. — XXXI., the Confirmation service, and the Communion office ; together with personal interviews and special prayer. If during the year there were any adults to be baptized, or converts from Romanism, I had them join these classes. I wish also to place it on record that, so far as I was permitted to know, there was no one department of the church work where there was so much evident blessing of the Holy Ghost as in that of confirmation classes. The reflex blessing upon my own soul constituted one of the greatest joys of my ministry. The average number of Sunday evening communicants for this year up to date exceeded that of any previous year, reaching two hundred and forty-nine.

On Monday I tried to rest. For Tuesday evening I had an invitation from the representatives of St. Nathaniel's dear people to meet them in the great parish hall, that they might collectively say farewell to me.

A cutting from the *Courier* describes it (see Appendix S).

Now the ordeal of saying farewell to the dear flock on the following evening in church had to be gone through.

Whilst waiting in the vestry for the service to commence, I made the following entry, after my name and text, as preacher : ' This evening I take my leave of the beloved flock and parish of dear St. Nathaniel. My prayer is : O God, accept what was Thine own ; and pardon what was mine. R. Hobson.'

The church was full ; there was a tearful response to my farewell, after a pastorate of thirty-three years. I felt God would give me the needed strength, and, blessings on His Name, He did. In point of strength I was a surprise to myself. I felt the Lord, the Spirit, was blessedly present.

I knew I dare not venture to do what my heart wished me to do, viz., to shake hands with each. It would certainly have overpowered me. Having pronounced the benediction as pastor for the last time, I left the pulpit, got out as quickly and privately as possible by the vestry door, and went back to the vicarage, weeping all the way.

The *Liverpool Courier* of the following day described the service (see Appendix T).

On Saturday, June 1, I sailed, accompanied by a niece, to New York, on a visit to relations, both in the United States and in Canada ; hoping, too, that the dry heat of the West might be found beneficial to me.

On arrival at the landing-stage, a large number of the dear people I loved to call my own were assembled there to see me off.

This was like the last feather ; still, the Lord upheld me, but it was just heartrending all the same. If I had been their earthly father going away never to return, it could not have been much more distressing.

Many got permission to see my allotted state-room, and as the s.s. *Campania* moved off they sang ' God be with you till we meet again,' and cheered until they must have been hoarse, waving farewells up to our passing out of sight. Then began the real struggle of my heart's affections and what I believed the Divine Will in the matter. If the Lord had not sustained me I must have sunk under it.

God, who had ever been my God and Father in Christ, gave me favour in the eyes of those in authority on board. They placed at my disposal, not the state-room I had engaged, but one just four times its value, with a porthole, and showed me many little extra attentions throughout the passage. This kindness was also repeated on the return voyage.

Truly, I have, I think, more cause to bless God than any of His dear people. All through my life He has been more gracious than either tongue or pen can describe. ' What have I that I have not received ? ' is absolutely true ; and it is all of God's sovereign grace in His dear Son. I might have been anything, if grace had not found and sustained me. I have indeed no stone to throw at any poor fallen fellow-man, as there never was, nor is there, anything in me by nature more than in another.

I have truly many crowns to lay at the feet of my dear Lord Jesus Christ, which through the grace of God I shall lay there ! Hallelujah !

When crossing to New York, I poured out my heart, in my state-room, to the one great companion of my life, the blessed Lord Jesus.

> ' What a friend we have in Jesus,
> All our griefs and sins to bear ;
> What a privilege to carry
> Everything to Him in prayer.'

I conducted divine service on board on the Sunday, though it tried me to the uttermost.

On arriving in New York, I was interviewed by a representative of the *Globe* newspaper, who inquired if I had ' come over to extend the work of the International Police Christian Association in New York City.' ' No.' ' I wish you had, for the New York police are a terrible set,' was his rejoinder.

Whilst I was in America I had in fuller force the realization of my changed position, brought about by resigning my benefice. As to that being the right thing, and therefore having God's approval, I had not, nor have I now, the slightest doubt ; but it was only natural that there should constantly arise a feeling of poignant grief, of heart sorrow, of soul solitariness, of isolation, even of desolation.

Whilst thus troubled in spirit, it occurred to me that the best way to soothe it would be to give my mind occupation ; and there seemed a fitness that that occupation should be by writing out a record of God's gracious dealings with me during the seven decades of my life.

I therefore resolved to take up that work, though in much weakness of both mind and body ; and, going on with it little by little, I have at last brought it to a conclusion. It may not satisfy the expectations of my readers, for it has not realized my own ideal ; but I have found it at least a real solace, and for that I thank God.

In the light of Psalm lxxxvii. 5, 6, how poor are one's efforts to tell of the Lord's doings in any one person, place, or church.

How inconceivably blessed must be the birth of a soul into God's family, when God Himself records such in the Book of Life.

By the grace of God I have been enabled to keep this before me during the whole of my ministerial life, whether as a layman, or as an ordained man, for fifty years ; and I have sought to illustrate it in this autobiography.

I refer with pleasure to the great change which has taken place in the United States with regard to England since I was there in 1885. At that time, I, as a ' Britisher,' had my corns trodden on at almost every turn ; this time ' no dog wagged his tail ' at me or at anything British. Doubtless John Bull's kindly attitude towards ' Cousin Jonathan ' during the Cuban War was mainly responsible for so welcome a result ; though apart from that there has been a growing feeling of friendliness towards the ' old country.'

With regard to Canada, I found its inhabitants— judging from my experience of Ontario and its neigh-bourhood—as loyal and devoted to the English throne and Constitution as any North of Ireland Orangeman ; they treat with scorn even the bare idea of ever becom-ing detached from the British Empire, and being annexed by the American Republic.

Having had a long rest in Fulton, N.Y., I found the dry, warm atmosphere suited me well. My nieces and I visited ' The Pan American ' in Buffalo, staying at Niagara ; the next day, President McKinley, visiting that grand Exhibition, was shot on the very steps on which we had stood, leading up into the Temple of Music. We next journeyed to Hamilton, Canada, staying with a relative, a barrister ; and, though weak, I preached in two churches there, to very goodly-sized congregations.

Thence we went to Whitby, on Lake Ontario, and stayed with another relative, a marble Merchant. There I preached four times in the Bay church, by the side of which several of my relatives lie until the resurrection morn. I felt greatly revived by the breezes from that fresh-water inland sea.

Returning to Fulton, and having stayed altogether three months, we re-embarked on the s.s. *Campania* at New York, landing at Queenstown. I felt much more equal to conducting divine service on board when on the homeward voyage than I had done when outward bound.

The following winter I spent in Cannes, residing partly

in that sanctified private Clerical Home of Rest, Villa Mauvarre, where I began to write my autobiography.

I helped the chaplain of Trinity Church in the services, and gave a course of Bible readings in his drawing-room. The attendances were good, and included some of the English and German nobility. I also had a little service on Sunday evenings in the Mont Fleury Hotel.

The efforts made by British Christians to give the Gospel to the native Romanists whose ears are actually open to hear it, greatly delighted me; as did the successful efforts on behalf of English women and men servants at Mauvarre, in which I was able to assist; after those services seven men professed to have received Christ.

Like most visitors to Cannes, I sailed out to the Island of St. Honorat.

This island, where St. Patrick is said to have been educated, has a history somewhat similar to that of Iona.

When exploring the island, I visited the monastery, and was most courteously received, being conducted over the place by a priest who understood English well.

As he was showing me out, I asked if he had a few moments to spare for a little conversation.

' Yes,' he replied brightly, ' but in fifteen minutes the noon bell for prayers will be tolled ; go on.'

' I noticed you genuflected in the chapel : why ? '

' I did so to Christ in the Blessed Sacrament on the Altar.'

' How do you know that Christ is there ? '

' The Catholic Church teaches it.'

' You mean the Roman Church ? '

Yes ; I know Protestants do not believe that our Church is the Catholic Church.' Then, looking at me rather thoughtfully, he added, ' Well, it is strange ; I was thinking particularly on that subject this morning.'

' The Roman Church has no warrant that I can see for that dogma, from either Scripture or philosophy ; may it not be idolatry to worship that which is a lifeless thing ? '

' I will not go,' he replied, ' to Scripture or philosophy ; I would rather put it to you in this way : Can you not suppose that God could suspend the body of Christ under, and yet apart from, the accidents of the Sacrament ? '

' The question is not what God could do, but does God do as you say ? Do you then give up Scripture and philosophy in proof of your position ? '

' Can you not really suppose that God could and might suspend Christ in the Blessed Sacrament, apart from the accidents ? ' he asked

' No, I cannot, as there is no proof in either Scripture or philosophy for such a supposition ; nor is there in nature a parallel for it.'

' I grant there is no parallel in nature, but may not Almighty God do so ? '

' No ; God never works a contradiction. Your position rests upon a groundless assumption ; since you allow that there is no warrant for such a thing in Scripture or philosophy, nor yet a parallel in nature.'

' Is it possible you are not able to suppose as I have proposed ? '

' Quite impossible. It is silly ; it is foolish ; it is nonsense.'

Here he remarked that he must go. I cordially offered him my hand, which he accepted. I then said, ' Brother, we shall probably never meet again ; may I hope you will do as I do, trust in the Lord Jesus alone, as your sole Saviour ? ' His reply was, ' I will.' The bell began to toll, and he hurried off, with the words ' God bless you ! ' in his ears. I came away in prayer for that amiable poor priest.

God be gracious to Roman priests. I do love to speak to them. So few Protestants seem to think of reaching them.

Whilst at Cannes I had the pleasure of meeting that truly Apostolic Bishop, Dr. Moule, of Durham. I carried away sweet recollections of the place and neighbourhood.

On returning to England, I came to Southport, and

soon after I preached in my 'turn,' on a Sunday afternoon in the Cathedral, and in the evening in dear St. Nathaniel's. What a joy to me it was to greet the flock from the old pulpit once again! And the joy was mutual. The evening service and sermon were, however, very trying to me.

I thank my heavenly Father that He has left me still one most blessed thing which I can do: that of interceding with Him for His Church all over the world; for the Church of England; for Missions; for the Diocese of Liverpool; for dear St. Nathaniel's; and for my relatives and friends.

And now, in the twilight, thank God, I have the assured confidence that 'He who separated me from my mother's womb, and called me by His grace to reveal His Son in me,' will keep me for His kingdom and glory; meantime, I trust, too, 'My meditation of Him shall be sweet' (Psalm civ. 34).

I.

When languor and disease invade
This trembling house of clay,
'Tis sweet to look beyond our cage,
And long to fly away.

II.

'Sweet to look inward, and attend
The whispers of His love;
Sweet to look upward, to the place
Where Jesus pleads above.

III.

'Sweet to look back, and see my name
In life's fair book set down;
Sweet to look forward, and behold
Eternal joys my own!

IV.

'Sweet to reflect how grace divine
My sins on Jesus laid;
Sweet to remember that His blood
My debt of sufferings paid.

V.

' Sweet in His righteousness to stand,
Which saves from second death ;
Sweet to experience, day by day,
His Spirit's quickening breath.

VI.

' Sweet, in the confidence of faith
To trust His firm decrees ;
Sweet to lie passive in His hands,
And know no will but His.

VII.

' Sweet to rejoice in lively hope
That when the end shall come
Angels will hover round my bed,
And waft my spirit home.

VIII.

' If such the sweetness of the stream,
What must the fountain be ?
Where saints and angels draw their bliss
Immediately from Thee ! '

My self-imposed task is fulfilled ; my desire to record
God's goodness has been granted. For my own sake I
regret that the work is finished ; for the Truth's sake I
rejoice, and am thankful that the Lord has graciously
spared me to conclude it.

And what is ' the conclusion of the whole matter ' ?
It is that in these latter days God's glorious Gospel of
Salvation by Grace, Justification by Faith only,
Sanctification by the Holy Spirit, the only real, God-
inspired Gospel, has the same convicting, convincing, converting power that it had in Apostolic days ;
that it needs no worldly, sensuous, or other adjuncts ;
and that it will ' have free course and be glorified ' to
the saving of sinners, as much in chapel, mission-hall,
schoolroom, or the open air, as in church or cathedral.

Such a Gospel the Lord lovingly made known to me
when a boy, enabled me to grasp, believe and accept,
and built me up in during my youth. He gave me
opportunity and ability, first to proclaim it, for eleven
years, to my poor Popish fellow-countrymen ; and subsequently, after student days, when an ordained minis-

ter, for three years, as curate to a rich congregation, and then, for thirty-three years, as vicar of a poor parish.

On the proclamation of that same Gospel in those respective spheres of labour, the Lord bestowed His blessing; so that alike in Ireland and in England, at Drogheda and at Dundalk, at Birkenhead and at Windsor, it won numbers of souls for Him.

And what thanks are due to Him for His constant care of, and His great goodness to, me His unworthy and ' unprofitable servant.' How He has led, guided, upheld, kept me! How having showed me the right way, He has graciously inclined my feet to walk therein! How He has ' put into my mind good desires,' and in spite of all my naturally sinful tendencies, has enabled me ' to bring the same to good effect ' by, in His strength, living something of the Christ life amongst my people and before the world.

Oh, how I do bless and praise His holy Name for all that He has been to me, for whatever of good He has allowed me to be to others! I look forward to that glorious gathering whereat, when called with my faithful fellow-servants, by His marvellous condescension, to enter into the joy of our Lord, I shall recognize amongst that blessed company many, very many, scores, hundreds, yea thousands, of saved souls, to whom my ministrations in the Lord were owned by His Holy Spirit.

To Thy honour, O my God, I send forth this book, as my thankful testimony to Thy loving kindness towards myself, and to the share which Thou hast permitted me to have in bringing others to Thee.

Looking back on the past, and forward to the future, in all humility I appropriate those gloriously inspiriting words of the great Apostle, ' The time of my departure is at hand. I have fought a good fight, I have finished my course, I have kept the faith : henceforth there is laid up for me a crown of righteousness, which the Lord, the righteous judge, shall give me at that day : and not to me only, but unto all them also that love His appearing ' (2 Tim. iv. 6-8). Amen.

MY EVENTIDE.

IN issuing the fourth edition of my autobiography, 'What hath God wrought,' it has occurred to me that I ought to take the occasion to let my friends and readers know something of the way my Heavenly Father has led, cared for, and used His servant thus far during my eventide.

I wish then in the first place to state that on my return to England from Cannes I soon took up my abode in a hydropathic establishment in Southport, where I had spent more than one holiday, and made my spiritual home in All Saints' Church. I knew, too, that residence in Southport was near enough, and yet not too near, to ever dear St. Nathaniel's, the sphere of my main life work, where, on the cordial invitation of my Successor, I have preached from time to time ; besides taking special marriages and funerals, as I had promised to do in certain cases. Also it met my beloved Bishop's requirement, as Canon, to reside in the Diocese ; thus I have kept up an official connection, though not a parochial one, in the Church. I may say here that, notwithstanding the saying of a witty Coroner, ' The sea saw it and fled,' I consider Southport the handsomest town in the North of England, and a most suitable residence specially for old people : that while it is a very rich and a very worldly place, yet many of the servants of God reside there.

But why settle in a hydro, where gaiety is said to abound ? This needs an answer.

Having had many years' experience of the healing effects of hydropathic treatment, I felt that to have such now might, under God, soothe and relieve, if not heal, my sadly ailing body.

Happily, I was in the main right. I knew also that I would have some outlet there for my soul's yearnings,

in a unique form, in having as a fellow guest access
to a class of people most difficult to reach by the
Minister of Christ, viz., merchants and tradesmen,
many of whom come there with weary heads and
sad hearts, when they would likely give ear to the
unofficial, tender, and sympathetic approach of a fellow
resident to pour in the oil and wine of the Gospel of
Christ. This I was keen to do, and thank God I never
met with a repulse, but quite the contrary.

I thought it probable that to conduct daily prayer
would fall to my lot, with a varying attendance from
ten to seventy persons, which it did.

During my residence there I knew I would meet
many of the Lord's own dear people with whom I
would have sweet fellowship in the Lord.

The visiting physician said to me, ' Why, this hydro
is like a little parish for you.' I found it so.

I feel I ought to put it on record that, by the help
of God, during my time there, while I sought to be
bright, affable, and friendly with all, I lived largely a
separate life, that so far as amusements went I was
not even once present at whist, bridge, theatricals,
billiards, or dancing ; I did join in croquet and
bowls occasionally.

Such things did not appeal to me. I had other
resources which more than satisfied my head and
heart, in God, and His Christ, by the Holy Spirit, in
the Word, and in sacred work.

Another important sphere for work was thrown open
to me by the Vicar of All Saints' giving me a *carte
blanche* to do as much or as little as I was able, whether
in the churches or parish, without holding me specially
responsible. Hence, I preached occasionally, assisted
in the services betimes, gave courses of Bible readings,
took confirmation classes, visited in the parish, and
particularly the sick of all classes. The latter work
being very congenial to me, as I ever sought not only
to win souls but to be a ' son of consolation.'

I found, too, a wide opening for sowing the seed of
the Word on the seats of the promenade and in the

parks, where I met with some of God's precious jewels, but never a rebuff except one. I was ever a strong believer in personal dealing with individuals as to the soul.

The preceding formed in the main the scope for my efforts for God.

Some of my friends chided me for attempting to do anything but rest from working. Though I knew I was ailing in several ways, including weakness of the heart, shattered nerves, chronic bronchitis and rheumatism, yet I could not rest if perhaps I might pluck a brand out of the fire or dry a tear. I knew that while God uses giants in His service He also uses ' the still small voice.' I could not be quiet, for the fire of the Lord burned within me.

Happily I had retained my modest library. I kept in touch with the work of God both at home and abroad. As time went on I found myself better able to rest in the way of sleep, and my appetite slowly improved. Though easily tired, I took as much exercise in the open air as possible, and while I had no hard and fast rule to live by, yet I sought to live by the day, and to press into it all that love enabled me to do for the Master.

I thank God that while weakness marked my general health, I had scarcely any pain whatever.

I must note here that God abundantly supplied all my temporal wants ; that the ninth decade of my life contrasts with the second. Not that God loved me in the one less than in the other. I thank Him that out of His abundant supply, and living a simple life, I have been able to give back to Him one-fifth of that which He so graciously gave me.

One other cause of restfulness was, while able to do some work, I ever felt fully satisfied that in having resigned my Benefice I had not made a mistake, and further, knowing that in my successor, the Rev. D. H. C. Bartlett, the right man was appointed, whose ministry is being much owned and blessed by God the Holy Ghost ; who, in Vestry assembled, most cordially referred more than once to the real, solid, and spiritual character of the work in the parish of his predecessor.

Having thus far indicated the Lord's gracious dealings with me in my retirement on the plain of service, I shall give an inlet to His most gracious dealings on the plain of my own personal experience as before Him.

To reveal one's inner life is a very sacred thing. Is there not, however, an example for it in Holy Scripture, where the Psalmist says, ' Come and hear, all ye that fear God, and I will tell you that He hath done for my soul.'

Referring, then, to the desire expressed at the end of my autobiography, that my ' meditations of God might be sweet,' I rejoice to state that that prayer has been more than fully realized in my habitual fellowship with ' the Father, and with His Son Jesus Christ,' which is the privilege of all God's dear children.

This blessed and soul-absorbing fellowship being attained through the teaching of God the Holy Ghost in the Word, reached me very soon in my eventide to a degree which I had never known before except when in Palestine, where I was well nigh ' out of the body,' when I felt as if I could scarcely remain on the earth even to do His will because of the intense longing to be in God's immediate presence.

I do not attempt to define this fellowship, including companionship, and partnership, with the Father and His Son, as it is not a subject here so much for definition as a note of personal experience.

I bless God that the enjoyment of this fellowship has been mine all through my eventide ; hence the restfulness, contentment, peace, happiness, and joy in God which has all along filled the soul of His worn-out servant.

Oh, how comforting it is to know that if this fellowship is interrupted, as in Adam's case, God has provided means of restoration in the precious blood of

Christ which cleanseth us from all sin. From this height of privilege how poor one's past life looks ! How deficient even one's ministerial life appears ! What a powerful incentive to contrition, humiliation, and repentance.

In the light of this fellowship I have been taught much as to the deeper meaning of the words : God, Bible, man, sin, grace, love, mercy, righteousness, redemption, blood, intercession, the coming One, heaven, and hell ; and I may add the inner meaning of the Word of God which has been a great comfort to me.

A young Christian recently addressing me, said, ' Canon, I suppose satan never tempts you now, as he sees there is no use in doing so ? ' Oh, my young brother, if you should live to my age you will find it very different. There is no safety for the old or young of the servants of God, but under the cover of the precious blood of Christ. ' They overcame him '—the dragon, Satan—' by the Blood of the Lamb and the word of their testimony.' That the warfare with the world, the flesh and the devil ends only with death ; there is victory only all along the line even to the last struggle, through the Blood of the Lamb.

Now, while I know something of the spiritual health, vigour, and joy, there is in being actively engaged in work for God, specially when the valleys are being filled, the mountains made low, the crooked places straight, and the rough places plain, I have in my eventide the blessedness of fellowship with God in a measure unknown till then, though only accompanied by a very feeble service in the way of His commandments.

This fellowship is more than an antidote to that very humiliating description of old age in Ecclesiastes xii., also against what is found so much amongst old people, viz., discontent, impatience, complaining, and selfishness.

A lad said to his father, ' Papa, will Grandad go to Heaven ? ' ' Yes, I feel sure he will.' ' Well, then,' replied the boy, ' I do not wish to go there ! '

Oh, for the Psalmist's description of old age, viz.:
' The righteous shall flourish like the palm tree : he
shall grow like a cedar in Lebanon.'

' Those that be planted in the House of the Lord
shall flourish in the courts of our God.'

' They shall bring forth fruit in old age : they shall
be fat and flourishing.' Psalm xcii., 12-14.

Dear Bishop J. C. Ryle used to say, Let us not
only live well, but finish well.'

Now I shall illustrate how God has graciously used
His servant in his eventide.

It is not easy to estimate spiritual results ; they
cannot be measured by tape, nor counted by heads ;
still, signs do follow. I believe every worker for
God is warranted in looking for results ; while we
know that spiritual work is pre-eminently the work
of faith.

As for my own part, I ever have expected such,
whether among Romanists in Ireland or in work in
England, and, thanks to His Holy Name, He has ever
given abundant evidence of His own presence and
blessing in abiding results. It is with thankfulness I
am able to record that such tokens continue during
my eventide.

Very many instances of abiding blessing from the
daily prayer in the hydro could be recorded. Space
will not allow of scarcely any reference to the work
there, which was indeed very varied.

A young Man writes : ' You will remember the
little prayer you taught me in the hydro, Southport,
several years ago. viz,, " Oh God, for Jesus Christ's
sake send me Thy Holy Spirit." I wish to tell you
that that prayer has never left me, and that now I
feel as if I must enter the ministry of the Church,
although I have served Articles for a profession and
have made a good ' start.'

Though a non-smoker, I used to go into the smoke-
room, where men speak their minds freely on many
topics, including religion and its professors, whether
lay or clerical. I do not wonder that many such men

do not go to church. I was able, however, to lead up
betimes the conversation to that which was better and
abiding. I ought to say at the same time, I found
among them strong admiration for real goodness. This
is that which gains attention for vital and eternal
things. While the opposite is a fearful stumbling-block,
whether in ministers or people. How often had this
fact led me to cry, ' Lord, take care of my character,
and of my influence for Thee, and for the sake of the
people.'

A solemn warning. A fellow guest asked me : ' Have
you heard our minister preach ? I replied, ' No.'
' He is a very clever man. Why, he is an astronomer !
he told me that he has been looking at Mars for twenty-
five years.' ' Indeed. Have there been any conversions to God through his ministry ? ' ' Not one ; we
should be surprised to hear of one.' ' Think you, if he
had been looking at Jesus all that time there might
have been such ? ' No reply. ' Have there never been
conversions in your place of worship ? ' ' Oh, yes ; I
recollect many years ago I myself brought forward
eighteen persons to be enrolled as members from my
Bible Class on their professed conversion ! There is,
however, a large congregation, and they paid four
thousand pounds for their organ.' ' But no conversions ! ' ' Not one.' ' Nero fiddles, while Rome is
burning ' ! !

Although I never had a doubt as to the will of God
in reference to the resignation of my benefice, yet the
separation from the work, and from the beautiful flock
which God had given me, was such a trial to my
affections that I felt as if I would die of grief.
I cried and cried to my Heavenly Father for relief to
my burdened heart. It was some months after when
the answer came in an unexpected manner, in that
God begat the thought within me, viz., to give to the
Church and the world an outline of my life. I felt
that this was the one thing I could do.

Now I must say that if the writing and publishing
of my autobiography did no more than the rest and

ease it brought to my poor heart, it has not been published in vain ; it is true, that amongst books published in faith, prayer, and tears, my autobiography certainly has a place. It is equally true that whether it be the author, or the book that is considered, they illustrate how God chooses and uses the weak things of this world to glorify His Holy Name.

Now who can tell the happiness it has been, and is, to me, that when my physical and mental powers, so limited to serve God, my book circulates and is being used and blessed by Him, far and wide, more or less, to those whom I could not ever hope to reach, including our late beloved King Edward VII., four Archbishops, thirty-three Bishops, numbers of the clergy and ministers of all denominations, titled people, and hundreds of Christian workers throughout the land, as is evident by verbal testimony, but specially by letter.

For example, one writes : ' Your book has been the means of my conversion to God.'

Another : ' My lost faith in Christianity has been restored by your book.' Thus wrote a minister.

Another : ' Your book has revolutionised my methods in my parish work.'

While the more frequent testimony is : ' Your book has been an inspiration to me in my work for God.'

So numerous and precious are these letters that I am having them bound in two volumes.

Verbal testimony : —

' Your life has been a wondrously varied one. I have read it, and I am not ashamed to say, it made me cry, it made me laugh, it made me pray, it made me praise ! '

Again : ' Your autobiography most conclusively illustrates the fact that controversy is not incompatible with deep spirituality.'

It is said by some that the middle classes are not so accessible for pastoral visitation as the lower classes. This is not my experience in Southport, nor yet was it my experience at Christ Church, Claughton, Birkenhead, when curate there, where the congregation was almost composed of the upper middle class. I shall only cite a few cases.

In visiting a lady in Southport I said, Shall we have prayer ? ' She lifted up her hands and exclaimed, ' Oh, yes ; you are the first clergyman who ever proposed to have prayer with me, though many of them kindly call.

Another : ' My husband was much impressed by your prayer when you called last. Now I wish to tell you, you are the only clergyman who offered prayer in our house though we have been in this town seventeen years, and have been regular churchgoers, while I am a communicant.'

Another : ' Thank you for that prayer ; it is a great comfort,' adding, ' We never had a clergyman who bent his knee in this house before.'

Another : I have been visiting for seven years a chronic invalid of forty-five years' standing, occupying one small, neat little room, a happy, Christian, residing in classic Lord Street ; but the vicar of the parish has prayer with that sufferer when he visits there.

It is much more easy to do than to suffer ! In visiting this chronic suffering saint of God I have learnt more than one salutary lesson !

We seem to forget that many an aching heart lives in the ceiled house or steps into a carriage.

Returning after a walk to my rooms, I heard a man had called to see me ; he also called next day and I was out again, but he left his card with a few words written on it. It struck me that he was a gentleman in distress. A postal order was on my table ; I put it in an envelope with a few sympathetic words, sending it to him.

The following day he called, and as he entered my study smilingly, I noticed the order in his hand, and holding it up he said : ' Thank you, this is not what I want. I am one of the Squires of Lancashire ! ' Then his countenance changed, and with tears in his eyes, and in a low voice, said : ' I am in distress about

my soul; can you help me?' Sit down, my dear
friend, I said, and open your grief. I reserve his
inner struggles. However, he said: 'My father died
while I was young, and my mother died some time
ago. If ever there was a saint on earth, she was one.
She was determined to have me a Christian, but when
I was a man *I would have none of it.* I have now been
led to think differently. I have come to you because
my mother named you and your work in Liverpool to
me more than once. I thought you would understand
and help me. I do not think the vicar of my parish
would.'

I soon found how deficient of God's way of salvation
he was, and also nibbled and pinched by unbelief. He
continued to call as arranged once a week for some
months. He took copious notes for consideration at
home of the way of life and of answers to his questions,
bringing me a bunch of flowers each time.

He did receive some light and relief to his burdened
heart, but not assurance of interest in Christ. The
connection was still kept up, and I did not cease to
pray for him.

One day, to my delight, I had a letter from him
written with a full and happy heart, opening with
these words and written in capitals: ' DEAR CANON,
AT LAST I HAVE FOUND THE PEARL!!' My
heart replied 'Hallelujah.'

When poorly one day, a Christian gentleman
called to ask me to visit a lady dying of an incurable
disease, and in great distress about her soul, and adding
that he considered the middle class greatly neglected
as to their souls. When I stood at her bedside, that
emaciated sufferer began at once to unfold her great
distress of mind as to her eternal destiny. Her case
was this, so deep was her consciousness of her departure
from God that she felt God *could* not receive her, not
that He would not but that he *could not,* and yet in
her home and among the wide circle of friends she was
beloved. I arranged to visit her once, twice, or a

third time each week, as she might be able to bear it. Some time passed over during which she was ever eager to hear and to join in prayer, and yet her soul had no resting-place. Her great fear, that God could not forgive her really, yet remained. One day, calling as usual, in faith and prayer, relying on 2 Cor. v. 21, I said to her, ' Now, my dear, God has given me a special message for you to-day.' And quoting that precious passage, I then said : ' Why, this passage tells you, in other words, that the Blessed Jesus, as it were, *stood in your shoes*, paid your debt, met all your liability, atoned for all your sins past, present, and to come.' When she at once said : ' What is that you say ? Stood in my shoes ? I never heard that before.' I assured her on the authority of God's word that such in effect was the case, and she replied : ' Oh ! I see now, I may, and I will believe that God can and will forgive me.' Here, thank God, rest and peace followed.

Some time after I had a telephone call from her On entering her room, her Christian sister said to me : ' Canon, my sister has one word for you—one word ! She will now give it to you herself.' When the dear one, lifting herself up, and in an assuring tone, looking at me, without any preface uttered the word ' Happy ! ' and then sank down. I responded : ' Thank God, that is a glory note—Hallelujah ! God makes all happy who trust in Him.'

Now to be happy under such conditions seems an impossibility. Could it be that a loving wife and mother, with a devoted husband and darling little ones, and in a good position, with her poor body wasted to five stones in weight, and death near, could be happy ? I say it is only by a miracle of grace that such could be. But the greater burden had been removed, and her poor distracted mind and heart had found rest and peace in that God Whom she had thought could not forgive her, but actually had done so ; glory to His Holy Name.

I interred her remains in sure and certain hope of eternal life—thank God. To be the messenger of the

Lord of Hosts to such a case, is it not worth more than a life of eight decades ?

I rejoice to state I have found several true Christians among the Bath-chairmen of Southport. One day I said to one of them, ' I am going to preach in the church you attend on Sunday evening next.' ' I'm glad,' was the reply. ' Shall I tell you my text ? ' ' Do.' ' A man in Christ.' ' That's a big text,' said my friend. Do you know it ? ' Oh, yes.' Do tell me what you think it means ? He paused and replied, ' In Christ by the gift of the Father ; in Christ by the purchase of Christ on the Cross.' Here another pause. I said, ' Go on.' ' In Christ by faith, and in Christ by our lives.' ' Give me your hand,, I said ; ' why, you understand it as well as Matthew Henry, the great Bible commentator.' He is now hopelessly ill. Having been absent for a little time, on visiting him I asked, How are you ? ' Oh, pretty well.' How is your soul ? ' Well, I have had all this time the three " knows " you left me, viz. : I know in whom I have believed ; I know all things work together for good ; I know I have a home, a house of God in the heavens. I have been living on these three " knows." ' This dear man told me that it was in a Confirmation class over sixty years ago held by the Rev. Charles Hesketh, then Rector of North Meols, and Lord of the Manor, Southport, he was led to Christ.

Another with a strong Yorkshire accent, meeting me on a Monday in the street, and taking my hands into his, exclaimed, ' Sir, Oiv good news for you,' and looking me in the face with tears rolling down said, ' Yesterday mornin' at our prayer-meetin' four young fellows, no one askin' them, confessed Chroist, and then in the evenin' foive more on 'em stood up and said they had given their hearts to Chroist. Now isn't four and foive noine, then there is noine on 'em saved.' We thanked God openly in the street, not careful who might think us crazy. Would to God that the holy joy that filled that dear man's heart might under similar circum-stances fill the hearts of Christian workers everywhere

For over eight years, I have been stopping in the street to say a kind word to a poor little crippled man, who sits on a seat resting on two wheels, by means of which he wheeled himself into the Leicester Street end of Lord Street, and who has sat there on fine days for eleven years, that he might receive coppers from the passers-by. I had known him as a Christian. I said to him one day, May I ask if you ever do anything for the Lord ? ' Yes, a little bit.' Oh, do tell me what that little bit is ? ' I teach in the Sunday-school.' I was amazed. He might have added, as I afterwards found, ' I am Chairman of the Christian Endeavour in the chapel I attend.' What Christian can be idle after such an example ?

I am thankful to state that at times during my eventide when I felt somewhat stronger I used to offer, as I was led, to conduct a Mission in certain parishes, not for the usual ten days, but for three weeks, that is, spreading the work usually done in the conventional ten days over that period, which enabled me to have a rest at intervals. This plan worked well. The visible results varied, but there were always some.

In one parish the attendance at church was doubled and the communicants quadrupled. In another parish, All Souls', Blowick, forty testified to have received blessing. One of them, a youth learning a trade, took my attention specially. I took him in my rooms four evenings a week for Bible study for two years, and so marvellously did God open his way that he is now an undergraduate in the University of Toronto for the Ministry in the Church of God.

There were other very interesting cases.

I took part in a twelve days' mission, my co-Missioner taking it for seven days, in which I helped. His aim was conversion. After he left I carried it on for the remaining five days, when I aimed at edification. At the end of the Mission, on the invitation of the Vicar, three hundred and twenty applied for memento cards of blessings received.

God also still makes my retirement smooth and

happy by the many kind friends, which He almost
seems to have reserved for my old age. But especially
one dear brother in the Lord, whose soul and mine are
knit together (see photo annexed) ; whose love and
fellowship in Christ are a real stay to me in my eventide.

There is so much of heaven in his soul, as seen in his
Christ-like life ; in his justness and generous dealing
with his vast number of workpeople ; his Evangelical
Hall for their souls' good ; his own old-age pension for
their benefit ; his Medical Mission for the entire region
where he resides ; his trained, converted to God, nurses,
for the sick and dying ; his thirst to bring the souls of
his fellow men to God and righteousness ; his princely
liberality to spiritual work ; as well as in his own personal service in good work of all kinds since he first knew
the Lord, now over forty years, during which it has
been my great privilege to have known him. And yet
the language of the Communion Office, in the General
Confession, as we approach the Holy Table, is not too
deep for him as before God. While one of Lancashire's
Merchant Princes, yet his faith in God is as simple as
that of a child, hence his radiant life. Praise God.

Neither the " higher nor the lower critics," give him
any trouble. He often says that " the beginning and
ending of his theology is John iii. 16."

Oh, that there were many such in the land ! If so
there would be little room for trades unions, and no
decay in true religion.*

God in His Providence has made me, as it were, the
connecting link of a very large number of relatives :
I have sought more than ever to make my correspondence with them to bear a message from the God of
grace and truth. This I have also done in a similar
way with my outer circle of ordinary correspondents.

During my life I have had some narrow escapes,
specially in the mission field in Ireland, and yet never
had a scratch.

God's care for His weak one, recently, was thus manifest : I had preached in my turn as Canon in the
Liverpool Cathedral to a crowded congregation one

* While these lines were in the press, it hath pleased God to call unto
Himself the soul of my dear and beloved friend.

Sunday afternoon, and while leaving it and standing on the steps leading into it, where a number of my old parishioners were waiting to have a word with their old Pastor, I slipped and fell from the sixth step right on my face and hands to the ground, but clear of the steps. On being picked up I exclaimed, ' Thank God there are no bones broken—the Lord let me down gently ! ' It was very singular that when falling I was not in the least alarmed. On the contrary, I had, like a flash, a comfortable feeling, I did not in the least feel the impact with the ground. How true it is ' The hairs of your head are all numbered,' or (with William III.) ' Man is immortal till his work is done.'

On reflection afterwards I confess I had the feeling that if the fall had been fatal, it would not have been amiss if I had been taken home to the ' many mansions ' from the steps of the Cathedral, and specially after having poured out my soul in preaching, in the service that afternoon, on Revelation i., 5, 6, ' Unto Him that loved us, and washed us from our sins in His own blood, and hath made us kings and priests, unto God and His Father ; to Him be glory and dominion for ever and ever. Amen.'

The Lord had yet something for me to do.

Amongst the many tokens of God's approval and blessing during my eventide I shall only mention another, viz. : On attaining my eightieth birthday the officials and friends of All Saints' Church, Southport, where I have worked well nigh since my retirement, now eleven years ago, indicated by the following address their kind appreciation of my feeble, yet willing, services. The address, beautifully illuminated and framed, was publicly presented at a large gathering. It is as follows :—

ALL SAINTS' PARISH, SOUTHPORT.

To the Reverend Richard Hobson (Honorary Canon of Liverpool)

On behalf of the congregations of All Saints' Parish Church, All Souls' Church, and Wennington Road

Mission Room, and on behalf of our parishioners and friends generally, we desire to congratulate you heartily on the attainment of your eightieth birthday. We embrace this special occasion to express our deep sense of your spiritual work in our churches and parish as a volunteer helper, and our gratitude for services rendered over a long period of time, and continued to this day in spite of advancing years.

Long before you were obliged by ill-health to resign your own living, you conducted Missions in our parish, and since you resigned it you have conducted Missions, given Bible readings, presided at our prayer meetings, conducted confirmation classes, preached in our pulpits, and assisted in our churches, and devoted yourself to parochial visitation, especially amongst the sick and dying. We would also record our appreciation of your unflinching fidelity throughout your long ministry to the Holy Bible, and Doctrines of Grace, and to the Protestant and Evangelical teaching of our beloved Church of England, and our joy at the success which has attended your ministry. Allow us to congratulate you on the large circulation of your autobiography, ' What hath God wrought,' which recounts God's abundant blessing on your arduous and strenuous life, spent in the forefront of the Lord's battles for over fifty years. That your days may be prolonged and that you may be spared many years to go in and out amongst us, carrying a bright and happy influence into many homes, is our ardent prayer, and our earnest wish is that you may have an ever-increasing enjoyment of the fellowship which God's children have with the Father, and with His Son Jesus Christ, until the Master's Voice calls you to ' Come up higher,' and you pass to His presence ' until the day breaks and the shadows flee away.'

C. T. PORTER, *Vicar ;* JOHN E. WILLETT, J. WAGSTAFF, *Wardens ;* J. H. CHISHAM SMITH, W. E. WINGFIELD, *Curates ;* J. J. COCKSHOTT, *Lay Representative.*

Replying after the presentation, Canon Hobson said : ' Dr. Porter, Fellow Parishioners, and Friends,—That the Emperor Francis Joseph, Lord Roberts, and such noted personages should have their birthday publicly honoured is not to be wondered at ; but that my birthday—even though it were my eightieth birthday— should be noticed, is indeed very exceptional. I would not be human if I were not very deeply sensible of the honour done to me by you in the presentation of this artistically illuminated address, and its accompaniments, on this day. You will allow me to say that though this presentation makes the seventeenth I have had during my ministry of fifty years, that it is all the more prized by me, coming as it does when my feet have well nigh touched " the margin of the river." On my retirement from active ministry in the Church of God and residence in Southport, that I should find a spiritual home in All Saints' Church is natural, because it is so thoroughly Evangelical, and that its worthy Vicar (Dr. Porter) is one of my oldest friends. I am really his debtor in that he has allowed me the great privilege, of assisting in Divine Service and of visiting in the parish whomsoever I could and how I could. I know that work for God is in itself its own reward, yet, at the same time, the approval of one's co-workers in the Kingdom of God is much to be thankful for, as in this instance. Your recognition of my fidelity to the Holy Bible as God's revelation of Himself to the sons of men, the doctrines of grace as taught therein, and of Evangelical Protestantism causes me to feel modest yet thankful. Here I wish to say I believe that a return thereto, with a plain service, is the real antidote for decaying congregations, whether in Church or Chapel. Thank you for your recognition of my autobiography, which God is so much using, as indicated by the testimonies which continue to flow in. I do confess I feel it a great consolation in the twilight of my life that it in some measure supplies the complement of the activities of my former life. I shall only add that of the life of which it is but a sidelight I can truly say, " Blessed Lord Jesus, accept what is Thine Own and pardon what is mine." I do very earnestly reciprocate your prayers for me. I shall not cease to pray for you and the Church of God, which He hath purchased with His Own blood. I thank you all for your uniform kindnesses to me, and do assure you it will ever be my joy to be your servant for Christ's sake.'

Allow me in conclusion to say, that although I am in my eighty-second year, I do not feel old, for my faith, hope, and love to God, and His Christ, are as strong, if not stronger, than ever, while my heart is as buoyant, young, fresh, green, and tender as ever. At the same time, I know that God is taking down my tabernacle, though very gently : in a word, I do know that while the house of David waxes stronger and stronger, the house of Saul waxes weaker and weaker.

I shall only add, that as the time yet remaining of my earthly life must be short, I do crave the prayers of my dear friends that I may be kept in still close fellowship with the Father and with His Son Jesus Christ, and that I may be used yet—despite of failing strength—in bringing souls to God, which is still the ruling passion of my life.

> ' Happy if with my latest breath,
> I may but gasp his name,
> Preach Him to all, and cry in death,
> Behold, behold, the Lamb.'

Glory be to the Father, and to the Son, and to the Holy Ghost ; as it was in the beginning, is now, and ever shall be : world without end. Amen.

Southport.

February, 1913.

APPENDICES.

INTRODUCTORY NOTE.

SO numerous and varied are the testimonies to [the work in which God was most graciously pleased to use the writer of this book, that their incorporation into the body of it would, by destroying the continuity of the narrative, detract from its interest.

The intention of this autobiography is not that the author's life shall be seen in his sermons or in his letters ; but that the results of, and the witnesses to, the work which he was enabled to do, should be placed on record, to the glory of God, and for the encouragement of His servants.

To the furtherance of that object these various tributes are collated as appendices, for consecutive perusal.

APPENDIX A.

WILL OF PATRICK WILLIAM McCONVILL, REFERRED TO ON PAGE 26.

' LIVERPOOL,
' *November* 8, 1881.

' In the name of Father, Son, and Holy Ghost. Amen. I, Patrick William McConvill, being of sound mind, hereby leave, by this deed of trust, the proceeds of my little effects to the Irish Church Missions to Roman Catholics, having first paid my debts as hereinafter named. I wish J—— K—— to see these things carried out after my burial. I die in the faith of the Lord Jesus Christ, my only Saviour, in whom I am safe for ever. I bless Him who found me, a poor ignorant Romish zealot, twenty-three years ago, and brought me out of Popish darkness into the true light of God's Holy Word. I thank Him I never had the desire to return to the Church of Rome. I had all that my soul required in the Church of Ireland,—England. God is my Father, Christ is my Elder

Brother, and only Priest, and I am comforted by the Holy
Ghost. I know that to be absent from the body is to be
present with the Lord. I wish to add I die grateful to God
for the many kind friends He gave me since my conversion,
especially John Murphy, Esq., J.P., and James Barton, Esq.,
and many others. I hope the Rev. R. Hobson, my Father in
Christ, will bury my body, in sure and certain hope of the
resurrection to eternal life. May God send the Gospel to all
my fellow-countrymen in dear old Ireland.

'(Signed) PATRICK WILLIAM McCONVILL.'

APPENDIX B.

ADDRESS AND PRESENTATION FROM RESIDENTS IN DROG-
HEDA, DUNDALK, AND NEIGHBOURHOOD, REFERRED TO
ON PAGE 33.

'DUNDALK,
'*January* 10, 1863.

'DEAR MR. HOBSON,
'As the time of your leaving Dundalk is now at hand,
it becomes at once our duty and our pleasure to record the
high estimate we have been led to form of your character and
worth, during the period of your most active and useful
labours in our midst.

'We feel sure those labours have been " as to the Lord,
and not to men," and that the privilege of the work is to you
a full reward. Yet we feel it right to bear a testimony to
others who may not have known you before, that the Lord
has acknowledged your work here—which was indeed but His
work—and made you a blessing, both by the wayside, and
from house to house.

'You now go from amongst us accompanied by our most
cordial wishes for your future, that you may be continually
more qualified for ever greater usefulness. In your further
studies to that end, may you have, above all things, the Spirit
of God as your Teacher, your Guide unto all truth.

'Accept the Book in which we enclose this little farewell
tribute, and the purse of money which accompanies it;
believing that the few names which follow represent but to
a small extent the regrets at your departure which is felt by
very many amongst the people of this town and county.'

(Here followed fifty-two signatures, including
Magistrates, Merchants, Clergymen, etc., of
the County.)

APPENDIX C.

ADDRESS AND PRESENTATION FROM FELLOW STUDENTS
AT ST. AIDAN'S COLLEGE, REFERRED TO ON PAGE 38.

' *To Richard Hobson, Esq., Student of St. Aidan's College.*

' ST. AIDAN'S COLLEGE, BIRKENHEAD,
November 11, 1864.

' DEAR MR. HOBSON,

' We the undersigned, Students of St. Aidan's College,
hereby testify the high sense of respect, esteem, and affection
which your truly evangelical piety has created in our minds ;
in testimony whereof, however feeble, we desire your acceptance of the accompanying Works, as a humble but heartfelt
expression of our feeling toward you.

' It gives us unfeigned pleasure to know that, so soon as you
leave our College, you will at once enter upon the high and
holy duties of your sacred calling, in a portion of our beloved
Church so near to us as Christ Church, Claughton.

' And that your useful life may be long preserved to enjoy
the fruits of your labour of love, in feeding the Flock of
Christ, instructing the young, consoling the aged, preaching
the glorious Gospel to the poor, is our sincere humble prayer.'

(Here followed twenty-one signatures).

APPENDIX D.

I. ADDRESS AND PRESENTATION FROM BIBLE - CLASS,
TEACHERS, AND CHOIR, AT CLAUGHTON, REFERRED
TO ON PAGE 47.

II. ADDRESS AND PRESENTATION FROM SUNDAY SCHOOL,
CLAUGHTON, REFERRED TO ON PAGE 47.

III. ADDRESS AND PRESENTATION FROM CHURCH INSTI-
TUTE, CLAUGHTON, REFERRED TO ON PAGE 47.

' Presented to the Rev. Richard Hobson, Curate of Christ
Church, Claughton,

By his Bible-class, the Teachers, and Choir, a set of Robes
and a Purse containing Thirty pounds, as a feeble expression
of their appreciation of his ability, faithfulness, and zeal in
unfolding the deep truths of God's Holy Word ; and also of
his kind Christian sympathy, manifested to all ministerially
associated with him in this portion of the Lord's vineyard.
2 Tim. iv. 1-5.

' *July*, 1867.'

(Here followed seventy-two signatures.)

'*To the Rev. Richard. Hobson, Curate of Christ Church, Claughton.*
' REV. AND DEAR SIR,
     ' We, the undersigned, Superintendent and Teachers of Christ Church Sunday School, Claughton, in the prospect of your intended removal from this Church and neighbourhood consequent upon your preferment to a more responsible and extended sphere of labour and duty, in presenting the accompanying pocket Communion Service for your acceptance, desire to express our sincere regret in losing, as we feel we do in your departure from among us, a faithful Pastor and a sympathising friend.
     ' We shall always gratefully remember with what loving zeal and unwearied activity you have ever laboured to promote the interests and welfare of our Sunday Schools, and while acknowledging with devout thankfulness to God the blessings and success which have attended your evangelical efforts, we earnestly pray that your labours in the cause of Christ may still continue to be abundantly blessed and prospered, so that in the day of the Lord the reward of those who " turn many to righteousness " may be plenteously bestowed on you.
     ' *November,* 1868.'
                    (Here followed forty-one signatures.)
            ' *To the Rev. Richard Hobson.*
                    ' CLAUGHTON,
                            ' *November* 30, 1868.
' REV. AND DEAR SIR,
     ' It is with much regret that the members of the Claughton Church Institute learn of your removal from amongst us, to another sphere of labour, whereby we are deprived of your valuable services as Vice-President of our Literary Society and of the good example of your daily walk.
     ' We feel, however, that our loss is your gain, and we heartily congratulate you on the substantial evidence of trust and confidence in you that your appointment to an important charge in Liverpool denotes.
     ' May the same God, who has so abundantly blessed your labours in Claughton, abide with you in your new home, and may you by His blessing be the means of spreading His kingdom, and turning many to righteousness.
     ' The undersigned members of the Institute beg your acceptance of the accompanying Timepiece, as a small token of their appreciation of your character as a Christian, and a lasting memorial of their esteem and affection for you as a friend.'
                    (Here followed forty-two signatures.)

APPENDIX E.

ADDRESS AND PRESENTATION FROM ST. NATHANIEL'S
MEN'S BIBLE-CLASS, REFERRED TO ON PAGE 68.

' *To the Rev. Richard Hobson, Incumbent of St. Nathaniel's
Church, Windsor.*

' LIVERPOOL,
' *December 26, 1870.*

' REV SIR,

' We, the members of your Sunday Afternoon Bible-
Class, feel that we cannot allow this our first Annual Tea
Meeting to pass, without giving expression to our high
appreciation of your uniformly kind and self-denying efforts
for our welfare, both spiritual and temporal, in common with
the welfare of the whole district, and to beg your acceptance
of this Address, together with a Study Table, which we
sincerely hope may, whilst proving a convenience to you in
preparing for our edification, also serve as a memento of the
respect and love with which you are regarded by us.

' That God may long spare you to continue your " work of
Faith and labour of Love " is the prayer of each member of
the Class.

' Your brethren in Christ,

' (Signed) JOHN CORNWALL,
' („   ) W. H. HAWKINS, JUNR.,
' On behalf of the Members
of your Bible-Class.'

APPENDIX F.

EXTRACT FROM THE LIVERPOOL *PORCUPINE*, REFERRED
TO ON PAGE 144.

From the Liverpool ' Porcupine.'

' Between Falkner and Upper Parliament Streets there lies
one of the most wretched and squalid districts of the city
notorious for such evils. Harding Street, with its filthy courts
and miserable alleys branching from it, should decidedly be
improved. At present there is a Minister of the Church of
England who is bravely battling to stem the loud and stunning
tide of human care and crime which floods this corner of the
city.

' The evil tide is too strong for one man's efforts ; the surroundings of the site are adverse to his endeavours to humanize
the denizens of the district, the majoriiy of whom profess a

creed which is hostile to his teachings, and who look sullenly on him and his helpers.

' Unless the cause he is struggling for is aided by an improved scheme of dwelling-houses, in place of the present pig-stys where they herd, and by a religion of sanitary science and plenty of sweepers, the outlook will be gloomy.

' This is indeed a neglected spot of foul dwellings, and fouler people, with but one small oasis in their midst, a church and its pastor. " But what are they amongst so many ? " '

NOTE.—That the majority in Harding Street professed a creed hostile to Protestantism, I admit, but they certainly did not look with hostility on either myself or my helpers. R. H.

APPENDIX G.

EXTRACT FROM BISHOP J. C. RYLE'S SPEECH AT THE DERBY CHURCH CONGRESS, REFERRED TO ON PAGE 153.

The Bishop continued :

' Now I confidently assert that the English working man is peculiarly open to sympathy, and the clergyman has peculiar opportunities for showing it. The working man may live in a poor dwelling, and after toiling all day in a coal-pit, or cotton-mill, or iron-foundry, or dock, or chemical works, he may look rough and dirty. But after all, he is flesh and blood, like ourselves. Beneath his outward roughness he has a heart and a conscience, a keen sense of justice, and a jealous sense of his rights as a man and a Briton. He does not want to be patronized and flattered, any more than to be trampled on, scolded, or neglected ; but he does like to be dealt with as a brother, in a friendly, kind, and sympathetic way. He will not be driven, he will do nothing for a cold, hard man, however learned he may be. But give him a clergyman who really understands that it is the heart and not the coat which makes the man, and that the guinea's worth is in the gold and not in the stamp on it ; a clergyman who will not only preach Christ in the pulpit, but come and sit down in his house, and take him by the hand in a Christlike way, during the week ; a clergyman who realizes that in Christ's holy religion, there is no respect of persons, that the rich and the poor are " made of one blood," and need the same atonement, that there is but one Saviour and one fountain for sin, one heaven for both employers and employed ; a clergyman who can weep with those that weep, as well as rejoice with those that do rejoice, and can feel a tender interest in the cares, the troubles, the

births, the marriages, the deaths, of the humblest dwellers in
his parish ; give the working man a clergyman of that kind,
and, as a rule, that man will come to church.

' I invite the special attention of my clerical brethren to
this point.

' We live in days when public work of all kinds every year
seems to absorb more of a clergyman's time. Committees,
Bible Classes, Lectures, Meetings, frequent services, are
rapidly increasing so much that they seem to leave ministers
no time for house-to-house or family work, and for winning the
confidence of individual souls. I warn you to be on your
guard. All the public work in the world, however good, will
not compensate for the loss of opportunities for cultivating
relationships of sympathy between yourselves and your people.
Make time for going amongst them, sitting down with them,
holding friendly intercourse with them, and in the long run
you will find the time was well bestowed. I am not speaking
theoretically only ; I have seen proof upon proof that I have
warrant for what I say, both in colliery districts and in towns.
I give one and so conclude my paper :

' I know at this moment a parish of 4,500 people, in Liverpool, with not a rich man in it, but only small shopkeepers,
artisans, and poor. There are only 13 families in it who
keep one servant, and not one which keeps two. There are
195 houses with more than one family in each. There are 133
families living in cellars. Many of these cellars are within a
few yards of the church, and under its shadow. In short, that
this is a thoroughly poor working-class parish, nobody will
deny. Now what is the Church of England doing in this
parish ? Listen, and I will tell you. In a plain brick church,
holding 1,000 people, built thirteen years ago, there is a simple
hearty service, and an average attendance of 700 on a Sunday
morning, 300 in the afternoon, and 950 in the evening. In
three Mission Rooms there is an average attendance of about
350 in the morning, and 450 in the evening. The total number
of communicants is 800, almost all of the working classes,
and nearly one half men. I myself helped to administer the
consecrated elements to 395, and I saw the hands which
received them, and I know by those hands that many of them
were dock-labourers, and foundry-men.

' The worthy minister of that parish began his work alone,
about fourteen years ago, with four people in a cellar. He
has seen a church built ; he has now with him one paid curate,
one paid Scripture-reader, one paid Bible-woman, and a paid

organist. But he has 82 voluntary Sunday-School teachers, 120 Church-workers, 17 Bible-classes with 600 adults on the register, and 1,700 Sunday scholars. The practical and moral results of the Church work in the parish are patent and unmistakable. Of course some remain to this day unaffected and careless. But the congregation raises £800 a year for the cause of God. There are 1,100 pledged abstainers in the district. There is not a single house of ill-fame, nor a single known infidel, in the parish. These are facts, simple facts, which anyone who visits Liverpool may, if he likes, verify for himself.

'The Incumbent of this parish is a quiet, unpretending man. . . . But of one thing I am certain : he is a man who tries to preach Christ in the pulpit, and to visit his people in a Christlike, sympathizing way as a pastor, at the rate of seventy-five families a week ; and to these two things I attribute his success. Of course men cannot command success under any circumstances. " It is the spirit that quickeneth." '

APPENDIX H.

ADDRESS AND PRESENTATION FROM ST. NATHANIEL'S CONGREGATION, REFERRED TO ON PAGE 168.

' Rev. and Dear Sir,

' Having happily passed through the crisis occasioned by your acceptance of the Vicarage of Garston—so earnestly pressed upon you by the Bishop—and prevailed upon you to cast in your lot with us, we think the time opportune to bear testimony in a tangible form and public manner to our sense of indebtedness to you for your indefatigable and highly spiritual labours amongst us ; to our sincere admiration of your devoted and consistent life, and to our grateful appreciation of your consent to remain with us, in response to our urgent appeals.

' We are glad, as we are bound, to testify that to all you have been a ready friend and counsellor, a worthy example, and a teacher of influence and power ; to many the honoured instrument who led them to the Saviour ; and to not a few, when breathing the glad tidings of the Gospel into the ears of the sick and dying, a welcome ambassador of the Lord of Life.

' In the discharge of the functions of your sacred office, you have ever sincerely sympathized with the poor of your flock, and have been ready with a cheering word and helping hand when hope had almost gone ; in return for which you now enjoy a wealth of real affection more valuable than honour and fame.

' The fulness of the joy of having you still as our pastor is somewhat interfered with by the consciousness that your health is not as good as you could desire. In the hope of your being able to secure a respite from your arduous labours by rest and a change, we ask you to accept the accompanying purse of money, and thus allow us to share with you the cost, as we hope eventually to enjoy with you the advantages of renewed strength and vigour.

' We congratulate you on the result of your unwearied labours during the sixteen years of your successful pastorate, and we bear faithful witness to the acceptability of your ministrations to all classes.

' We thank you heartily for continuing to watch over our spiritual interests, and to superintend the extensive parochial machinery you have called into exercise, and we earnestly pray that God the Holy Spirit may continue to endue you with that power from on high which alone can qualify for the noblest work, that you may be long spared to us and to the Church, with every spiritual blessing in Christ Jesus ; and may be granted a rich harvest of rescued souls as the reward of an earnest life.

' On behalf of the parishioners, the congregation, and the various parochial agencies,

' We remain, Rev. and Dear Sir,
' Yours very affectionately.'

The address was signed by the churchwardens, sidesmen, curate, and two representatives of about thirty parochial agencies.

The purse contained £120.

The Vicar's reply :

' ST. NATHANIEL'S,
' *December* 31, 1884.

' MY DEAR BRETHREN IN THE LORD,

' Being fully aware that in withdrawing from the parish of Garston, in response to your loving entreaties, I was giving up a position possessing ample scope to work for God, and social advantages rarely to be obtained by an ordinary Presbyter, I can truly say I felt as if I could have given up anything for your sakes.

' I accept most gratefully your beautiful and generous gift as " an odour of a sweet smell, a sacrifice acceptable, well-pleasing to God."

' I am deeply touched by your tender solicitude for my health, which I trust is not so injured that the contemplated change and rest may not be sufficient to restore it if the Lord will.

' Since then, we still dwell together, let us specially rejoice in the manifested presence of God the Holy Ghost, in quickening power and sanctifying blessedness through the Word of God, in our parish.

' This is our real strength. Oh, may we never grieve the Holy Ghost. I am persuaded that this sacrifice and reciprocity of love in the Lord will evidently work for the advancement of the Gospel amongst us, which we so ardently desire.

' There is yet much land to be possessed.

' And now, Brethren, I commend you to God, and to the Word of His Grace, which is able to build you up, and to give you an inheritance among all them which are sanctified.

    ' Your ever affectionate Friend and Pastor,

               ' (Signed) R. HOBSON.'

APPENDIX I.

EXTRACT FROM SIR BALDWYN LEIGHTON'S SPEECH AT THE CHURCH CONGRESS, MANCHESTER, REFERRED TO ON PAGE 191.

' Now as to facts. What we want is sympathy and adaptation. We must get at the working man through the working men and Mission Halls, if we cannot speak to them in Churches, and not drive all the most religious into the ranks of Nonconformity because there is no place for them in the Church. Here is how a spiritually-minded Clergyman in Liverpool has solved these problems.

' Some nineteen years ago the Rev. R. Hobson took charge of a poor and degraded district in Liverpool, called St. Nathaniel's, Windsor, containing about five thousand people.

' His first service was in a cellar, which I visited myself, and his first congregation consisted of four persons, recalling the words " where two or three are met together." The men, women and children that were reached by his ministry last Sunday amounted to nearly four thousand.

' Owing to the Irish population, and a seafaring contingent and other causes, Liverpool is not an easy town to work in ; and Windsor, according to the best opinion, was a district where humanity was at its lowest level a few years ago.

' Yet such have been the effects of Mr. Hobson's ministry at St. Nathaniel's that there is not now a single known atheist in the district, and public opinion will not allow of a single disorderly house within that border.

' A Church has been built, there are three Mission Halls, where services are being carried on by trained working men every Sunday, one in Welsh for the Welsh population in that part of Liverpool, for whom there are forty Nonconformist Chapels, but there was only one Church of England place of worship, till this was opened by Mr. Hobson in the Jubilee year.

' Besides this, in summer he has open-air services conducted by working men four times a week, at one of which he himself attends, but takes little part in the service. He has twelve young working men in training as Evangelists, and has nearly two hundred Helpers, including Sunday School Teachers and Lady District Visitors. His morning service is a shortened one, omitting the Litany and Ante-Communion, with a spoken sermon ; and the Mission Services are going on at the same time.

' It may be added his professional stipend is under £230 per annum, and his people raise £800 for all purposes, in a district where not thirteen families can afford to keep one servant.

' There are eight hundred and seventy Communicants.'

APPENDIX J.

EXTRACT FROM THE *LIVERPOOL COURIER*, REFERRED TO ON PAGE 252.

' The history of the Christian Police Association movement in Liverpool will be looked upon with interest, in view of the large dimensions the association has assumed since its establishment some few years ago. It was here that the idea of establishing such an association first originated. About nine years ago three constables in the Liverpool force met regularly in a cellar in Upper Parliament Street, for the purpose of holding prayer meetings. By degrees their numbers increased until at length the little cellar became altogether inadequate to hold all who wished to attend, and more commodious premises had to be found. Through the instrumentality of the Rev. R. Hobson, Vicar of St. Nathaniel's, who took considerable interest in the doings of the policemen, a room affording more accommodation was secured ; but it was not long before this also became too small to hold all who came to the meetings. Consequently a hall had to be erected in Kingsley Road in order that the good work so simply begun might be successfully carried on. The influence exercised by these few earnest workers was not felt in Liverpool alone, but it gradually spread to other towns, where sympathizers were soon enlisted in the cause of the policemen. Some six years ago the headquarters of the association was established in London, and there are now one hundred and seventy-six branches flourishing in various parts of England, Ireland, Scotland and Wales, and the colonies.'

APPENDIX K.

LIVERPOOL COURIER'S REPORT OF CANON HOBSON'S RECEPTION, REFERRED TO ON PAGE 264.

'CONGREGATIONAL RECEPTION OF THE REV. CANON HOBSON.

' Last night a very affectionate welcome was given by the congregation of St. Nathaniel's to the Rev. Canon Hobson, on his return from Grand Canary, whither five months ago he went to recover his health.

' The Rev. gentleman's appearance showed how effectual his trip has been, and his crisp speech during the proceedings assured the congregation that their Pastor has lost none of his well-known fervour and persuasive eloquence.

' The gathering took place in the Church Hall. It was prettily decorated with fairy lamps, palms, ferns, and flowering plants, and there was an extremely large attendance of the congregation.

' On the Vicar's arrival he was welcomed by the Reception Committee, the whole gathering rising, and singing " Home, Sweet Home."

' The following address was read :

' " REV. AND DEAR SIR,

' " We, the Parishioners and Congregation of your dear St. Nathaniel's, desire to offer you a warm welcome back to us after a stay of five months in the Canary Islands. We thank God that—as we prayed for you—you have there enjoyed the calm of a time of rest, and there have largely found the needful to give again to us the toil of heart, of mind, and body as a faithful Pastor, as you gave it to us in the twenty-eight years before you left. In your absence we missed you as a leader, as a teacher, as an example, and as a comforter in the time of sorrow ; and now we pray that you may continue to be all these things to us, and to others for many years to come.

" Please accept the little present which accompanies this as a token of our high esteem in love for your work's sake, and believe us,

'" Yours affectionately, etc., etc."

' A Lady on behalf of the Ladies of the Church, presented Canon Hobson with a gilt enamel drawing-room clock.'

APPENDIX L.

ADDRESS FROM RESIDENTS AT LAS PALMAS, REFERRED TO ON PAGE 291.

' *To the Rev. Canon Hobson.*

' PORT LA LUZ, GRAND CANARY, ' *March* 22, 1900.

' REV. AND DEAR SIR,

' We, the undersigned, on behalf of ourselves and other residents in Port La Luz, desire on this the eve of your departure for England to express our grateful acknowledgment of the interest you have taken in our little Community during your stay in Las Palmas.

' We thank you especially for the religious exercises you conducted in the Sailors' Institute ; for your spiritual ministrations at the Seamen's Hospital, and at private houses in our midst ; for your kind attention and " word in season " to the sick and afflicted ; and for your Christian kindness and sympathy to all, and especially to those in sorrow and trouble.

' The words which you have uttered here in the Institute were words given you by God when alone with Him ; and as such they will live long in our minds.

' We appreciate those attentions more, knowing that they were generously bestowed out of a brief sojourn here for health and change.

' Whilst here you have not once turned a deaf ear to those who needed your help and comfort.

' We beg you to accept this heart-felt expression of our thankfulness.

' Both your words and your consistent Christian life have been a blessing to us.

' We earnestly pray God that you may have a favourable and a happy passage home, and be safely restored to your parish and people ; and that, in God's providence, you may be spared to be a witness for Him, and to lead many wanderers from the paths of sin and death to the marvellous light of the Lord Jesus Christ.

' We pray God you may comfort some on the voyage home to England.

' That the sojourn made so profitable to us may bring you that health and strength you require, is the hearty united prayer of your humble well-wishers in Port La Luz.'

(Here followed the signatures.)

APPENDIX M.

LIVERPOOL COURIER'S ACCOUNT OF ' WELCOME ' TO CANON HOBSON, REFERRED TO ON PAGE 291.

' HOME-COMING OF THE REV. CANON HOBSON.

' A large audience, comprising members of St. Nathaniel's Church, and of the P.S.E. Brotherhood, assembled in the Windsor Mission Hall, the occasion being the Welcome Home of the Rev. R. Hobson, the esteemed Vicar, who has just returned from a visit to the Canary Islands for the benefit of his health.

' The proceedings were of a most enthusiastic character, and nothing could have exceeded the welcome which the Vicar received.

' The following resolution was proposed, seconded, and carried with the greatest enthusiasm : " That this meeting of the congregation of St. Nathaniel's Church begs to accord to their esteemed Vicar, Canon Hobson, a most warm and heart-felt welcome upon his return after a short stay in the Canary Islands.

' " It begs to assure him of the earnest prayers and sincere sympathy of his congregation regarding the cause which has necessitated his temporary absence from them, and it also assures him of the devotion which it feels towards him, re-membering the Christian zeal, courage, and sympathy which he has ever displayed in his life-work of thirty-one years in their midst.

' " It prays that he may, by the grace of God, be thoroughly restored to health and strength, and that as Pastor of the congregation, he may be enabled to carry on the work of ex-tending the Master's kingdom for many years to come."

' The Vicar, in his reply, assured his people that he would remain with them to the last.'

APPENDIX N.

FUNERAL SERMON PREACHED BY CANON HOBSON, IN
LIVERPOOL CATHEDRAL, ON THE LATE BISHOP
RYLE, REFERRED TO ON PAGE 293.

' IN MEMORY OF
J. C. RYLE, D.D., LATE BISHOP OF LIVERPOOL.
Sermon preached in Liverpool Cathedral at the 3 o'clock p.m.
Service on Sunday, June 17, 1900,
BY CANON HOBSON.

Revelation xiv. 13.

' I have chosen this text as suitable for the occasion, having
seen it in large letters on the paper with the hymns sung at
the funeral service of our late revered Bishop on Thursday
last ; probably intended to express the belief of those who
placed it there as to the blessed state of his soul.

' The command to St. John to write, and the endorsement
thereof by the Holy Spirit, give immense importance to the
weighty and most comforting words of the text : " Blessed
are the dead which die in the Lord from henceforth : Yea,
saith the Spirit, that they may rest from their labours ; and
their works do follow them."

' Let us look at the text as it stands :

' 1. " Dead." There is little said in Holy Scripture about
death-beds. There is enough concerning the future state ;
while immense stress is laid on our life here. Death is not
part of our original nature. It is the result of a foreign introduction into our being. Hence it is that all shrink from
death. This was so even with Christ Himself. We seem to
think everyone will die but ourselves, yet all must die, and
after death the judgment.

> " And am I born to die,
> And must I suddenly comply
>   With nature's stern decree ?
> What after death for me remains,
> Celestial joys, or hellish pains,
>   To all eternity ? "

' 2. " In the Lord." That is, in Christ. There are two
senses of being in the Lord, viz., as fruit-bearing or non-fruit-
bearing branches, that is, internally or externally ; in other
words, members of the invisible or visible Church ; like the
wheat and the tares, the good and the bad fish, the wise and
the foolish virgins. " In the Lord " here means in Him as
fruit-bearing branches ; and as such deriving sap and fruitfulness from Christ the true Vine. To be " in the Lord " is to

be united to Him by living, loving faith. It is to be in Him as Noah was in the Ark, as the man-slayer was in the City of Refuge, as a living limb is in a living body. It is idle to speak of this union being true of the baptized as such.

'"Blessed," happy : note, not miserable, not in suffering, not being disciplined, not rendering satisfaction for sins, not in darkness ; but happy, blessedly happy, with the Lord. Remember the climax prayer of Christ : "Father, I will that they also whom Thou hast given Me be with Me." That is to be happy indeed !

'"From henceforth." That is from the moment the soul leaves the body of the individual who is in vital union with Christ. Thank God : Hallelujah !

'Why is this ? (*a*) Because there is no condemnation to them which are in Christ Jesus ! ; (*b*) because the Blood of Jesus Christ cleanseth from all sin ; (*c*) because in this life the soul of such is made whiter than snow ; (*d*) because the true believer is justified, acquitted. Hence such are perfect ; because as He—Christ—is, so are they in this world. Thank God that is the present standing of all who are in Christ by living, loving faith. This pulverizes purgatory and all its approaches.

'Is not this the teaching of the Book of Common Prayer, and of the Homilies ?

'Thus, in the Burial Service : "Almighty God, with whom do live the spirits of them that depart hence in the Lord, and with whom the souls of the faithful, after they are delivered from the burden of the flesh, are in joy and felicity."

'The Homily on Prayer has these words : "The Scripture doth acknowledge but two places after this life : the one proper to the elect and blessed of God ; and the other to the reprobate and damned souls."

'Again, "Let this and other places be sufficient to take away the gross error of purgatory out of your heads ; neither let us dream any more the souls of the dead are anything holpen by our prayers ; but as the Scripture teacheth us, let us think of the end of the soul of man passing out of the body, going straightway either to heaven or hell, whereof the one needeth no prayer, and the other is without redemption." Could anything be more conclusive ?

'It is not true, as it is sometimes said, that prayers for the dead are now "by lawful authority" used in the Church of England ; for the two Houses of Convocation together have not lawful authority to add or take away from the legal standards of the Church of England ; any more than the Cabinet has power to make laws for this realm apart from the Sovereign, the Lords, and the Commons.

' The truth is, the Church at the Reformation deliberately, and of set purpose, cast out prayers for the dead. Let us not forget that the Church, being " by law established," is governed by the State, that is, by Parliament ; which is now our protection from the errors of even an Archbishop.

' " Yea, saith the Spirit." The Holy Spirit witnesseth to this great and all-important truth ; not to make it more certain, but for the confirmation of our faith, so that death may be met with confidence : in fact, in the light of the Spirit's witness, death becomes the next best blessing to Calvary ; because the death of believers enables them to enter that door of Life which Christ's death opened for them.

' " Rest from their labours." How can this be, if purgatory is a place of liquid fire on the one side, and cold water on the other, as described by an eminent Cardinal ; or, as Ritualists put it in a milder form ? Why, then the real labour begins ! God's Word and our Church teach nothing of the kind ; but rather, that when the believer's soul leaves the body, it enters into " rest, sweet rest," " joy, glad joy," in the presence of the Lord.

' " The works follow." The ticket of admission into heaven is the righteousness of Christ ; while works do follow, in that God is not unrighteous to forget the works of faith and labour of love of His dear people : no, not even a cup of cold water. Then their works follow, too, in that being dead, their deeds and holy lives testify whose they were whom they served, to the lasting benefit of the survivors.

' This, I take it, was the teaching of our late beloved Bishop on this subject. I do not claim for him infallibility or impeccability ; in a tribute to the late chief shepherd of this Diocese I would strike the note of praise to the glory of God. I do not ask your prayers therefore for his soul ; but, to praise God for all He accomplished by His faithful servant.

' To praise God for all those who have departed this life in His faith and fear is our duty and privilege. God Himself graciously commended Moses after his death—viz., " Moses My servant is dead." This was sublime " In Memoriam."

' A great man has just now fallen in Israel, in the decease of the dear Bishop. Yes, he was great through the abounding grace of God. He was great in stature ; great in mental power ; great in spirituality ; great as a preacher and expositor of God's most Holy Word ; great in hospitality ; great in winning souls to God ; great as a writer of Gospel tracts ; great as an author of works which will long live ; great as a Bishop of the Reformed Evangelical Protestant Church of England, of which he was a noble defender ; great as first Bishop of Liverpool.

' I am bold to say, that perhaps few men in the nineteenth century did so much for God, for truth, and for righteousness, among the English speaking race, and in the world, as our late Bishop.

' Let us again with joyous hearts ascribe all the praise and glory—not unto us, not unto the man—but to Him to whom it is most justly due, our Covenant God, Father, Son, and Holy Ghost. In conclusion :

' Are we in the Lord, each one ?

' Are we fruit-bearing branches ?

' Have we our " fruit unto holiness, and the end everlasting life " ? '

APPENDIX O.

LIVERPOOL *PORCUPINE'S* NOTICE OF ST. NATHANIEL'S SERVICE, REFERRED TO ON PAGE 295.

(From the ' Liverpool Porcupine.')

' PEEPS AT POPULAR CHURCHES : WITH THE BISHOP AT WINDSOR.

' By a Peripatetic Pagan.

' I do not wish you to infer, Church reader, that Francis James—the gentle prelate who bosses this Diocese—and I have been enjoying a brief and well-earned holiday in the little Berkshire town, whose chief glory is the stately residence of Her Majesty. Nothing of the sort. I only desire to draw your attention to the coincidence of his lordship and I together visiting St. Nathaniel's Church, Pine Grove, Windsor, Liverpool, on last Sunday morning. We cheered the heart of that sturdy veteran and champion Low Churchman, Canon Hobson, who for three decades has worked with tireless energy and indomitable perseverance in this congested parish.

' It takes a bit of finding. Through a mazy labyrinth of small streets I at last entered the desired haven. The Bishop was, of course, the cynosure of all eyes, while yours truly occupied a remote seat in the rear of the Church.

' I was at once struck with the severe simplicity, yet extreme

heartiness, of the service ; and the truly devotional manner in which the beautiful collects and prayers of our glorious Church liturgy were read and responded to, made me consider the advisability of changing my pseudonym, and saying with Agrippa, " Almost thou persuadest me to be a Christian."
' When I first " diaryized "—copyright word—St.Nathaniel's on my list of popular churches, I intended to give a sketch of Canon Hobson, and describe an ordinary Sunday morning service. But it so happened that I dropped in on the annual Harvest Thanksgiving day ; when the Bishop had arranged to preach for the Windsor Ragged Schools, at which 16,000 free meals were given last year.
' The Church was in every part crowded to its utmost capacity, though there was no " draw " in the shape of market-garden decoration ! which many people erroneously fancy must be associated with real harvest festivals.
' Evidently Canon Hobson and his people have put into practice Paul's advice to the Phillippians, " In everything by prayer and supplication with thanksgiving let your requests be made known unto God," and the heartiness of their thanksgiving on Sunday morning was far more effective than any amount of horticultural ornaments.
' There was no straining after effect in any part of the service, the Bishop, parson, and people, all spoke in psalms and hymns and spiritual songs.
' The ordinary choir was augmented by a number of school-children, and as their fresh voices re-echoed through the sacred fane in the special hymns chosen for the occasion, I was more than ever convinced that Canon Hobson's evangelicalism is as judicious as it is conformable to the rules of the Prayer-Book and to Holy Writ.'
The collections amounted to £81. This was more than was actually required. Thank God !

APPENDIX P.

CANON HOBSON'S CIRCULAR LETTER TO HIS CONGREGA-TION, REFERRED TO ON PAGE 298.

' *To my Beloved Brethren of the Parish and Congregation of St. Nathaniel.*

' My heart is very sad as my pen traces the words I now address to you. How can I write the word I now send to you ? That unwelcome word which I am bound to write at this time, the word Resignation ?

' I have written it ! What does it mean in this communication ? It denotes that I have virtually resigned the Benefice of St. Nathaniel, Windsor, West Derby, Liverpool, and thus in effect cease to be the Pastor of you, my beautiful flock for, whom I have laboured " in season, out of season," according to the powers, gifts, and graces given to me for the last thirty-three years, which has been to me in the main my life-work.

' It will be news to you that on the first day of the new century I entered upon my Jubilee year as a wholly separated man for work in the Lord's Vineyard, having been engaged as a lay Missionary in Ireland before entering the ordained Ministry of the Church.

' I have therefore been blowing the silver trumpet of free grace for fifty years. Oh, what a privilege to have given my little all for half a century to Him who gave His all for me. Thank God, I have not been ploughing on the rocks !

' You know how since eighteen hundred and eighty-five I have broken down five times, under the loved burden of this poor and trying parish. I never fully recovered from my severe illness in eighteen hundred and ninety-two. Since then my nervous weakness and chest trouble have gradually increased, until they seem to have become hopelessly chronic. I feel myself spent, worn out ; hence my resignation. Fidelity to God, in caring for the souls of the people, forbids that I should seek to hold a position to·which I feel no longer equal.

' You know I am not deserting a sinking ship, as St. Nathaniel's was never stronger, numerically or financially, than at the present time. There are eight hundred and eleven Communicants on the roll up to date, whose names and addresses were handed to my successor, together with the names and addresses of the seventy-eight newly confirmed, who received their first communion at my hands, making altogether eight hundred and eighty-nine ! While my stipend the first short year was £75, I leave an income of £450, with a Church, three Halls, and a Vicarage, without one penny of debt. Would I resign such at random ?

' I want you all to join in prayer that the Good Shepherd of the Flock may send a minister who will feed you with a generous and liberal hand, in leading you beside the green pastures and still waters of God's Holy Word and Ordinances.

' I shall not say farewell yet ; but pray that " the God of all grace " may be your everlasting portion.

' Your loving Pastor,
' R. Hobson.'

APPENDIX Q.

(Extract from the ' Liverpool Courier,' March 16, 1901).

'RETIREMENT OF CANON HOBSON.

' A ZEALOUS PARISH CLERGYMAN.

' Churchpeople throughout the Diocese will hear, with deep regret, that in consequence of physical exhaustion and chest trouble, the Rev. Canon R. Hobson, Vicar of St. Nathaniel's, Windsor, has resigned his benefice, although the resignation will not take effect until the 30th of May. To his parishioners, by whom the Canon is beloved, the news of the severance will occasion profound sorrow, but by none will the breaking of old ties be more keenly felt than by the reverend gentleman himself. Acting under the advice of his medical advisers, Sir William Gowers and Dr. Alexander, Canon Hobson feels that, if he has yet to live, absolute rest is imperative, and that he dare not, from fidelity to God and the souls of those committed to his care, continue to hold a position to the responsible demands of which he is not equal. Bishop Chavasse has been slow to part with such an esteemed and zealous incumbent, and, with that kindness of heart which distinguishes him, has offered to supply Canon Hobson with an additional curate to relieve him of part of his duties. While deeply grateful for his lordship's consideration, the Canon feels that the time for his retirement has come.

' Canon Hobson, who is in his seventieth year, was born in the picturesque village of Donard, County Wicklow, and has now attained to his fiftieth year in special work for God. Having been engaged in connection with the Irish Church Missions for eleven years, he passed, with first-class honours, through St. Aidan's Theological College, Birkenhead, and afterwards matriculated at Trinity College, Dublin. He was ordained in 1865 by the then Bishop of Chester (Dr. Graham), and for three years was curate of Christ Church, Claughton, under the late Dr. R. P. Blakeney. Then he entered upon the great work of his life in the district of Windsor, in this city. The Church at that time was not built, the district being part of St. Clement's. Mr. Hobson began his work in a cellar, and at his first ministration of the Sacrament there were eight communicants. He soon became noted as a hard-working minister, and after the church of St.Nathaniel was consecrated on the 17th July, 1869, by the late Bishop Jacobson, large congregations were soon drawn to the services. Then began that wonderful development of church life in the district which has made St. Nathaniel's Parish one of the most notable in the diocese. There is now a completed church, with tower, peal of bells, and clock, and the church is lighted with electricity, while there are three halls—Windsor Mission-hall, Harding Street Mission-room, and the Jubilee Hall—and a vicarage, all entirely free from debt, no less a sum than £60,000 having been brought together for all needs during Canon Hobson's incumbency.

' At the present time the communicants' roll numbers 811, and there are no fewer than 27 agencies, carried on by over 200 voluntary church workers, with the help of a curate, Scripture-reader, and Bible-woman. The work amongst men is a notable feature. The Church is in touch with nearly fourteen hundred men assembling in the church or mission-halls, in the way of Tontines, Young Men's Society, Work-men's Brotherhood, Men's Bible Class, and Special Services for men on Sunday evenings. The Ragged School, as a centre of Evangelical work, is another branch of Christian effort which has proved eminently useful. It embraces some 1,000 young and old, mainly young, of the waifs and strays class, to whom last year 16,541 warm, nourishing meals were given. This agency costs nearly £300 a year, and the money is raised absolutely by voluntary subscriptions. The work amongst women includes large attendances at Mothers' Meetings, while special care is taken of over 300 poor widows, irrespective of denomination. The Sunday School has a list of 1,200 children and 79 teachers. Moreover, there are 23 Adult Bible Classes on Sunday afternoons, attended by nearly 500 grown-up people. As to the Temperance cause, there are in the parish two prosperous total abstinence societies and four Bands of Hope. To bring his parish to such a state of efficiency, Canon Hobson has not only spared himself no pains, but he has been loyally assisted by his curates, and by as faithful a band of communicants as any parish clergyman could desire.

' When he first became acquainted with the district, it had earned the soubriquet of " The Roughs of Windsor," and it was not an uncommon thing to notice attached to advertise-ments for labouring men, " No Windsor man need apply." One street was absolutely given over to the social evil, of which there has not been a trace in the parish for some years. The result has been attained, not by appealing to the authori-ties, but by a raised moral standard of the people, through the instrumentality of the church. The parish has a population of close upon 7,000 people, composed entirely of the artisan class and the very poor ; in fact, there are only thirteen families in the parish who keep a servant. Always a thorough Protestant Evangelical Churchman, Canon Hobson's relations, throughout his ministerial career, with his Nonconformist brethren have ever been the most friendly character, and it was a pleasure to him to be present and speak at the laying of the foundation-stone of the enlarged Wesleyan Chapel in his parish. Moreover, he has always been on the most cordial terms with the Roman Catholics, who constitute one third of the parish. From them he has never received the slightest discourtesy, they having appreciated the fact that the Canon has ever sought to further the interests of all parishioners without distinction of creed.

' As is well known, the services at St. Nathaniel's Church are of the description now termed plain. The gown is used in the pulpit, the Psalms are read antiphonally, and there is a large and effective choir leading the congregation in plain chant and tune, in which the people heartily join *en masse.* It would require more space than is at our disposal to recount fully the great work which, under God, Canon Hobson has accomplished in St. Nathaniel's parish. No man could have been happier in his labour of love than Canon Hobson, and it was a striking tribute to the affection which his flock entertained for him that with tears in their eyes they implored him not to leave them, when in 1885 the late Bishop Ryle offered him a country living with a much higher stipend. Nay, more, a deputation of twenty-five went in a body to the Palace, and as the Bishop afterwards jocosely described the interview : " Although I reasoned with them for twenty minutes, trying to show that Canon Hobson ought to go to the country, if I had not acceded to their wishes they would have knocked my head off." Although since then Canon Hobson has five times broken down in health, he has never regretted having stayed at St. Nathaniel's, and now that he feels obliged to give up his charge, he finds it one of the greatest trials of his life.'

APPENDIX R.

CANON HOBSON'S FAREWELL LETTER TO HIS CONGREGA-
TION, REFERRED TO ON PAGE 298.

MY DEAR BRETHREN,

' How shall I say FAREWELL to you, for and amongst whom I have for thirty-three years given strength of body, soul, and spirit without reserve ? Is such a farewell a mere sentiment ; or is it a wrench of associations, ties, and affections, as real as is possible ? God knoweth !

' I do thank Him for having called me to work for Him in your midst ; I have never had a doubt that I was just where He would have me.

' And now, owing to my failing health, the time for parting has arrived. I do wish very tenderly to tell you how utterly unable I am to do that which my heart desires, viz., to say " good-bye " in each home ; you will therefore be so kind as to accept this farewell instead, as also a general parting word in our ever dear St. Nathaniel's on the evening of 29th of May (Wednesday), at eight o'clock (D.V.), which will be the last day of my Incumbency.

' FAREWELL, COMMUNICANTS ! You constitute the inner circle of the life of the Church. The Lord's Table is for His spiritual children. You know how I have ever looked to you for co-operation in every department of work, both in the Church and parish, where lay help can assist ; refusing, as I have done, all extraneous aid in these respects—only in £ s. d. have we sought assistance outside the parish—for the communicants are to the Church as the heart is to the body.

' FAREWELL, HELPERS IN CHRIST JESUS ! How much I owe you in the Lord ; you have been hands and feet to me in a thousand ways. I know your love and labour in Christ ; how, too, you have cheered your minister, in upholding his hands when ready to drop. It is obvious that what you have done, you have done for His Name's sake which is in itself its own reward. I trust you will ever abound yet more and more in work for God.

' TO THE UNSAVED IN ZION ! and to the many in the parish, utterly careless about their eternal interests, how shall I say FAREWELL to you ? Oh ! how I have prayed and besought you in Christ's stead to be reconciled to God. I take you to record this day that I am free from your blood ; you cannot say with truth, no man cared for your souls ; for the Christ, in all His power and willingness to save, has been presented to you in the open air, in cottage readings, and in your homes ; but, alas, thus far you have refused to hear " the voice of the charmer."

' My best farewell to you is, may God give you repentance unto life. Amen.

' FAREWELL, WELSH MISSION CHURCH ! Your regular services, having been begun and carried on under our direction and tender care since 1887, in the Jubilee Hall, make the prospect, now so near, of your getting into your own new church a joy to me. I trust the pure Gospel will ever be preached among you, and that, you each being born again, and living holy lives, we shall meet in our Father's home above. FAREWELL!

' FAREWELL, NONCONFORMISTS! with whom I have ever been in the most friendly relationship, and many of whom have joined the Church. There is no time, even if we wished, to have controversy with those who hold the Head—Christ.

' FAREWELL, ROMAN CATHOLICS! who form a third of the population ; I wish to state here to your credit, that in my goings in and out amongst you, all those years, with the Gospel Message, you have never resented my advances by a discourteous word, though not a few received Christ and joined the Church, including two priests of your Communion. I believe you have been long since convinced I have ever been a real and true friend to you, though a strong Protestant. Lovingkindnesses go a long way with all of us !

' FAREWELL, POOR WIDOWS! You have had a real place in my heart ; for who is so desolate as a poor widow ? I know some of you " are widows indeed," loving and serving God. FAREWELL!

' FAREWELL, RAGGED SCHOOL CHILDREN! Your looks and smiles have more than compensated for all the labour in providing you with good cheer.

' Space will not permit me to do more than simply say farewell to the Sunday School Teachers ; the Workmen's Brotherhood ; the Young Men's Society ; Men's Service on Sunday Evenings ; four Tontines ; the Bible-Classes ; the Lady District Visitors ; the Total Abstinence Societies, and Bands of Hope ; the Choir, Wardens, and Sidesmen ; and, though last, not least, to our dear old venerable octogenarian sexton, who has been a real and successful helper in many ways.

' FAREWELL TO ALL EXTRA PAROCHIAL BENEFACTORS! I feel it my duty to thank all those kind and generous friends outside the parish, who have from the beginning so cheerfully helped us by subscriptions and donations, without which we could never have accomplished what has been done.

' I specially desire to place on record my deep sense of gratitude to my dear friend the worthy Vicar of All Saints' Church, Southport, the Rev. Dr. Porter, and to his generous congregation, for having taken St. Nathaniel's under their wing ; in that I was cordially allowed to plead the wants of this parish in All Saints' Church once a year for many long years.

' FAREWELL TO OUR DEAR ST. NATHANIEL'S CHURCH! Truly that sacred Fane has been none other than the House of God, and the very gate of Heaven to vast numbers, who have been drawn thither by the magnetic power of the uplifted, blessed, personal, Lord Jesus in ritual, and life, and language " understanded of the people." Oh, the number of persons brought to God in that parish, and specially in the Church, all those years, many of whom have grown up stalwart Christians, and are now pillars in the house of our God !

' May it continue more and more to be the spiritual birth, place of precious souls, and a well of living water for all who are athirst for God.

' The people call it " Our Church." Its plain, hearty service suits them. May growing numbers worship there.

' FAREWELL, LECTERN ! on which rests that most precious jewel, God's Holy Word ; and from which that Word is read, that thereby " Lessons " of truth and godliness may be learned by God's waiting people.

' FAREWELL, PULPIT ! whence, for thirty-two years, I have, as God's ambassador, " not fearing the face of man," sought to proclaim, as He has taught me, " The Whole Counsel of God," " Ordered in all things and sure," as set forth in God's Word, and in the standards of our Evangelical Protestant Church.

' FAREWELL, FONT ! Kneeling there, how I have pleaded with God for the spiritual regeneraton there and then of those being baptized thereat ; and, in the language of faith, hope, and love, have thanked Him for so great a gift. Why should less be expected ?

' FAREWELL, READING DESK ! Oh, how privileged to have been permitted all those years to lead the Lord's people in the sanctuary to the throne of the heavenly grace. How I sought to be preserved from a perfunctory rendering of the Service.

' FAREWELL, HOLY TABLE ! Oh, my God ! Oh, my Saviour ! Oh, Holy Ghost ! triune Jehovah ! what gatherings of Thy children we have had around Thy Holy Table, to feast in our hearts by faith on the " benefits " derived from our once crucified, but now risen and ascended Lord. Have not our vessels often overflowed, when He thus brought us into His banqueting House ?

' FAREWELL, HOLY TABLE, FAREWELL !

' FAREWELL ALL ! To all, I say FAREWELL. Do not blame me for feeling our separation so deeply as I do It would be strange if I did not. It is no small consolation to me under it, that instead of being regarded by you as an old fossil, who had worn out your patience and let the work of God drift, I have in you a wealth of affection above all price ; and that I leave the cause strong and healthy, as indicated by nearly five hundred communicants this Eastertide.

' OH, MY FLOCK ! MY BEAUTIFUL FLOCK ! How shall I leave you ? I know you are infinitely dearer to Christ, the Great Shepherd of the sheep, than to me. I know God is too wise to err, and too loving to be unkind. There I leave you, and there, too, I seek rest.

' Your loving Pastor,
' R. HOBSON.'

APPENDIX S.

LIVERPOOL COURIER'S DESCRIPTION OF THE CONGREGA-
TIONAL FAREWELL TO CANON HOBSON, REFERRED
TO ON PAGE 301.

' A WORKING-MAN PASTOR AND HIS PEOPLE.
' *Presentation to the Rev. Canon Hobson.*

' The Windsor Mission-Hall was last night packed with a large congregational meeting on the occasion of a farewell presentation to Canon Hobson, who is retiring, owing to ill-health, after thirty-three years of faithful and loving service as vicar of St. Nathaniel's Church. Mr. Thomas Stubbs presided, and the large gathering included Dr. Chavasse (Bishop of the diocese), Canon Herbert Jones, Canon Burbidge, the Revs. Dr. Porter (Southport), Dr. Oliver, R. B. De Wolf, W. B. Irving, R. M. Ainslie, E. A. St. Duke, Aldermen Burgess and Roberts, J. Lea, C.C., W. Bullen, C.C., J. Jones, and many representative clergy and laity of the diocese. Letters couched in terms of deep appreciation of the Canon's labours in con-nection with St. Nathaniel's parish were read from Mr. S. W. Higginbottom, M.P., Mr. A. L. Jones, Mr. A. F. Warr, M.P., Lord Claude Hamilton, Alderman Evans, Canon Spooner, Canon Woodward, Archdeacon Madden, Alderman Bartlett, and others. Archdeacon Taylor was prevented from attending as he had hoped.

' The Chairman said the secret of Canon Hobson's great success and powerful ministry in St. Nathaniel's parish was his wonderful parochial work. Soon after the church was con-secrated, an epidemic of small-pox broke out in the locality, and Canon Hobson visited every case, coming out scathless, to the great astonishment and relief of his friends. Canon Hobson, in that poor parish, had used his own money freely in relieving the necessities of the poor, whom he continually went

amongst. (Hear, hear.) The pastoral work, which made
Canon Hobson's success, had been continued right up to the
very last, and within the last few months he had seen Canon
Hobson at the side of a sick-bed, when the Canon was more
fit to have been in bed himself. (Applause.) The Canon's
visitation, his kindness, and his deep sympathy, were what had
implanted the love in the people's hearts, and made it possible
for him to achieve what he had. (Applause.) The Canon
was not so young as he was when he came amongst them
thirty-three years ago, and it was very sad for the people who
had known him all those years, and benefited so vastly from his
ministry, to see him leaving them, but they knew his heart and
his prayers would be with them, and they wished him all peace
and happiness in the years that were to come. (Applause.)

'Mr. Derbyshire (senior superintendent of the Sunday
School and Band of Hope), Mr. Haselden (manager of the
Brotherhood), Mr. W. J. Wright (superintendent of the Sunday
School and Band of Hope), and Mr. S. Hayes (churchwarden
and superintendent of the Ragged School) each spoke in
affecting terms of an almost life-long association with Canon
Hobson and his wonderful work, and of the inexhaustible
sympathy, love, and forethought which he ever displayed
throughout the long years of his arduous ministry. They
agreed in describing him as the working-man parson, who
preached and lived Christ, and set the example of a self-
sacrificing, manly Christian, who never betrayed the confidence
of his people, and left the parish at last with not one halfpenny
of debt upon any of the Church's agencies.

'Mr. John Lea, C.C., speaking as a Presbyterian, said no
one could speak too highly of Canon Hobson's work, which
extended beneficially beyond the bounds of parish and of
denomination, and was sincerely recognized by the Nonconformists of the city. (Applause.)

'Dr. Chavasse then made the presentation, which consisted
of a cheque for 500 guineas, accompanied by an illuminated
address. The wording of the address was as follows :

'" REVEREND AND DEAR SIR,

'" It is with deep grief that we, as parishioners and
members of the congregation associated with St. Nathaniel's
Church, Windsor, Liverpool, are called upon to part with you
as our vicar and devoted pastor, and our personal friend. But
living as we do in a world of parting and separation, it might
almost be said that in our sorrow there is something which
may be called a solace, for we grieve not ' as those without

hope.' It cheers us, and we are sure it will cheer you, to feel that your life for fifty years has been wholly spent in the Master's service, and it cheers us more to know that out of those busy and successful years nearly thirty-three have been given to us. Very full of work, and at the same time, very full of reward, these years have been. How many tears have been dried, how many torn hearts have been bound up, how many wanderers led home, how many souls won for Christ, how many hopes called into being, how much calm inspired to anxious souls, how much comfort to tired ones passing through the ' valley of the shadow of death,' and, all the time, how much honour and how much glory given to the Saviour, we may not know—perhaps it were better not to know till the dawn of a better day, till the Lord of Life ascends the eternal throne. In those sacred memories you will, sir, come back to us and we to you, when you seek in sunnier climes some at least of the strength you have spent so generously in our behalf. Our love and prayers will follow you, and we hope again to meet you when rest and change have done their wished-for work. Only as a proof of sincere affection we ask you to accept this purse of gold, and with our tears and with our sincere affection,
 ' " We remain, reverend and dear sir,
  ' " Your devoted people and attached friends,"
   ' (Then follow the names of the officers and
    committee.)
 ' The Bishop, in requesting the Canon's acceptance of the cheque and address, said those gifts were an expression of gratitude for the great work God has chosen him to do. In thirty-three years he had brought together no less than £60,000. He had covered their parish with a network of parochial buildings hard to beat in Liverpool or elsewhere. (Applause.) Far more, their offering was an expression of their gratitude for that building of living souls which God had used him to build up at a cost of so much prayer and effort, and of his very life-blood. (Applause.) When Canon Hobson went away he would not leave merely behind him a good church, a good school, and a noble parish hall, but what was far better—a congregation of earnest Christian men and women, built upon Christ, and eager to carry on the good work their old minister had let drop from his hands. (Applause.) Such men were the very best Church defence, and if the Church of England were manned with such men as he, there would never be any need for any Church defence meetings. (Applause.) As his Bishop he thanked Canon Hobson through them for being a

very defence of their great historic Church of England in these troublous days. (Applause.) He thanked him also for being a bulwark of their common Christianity. They heard it said on all sides that Christianity had had its day. They had only to point to what God had done in St. Nathaniel's through Canon Hobson, to show that that statement was absolutely untrue. (Applause.) He thanked him also that he had done his work on strictly spiritual lines. He thanked God that their congregation had been gathered together by the use of such means as the most spiritual man amongst them must feel that their Lord approved. Too often in their churches to-day, in their eagerness to secure money or gather congregations, methods were used which he could not help but call " of the world, worldly." (Applause.) Canon Hobson had shown them that the Gospel faithfully and fully preached, and lived out in a life of love and self-sacrifice, had lost none of its power, even at the end of the nineteenth and the beginning of the twentieth century. (Applause.) Those gifts were an expression still more of love. (Applause.) It was the good pastor who was much loved, and the longest remembered. Canon Hobson had gone amongst them as a minister of Christ, binding up the broken hearts, drying up the falling tears, and helping the fallen, strengthening the weak, reclaiming the backsliders. Whilst they looked with thankfulness and admiration at the work he had done, they would remember him best, not because he had been a great church builder, but because he had been their truest friend and Christ-like pastor. (Applause.) Those gifts were, furthermore, an expression of hope that, after he had taken his needed rest, his life would be spared for many a day to help them, and to help the Church at large, by his intercessions, his sympathies, his counsels, and his example. (Applause.) Above all, they must show their gratitude by not allowing the Canon's work to suffer, and by extending the right hand of brotherly welcome to his successor. (Applause.)

'Canon Hobson, who was deeply touched, expressed his heart-felt gratitude and affection for the expression of their appreciation of his work. He could not doubt, after the experience of his thirty-three years' ministry amongst them, either their appreciation, their affection, or their love. (Applause.) The winning of hearts was the greatest reward the Christian minister could obtain, for that could not be bought with money. (Hear, hear.) He came to Liverpool as a young man with the greatest aversion to the city, but he had lived and laboured for all those years amongst the people, receiving the greatest sympathy and kindness from all denominations and sects, and he left them with the words " St. Nathaniel's " graven upon his heart. (Applause.) '

APPENDIX T.

LIVERPOOL COURIER'S ACCOUNT OF CANON HOBSON'S FAREWELL SERVICE AND SERMON, REFERRED TO ON PAGE 302.

' REV. CANON HOBSON'S FAREWELL.

' The Rev. Canon Hobson, Vicar of St. Nathaniel's Church, Windsor, on Wednesday, May 29th, took farewell of his congregation, amongst whom he has worked with the greatest acceptance for thirty-three years.

' For some time the Canon has been in failing health, and to the deep regret of all in his district, he has found it necessary to retire. The church was crowded to its utmost capacity, and the service was throughout of a most affecting description. The prayers were read by the Rev. J. J. Cuningham, and Canon Hobson preached from the text " I have no greater joy than to hear that my children walk in truth " (3 John 4). He alluded in touching language to the close relationship which existed between pastor and people, and said he had no greater ministerial joy than to know that his children, represented by all who had been under his spiritual charge, walked in truth. He bade an affectionate farewell to St. Nathaniel's Church, and everything associated with it, with the congregation, and all agencies engaged in its work. He trusted when he was gone he would hear they were still bound together, labouring together, and working together, helping his successor, who, he believed, was a man of God. They must not forget that they were not all exactly alike, but he commended his brother in the ministry to them ; he did it for the Lord's sake, for their sake, and for his sake. Had he the least idea that a wolf could possibly enter into the fold he would have hung on to the very last, but he knew such, under God's providence, was not likely. He bade all an affectionate farewell, and hoped God would bless them in the work in which they were engaged. After the choir had, at the Vicar's request, rendered the " Hallelujah Chorus," the congregation, with visible signs of grief, sang the hymn " Farewell, faithful friends," to the tune of " Home, sweet home," and the Benediction closed a most touching service.'